KW-221-672

Durham Hearth Tax
Lady Day 1666

Issued by

The British Record Society
[Index Library 119]
Hearth Tax Series Volume IV

in association with

British Academy Hearth Tax Project

General

The fireplaces illustrated on the jacket come from various parts of England and Wales and reflect a wide social spectrum from the major gentry (Little Moreton Hall) to yeoman farmhouses (Valley Farm; Glencoyne). Unfortunately, few seventeenth-century fireplaces in small, single-hearth houses and cottages survive unaltered, and it has proved impossible to find suitable illustrations of them. However, the simple timber chimney and fireplace of Tŷ-Mawr, the brick one at Valley Farm, and the cooking hearth of Glencoyne, are typical of the period and could have been found in many smaller houses and cottages.

DESCRIPTIONS

Front jacket

Top left: Little Moreton Hall, Cheshire. Decorative fireplace in the chamber over the porch. The house was owned by the powerful Moreton family, whose wealth was based on land, The fireplace is part of the late sixteenth-century additions to the medieval house. By the seventeenth century there were around twenty fireplaces. © Jeremy Milln

Top right: Wickens, Charing, Kent. Fireplace with plaster overmantel in the chamber over the parlour. The house was built around 1600 by the Dering family, who were minor gentry. Six hearths were charged to the hearth tax of 1664. © Sarah Pearson

Bottom left: Valley Farm, Flatford, Suffolk. A late-medieval yeoman's house; in the sixteenth century a brick fireplace and ceiling (now removed) were inserted into the open hall. By the late seventeenth century a second stack with one, or possibly two, fireplaces had been added to heat the adjacent cross wing. © John Walker

Bottom right: Tŷ-Mawr, Castell Caereinion, Montgomeryshire. An open-hall house built in 1461. In the sixteenth century a half-timbered fireplace was added, and later an upper floor inserted (now removed). Tŷ-Mawr means 'great house', and although probably a long-house, with animals at one end, and only one hearth in the 1660s, this was a dwelling of high status in the region. © Peter Smith

Outside back jacket

Glencoyne Farm, Ullswater, Cumbria. A rare surviving open fire, complete with hearth furniture set within a typical northern firehood. The large space was lit by its own window, to the right of this photograph of *c.* 1900. The house received its present form in 1629. It was owned by a family called Harrison, one of whom was taxed on three hearths in 1674. Reproduced by courtesy of the Museum of Lakeland Life, Kendal, Cumbria.

County Durham Hearth Tax Assessment Lady Day 1666

Introduced by
Adrian Green

Text edited by
Elizabeth Parkinson

Under the general direction of
Margaret Spufford

Published by The British Record Society
c/o Patric Dickinson
The College of Arms
Queen Victoria Street
London EC4V 4BT

ISBN 0-901505-46-3

Printed in Great Britain

Gregory King's topographical drawing of Bishop Auckland, from 'Durham Church notes' between ff. 10v. and 11. Reproduced by kind permission of the College of Arms.

Contents

Plates (after page lxiv)
Plate 1: Low Woodifield Farm
Plate 2: Slashpool Farm, Hett
Plate 3: Greystone Hall
Plate 4: Great Chilton Farm
Plate 5: Great Chilton Farm, parlour fireplace
Plate 6: Great Chilton Farm, hall fireplace
Plate 7: Tudhoe Hall
Plate 8: West Auckland Old Hall
Plate 9: West Auckland Manor House
Plate 10: New House, Ireshopeburn, upper Weardale
Plate 11: Bank House, Wolsingham
Plate 12: Abbey House, from Dun Cow Lane, Durham City

Figures
Frontispiece: Gregory King's topographical drawing of Bishop Auckland.

Preface

by Margaret Spufford

The Hearth Tax is the last great pre-nineteenth-century tax covering the whole of England and Wales that has not been fully exploited until now. From Professor Darby's *Domesday* series of analyses to Dr Glasscock's 1334 subsidy, Dr Fenwick's late fourteenth-century poll tax, and Dr Sheail's 1524–5 subsidy analyses, we gain pictures of the relative distribution of population, wealth and, more dubiously, poverty right across the country. The Hearth Tax of the 1660s and 1670s has never been systematically analysed, tabulated and mapped. This is the fourth volume in a series that is attempting to do just that.

Because the Hearth Tax was in force from 1662 to 1689 there are numerous returns from which to pick the best, although Tom Arkell's and Nat Alcock's Warwickshire is the only county for which all eight possible returns survive. Four survive for Durham. It gives me very great pleasure to write a preface to the Lady Day 1666 Hearth Tax Return for County Durham, with a splendid Introduction by Adrian Green. This is all the better because he was able to include a comparison with the return for Lady Day 1674. The latter contains more entries, but the former lists far more legible names, and has therefore been preferred for publication. It is very good to have his commentary on both.

It is the first major tax to contain lists of those who were exempt on the grounds of poverty. No other tax gives any indication of the invisible part of the iceberg, the non-taxable. Even though, as this volume shows, the exempt are likely to be under-recorded, these lists present a new resource. The exemption certificates were only very cursorily listed in the great E179 project to list all taxation records in the PRO, now the National Archives. In our Norfolk towns volume, we printed exemption certificates for the first time, but could not at that stage integrate them with a full return. We are proud that in this volume we have been able to fill some of the gaps, where the exempt are not given in the surviving returns. (Table 8). We now know that there were at least 117 non-payers living in Barnard Castle in 1671, alongside the 150 taxed there in 1674, just as we know that Gateshead High Ward contained at least 145 non-payers against the 140 payers of 1674. These exemption certificates have had a very chequered history, including being stored in two enormous bins in the Royal Mews, to the delight of the rats resident there. They were removed from these bins by gangs of labourers, sustained by 'strong stimulants' whose sensitivities towards paper conservation were not as great as ours. See p.178. They sold some to a glue factory.

I hope in future the British Academy Hearth Tax Project will be able to include exemption certificates to fill gaps in all forthcoming county volumes, as we have in this quite novel way here. Our ability to do so may depend on obtaining a sufficiently substantial grant from the Economic and Social Research Council, or another major funding body, to cover the expenses of sorting and cataloguing the remaining mass of certificates.

Naturally, once there are so many returns for a tax, and so many exemption certificates, it becomes more and more possible to point out that there are defects in the surviving records; – copying of previous assessments, or exemption certificates, for instance. When only single records of a tax survive, such comparisons are impossible and defects remain invisible to historians. We are much more able to be critically aware of the value of the records that we have. The Hearth Tax has left the fullest and best set of tax returns that we have, compared with its predecessors, which we have never been able to assess accurately.

We are also extremely lucky to have in Adrian Green an Introducer who is as able to write about vernacular buildings as he is about the social history of a county which was rapidly industrializing and enclosing for commercial agriculture. His work compares with Sarah Pearson's preceding volume on Kent. It is particularly interesting that we have in these two volumes dramatic contrasts of poverty and comparative prosperity. The reader only needs to compare the histograms for Durham and Kent to see this north-east – south-east comparison (Fig.2 p.xciii). There is indeed as great a contrast as I imagined there would be. There was no need, in prosperous Kent, to create a band for taxpayers, or indeed for those exempt, with over 70% of householders living in a house with only one hearth. In County Durham there certainly was (Map 9, p. liv). Dr Green uses the Hearth Tax to paint a picture of a heavily industrialising north of the county, along the coal-mining parishes of Tyneside. This created a large market of wage-labourers dependant on purchased foodstuffs. In response, the south-east of the county, along the Tees valley saw a great wave of enclosure between 1630 and 1680. Engrossing yeomen expanded their farms over many of their predecessors' plots. Some of the patterns identified by Dr Green we now know as 'normal'. Everywhere river valleys were more thickly settled, with more larger houses. Urban and rural houses were different, with many more small houses with more hearths in the towns and suburbs, and far fewer such houses in the countryside. Where there was a gentry house, the surrounding households generally had only one hearth, and all but the labouring poor had left.

We are convinced that the historian cannot discuss intelligently a tax on the number of hearths without also discussing the chimneys and the types of buildings themselves. It is therefore our hope that this series may put back on the agenda amongst the rest of material culture, the discussion of vernacular buildings in the 1660s and 1670s. We hoped that vernacular architecture had been firmly established on the historical syllabus in the 1970s, but it disappeared again. I hope very much that this series may lead to a reconsideration of its importance.

I am grateful to the British Academy for making the Hearth Tax Project one of its new British Academy Research Projects in the spring of 2004. The Hearth Tax project is doing well. We are now working on sixteen further volumes.

Margaret Spufford, Director, British Academy Hearth Tax Project, Roehampton; General Editor, Hearth Tax Series, British Record Society

All Saints Day 2005

ACKNOWLEDGEMENTS

Margaret Spufford would like to thank Roehampton University for giving its support to the Hearth Tax Project. She would also like to thank the British Academy for contributing via its Small Grant Scheme to the pre-publication costs of this volume for County Durham, and then for adopting the whole project as an Academy Project. The Nuffield Foundation also gave us a Small Grant to enable Duncan Harrington to transcribe Durham exemption certificates. The Aurelius Trust also made us a very welcome grant. The Mark Fitch Fund contributed to its publication costs. The Pilgrim Trust gave us a sum to contribute to the creation of the digitised maps at the beginning of the Project.

Sarah Pearson continued to support us in every way possible when we needed her advice on buildings. Margaret would like to thank for their remarkable patience Sue Stearn, the statistician who produced the tables from the data, and Mike Shand, the cartographer who presented them in digital map form, so rendering comparison with our earlier volume on Kent immediately possible. Alasdair Hawkyard is a most assiduous palaeographer to the series. Professor Brian Roberts has not only made his terrain map available for County Durham, but with great generosity has promised us use of all the other county terrain maps from his *Atlas* for our future volumes. He in turn is indebted to Stewart Wrathmell and English Heritage. Phillip Judge draws seventeenth century town plans for us. Robert Yorke, Archivist of the College of Arms, was extremely helpful in finding the Prospects drawn by Gregory King as a seventeen-year old. We are grateful to the College for its permission to reproduce two of them in this volume. The photographs of documents in the National Archives were kindly provided by Duncan Harrington. John Price who joined the project as my Research Assistant in 2005 has moved mountains. Sarah Wroot has also showed infinite patience in seeing the volume through the press. Lastly, she would like to thank Adrian Green for his excellent Introduction and Elizabeth Parkinson, who has been a most assiduous editor of the text, originally transcribed by Gwyn de Jong in the Netherlands.

There were also the eighty people who came to a conference jointly sponsored with the Vernacular Architecture Group at Rewley House in Oxford, in October 2004 on 'Vernacular Buildings and the Hearth Tax' and demonstrated in the most lively way possible their enthusiasm for the subject. They give us hope for our future. The proceedings are being published as a Research Report by the Council for British Archaeology, edited by P.S.Barnwell and M.Airs, *The Later Stuart House: Vernacular Buildings and the Hearth Tax*, York, 2006.

ACKNOWLEDGEMENTS

Adrian Green would like to thank Margaret and Peter Spufford, Susan Rose, Sarah Pearson and Elizabeth Parkinson for their advice and support throughout. He is also grateful to Professor Keith Wrightson of Yale University, for his role in the early stages of this volume. Prof. Brian Roberts and Dr Helen Dunsford in the Department of Geography, Durham University, provided crucial assistance in preparing the maps; Jeremy Hutson shared in the research on Tudhoe, and Martin Roberts alerted him to John Kay's notebook and made useful comments on a draft of the Introduction. Adrian is also grateful to his colleagues in Durham History Department, Christian Liddy, David Craig and Christopher Brooks. He is especially appreciative of those people who allowed buildings in their care to be inspected. Adrian was also encouraged by students and various seminar and conference audiences, who showed more interest in the hearth tax than might be expected. Certain friends, meanwhile, issued a challenge by endorsing the view that "the hearth tax is boring". He has tried to prove that remark wrong.

County Durham at the Restoration
A Social and Economic Case-Study

by Adrian Green

This introduction is intended to indicate some of the ways in which hearth tax records can be used by historians of all kinds. Further guidance can be found in Kevin Schürer and Tom Arkell's *Surveying the People*, and there are useful introductions to other counties with published returns, notably for Nottinghamshire and the previous volumes in this series on Kent and Cambridgeshire.[1] This volume covers historic County Durham and publishes the transcript of the Exchequer records for Lady Day 1666. The Palatinate of Durham included detached areas in Norhamshire, Bedlingtonshire and Islandshire, and the hearth tax for these areas was enrolled with this Durham return but will be analysed separately in the Northumberland volume in this series. Exemption certificates from the 1670s have been printed in Appendix IV for those places without non-payers in Lady Day 1666. A table of hearths and households for Lady Day 1674 is also included, as it is always wise to use more than one hearth tax return to compensate for under-recording. Together 1666 and 1674 provide the most comprehensive coverage of the county, and both are analysed in the introduction. The 1666 transcript, tables and maps are intended to provide comparability with the records for other counties published in this series.

Changes in the number of hearths or households between 1666 and 1674 may relate to real changes in population and wealth, but can also reflect variations in the degree of recording. These were largely a product of the national administrative context, explained below by Elizabeth Parkinson. The local administration also affected recording, and this is explored through the surviving lists made by local collectors. Understanding these administrative issues is essential, as only through appreciating how the tax was collected can we make the best use of the information it provides. The central section of the introduction discusses the transcript and maps to indicate what the Lady Day 1666 Exchequer Return does show. Preceding this is an account of the broader social and economic context, and following the discussion of the hearth range tables and maps, is some further analysis of the detail for status, women and families in 1666. The final section discusses houses and the hearth tax.

The Politics of the Hearth Tax in Durham

Tax collection and its assessment was a political issue. The hearth tax records were

---

[1] K. Schürer and T. Arkell, eds. *Surveying the People*, (Oxford, 1992). W.F. Webster, ed. *Nottinghamshire Hearth Tax 1664:1674*, with an introduction by J.V. Beckett, M.W. Barley and S.C. Wallwork, Thoroton Society Record Series, 37 (Nottingham, 1988); Nesta Evans, ed. *Cambridgeshire Hearth Tax, Michaelmas 1664*, British Record Society, Hearth Tax Series, I (London, 2000); Sarah Pearson, 'Kent Hearth Tax Records: Context and Analysis', in D. Harrington, ed. *Kent Hearth Tax Assessment, Lady Day 1664*, British Record Society, Hearth Tax Series, II (London, 2000).

the product of central authority and county government, but were also generated amidst parish politics. Appreciating the community context, and the ways in which churchwardens and local constables acquitted their responsibilities, can help us to understand the creation of these records and why the apparently straightforward lists of names and hearth numbers entered into the Exchequer Rolls need to be interpreted with care. Ultimately, the encounter between tax collector and tax payer represented an interface between the state and the private realm of the household. At a more immediate level, the collection of taxes involved interactions between neighbours. The operation of state authority was highly localised, and depended upon local participation in office-holding being regarded as an aspect of good neighbourliness.[2] This was a system that relied upon agreement between central and local conceptions of authority and appropriate taxation. Since the household was the fundamental social unit, the extension of taxation to hearths had some logic. From outside the house, a smoking hearth signified a functioning household and chimneys were regarded as symbolising wealth. This provided a justification for the tax, but many disagreed that any such constant tax on wealth should be levied, and there were various degrees of opposition to both the collection of the money and the assessment process, which could require entry into the household to inspect the number and functioning of hearths. There was some irony in resenting the internal inspection of hearths, as from outside the house chimneys made a social statement. Chimneys proliferated on higher status houses and appeared as a marker of more moderate wealth on middling homes. The stepped profile of projecting external stacks on even single-hearth houses, built in County Durham as across England, was a marker of status and wealth, which had not been so obvious a feature of smaller houses a generation earlier. Many of those exempted from the tax occupied homes that must have lacked a chimney stack, and the possession of a chimney came to qualify a household as respectable in this period.

Restoration taxation had a particular political context in County Durham, which was geographically co-terminous with the Palatinate or Bishopric of Durham. Before the civil war, the bishops held considerable secular powers within the Palatinate, and these were enhanced by their additional role as lord lieutenants of the county.[3] The civil war and commonwealth saw the dismantling of this system of local government. In the late 1640s parliament ordered the preparation of a scheme for establishing an administration parallel to neighbouring counties, and during the 1650s the county came under the full jurisdiction of Westminster. At the Restoration, Bishop Cosin was equipped with the rights and privileges of his predecessors and the church estates were restored. The reported enthusiasm which greeted Cosin's entry into the Bishopric and City

---

2   See J. R. Kent, 'The Centre and the Localities: state formation and parish government in England, c.1640-1740' *Historical Journal* 38, 1995, pp. 363-404.
3   See G. T. Lapsley, *The County Palatine of Durham: A Study in Constitutional History* (New York, 1900); M. E. James, *Family, Lineage and Civil Society: A study of Society, Politics and Mentality in the Durham Region, 1500 to 1640* (Oxford, 1974).

of Durham in 1661 has been taken to imply that the Restoration was regarded as a deliverance from uncertainty.[4] A portion of the population was undoubtedly sympathetic to a return to the order and authority of the 1630s, when some communities had shown an appetite for Arminianism and the county generally acquiesced to the payment of Ship Money in 1636.[5] Yet the Restoration actively circumscribed the political, religious and economic freedoms enjoyed by some of Durham's populace during the 1650s. Individuals, including some former tenants, had been able to purchase the freeholds of sequestrated lands and houses. The restoration of the Bishop's and Cathedral Dean and Chapter's estates, by far the largest landlords in the county, entailed the widespread loss of freeholds and the payment of arrears on the restored leaseholds (in some cases these arrears were not cleared until the end of the century).[6] The propertied inhabitants of Durham also lost their representation in parliament, briefly gained in the 1650s but reverting in 1660 to virtual representation via the bishop in the House of Lords.[7] Traditionally, lack of representation in parliament went with lack of central taxation.[8] The imposition of the hearth tax in 1662, might therefore be expected to have fuelled resentment towards the Restoration regime.

As Braddick has argued, the hearth tax was part of a move towards greater centralisation in the operation of state authority, as the sixteenth- and early seventeenth-century ideal of administration operating by virtue of the authority of élites in each locality was fractured by the experience of civil war and the commonwealth regime.[9] The hearth tax was a product of the need for greater fiscal supply to the crown, but it was also part of a Restoration emphasis on control that manifested itself in an inclination to compile lists. Coleby suggests that payers, defaulters and those exempt for taxation purposes were listed as part of the determination by the landed élite and the established church to re-establish and maintain its economic superiority, spiritual power and social control.[10] In the Palatinate of Durham generally, it was the bishop who held the reins of local office before the civil war and who regained the saddle in 1660, and Bishop Cosin exemplifies the Restoration reassertion of control. The hearth tax lists were both a mechanism and record of that control, and its limitations.

Resistance to the hearth tax took a variety of forms, and in some communities local officials were slow to cooperate in the first years of the hearth tax. In parts of Easington Ward the high constables made no returns regarding the arrears

[4] G. Ornsby, ed. *The Correspondence of John Cosin, Bishop of Durham, Vol. II*, Surtees Society 55 1870, p. 21; J. G. Hoffman, 'John Cosin, 1595-1672: Bishop of Durham and Champion of the Caroline Church' (unpublished University of Wisconsin-Madison PhD, 1977) pp. 308 and 334.
[5] James, *Family, Lineage and Civil Society*, pp. 108-137; Lapsley, *County Palatine*, pp. 294-300.
[6] J. Morin, 'Merrington: Land, Landlord and Tenants 1541-1840: A Study of the state of the Dean and Chapter of Durham' (unpublished University of Durham PhD, 1998); P. Mussett with P. G. Woodward, *Estates and money at Durham Cathedral 1660-1985* (Durham, 1988).
[7] A. Heesom, 'The Enfranchisement of Durham' *Durham University Journal* 80 (1988), pp. 265-85.
[8] see Lapsley, *County Palatine*, pp. 294-300.
[9] M. J. Braddick, *State Formation in Early Modern England, c.1550-1700* (Cambridge, 2000).
[10] A. M. Coleby, *Central Government and the Localities: Hampshire, 1649-1689* (Cambridge, 1987), pp. 87-155.

of the 1662 and Lady Day 1663 collections and some of the constables in every
ward acted similarly.[11] Further lassitude is revealed in Gateshead, where parish
officials allowed a very large number of households to be returned as exempt. For
the county as a whole there were considerable arrears by 1664, as the first four
collections of the hearth tax in Durham only collected sixty-five per cent of those
hearths or households that were assessed. Assessment itself had been limited,
and Michaelmas 1665 witnessed a fourteen per cent increase on the number
of chargeable hearths recorded a year before. Most other parts of England and
Wales did not experience the same degree of initial difficulties in making an
assessment and extracting collection.[12]

 Disorderly opposition occurred elsewhere in the north of England. In 1666
there were hearth-tax riots at Hexham in Northumberland and in Newcastle
upon Tyne, and there was sporadic disorder in the North Riding of Yorkshire.[13]
No disorder against the hearth tax is recorded in the Palatinate of Durham.
Given the degree of resistance to the tax's collection between 1662 and 1664, it
seems unlikely that this reflects any great acquiescence to its legitimacy and more
accurately reflects the success of the county government in ensuring order. As for
instance, when Cosin warned his deputy-lieutenants to guard against disorder
resulting from rumours connected with the Great Fire of London in 1666, and
they responded by issuing instructions to their officers 'to double their guard,
and to keep patrols constant in the night, that we might not be surprised or taken
unprovided'.[14] Within this context of control, the collection of the hearth tax was
presumably conducted in such a way that local grievances were catered for. This
has implications for the reliability of the data compiled in the Exchequer returns,
as any leniency in assessment would have reduced the recording of householders or
their number of hearths. Surviving lists of assessment and collection for specific
localities in County Durham reveal significant discrepancies with the central
records, and the degree of recording was directly related to the administrative
context of the tax. Furthermore, under-recording of hearths and households may
well relate to lenient practices at a local level that the tax collectors (and payers)
regarded as legitimate — with or without the sanction of higher authority.
We will miss much of the hearth tax returns' potential for understanding late
seventeenth-century society, if we regard the difficulties in the data as simply the
result of administrative error. As Braddick has shown, the social and political
dimensions of taxation were bound up with the creation of these records.

[11] NA E179/106/20 and 21, including places as diverse as Teesdale Forest, Piercebridge, Darlington,
    Stockton, Sedgefield, Jarrow, Ryton, Sunderland and St. Nicholas, Durham City.
[12] E. Parkinson, 'The Administration of the Hearth Tax, 1662-1666' (unpublished University of
    Roehampton PhD, 2001), p. 134.
[13] M. J. Braddick, *The Nerves of State: Taxation and the Financing of the English state, 1558-1714*
    (Manchester, 1996), pp. 234-5; J. D. Purdy *Yorkshire Hearth Tax Returns* (Hull, 1991), pp. 19-29; D.
    Smith, 'Northumberland Hearth Tax 1664' *Journal of Northumberland and Durham Family History
    Society* (April 1978), pp. 88-89.
[14] P. Osmond, *A Life of John Cosin Bishop of Durham 1660-1672*, (London, 1913), p. 274

The Administration of the Hearth Tax

The hearth tax was first levied in 1662 to provide King Charles II with some much-needed money. The Act introducing the tax stated that 'every dwelling and other House and Edifice....shall be chargeable.... for every Fire hearth and Stove....the sum of Twoe shillings by the yeare'.[15] The money was to be paid in two equal instalments at Michaelmas (29 September) and Lady Day (25 March). Payment was to be made by the occupier or, if the house was vacant, by the owner according to a list of named householders with the number of their hearths. Exemption from payment was allowed for certain properties. Throughout the twenty-seven years of its life from 1662 to 1689 several different administrative systems were tried in order to improve the yield.[16] These included unpaid local government officials, professional tax collectors, private agents and finally a central commission.

The sheriffs' administration Michaelmas 1662 to Lady Day 1664
Initially, the tax was managed by the existing machinery of local government within each county, thus the petty constables, high constables and sheriffs were involved. Under the 1662 Act, each petty constable was responsible for notifying the householders within their jurisdiction that they must provide a self-assessment of the number of hearths in their occupation. From these self-assessments, the petty constable had to compile a list of the liable hearths with the names of the occupiers, and those of the owners if the property was empty, and deliver it to the next meeting of the Quarter Sessions. Here, the clerk of the peace was responsible for collating the constables' returns into a single county list to be inspected by three Justices and enrolled in duplicate. One copy was to be delivered to the Exchequer within a month of the Quarter Sessions meeting, as the authority for collection. The other was retained locally for the sheriff as a check on the amount of money to be collected.[17] Provision was also made for the recording and enrolment of any change in hearth numbers in the subsequent collections.[18]

The 1662 Act laid down strict time limits for the collection of the money at each stage of the process from petty constable to high constable to sheriff. The sheriffs were responsible for the safe transmission of the money to the Exchequer in London, it was to reach the Exchequer within sixty days from the time the tax was collected from the occupier. Expenses were allowed for each official involved, totalling seven pence for each pound collected. For the first collection, less than a fifth of the assessed total revenue had reached the Exchequer within

---

[15] 14 Car.II c.10, s.1.
[16] Outlined by C. A. F. Meekings in his introduction to *The Hearth Tax 1662-89: Exhibition of Records*, Public Record Office (London, 1962). T. Arkell gives a clear description of the legislation in 'Printed instructions for administering the hearth tax' in *Surveying the People*, pp. 38-64.
[17] 14 Car.II c.10, s.2-5.
[18] 14 Car.II c.10, s.14. These documents were known as schedules of variation.

the prescribed time limits.[19] The proceeds of the ensuing Lady Day collection took even longer to reach London. Thus after only two collections, parliament was forced to introduce a revising Act passed on 27th July 1663.[20] The poor yield was thought to be due entirely to under-assessment so this procedure was tightened up. Now every dwelling had to be viewed by the petty constable and two substantial inhabitants to check the householder's notification. The constable had to record all hearths both liable and not liable with their occupiers, and have the list verified by the high constable and signed by two justices before being returned to the clerk of the peace for enrolment at the Quarter Sessions. The Exchequer's aim was that by noting both liable and not liable hearths and householders any omissions could be traced. The additional work required for assessment delayed the compilation of the Exchequer duplicate. It was thus not effective until the 1664 Lady Day collection and sometimes not even ready for that one.

In most counties sheriffs were appointed annually, but Durham had an hereditary sheriffess in Anne, Countess of Pembroke, and all four collections between Michaelmas 1662 and Lady Day 1664 were delegated to her under-sheriff, Sir Thomas Davison.[21] This shrieval continuity might be expected to have encouraged efficiency, but Davison only managed to collect about sixty-five per cent of that assessed. Some of the difficulties were practical, such as the death of Robert Thompson and Philip Ripon, petty constables of Darlington borough,[22] and the physical remoteness of townships without a petty constable.[23] The large degree of under-collecting, however, reflects more wilful non-cooperation by the constables, as revealed in the Durham returns of 1662 and Lady Day 1663.[24] The accounts show a charge in Durham of 17, 624 hearths in 1662 which decreased to 12, 966 hearths for the Lady Day 1664 collection.[25] In Durham as elsewhere, the stricter assessment procedure did not result in an increased number of liable hearths.

The first receivers' administration Michaelmas 1664 to Michaelmas 1665
The revision of 1663 had hardly been introduced before the Lord Treasurer Southampton realised that it was unlikely to improve matters. A second revising act was therefore passed on 17 May 1664.[26] These changes generally took effect from the fifth collection at Michaelmas 1664. Responsibility for assessment and collection was now removed from the local government machinery and taken

---

[19] Calculations from the entries in NA E401/1935, 53-109 show that £11,205 had reached the Exchequer by 31 December 1662. The yield of the first collection was estimated from the assessments to be about £80,000.

[20] 15 Car.II c.13.

[21] C. A. F. Meekings, *Analysis of Hearth Tax Accounts 1662-1665*, List and Index Society, 153 (London, 1979), pp. 81-2.

[22] see NA E179/106/23.

[23] See Quarter Sessions Book 1664, f.225.

[24] NA E179/106/20 and 21.

[25] Meekings, *Hearth Tax Accounts 1662-1665*, p. 81.

[26] 16 Car.II c.3.

over by professional collectors, known as sub-collectors or chimney men, under the supervision of a receiver for each area. The areas of administration were also simplified. The smaller counties were combined and most cities and towns were incorporated with their surrounding county. In an attempt to improve efficiency, the poundage for the receivers was increased from seven pence to one shilling in the pound, out of which they had also to pay their sub-collectors. The house searches were now undertaken by the chimney men. They could levy the tax on demand but the use of distraint required an hour's notice and the presence of the petty constable. Most of the receivers were appointed in July 1664, but with their teams of sub-collectors to organize, the work was not started until after the 1664 Michaelmas collection was due.[27] With an overdue collection undertaken by paid tax collectors, assessment and collection were now undertaken simultaneously.

The receiver appointed to administer the county palatinate of Durham in July 1664 was William Christian 'of Southwaite' in Cumberland.[28] He had both influential connections and some financial experience, and was a member of the Merchant Venturers of Newcastle.[29] His efficiency produced an increase in the number of liable hearths by 2531 to 20,155 for which he was allowed a reward of £379 13s 0d.[30] His record of payment was quite good but the high level of arrears from the sheriffs' time, which he was commissioned to collect, meant that he only managed 51 per cent of that assessed.[31] Nationally, the receivers' work was disrupted by the outbreak of plague, and slow payment to the Exchequer compounded the king's difficulties in funding the war against the Dutch. To remedy this, the receivers were hastily replaced in the spring of 1666. By this time, some of them had already begun the current Lady Day collection and so had to hand over an unfinished collection to their successors.

The first farm Michaelmas 1666 to Lady Day 1669

The successors were a consortium of City merchants led by Sir Richard Piggott, who paid the government up front for administration and collection.[32] The consortium itself managed London and Middlesex and leased out the rest of the country to sub-farmers. In Durham, the receiver William Christian was replaced in the summer of 1666 by a sub-farmer, William Applegarth of Carlisle, who in turn appointed Thomas Sewell as his deputy. The administrative area was now enlarged to include Northumberland, Berwick upon Tweed and Newcastle upon

27 *Calendar of State Papers Domestic 1663-4*, p. 530.
28 NA T51/36, f.178. Family tree in W. Hutchinson, *History of Cumberland* (Carlisle, 1794).
29 *Extracts from the records of the Merchant Adventurers of Newcastle upon Tyne*, ed. by F. W. Dendy and J. R. Boyle, Surtees Society 93, 1894, vol. 1, p. 216. Appointed as customer at Carlisle in 1663, he was known to George Williamson (brother of an under-secretary to the secretary of state, Sir Joseph Williamson) and Daniel Fleming (first sheriff of Cumberland after the Restoration and a justice in Cumberland, Westmorland and Lancashire) *Calendar of State Papers Domestic 1661-2*, p. 630; *CSPD 1663-4*, p. 274; *CSPD 1665-6*, p. 436.
30 Meekings, *Hearth Tax Accounts 1662-1665*, p. 84.
31 Parkinson, 'Administration of the Hearth Tax', p. 141.
32 City merchants advanced an initial £250,000 on which interest was paid at the rate of 6% whilst their subsequent annual rent was fixed at £145,000.

Tyne — the same area as was used for the farm of the Excise. The list transcribed in this volume is headed a '...survey made by William Applegarth and Thomas Sewell... For the halfe-yeare ending 25 March 1666', and the last 16 membranes list the non-solvents. The very high number of exempt may include some of those who did not pay, to cover Sewell's failure to collect.

The farmers were supposed to start with the 1666 Michaelmas levy, but they agreed to complete the previous 1666 Lady Day collection begun by the receivers and return the books to the Exchequer, who had already mortgaged the proceeds of this collection to the City. The contract was meant to last for seven years but an option to surrender after three was included. The farmers were unable to recoup their rent partly because the Fire of London directly reduced their yield, and increasing opposition to the tax (seen in riots, obstruction of the tax collectors and even obstruction by the justices) made it more difficult to collect.[33] The two previous administrations had employed local officials who were aware of how far they could go in collecting the money. The farmers' men, ignorant of local conditions, tended to impose a stricter regime, thus increasing opposition to payment. Such an unsatisfactory administration could not last so the farmers invoked the option to surrender after the Lady Day 1669 collection. They informed the government in November 1668 of their plan but parliament took over a year to decide what to do.

The second receivers' administration Michaelmas 1669 to Lady Day 1674
Eventually in the spring of 1670, a second receivers' administration was set up, following the recommendation of a report prepared by Richard Sherwyn, a Treasury clerk, and Colonel William Webb, the farmers' auditor. By this time, the two collections for Michaelmas 1669 and Lady Day 1670 were overdue. The tax was to be managed centrally by Sherwyn and Webb as agents for the tax, from an office in London, although they were still answerable finally to the Exchequer.[34] They streamlined the organisation. The earlier system of returning duplicates to the Exchequer with one copy being retained locally was revived. A system of graduated poundages was introduced based on the size of the collection area and the density of population. The sparsely populated areas of Cumberland, Cornwall, Durham and Northumberland rated a poundage of two shillings for every pound collected compared with that of one shilling and sixpence in the more compact areas of Hertfordshire and Surrey. This administration lasted until the 1674 Lady Day collection when the Lord Treasurer Danby decided to farm the tax as a way of reducing expenditure and increasing revenue.

In Durham in 1670 Applegarth had to hand over his books to Christian, who was now reappointed as receiver for Durham, together with Northumberland,

---

[33] See NA PC2/59, f.218; L. M. Marshall, 'The Levying of the Hearth Tax', *English Historical Review*, vol.51 (1936), pp. 628-646; M. J. Braddick, *Parliamentary Taxation in Seventeenth-Century England* (Woodbridge, 1994), pp. 252-266.
[34] NA T51/36 f.197, *Calendar of Treasury Books*, III, p. 382.

Berwick upon Tweed and Newcastle upon Tyne.[35] Few of the first receivers were reappointed second time around, but Christian benefitted from his close links with Williamson (who was reappointed for Cumberland) and his prominence in several financial spheres.[36] Christian's sureties for the hearth tax were Sir Francis Anderson and Jeremy Tolhurst of Newcastle and a mercantile relative Thomas Christian of Liverpool. Their joint obligation was £32,000.[37] These merchant links must have aided the transfer of the collected money to London, principally by bills of exchange. No doubt building upon the stricter farmers' administration, Christian's charge for 1669-70 (omitting the detached portions of Norhamshire, Islandshire and Bedlingtonshire) increased to 24,155 hearths. By 1674 it had decreased to 23,323 hearths, and there was a suspicion that the justices were granting too many exemptions.[38] We can only guess at the number of exemptions allowed from 1671-3, for the Hearth office mislaid Christian's certificates so that his accounts for 1671-3 were declared on the level of exemptions for 1669-70.[39]

The second and third farms: Michaelmas 1674 to Lady Day 1679 and Michaelmas 1679 to Lady Day 1684, and the Commission: Michaelmas 1684 to Lady Day 1689

The farms were administered centrally without recourse to sub-farming and organized from an office in London. The terms of the contracts were such that the farmers had to allow Treasury access to their records.[40] By 1684 it appeared to the government that the farm was making undue profits, so the administration was returned to a system of direct collection managed by a Commission, who also managed the excise. This continued for a period of five years until 1689. By now William and Mary were on the throne and in order to gain popularity for their regime they agreed to abolish the tax in England and Wales. As it was one of the few taxes to have been granted in perpetuity, it could only be repealed by an Act of Parliament which took effect after the 1689 Lady Day collection.[41]

The yield of the tax

At first the government was hoping for an annual yield of around £300,000 but this was purely notional since nobody knew the total number of hearths in England and Wales.[42] In fact this was a hopeless overestimate, hence the

[35] *Calendar of Treasury Books*, III, pp. 557 and 567.
[36] Both men were appointed as joint farmers of the excise in 1671, see *Calendar of Treasury Books*, III, p. 833. In 1673, Christian was a receiver of subsidies and of the eighteen months tax, and leased several mine fields. *Calendar of Treasury Books*, IV, pp. 68, 101 and 136.
[37] NA T51/36, f. 178.
[38] C. A. F. Meekings, *Analysis of Hearth Tax Accounts 1666-1669*, List and Index Society 163 (London, 1980) pp.36-7. See *Calendar of Treasury Books*, IV, p. 679.
[39] NA E179/327/3.
[40] C. D. Chandaman, *The English Public Revenue* (Oxford, 1975), p. 101.
[41] I Wm.& M. c.10.
[42] Lord North believed it to be worth £500,000 and Treasurer Southampton 'at least £300,000 per annum', see British Library Harleian MSS 1243, f. 202.

frequent reorganizations in vain attempts to reach this target. Under the sheriffs' administration from Michaelmas 1662 until Lady Day 1664, the net yield of the tax was about £115,000 per annum. The change to the first receivers from Michaelmas 1664 to Michaelmas 1665 did not improve matters for the net yield fell to an average of £112,500 per annum. Under the difficult conditions of the farm from Michaelmas 1666 to Lady Day 1669 the annual yield fell further to around £103,000. During the second receivers' administration from Michaelmas 1669 to Lady Day 1674 the net receipts shot up to £145,000 per annum, a figure maintained during the second farm. For the third farm from Michaelmas 1679 to Lady Day 1684 the net yield averaged about £157,000 with a surplus to the farmers of at least £50,000. Under the Commission from Michaelmas 1684 to Lady Day 1689, the net receipts reached a record level of around £216,00 per annum.[43]

In County Durham, the yield of the tax increased markedly during the receiver's administration from Michaelmas 1664. No doubt they worked more assiduously as their reward was governed by the yield of the tax. In Tudhoe township for instance (see Appendix II), in the first collection of 1662 twenty-nine chargeable hearths were returned, but by 1665 this had risen by fifty-two per cent to forty-four hearths. Thereafter, the number of charged hearths returned to the Exchequer for Tudhoe remained fairly consistent. It rose from forty-three hearths in 1666 to forty nine in the most thorough collection of 1670. In Lady Day 1674, twenty-three householders paid tax on forty hearths, plus thirty-four non-liable — ten to twenty per cent lower than the 1670 assessment. Tudhoe's experience may have been paralleled in other parts of the county with both 1666 and 1674 representing effective but not exhaustive assessments.

Exemption

Initially the clauses of the 1662 Bill made no mention of exemption, but conditions for non-liability were hastily added as amendments during the Bill's passage through parliament. Three exemption clauses were included in the 1662 Act. The first exempted any householder already excluded from paying the local rates to church and poor where such non-payment was 'by reason of his poverty or the smallnes of his Estate' and not because the landlord paid the rates for his tenant.[44] The second clause exempted those houses whose rentable value at market rates was not more than twenty shillings per annum and whose occupiers did not have or use any land or tenements of their own or others exceeding that value nor 'hath any Lands Tenements Goods or Chattels of the value of Ten pounds in theire owne possession or in the possession of any other in trust for them'.[45] Anyone in this category required a certificate signed by the minister and at least one of the churchwardens or the overseers of the poor of their parish

[43] Chandaman, *English Public Revenue*, pp. 91-106.
[44] 14 Car.II c.10, s.16.
[45] 14 Car.II c.10, s.17.

and certified by two justices. These certificates were valid for one year or two collections. In practice, there was much overlap between these two categories of exemption, causing confusion as to who required a certificate.[46] In addition, the involvement of the parochial officials introduced a second group of administrators whose areas of jurisdiction sometimes differed from those of the secular officials (hence the sometimes different areas for payers and non-payers in the Exchequer Returns). The third clause excluded three different types of hearth, namely those hearths in any hospital or alms house (except those with an annual income over one hundred pounds a year), those in any 'Blowing house and Stampe, Furnace or Kiln', and any private ovens.[47] Again poor drafting of this clause of the Act did not make it clear that smiths' forges and bakers' ovens were liable, thus creating a fertile area for dispute.[48]

The grounds for exemption were further tightened under the 1664 Act. Firstly, no dwelling with more than two hearths could be exempted for any reason whatever. Secondly, any landlord who attempted to decrease their tenant's liability subsequent to the passing of the 1663 Act, by letting land apart or further sub-dividing houses to produce rentals of not more than twenty shillings per annum, was to be made liable for their tenants.[49] In addition from 1664, no property that was then chargeable could subsequently be made not chargeable unless it became ruinous. The application of the exemption criteria in Durham, in both the 1666 return and 1670s records, is discussed below.

The survival of the lists and their diversity

The records of the tax include lists of householders with their hearth numbers, exemption certificates, and papers dealing with the arrears and the audit.[50] The following discussion is restricted to the first two types since these are the two most frequently consulted. At the National Archives, the survivals are limited to the two periods when the Exchequer was responsible for the accounts, namely 1662-6 and from 1669-74. As to which records have survived, much is due to chance. Seaman has pointed to the hazards endured by these documents whilst being stored in chests, sheds and bins accessible to rats and affected by damp.[51] This has resulted in a patchy coverage of England and Wales with documents in varying conditions and legibility. Most counties have at least two surviving duplicates.[52]

---

[46] This confusion continued in the 1670s. See T. Arkell 'Identifying regional variations from the hearth tax', *The Local Historian*, (2003), vol. 1, pp. 148-174.

[47] 14 Car.II c.10, s.19.

[48] *Calendar of Treasury Books*, I, p. 689; III. p. 352; V, pp. 159, 417 and 472.

[49] 16 Car.II c.3, s.5 and 6.

[50] The lists of householders comprise those made by the constables or the high constables, the sub-collectors books and the county lists. Records concerning the arrears and the accounts can be found in NA classes E179 and E360.

[51] P. Seaman, J. Pound and R. Smith, *Norfolk Hearth Tax Exemption Certificates 1670-1674*, British Record Society, Hearth Tax Series, III (London, 2001) p. xxvii.

[52] See J. Gibson, *The Hearth Tax and other later Stuart Tax Lists and the Association Oath Rolls* (Federation of Family History Societies and Roehampton Institute, London, 1996).

Some local record offices have lists of householders amongst the Quarter Sessions papers, but generally less has survived locally.[53] In a few cases the local duplicate can be matched to its partner at the National Archives so that one can compare them.[54] Collections of estate papers may also contain some hearth tax lists,[55] as for Tudhoe in County Durham. A more unusual survival, is the notebook of the West Auckland constable. These surviving local records for County Durham are discussed below.

The first county lists for the Michaelmas 1662 collection were generally compiled during the summer of 1662 before the collection was due. Under the terms of the first act they should record the names and hearth numbers of those assessed as liable for the tax. For the Lady Day 1664 collection, both liable and not liable householders were to be noted in two parallel columns with their hearth numbers. Not all county duplicates conformed to this format, for the Durham and Newcastle lists omit the not chargeable.[56] Furthermore, the not chargeable lists may or may not include those hearths in liable dwellings exempted since the previous assessment for a variety of reasons.[57] As some of these lists were completed after the collection was made they record the names and the number of liable hearths paid up and those whose hearths were not liable. Meekings, however, has suggested that other lists were never used because they were drawn up so late that the original procedure was continued.[58]

For the Michaelmas 1664 collection to avoid making new lists from scratch, a different format was envisaged. Each receiver was to be given a copy of the Lady Day 1664 duplicate together with a manual and a specimen form showing how to update the list. Unfortunately the receivers were given copies of the 1662 assessment to amend, which omitted the exempt and so did not match the instructions.[59] Such confusing instructions for newly-appointed officials has resulted in much variation in the amount of information recorded.[60] In

---

53 Bristol, Denbighshire and Warwickshire are better represented at the county record offices. See Bristol Record Office F/Tax/A/1; National Library of Wales Chirk Castle B64-68 and 74; Warwickshire Record Office Q.S.11/1-63.

54 Both 1664 Lady Day duplicates for most of Kent have survived, as transcribed by P. Hyde and D. Harrington in *Hearth Tax Returns for Faversham Hundred 1662-1671*, Faversham Hundred Records, vol. 2 (1998), pp. 37-48.

55 Amongst the Fleming Papers in the Kendal Record Office is a transcript of the 1674 list for the county of Westmorland, Kendal Record Office, WD/RY/box 28, transcribed in Cumbria Family History Society, *The Westmorland Hearth Tax 1673*, (Cumbria Family History Society,1998); In the Suffolk Record Office are constables' returns for Blackbourne hundred HD1538/2 transcribed by S. Coleman in 'The Hearth Tax returns for the Hundred of Blackbourne, 1662M', *Proceedings of the Suffolk Institute of Archaeology*, vol. 32, pt. 2 (1971), pp. 168-192; the Essex County Record Office has exemption certificates dated 1668, see Q/RTh2.

56 For Durham see NA E179/106/27, for Newcastle see NA E179/254/20.

57 See Parkinson, 'Administration of the Hearth Tax', p. 158.

58 C. A. F. Meekings, ed. *Surrey Hearth Tax 1664*, Surrey Record Society, vol. 17 (1940), p.xxxi.

59 The slow return of the Lady Day 1664 lists to the Exchequer meant that there was insufficient time to have them copied and re-issued to the respective receivers. See Arkell, 'Printed instructions for administering the hearth tax', pp. 38-64.

60 The Cambridgeshire, Rutland and Somerset lists conform to the specimen form with detailed annotations whilst Durham and Hampshire have no annotations in their chargeable/not-chargeable layouts. See NA E179/84/437; E179/255/9; E179/256/16; E179/245/27 and E179/176/565.

addition, since none of the receivers completed their lists for enrolment whilst still in office, their duplicates or schedules of variation are in effect a combined assessment and return of those who had or had not paid, covering one, two or all three collections from Michaelmas 1664 to Michaelmas 1665.[61]

The surviving county lists for the Lady Day 1666 collection present a different picture again. Although in theory a shared collection, it is not always easy to establish from the returns the division of responsibility between receiver and farmer.[62] Some of the parchment records show evidence of enrolment, whilst in some counties paper books (earlier documents in the recording process) were returned noting the money collected and from whom.[63] This information was essential to prevent double payment. Since these lists were compiled after the collection was made, many, but not all record those who paid and those who did not. Others record the householders as 'solvent' or 'non-solvent' or chargeable and not chargeable. In some cases the not chargeable entries may not be all that they seem for there is a possibility that in some places the householders were noted thus to conceal the failure of the farmer to collect.[64]

The second receivers were issued with instructions by the Hearth Office as to how to compile their lists for the collections Michaelmas 1669 to Lady Day 1674. Unfortunately no copy has survived. The duplicates dated Michaelmas 1670 cover the two retrospective collections of Michaelmas 1669 and Lady Day 1670 and the current collection of Michaelmas 1670. Many of the surviving lists record the liable householders separately from the not liable, with the occasional annotation which may refer to all or only one of the three collections involved. For the 1671 collections some receivers produced a schedule of variations just recording the changes since the previous list. Between 1671 and 1674 each county or administrative area produced a varying number of duplicates of a generally similar format. In all these duplicates of the 1670s the recording of the not liable varies. Where the exempt are noted they appear under a variety of headings such as 'discharged by (legal) certificate', 'under the value' and 'poor', 'not liable', 'non-solvent' , 'receive alms of the parish' or 'take collection'. Some may also be noted in numerical terms often as those receiving alms.

If few exempt householders are recorded on the duplicates, their names can be found on the surviving paper exemption certificates. Until the Lady Day 1664 collection, such documents were only required for those exempted under the rental criterion or where a non rate-paying householder had been entered in error in the list of liable householders. Many of these records were issued on an individual basis. The enrolling of what should have been all the not liable by

---

[61] Herefordshire has three lists for the individual collections, see NA E179/119/485/4, E179/485/3 and E179/119/486 whilst Somerset has one for all three see NA E179/256/16. The not chargeable are omitted in the Berkshire list NA E179/76/460.

[62] For Durham see NA E179/106/28.

[63] The Treasury Commission in June 1668 appeared to waive the need for lists to be signed by the Clerk of the Peace in order to speed up the audit. See *Calendar of Treasury Books*, II, p. 583.

[64] Suspiciously, in the Breconshire and Glamorgan lists the numbers of not chargeable within the chargeable section are frequently multiples of five. See NA E179/219/63 and E179/221/297.

name under the 1663 Act required a huge increase in certificates. To save time most were now issued on a parochial basis rather than individually. Many of them cite the rental criterion but others use incorrect phrases such as 'in regard of their indigencie and povertie ought to be exmptd'.[65] A few printed certificates of the first receivers' administration, Michaelmas 1664 to Michaelmas 1665, have survived which rehearse the first two exemption clauses as given in the 1662 Act.[66] By the 1670s Sherwyn and Webb organized printed versions for every county. The preamble at the top of the certificate may state some or all of the statutory exemption clauses from the 1662 and 1664 Acts. In addition, from 1672 the reverse of the certificate often lists the main grey areas of abuse to remind the administrators how the law should be interpreted.[67] This however is no guarantee that in practice the officials followed the wording exactly.

Lists of named householders with the number of their hearths appear very straightforward but such information cannot be taken at face value. In theory, the name should refer to the occupier but in practice, if the property was vacant it may be the landlord or the owner. Generally the hearth number represents a single building but sometimes it refers to part of a sub-divided house or even hearths in several buildings. The completeness of each list also varies for a multitude of reasons such as the diligence or confusion of the officials compiling it, the changes in the law, and the timing of these changes. Furthermore such differences may not be consistent within one county. There is no single way of testing the comprehensiveness of a list, but comparison with others of different dates, or with surviving parochial records of the same date may throw some light on the level of omissions.

Local Collection and Source Difficulties

Local lists provide a means to test the source difficulties of the tax. An almost complete sequence of papers from 1666 to 1675 for Tudhoe township provide details of ownership, occupiers and alterations to houses (Appendix II). Tudhoe lies four miles south-west of Durham City; a nucleated village around a large open green, with some houses away from the village at Watergate and Butcherbank. The Tudhoe constables listed households topographically; in some years differentiating the east and west rows on either side of the green, and listing the outlying houses separately. The village was inhabited mainly by farming tenants and their labourers, with land-sale coal mining providing some additional employment.[68] Most of the freehold land was owned by individuals resident elsewhere and only the most established yeomen and husbandmen families held the freehold to their house. The constables themselves headed chargeable single hearth households in Tudhoe, being of similar status and means to most of their

---

65 This 1663 certificate for Prees in Shropshire exempts 82 persons NA E179/225/24.
66 These refer to Surrey and are in NA E179/346.
67 Some examples can be found amongst the Lincolnshire material in NA E179/334.
68 see J. U. Nef, *The Rise of the British Coal Industry*, vol. I (London, 1966), p. 39 and 137n.

neighbours. The gentry Salvins, of Croxdale Hall, acquired land in Tudhoe during the 1630s and established a residence there by the 1660s.[69] The Salvins became the dominant landlord from the 1690s, and the hearth tax lists survive among their papers in Durham Record Office, along with a list of freeholders.[70]

Tudhoe's local hearth tax records can be compared with the Exchequer Returns for 1666 and 1674, and the 1670s exemption certificates (see Appendix II). In common with most rural settlements in the county, the majority of households were single hearth with the remainder predominantly having between two and four hearths. Only two entries record over four hearths. The gentry household of the Salvins had five hearths, and they were remodelling Tudhoe Hall in the 1660s and ended up with eight hearths.[71] A yeoman family, the Byerleys, seemingly had two households within one house. The Byerleys were listed as father and two sons with five hearths in 1666 and 1668, but in other years and in the 1666 Exchequer Return, William Byerley senior and junior are listed separately for two and three hearths. In 1670 the constable recorded that one of their five hearths was 'not paid for W.B. senior pretending it a Butcher Shop'. 'Pretending' meant not so much evasion as presenting for the justices to decide whether such a non-payment was allowed by law. This may have been regarded as a legitimate claim to avoid two middling households being taxed at a rate thought to be more appropriate to the wealth of a gentry household.[72] The 1666 Exchequer Return merely lists two separate occupiers as was required by law.

Several Tudhoe houses were being altered during the 1660s, expanding from one to two hearths, or two to three, and two houses had a chimney stack pulled down. The loss of chimneys may reflect reduced circumstances. In 1666, Richard Haward lived with his infants in a single-hearth house and was exempt from the tax, but by the beginning of 1670 the house was empty and by Michaelmas of the same year 'uninhabitable'. In more cheerful circumstances, a reduction in the number of chimneys between hearth tax assessments can relate to ongoing programmes of rebuilding, as at William Dell's single-hearth house, where between 1666 and 1667 'the old House [was] pull'd down ye last winter; and rebuilded this Spring; the Hearth layd againe April 29th 1667'. The rebuilding of Dell's house entailed no increase in the number of hearths, but the standard of accommodation was presumably improved. The hearth tax does not appear to have been a sufficient imposition to warrant the demolition of chimneys in order to reduce taxation, though it may have inhibited less wealthy households from expanding their number of hearths when they rebuilt.

The hearth tax shows a solid core of Tudhoe residents through the 1660s and 1670s, with the addition of a few houses, such as Anthony Harper's at the end of

---

[69] A. Green 'Tudhoe Hall and Byers Green Hall, County Durham: seventeenth and early eighteenth century social change in houses', *Vernacular Architecture*, 29 (1998), pp. 33-41.

[70] Durham Record Office, D/Sa/E882-890.

[71] With three unused, probably in the garrets leaving five hearths in use by the household below.

[72] See M. Spufford, '2000 Phillimore Lecture: The Scope of Local History and the potential of the Hearth Tax Returns' *The Local Historian* Vol. 30, 4, 2000, p. 206.

East Rawe. There were some alterations in the heads of households, where they passed from father to son or, in more cases, from husband to widow. In contrast to this family continuity, other householders only appeared for periods of a few years. This indicates movement into and out of the village, and insecurity of employment may have encouraged such mobility, though this was not so extreme as in the sea-sale mining areas in the north of the county.[73] The exempt households at Tudhoe had a solid core, but there was some oscillation with a few households shifting in and out of the not liable category. For the able-bodied this may relate to the vicissitudes of waged employment, but in most cases exemption was part of the life cycle, when older inhabitants were unable to earn enough to sustain themselves without support from the parish and consequently received relief from taxation. Movement between the exempt and the chargeable category in the hearth tax records may also be explained by the particular motivations underlying the compilation of different records. Levine and Wrightson found that some taxpayers at Whickham listed in the 1666 assessment were exempt in the return of the same year, which might relate to real impoverishment but more likely reflects assessors maximising payers who were found to be exempt on collection.[74]

The local lists for Tudhoe can also be used to test the degree of under-recording in the Exchequer Returns. The 1670 assessment provides the most complete index of Tudhoe households and their hearths; its thoroughness a result of Michaelmas 1670 being an entirely new administration of the tax.[75] It probably represents a full survey of the township, listing householders with their hearths in topographical order, with some of the non-liable intermingled with the chargeable. Sixty-five households are recorded, and the parish officers' certificate for 1670 records an additional thirteen as exempt. The total of 78 households includes 46 charged and 32 exempt, of whom nineteen were presumably granted exemption on the grounds of the value of their property. All other years give lower figures. Some of the local records must therefore include a degree of under-recording, unless they precisely match fluctuations in population. If 1670 is taken as a benchmark, then the under-recording of households in the 1674 Lady Day Exchequer Return is 40 per cent; as high as that suggested by Husbands nationally.[76] One must remember however that differences between lists may not only indicate changes in population but also changes in interpretation of the law.

---

[73] D. Levine and K. Wrightson, *The Making of an Industrial Society: Whickham 1560-1765*, (Oxford, 1991), pp. 168-71.

[74] Levine and Wrightson, *Whickham*, pp.153-4, found a disparity at Whickham between 252 names in 1665 and 390 in 1666, explained by the administrative changes to the hearth tax, but which may still reflect population changes.

[75] William Christian was receiver for both the 1664-5 & 1670-74 administrations, Thomas Hall probably surveyed Tudhoe township as sub-collector.

[76] C. Husbands, 'The Hearth Tax and the Structure of the English Economy' (unpublished University of Cambridge PhD, 1985), though Arkell, 'The Incidence of Poverty in England in the later seventeenth century' *Social History* 12 I (1987), p. 30, doubts the validity of a 40 per cent omission rate based on population estimates for 1700.

Comparison between the various central and local lists for Tudhoe,[77] also suggests a lower degree of recording in the Exchequer records. The number of chargeable entries hovers around 30 in most of the lists, except for the 1674 Exchequer Return which records the lowest number, of just 23 householders as mentioned in the preceeding paragraph. In 1666, 30 chargeable households are recorded in the Exchequer Return, with 31 for the combined 1666 and 1667 constables' assessment. For the not chargeable, 32 are recorded in the 1666 Exchequer Return, 28 in the 1667 local list and 33 in the 1673/4 exemption certificate.[78] Some of those listed as not chargeable in 1666 may have included some who did not pay rather than those exempted in order to conceal the failure of the farmers to collect. Furthermore the proof of non-liability was the exemption certificate, so that they probably provide a more accurate reflection of the number of exempt than those found on the Exchequer Return. The 1674 Exchequer list records 23 charged households compared to 28 in the 1673 local list, with 34 'non-solvent' in the Exchequer Return and 33 exempted in the 1673 certificate. The Tudhoe lists suggest that under-recording did occur in the Durham hearth tax, most likely excluding the poorer households; a practice encouraged by population mobility. Moreover, between the local records and the Exchequer a loss of between ten and twenty per cent of households is known. Similar discrepancies between local lists and the Exchequer records can be found in West and St. Helen Auckland. In John Kay's notebook (Appendix III) an exemption certificate for 1671 records 30 names in St. Helen Auckland and 61 in West Auckland,[79] whereas the Exchequer Returns contain 27 in St. Helen Auckland, and 57 in West Auckland, and these lower figures are suspiciously constant between 1666 and 1674 in both communities — suggesting that exemption lists were replicated in the Exchequer Returns rather than accurately revised. The notion that 20 per cent under-recording in the 1666 and 1674 Exchequer Returns may be general, is supported by the under-recording rates calculated for other areas. In the West Riding of Yorkshire 20 per cent of the exempt, and in Nottinghamshire 25 per cent of households, were not recorded. While under-recording mainly omitted the poor,[80] tax evasion also occurred among the more prosperous. In Cambridgeshire there are instances of constables under-assessing themselves, and of higher hearth numbers being under-assessed, with eight instead of nine, or eleven instead of seventeen hearths.[81] Given the source difficulties, the Exchequer Returns cannot be taken as a complete index of the total number of households, or even always the correct number of hearths among the more prosperous.

---

[77] see Table in Appendix II.
[78] For 1675, see NA ER179/890; the 1673/4 exemption certificate is printed in Appendix IV.
[79] Kay's notebook: Churchwardens Exemption Certificate, September 1671.
[80] See Arkell, 'Incidence of Poverty', and Husbands in Schürer and Arkell *Surveying the People*, pp. 65-77, and N. Alldridge (ed.) *The Hearth Tax: Problems and Possibilities* (Hull, 1983) pp. 45-58.
[81] Evans, *Cambridgeshire*, p.xxiv-v, citing M.F. Pickles, 'Labour Migration: Yorkshire, c.1670 to 1743', *Local Population Studies*, 57 (Autumn 1996), pp. 32-33; Webster, *Nottinghamshire*, p. xxii.

At West Auckland, the notebook of John Kay, grieve, includes hearth tax lists for 1671, 1672 and 1675, notes on 1676 and 1677, and a list of constables from 1662 to 1700 (Appendix III).[82] There were two constables for West Auckland, one for the 'town' and a second for the outlying farms and hamlets, and the hearth tax lists were correspondingly drawn up in topographical order. Kay was an overseer of the administration of the township, and was closely involved with the gentry Eden family resident at West Auckland. Kay served as churchwarden and as constable in 1662, 1670 and 1700. His copybook is densely written, crammed with detailed lists relating to the administration of the township and his personal affairs, including his own payment of hearth money in 1676 and 1677.[83] In comparison to the Tudhoe constables, who paid on single-hearth households, Kay was a 'yeoman' and 'grieve' of more substantial status, assessed for three hearths in March 1666, 1671 and 1672. The purpose of the notebook was seemingly to provide a written record that would guard against legal or personal disputes, and it provides an insight into the contentious aspects of local office holding. Constables served in rotation on the basis of the location of their house, though in many instances the householder hired another person to perform their duties. Yet there were disputes over fulfilling the office of constable, and Kay records an agreement made in about 1700 that the owners or occupiers of houses should serve in rotation, 'whereas heretofore there haith very often and for the most part every yeare strifes and dessentes been raised [...] concerning the serving of the office of Constables'. Typically of seventeenth-century community relations, the dispute was resolved in the presence of an authority figure, John Eden esqr., and through appeals to good neighbourliness. The occurrence of such disputes partly explains why Kay kept such a careful record of the hearth tax collection in West Auckland. Inter-personal relations may also have resulted in some leniency for individual hearth tax assessments, though this is very difficult to detect and the general impression is that local office holders took their responsibilities seriously. Indeed, the assessment of liability and exemption in local lists is generally more comprehensive than the final returns included in the Exchequer Rolls. Even local lists, however, are rarely ever entirely complete records of the full number of households or hearths.

Historical Background

The Social and Economic Development of Seventeenth-Century Durham
County Durham was bounded by the North Sea to the east, the Rivers Tyne and Tees to north and south, and the Pennine watershed in the west (Map 1). The upland and lowland areas are respectively west and east of a line running in an

---

82 Durham University Archive (DUA), Halmote Court Doc. M. 95.
83 DUA Halmote Court Doc. M. 95, p. 2, 'Paid to Christar Dobeson Constable my harth money May 5th 1676 3s. 0d'; 'Paid to Jo Bell Constable my harth money Oct. 23 1676 3s.' and 'April 28 1677 Paid my chimney money to Rob. Middleton and Robt Andarson Constable for West Auckland'.

arc from Barnard Castle on the River Tees, through Bishop Auckland, Durham City and Chester-le-Street on the River Wear, to Gateshead at the River Tyne. The river valleys linked the lowlands to the uplands so that their watersheds shaped the pattern of social activity as much as the height of the land. The west of the county is in the High Pennines, with Teesdale and Weardale the focus of settlement and communication routes. Pennine spurs dissect the landscape to the east of this area, maintaining the distinctions between watersheds. The Tyne and Wear lowlands occupy the centre and north of the county; a further area of higher ground forms the east Durham plateau, extending almost to the coast, with the Tees lowlands in the south-east of the county. The geological and glacial activity that formed this landscape left lead in the Pennines, coal deposits mainly beneath the Tyne and Wear watersheds, and more nutrient rich soils in the Tees lowlands. The most productive agricultural land is in the south-east of the county, while in the uplands rough grazing characterises most of the ground above the more fertile river plains of Weardale and Teesdale.[84] The hearth tax maps show very well that the greatest density of settlement was along the Rivers Wear, Tees and Tyne.

The society and economy of County Durham underwent considerable change during the seventeenth century. While commonly regarded as a relatively 'backward' area in the sixteenth century, social and economic development had quite transformed the region by the late seventeenth century. The single most significant development was the expansion of the coal trade, ultimately dependent on increased demand for coal created by the growth of London. Starting from an already high base of 60,000 tons a year in the mid-sixteenth century, there was a ten-fold increase in the Tyne coal trade by the late seventeenth century.[85] By then, the Wear-side coalfield with Sunderland as its port, had developed into a rival to coal shipment from the Tyne. The expansion of coal mining was not limited to sea-sale markets; coal for land-sale was extracted from inland areas as far south and west as Chilton, Raby and Hamsterley.[86] By the end of the seventeenth century, the land-sale districts of Northumberland and Durham produced about 100,000 tons per annum; a sixth of the sea-sale trade.[87] Land-sale coal was mainly consumed as fuel in the houses of the region and to burn lime for fertilising fields. Coal of inferior quality from the sea-sale areas was used by industries on Tyne- and Wear-side, especially for glass manufacture and salt extraction from sea water. Industrial activity also involved lead mining in the Pennines and ship building on Tyne- and Wear-side. Many of the households

[84] See J. C. Dewdney (ed.), *Durham County and City with Teeside*, (Durham, 1970) and P. Brassley, *The agricultural economy of Northumberland and Durham in the period, 1640-1750* (New York, 1985) from J. Thirsk (ed.) *The Agrarian History of England and Wales, Vol. 5i, 1640-1750: Regional Farming Systems* (Cambridge, 1984).

[85] B. Dietz, 'The North-East Coal Trade 1550-1750: Measures, Markets and the Metropolis', *Northern History* 22 1986, pp.280-94, p. 286; see also, J. Hatcher, *The History of the British Coal Industry, Vol. 1, Before 1700: towards the Age of Coal* (Oxford, 1993).

[86] J. U. Nef, *The Rise of the British Coal Industry*, 2 vols (London, 1966), vol. I pp. 37-8.

[87] Nef, *Coal Industry* 1966 I, p. 36.

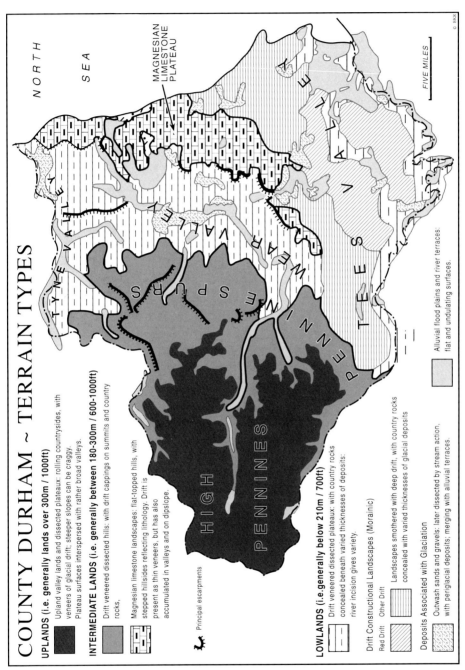

COUNTY DURHAM ~ TERRAIN TYPES

UPLANDS (i.e. generally lands over 300m / 1000ft)

Upland valley lands and dissected plateaux: rolling countrysides, with veneers of glacial drift; steeper slopes can be craggy. Plateau surfaces interspersed with rather broad valleys.

INTERMEDIATE LANDS (i.e. generally between 180-300m / 600-1000ft)

Drift veneered dissected hills: with drift cappings on summits and country rocks,

Magnesian limestone landscapes: flat-topped hills, with stepped hillsides reflecting lithology. Drift is present as thin veneers, but has also accumulated in valleys and on dipslope.

Principal escarpments

LOWLANDS (i.e. generally below 210m / 700ft)

Drift veneered dissected plateaux: with country rocks concealed beneath varied thicknesses of deposits: river incision gives variety.

Drift Constructional Landscapes (Morainic)

Red Drift   Other Drift

Landscapes smothered with deep drift, with country rocks concealed with varied thicknesses of glacial deposits

Deposits Associated with Glaciation

Outwash sands and gravels: later dissected by stream action, with periglacial deposits; merging with alluvial terraces.

Alluvial flood plains and river terraces: flat and undulating surfaces.

MAGNESIAN LIMESTONE PLATEAU

NORTH SEA

TYNE VALLEY

WEAR VALLEY

TEES VALLEY

PENNINE SPURS

HIGH PENNINES

FIVE MILES

© BKR

Map 1. Terrain types

recorded in the hearth tax, especially in the north of the county, were bound into this quasi-industrial economy.

Industrial employment created a large wage-labour population, increasingly dependent on purchased food-stuffs. Farming in the county altered in the seventeenth century in response to the demand presented by this local market for agricultural produce. This led to a greater specialisation in pastoral production, especially in the north of the county, where local farmers could easily supply dairy and livestock produce, whereas the market for cereals had to compete with imports, especially through Newcastle. The landscape was transformed as a large proportion of the open fields surrounding individual settlements were enclosed by freeholders and tenants. These farmers were prospering indirectly from the expansion of the coal trade, and often gained larger holdings at the expense of smaller farmers (invariably copyholders) who sought wages in agricultural, mining or other employment. The landlords, particularly the institutional estates of the church, were not especially active in encouraging enclosure to raise rents, though some gentry landlords were concerned to secure a food supply for their coal workers.[88] Whereas in many parts of southern England the enclosure of open fields took place after 1700, in County Durham most townfield enclosures occurred during the seventeenth century with the majority of documented enclosures between 1630 and 1680. Enclosures were concentrated in the lowland Tees valley, East Durham Plateau and southern Wear lowlands, as well as in the coal-mining parishes of the Tyne (Ryton, Whickham and Winlaton) and Wear (Herrington, Newbottle, Chester-le-Street and Lumley) valleys.[89] Seventeenth-century enclosures were particularly intensive in the south-east of the county, and were accompanied by depopulation.[90] By the late seventeenth century, a more commercial agriculture had altered the economy and society of many communities across the county.

Those who prospered in agriculture rebuilt the village farmsteads, and many nucleated settlements experienced the expansion of single houses over the house plots of several predecessors.[91] This trend was also present in towns, where seventeenth-century rebuilding often occured over two or more medieval tenements. Tenurial change contributed to the process of house rebuilding in both town and country, as copyhold tenure was replaced by commercial leaseholds from the early seventeenth century; encouraging landlords and tenants to engage in 'improvement' of land and buildings. In the coalfield, by contrast, traditional villages were subsumed by 'mining colonisation'; maintaining or extending the number of cottage holdings and converting surplus farmsteads into dwellings for

---

[88] R. Floud and D. McCloskey, *The Economic History of Britain since 1700*, 2 vols, 2nd edition (Cambridge, 1994), Vol. 1 pp. 117-8.

[89] R. I. Hodgson, 'The Progress of Enclosure in County Durham 1550-1870' in *Change and Continuity in the Countryside*, ed. by H.S.A Fox and R.A. Butlin (London, 1979) pp. 83-102.

[90] R. I. Hodgson, 'Demographic Trends in County Durham, 1560-1801' *University of Manchester School for Geography Research Papers* 5 (1978).

[91] B. K. Roberts, *The Green Villages of County Durham: a study in historical geography* (Durham Local History Publication No. 12, 1977), pp. 21 & 35-6.

persons not regularly engaged with agriculture.[92] Employment in lead mining led to similar changes in settlement, albeit on a smaller scale, in the Pennines to the west of Middleton in Teesdale and in the upper reaches of Weardale and on Derwentside in the north-west of the county.[93]

Seventeenth-century Durham was no isolated northern backwater, but there was continuity in the basically agricultural dependence of most of its population who continued to occupy small households which were far from prosperous in a largely rural context. Even in the most intensively mined parts of the county such as Whickham, continuity went alongside change, particularly in the more established households.[94] Conversely, it is too readily assumed that the character of settlement and society in the coal field was a creation of the nineteenth century. The later industrial character of the county had its antecedents in the seventeenth century with the pattern of industrial activity and settlement largely in existence by 1700. During the seventeenth century agricultural change and mining settlement modified the medieval pattern of settlement, characterised by dispersed settlement in upland areas, with greater nucleation, often around open greens, across lowland County Durham. The hearth tax appears during the period of greatest discontinuity in the county's settlement pattern and standard of housing between the medieval and modern eras. New mining settlements in the coal field, now either composed of nineteenth and twentieth-century terraces or deserted, began as seventeenth-century settlements; while isolated farms and the shrunken and deserted villages of south-eastern County Durham were a product of enclosure and the exodus of the poorer population to work in the coal field and elsewhere. This came about as a result of expanded opportunities for industrial employment, and the social polarisation of communities caught up in the process of enclosing fields and engrossing farmsteads, and were the most far-reaching aspects of County Durham's social and economic development during the seventeenth century.

Lady Day 1666

The Transcript and Maps

For purposes of administration, County Durham was divided into the four wards of Chester, Easington, Stockton and Darlington. These wards were further sub-divided for the administration of the hearth tax, with a separate ward for Durham City (see p. cxxv).[95] The Exchequer Return lists by place the names and

---

[92] Roberts, *Green Villages* i, pp. 4-5 & 20-1.
[93] A. Raistrick and B. Jennings, *A History of Lead Mining in the Pennines* (London, 1965).
[94] Levine and Wrightson, *Whickham*; see also A. Green, 'Houses and Landscape in Early Industrial County Durham' in *Northern Landscapes: Representations and Realities*, ed. by T. Faulkner and H. Berry (Boydell & Brewer, forthcoming).
[95] In Lady Day 1666 Haughton-le-Skerne parish is in Darlington Ward, though usually part of Stockton Ward. Durham City was formally part of Easington Ward until 1829. See P. D. A. Harvey, 'Boldon Book and the Wards between Tyne and Tees' in D. Rollason, M. Harvey and M. Prestwich (eds.) *Anglo-Norman Durham 1093-1193*, (Woodbridge, 1994), pp. 399-405.

number of hearths of those who paid the tax with those deemed to be exempt listed separately after all the chargeable, following the same order of wards with the omission of Durham City. In Table 6, pp. xcv–cxxiii, the non-payers have been placed with payers to ease comparison. It has taken some effort to co-ordinate them, since the township and town divisions, used to identify payers, were not necessarily consistent with the parishes or chapelries used for non-payers. This consistency even varied between years of the tax. We find it harder than contemporaries to co-ordinate lists of chargeable hearths, for collection, in 1666, by professional sub-collectors, with those of the non-chargeable, made by parish officers. In several cases the township units in the hearth tax do not appear with their formal parish, which indicates some rationalisation in the collection of the hearth tax.[96] The maps present the data by township, and since these usually relate to a single settlement, this provides a reliable guide to the social and economic profile of each community, and the differences between them. The Exchequer Return does not, however, distinguish nucleated from dispersed settlement, and individual places need to be compared with other sources (especially enclosure, estate or tithe maps). In many instances the entries in the hearth tax are in topographical order, but sense can only be made of this by comparison with other sources. Within this volume, the maps should be read in conjunction with the terrain map (Map 1) and tables.

Comparison of Lady 1666 with Lady Day 1674

Lady Day 1666 is the preferred assessment for this volume as it is in better condition and lists more legible names. Yet Lady Day 1674 actually contains the greatest number of entries among the Exchequer records extant for County Durham: 13,281 households, whereas Lady Day 1666 has 12,313. The difference mainly relates to the larger number of places with non-payers included in the Exchequer Rolls in 1674. The 44 per cent exemption rate for 1674 is therefore the more reliable, especially since Durham City is omitted from the non-payers in 1666. For the payers, although 1674 contains about 900 more entries than 1666, there is a considerable degree of consistency in the proportion of hearth numbers within the paying category (see Table 1). There is also broad consistency for the proportion of hearth ranges as a total of the recorded entries: in 1666, 69 per cent of all entries were for single hearths, with 73 per cent in 1674. This increase reflects greater recording. Around a quarter of households occupied the middling band of two to four hearths in 1666 and 1674, with the remaining 5 per cent having five hearths or more. Comparison by township may indicate changes in the number of households due to shifts in population, while increases in hearth numbers may relate to rebuilding. In many cases, however, differences between 1666 and 1674 relate to the degree of recording.

---

[96] For example, Tudhoe was formally part of Brancepeth parish, but is listed with Whitworth in 1666 and with Merrington in the 1670s exemption certificates (NA E179/327/3); Byers Green is also listed in 1666 as part of Whitworth, when its major portion lay within St. Andrew's Auckland parish.

Table 1: County Durham Hearths in 1666 and 1674

	1666	%	1674	%	1666 & 1674
Total entries	**12,313**	**100%**	**13,281**	**100%**	**100%**
Not chargeable	4,963	40%	5,870	44%	42%
Chargeable	7,350	60%	7,411	56%	58%
Breakdown of chargeable:					
1 hearth	3,826	52%	3,858	52%	52%
2 hearths	1,903	26%	1,711	23%	25%
3 hearths	685	9%	719	10%	10%
4 hearths	364	5%	397	5%	5%
5 hearths	196	3%	235	3%	3%
6 hearths	115	2%	168	2%	2%
7 hearths	75	1%	78	1%	1%
8 hearths	48	>1%	53	1%	1%
9 hearths	38	>1%	47	>1%	>1%
10+ hearths	86	1%	104	1%	1%

The Hearth Tax as an Indication of the Density of Population

The hearth tax returns of 1665 and 1666 have been taken to suggest a population of between 54,000 and 60,000 for County Durham.[97] Given the degree of under-recording this is probably an under-estimate; an alternative calculation suggests 70,000 on the basis of 1674.[98] The distribution of the recorded population is indicated in Map 2, on the basis of households per 1000 acres. Generally it confirms our picture of the topography and settlement pattern. The western uplands are sparsely populated, with dispersed settlement rarely amounting to more than fifteen households per thousand acres, and this pattern extends in the north-west of the county where the high ground continues almost to Chester-le-Street and the Tyne. In Weardale, only the towns of Stanhope and Wolsingham appear as significant population centres. Barnard Castle does not emerge so clearly, partly because the township extends over a relatively large area, but also because Lady Day 1666 does not include any non-payers for the town and the list of payers is incomplete. The area east of Barnard Castle to the Roman road (which marks the division between townships from Piercebridge north to Bishop Auckland) presents an area of more fertile, lower ground, with an unusually high rural population for the county: there were significant centres at Piercebridge

---

[97] Durham County Local History Society, *An Historical Atlas of County Durham* (Durham, 1992), pp. 40-1.

[98] Based on multiplying the number of households by 4.25 (mean household size), and inflating by 25 per cent to account for under-recording.

and Staindrop, and Gainford was unusually prosperous among rural Durham parishes, being more like Richmondshire south of the Tees.[99] East of the Roman road there were further significant populations around Darlington and the towns of Stockton and Hartlepool are clearly distinguished. The market centre of Sedgefield also appears amidst a more general pattern of lower population in the rural communities of south-eastern Durham. A further area of lower population density in the east of the county is apparent on the higher ground of the East Durham Plateau. Within the Wear watershed, most of the places with the highest population density are along the course of the River Wear. In the far north of the county, industrial employment created significant concentrations of population along the Tyne.

The places with the greatest density of population in the north of the county reflect industrial employment.[100] Whickham, Gateshead, Heworth and South Shields (with its salt pans) are all highly populous parishes on the River Tyne, with Ryton and Ebchester, to the west, similarly affected by immigration to the coalfield during the seventeenth century. Along the River Wear, the parishes of Sunderland, Monkwearmouth, Bishopwearmouth, and Houghton-le-Spring contained similar densities of population as a result of employment in coal mining. The maps for seventeenth-century waggonways and coal pits correlate with this density of population,[101] while salt pans and shipbuilding provided further employment nearer to the mouth of the Wear. The lower population densities for other northern Durham parishes (Jarrow, Whitburn, Lamesley, Washington and Chester-le-Street), reflect a lower intensity of mining.

Some of the places with the highest population density relate to towns. Durham City and its environs appear clearly, as do Hartlepool and Darlington. Townships containing a town but also large rural acreages will not show up so well on Map 2. Kirby provides a firmer identification of urban places by comparing population density in the 1666 hearth tax with land values in 1642, which shows six places with urban characteristics: Durham, Darlington, Gateshead, South Shields, Sunderland and Hartlepool. The market towns of Stockton, Bishop Auckland and Barnard Castle were distinct from these. They were more rural than urban, while the smaller market centres, such as Sedgefield and Staindrop, were found to be virtually indistinguishable from their rural hinterlands.[102] This pattern of urban places and market towns is confirmed in the average number of hearths per household (the mean hearth ownership,

[99] See J. D. Purdy, *Yorkshire Hearth Tax Returns*, Studies in Regional and Local History No. 7 (Hull, 1991).

[100] See R. I. Hodgson, 'Coal Mining, Population and Enclosure in the Sea-sale Colliery Districts of Durham 1551-1801' (unpublished University of Durham PhD, 1989).

[101] *Historical Atlas of County Durham*.

[102] D. A. Kirby, 'Population Density and Land Values in County Durham during the mid-seventeenth century' *Transactions of the Institute of British Geographers* 57 (1972), pp. 83-98, using Protestation Returns in the Book of Rates of 1642.

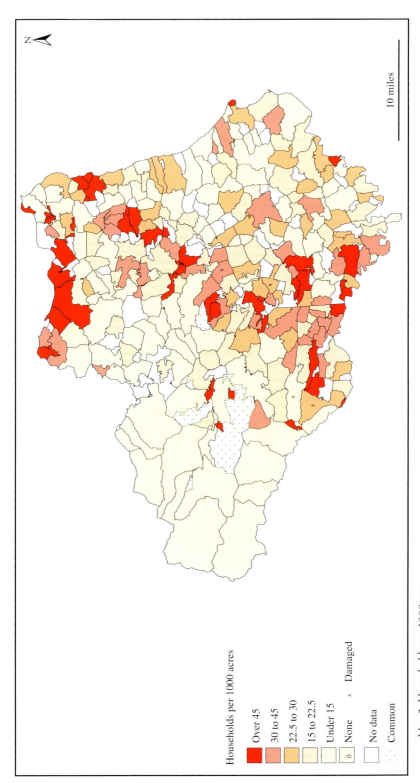

N

10 miles

Households per 1000 acres

■ Over 45
▨ 30 to 45
▨ 22.5 to 30
▨ 15 to 22.5
☐ Under 15
⊙ None   x   Damaged
☐ No data
⬚ Common

Map 2. Households per 1000 acres

calculated for 1674).[103] Across England, hearth ownership is generally higher in market towns and urban centres than in rural communities. There were 1.6 hearths per household on average for the county as a whole, with 2.16 among the payers (compared to a national average of 2.5 hearths per household). Following Kirby's definitions, the total mean hearth ownership for towns is 1.97, for urban centres 2.2 and for market towns 1.54. Stockton, Sunderland and Hartlepool have a lower average number of hearths per household, which may relate to their role as ports, whereas the inland marketing centres (including Bishop Auckland and Barnard Castle) have a higher mean hearth ownership. In short, there was greater prosperity in the inland towns than in the urban coastal communities. The remaining areas (both rural and industrial settlements) had 1.42 hearths per household on average.

The average number of households per settlement for 1674 produces a mean of 31.7 households per settlement for the entire county, but in non-urban areas 25.7 households on average. As in the maps of 1666, the highest number of households were located in areas bordering the Tyne, and somewhat less so between the Tyne and Durham City. In the south of the county, the next highest number of households per settlement were located along the Tees. This represents densely populated communities in the north of the county in the coal mining areas and larger communities in the rich farming land along the Tees and in relation to the marketing centres at Stockton and Darlington. When the larger towns are removed from the equation, the higher figures are again in the north of the county reflecting the non-urban nature of mining settlement. There does not appear to be a clear distinction between the upland and lowland areas, despite the contrast between dispersed and nucleated settlement. This fits Husband's conclusion that there was no strong correlation between the type of agricultural region and population density. Maps 2 and 3 similarly show no strong contrasts between upland and lowland.

The pattern of population density also needs to be placed in chronological perspective. Hodgson compared the 1563 Ecclesiastical Return with the 1674 hearth tax and 1801 census, and found a declining number of households in many settlements in south-eastern County Durham, while the rapidly developing coal field experienced population growth well in excess of the national average. He calculates a total of 8,495 households for County Durham in 1563; rising by 70 per cent to 14,561 in 1674. Most of this increase occurred in the north and east of the county, where industrial activity and relatively large populations were already present in 1563. The south and east of the county by contrast, had far more modest increases in household totals and in some townships population decreased, usually in association with the enclosure of townfields and lowland waste. In northern County Durham the industrialised centres expanded

---

[103] For further detail on mean hearth ownership, and mean households per settlement, see A. Green, 'Houses and Households in County Durham and Newcastle, c.1570-1730' (unpublished University of Durham PhD, 2000).

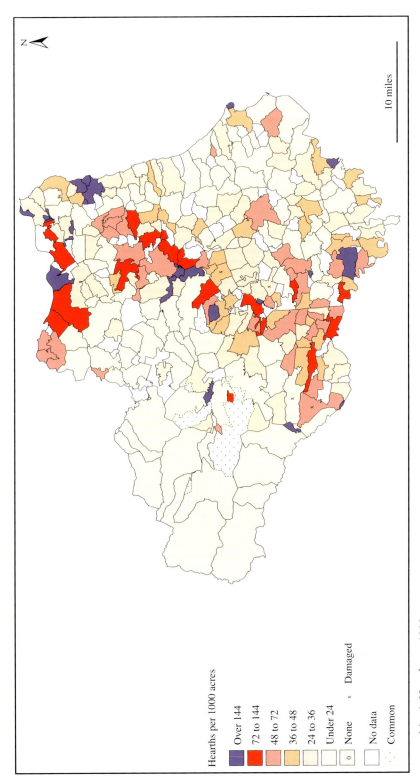

Map 3. Hearths per 1000 acres

Hearths per 1000 acres

Over 144
72 to 144
48 to 72
36 to 48
24 to 36
Under 24
None   x   Damaged
No data
Common

dramatically; Whickham, Gateshead and South Shields each increased threefold. Mining expanded through the seventeenth century, and Sunderland gained a greater share of the coal trade. Most of the newly worked coal came from the townships of Lumley and Lambton in Chester-le-Street parish, and the hearth tax returns give a high rate of exemption in these mining communities; 191 out of 241 households were exempt in 1674, with only 50 families deemed able to pay. Coal was also being mined on an increasing scale in the land-sale parishes and the parish registers indicate rising household totals in Brancepeth, Witton-le-Wear, Hamsterley and Cockfield. Hodgson's comparison of the 1674 figures with the national census of 1801 indicates greater rates of growth for the county as a whole (161.77 per cent against 71.4 per cent between 1563 and 1674) and new growth in older urban centres at Durham, Darlington, Staindrop and Barnard Castle and the ports of Stockton and Hartlepool. This contrasts with the fate of smaller and medium sized settlements in 1674, which continued a decline already in progress between 1563 and 1674.[104]

The Hearth Tax and the Distribution of Wealth

Map 3 shows hearths per 1000 acres, with a distribution closely connected to the density of population. Given that the majority of households had a single hearth (see Map 9), the density of hearths reflects population levels as well as houses with a greater number of heated rooms. Some of the places with the highest density of hearths contained large populations which were extremely impoverished by national standards: as for instance, at Whickham, where 78 per cent of all households had single hearths, and the exemption rate was 75 per cent. Moreover, the places with larger populations often contained the most mixed communities, and Whickham had a good spread of households with a wide variety of higher hearth numbers. Map 3 does not therefore present a straightforward index of wealth, and should be compared with the population density in Map 2. Places which have a high population density but a lower number of hearths in Map 3 are less prosperous overall, whereas those places with a high ranking in both maps may relate to either high levels of single-hearth households (as for example in the Tyne parishes and Sunderland) or prosperity (as in Durham City). Places with a greater hearth than population density were more prosperous, as the number of hearths is proportionally greater in relation to the number of households.

In the north of the county, the coal economy fuelled a considerable number of hearths along the Tyne and along the Wear, with further areas of population density and a greater number of hearths in communities through the centre of the county. In the triangle between Durham City, Chester-le-Street and Houghton-le-Spring, communities had a relatively high number of hearths owing partly to the prosperity generated by commercial and agricultural activity, and the presence of some larger houses, but also because there were a considerable number

[104] Hodgson, 'Demographic Trends'.

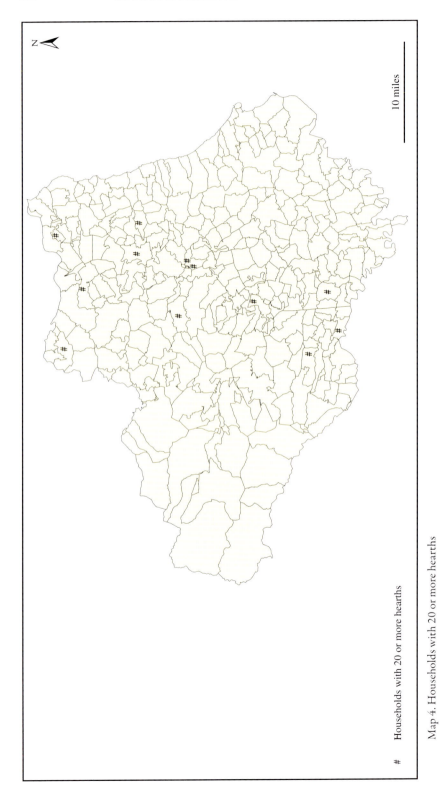

Households with 20 or more hearths

Map 4. Households with 20 or more hearths

of smaller houses with only one hearth. The settlements to the south and west of Durham City, and in the triangle between Barnard Castle, Bishop Auckland and Darlington, also contained a greater number of hearths, and this reflects a degree of greater prosperity by the standards of the county, as well as some larger villages. In the remainder of the county, the number of hearths is low except for places with a significant town, port or marketing centre: witness Stanhope, Wolsingham, Sedgefield, Stockton and Hartlepool. Exceptions to this pattern are due to particular circumstances; for example, Greatham, where the hospital boosts the number of hearths. Neither the uplands nor the eastern lowlands emerge as areas of significant prosperity. Generally, the majority of households contained few hearths, and the number of more prosperous households with a greater number of chimneys was insufficient to off-set this pattern, and produces few rural places with more than twenty-four hearths per thousand acres.

Although the density of hearths does not provide a straightforward index of wealth in County Durham, the hearth tax was based on the assumption that the more hearths an individual had the wealthier they were, and while there are problems with systematically applying this assumption, historians have demonstrated that there was some correlation between hearths and wealth. The following maps, in common with other volumes in this series, adopt a series of hearth-ranges which are believed to relate closely to social status and the wealth of their occupants.

Buildings with Twenty or more Hearths

Twelve buildings in the county are recorded as having twenty or more hearths in 1666 (Map 4). Three of these reflect the wealth of the church — the bishop's residences and Durham Cathedral. Several of the remainder were medieval castles remodelled in the sixteenth and seventeenth centuries. The others were large houses usually occupied by élite families that had gained prominence in the county in the last century, often funded from commercial wealth.[105] The county contains relatively few very large households, and no recently built palatial residences: Sir Arthur Haselrigg had created a neo-classical house at Bishop Auckland in the 1650s, but Bishop Cosin had removed it by 1666. Cosin's remodelling of Bishop Auckland may also be responsible for the reduction in the number of hearths, from 35 in 1666 to 26 in 1674: Gregory King's drawing (see frontispiece), shows the castle in 1666 and identifies Cosin's new chapel. Cosin also made alterations to Durham Castle in the 1660s and 1670s, and its assessment rises from 22 hearths in 1666 to 28 hearths in 1674.[106] The other major ecclesiastic was 'Mr Dean', with twenty hearths in 1666 for the Deanery and Cathedral complex. These twenty hearths do not relate entirely to the Deanery, and in common with most of the individuals assessed for twenty or

[105] S. J. Halliday, 'Social Mobility, Demographic Change and the Landed Élite of County Durham, 1610-1819' *Northern History* 30 (1994), pp. 49-63; James, *Civil Society*, pp. 67-74.
[106] See *The Correspondence of John Cosin*, II Surtees Society 55 (1870), pp. 332-383.

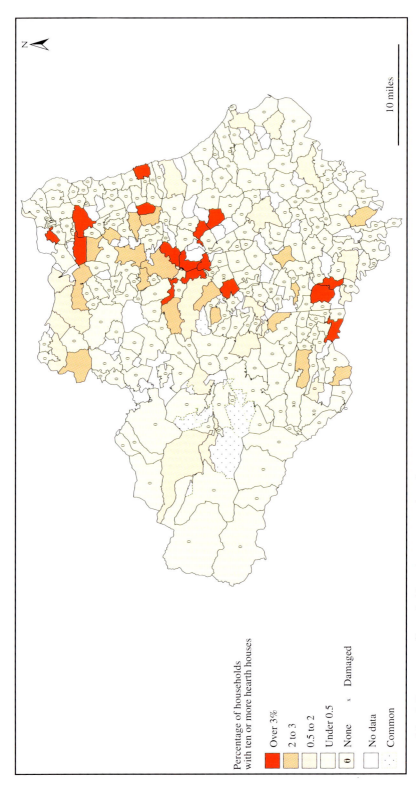

Map 5. Percentage of households with ten or more hearths

Percentage of households
with ten or more hearth houses

Over 3%

2 to 3

0.5 to 2

Under 0.5

None   x   Damaged

No data

Common

10 miles

more hearths, include other buildings in their ownership, though usually in the same complex or vicinity.

In 1666 all persons assessed for over twenty hearths were of high status. The very highest was for Lady Vane with 47 hearths at Raby Castle. After the bishop with 35 hearths at Bishop Auckland, the next highest assessments were for Ralph Wilson gent. at Lumley Castle with 32 hearths and Sir Thomas Liddell with 28 hearths at Ravensworth. We then drop to assessments of 25 hearths or lower: Sir Nicholas Coall was assessed for 25 hearths in Durham St. Giles; Jno. Jennings esqr. had 23 hearths for Walworth Castle; Sir Edward Smith had 22 hearths at Esh Hall; Sir Thomas Tempest, with 22 hearths at Ryton Woodside; Cuthbert Ellison gent., 22 hearths at Monkton Hall, while Gilbert Marshall gent. in Gainford had 21 hearths in and around Selaby Hall. [107]

In other areas of England, the presence of large gentry houses has been found to correlate with smaller communities. In Suffolk, places containing a house with over twenty hearths had on average 23.3 other houses, whereas villages without a large house had on average 33.3 houses. These were gentry-dominated communities with a relatively small population primarily consisting of labourers, and tending to exclude yeomen.[108] This pattern of greater gentry residences alongside smaller and less prosperous communities, did not exist in County Durham, at least for houses with over twenty hearths. The five rural places in 1674 with over twenty hearths, had on average 24.8 other houses per community, compared to 25.7 for all other setlements excluding large towns, and these five places varied in size of population.[109] South of the Humber, Husbands found that communities with a single dominating house of over twenty hearths and relatively few other houses were products of enclosure.[110] This was not the case in Durham, where enclosure before the 1670s was primarily the initiative of middling tenant farmers rather than landlords. Some of the gentry houses with between ten and twenty hearths show a closer correlation to smaller communities with lower hearth numbers.[111]

Households with Ten or more Hearths

Householders taxed on over ten hearths possessed considerable wealth, though not all such entries relate to single houses since some include a number of buildings under the same ownership, and several of the largest entries in towns will refer to inns. The housing market may have affected higher hearth numbers where individuals paid on houses owned for rent, though they ought only to have paid when empty and were usually assessed separately. Very large houses

---

[107] An inventory of Selaby in 1633 is printed in R. Surtees, *History and Antiquities of the County Palatine of Durham*, 4 vols. (1816-40), vol. 4, p. 18. Gilbert Marshall, a Parliamentary Commissioner for sequestrating royalist estates, had obtained Selaby from the recusant Brackenbury family by 1657.

[108] M. H. Johnson, 'A Contextual Study of Traditional Architecture in Western Suffolk, 1400-1700' (unpublished University of Cambridge PhD, 1989).

[109] These are Cold Hesledon and Dalton, Lumley and Lambton, Monkton, Esh, and Walworth.

[110] Husbands, 'Structure of the English Economy'.

[111] See, for instance, Hunstanworth and Archdeacon Newton in the tables.

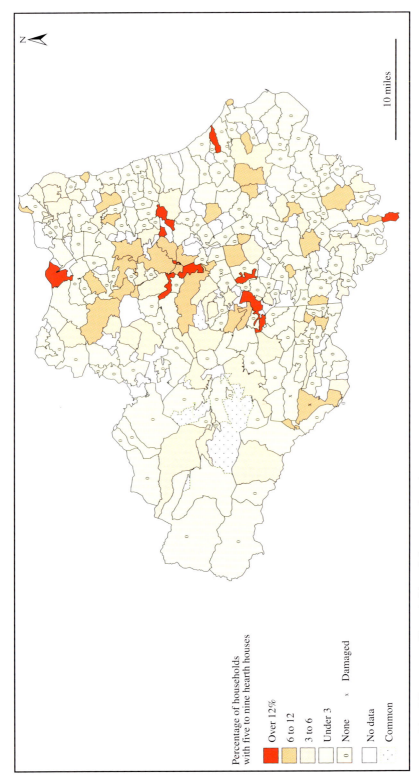

Percentage of households
with five to nine hearth houses

Over 12%
6 to 12
3 to 6
Under 3
None   x   Damaged
No data
Common

Map 6. Percentage of households with five to nine hearths

were also sometimes let and the hearth tax may record occupiers not owners. Nevertheless, Map 5 indicates the distribution of large houses, including those with over twenty hearths. Many of the most prominent houses had between ten and nineteen hearths, such as Brancepeth Castle, or Mr. Bowes with twelve hearths at Streatlam Castle in Teesdale, and Sir Christopher Conyers with fourteen hearths in Easington, partly for Horden Hall, on the coast. Some of the houses with over ten hearths were occupied by families who had established themselves in the county through clerical office; as for instance at Washington, Houghton and Gainford Halls.[112] On the Tyne, at Whickham, coal wealth supported the Blakistons at Gibside Hall, as well as the Claverings and Liddels. These gentry households were all headed by baronets: a 'distinctive élite, men of weight not only in parish but also in county society'.[113]

Across the county, the weight of the élite was thinly spread, with no large households in a majority of rural communities. The county contained relatively few large households, with a mere 86 entries in 1666, representing less than 1 per cent of all recorded households. In Kent, by contrast, there were 589 ten-plus hearth households in 1664, representing 2 per cent of the total.[114] The relative absence of families of great consequence was not a product of inherent lack of wealth, or even distance from London, but of the dominance of the Bishopric over land and office. The upside was that few communities were dominated by the great and the grand. In the west of the county there were concentrations in Stanhope and Wolsingham, and at Staindrop, but generally, even in the towns, fewer than 2 per cent of householders ran establishments with over ten hearths. In the south of the county, in the Tees lowlands, the very largest households tended to be clustered together rather than evenly spread, and this is even more pronounced in proportional terms in the north of the county, where communities either had several householders with over ten hearths or none at all. The larger households in this part of the county were often a result of commercial wealth, including those with a country seat within reach of Newcastle-upon-Tyne. The relative distribution of these is not always clearly apparent in Map 5, where the volume of less wealthy houssholds can reduce their proportional significance; as for instance, in the Tyne-side parishes of Gateshead, Whickham and Ryton. The geographical relationship between the production of this wealth and the residences where it was consumed was often closer than assumptions of sensitivity to pollution and even labouring populations allow. Coal-owners sometimes resided near their collieries, and there were a couple of large households in South Shields, where salt-panning fouled the air. It was not for want of wealth that no-one had a house with over ten hearths along most of the east coast, including Sunderland. The geography of wealthier folk dwelling in larger houses was not

---

[112] See D. S. Reid, 'The Durham Church Establishment: The Gentry and the Recusants 1570-1640', *Durham County Local History Society Bulletin* 22 (1978).
[113] Levine and Wrightson, *Whickham* p. 158.
[114] Pearson, 'Kent Hearth Tax', p. xli.

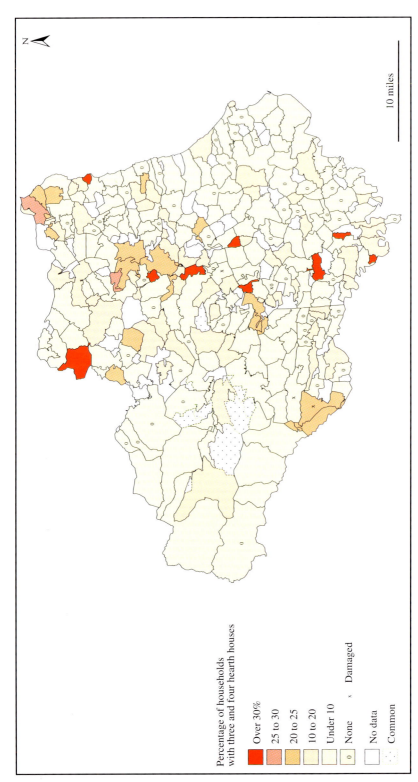

Percentage of households
with three and four hearth houses

Over 30%
25 to 30
20 to 25
10 to 20
Under 10
None   x   Damaged
No data
Common

10 miles

Map 7. Percentage of households with three and four hearths

only related to the economy of the county, but also to reasons of sociability, which were perhaps all the more pressing among a small élite.

The clustering of very large householders is confirmed by the similarity in location of those given status designations in 1666 (discussed below), not all of whom occupied houses with more than ten hearths. The location of individual large houses was the result of a number of factors, including the existence of a propitious earlier building, family landholdings, or the opportunity to purchase a landed estate, and a preference for dwelling near those of similar social standing. The greatest concentration of ten-plus households lies within a ten-mile radius of Durham City, indicating that proximity to the capital of the bishopric was important for access to administrative and social engagements, the law courts, and religious services for both Protestants and Catholics. This gentry presence in the central Wear valley was built on late medieval foundations. As Christian Liddy has demonstrated, in the fourteenth and fifteenth centuries the area immediately west of a line between Bishop Auckland and Durham attracted families wishing to establish gentry land-holdings, on what had previously been uncultivated land in the Pennine foothills. The wider distribution of larger households across the county also had its origins in the fourteenth and fifteenth centuries, when many of the established seventeenth-century county gentry families, major and minor, rose to prominence. Estates and houses established by the fifteenth century might also be taken up by new gentry families in the sixteenth and seventeenth centuries. Liddy has demonstrated that wealthier gentry estates were particularly prevalent in the Tees lowlands and along the coast, while the western uplands contained few gentry, of very limited wealth by national standards.[115] Some of the houses erected by the fifteenth-century gentry were still standing in the late seventeenth century as houses with between five and nine hearths.

Households with between Five and Nine Hearths
The distribution of five to nine hearth households in Map 6 is similar to that for the largest houses. The area around Durham City was a particularly prominent district for wealthier households, and there is a broad correlation in the contrasts between north and south, and the western parts of the county, though more places had households with over five hearths than over ten. The central Wear valley contained particular concentrations, especially in and around Bishop Auckland and Durham City, and along the Wear from Bishop Auckland to Sunderland there was a relatively high number of over 6 per cent or even over 12 per cent. The towns generally emerge with a significant proportion of householders with over five hearths, especially Gateshead and South Shields, with a lower proportion at Sunderland and Hartlepool, which represents a fair index of their relative prosperity. In the north-eastern corner of the county, salt-pans, ship-building, maritime and agricultural activity together generated enough prosperity to

[115] C. D. L. Liddy and R. H. Britnell (eds.) *North-East England in the Middle Ages* (Boydell and Brewer, 2005).

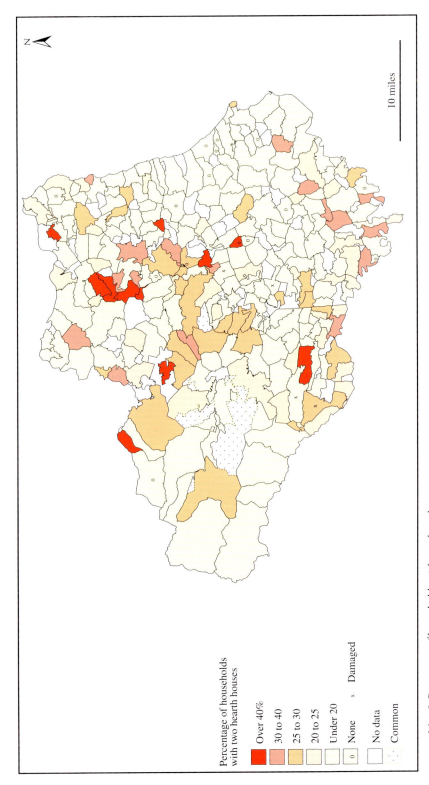

Percentage of households
with two hearth houses

- Over 40%
- 30 to 40
- 25 to 30
- 20 to 25
- Under 20
- None   x   Damaged
- No data
- Common

Map 8. Percentage of households with two hearths

support larger households in most of the townships between South Shields and Sunderland. By contrast, townships south of the Tyne, between South Shields and Gateshead, lack many houses with between five and nine hearths, even those where householders with over ten hearths are present.[116] This indicates a greater degree of social polarisation in these communities than was generally typical of Tyne-side as a whole. In the south and west of the county, the pattern of five to nine hearth households is similar to the distribution of those with over ten hearths, but many more townships had some houses of over five hearths throughout the watershed of the Tees. The economic and social centres of Middleton and Barnard Castle stand out in Teesdale, as do Stanhope and Wolsingham parishes in Weardale. Throughout the Tees lowlands there is significant clustering of larger houses, and Sedgefield does not emerge as a particularly wealthy town.

Across England, the five-hearth house has been taken to represent an important threshold for house size in relation to social status, as the gentry invariably occupied houses of five hearths or higher in the countryside. In Sussex and Warwickshire only gentlemen and yeomen occupied houses with over five hearths, while in larger towns the houses of gentlemen were somewhat larger, with around seven hearths the average in Warwick.[117] In Durham City, the gentry, merchants and professionals mostly lived in houses with between five and nine hearths, and in Whickham, households with five to nine hearths were those of the lesser gentry: 'the wealthiest and most prominent members of parish society', and this was generally true in the more rural parts of the county and in market towns.[118] In keeping with the narrowness of Durham's social élite, only 3 per cent of all households and under 5 per cent of the chargeable, lived in houses with over five hearths. Yet five hearths was not an absolute threshold for status or wealth, and across County Durham the lesser élite had a somewhat broader range of hearth numbers, with many persons of status in 1666 paying on houses with four or even three hearths (see Table 3). The differences between a four and a six-hearth house could be subtle, as the number of heated rooms did not necessarily correlate with the size or form of houses. Yet many of the lesser gentry were in relatively large, well-heated houses, and several of those with eight hearths in 1666 are described in the section on surviving houses below.

Households with Three or Four Hearths

Map 7 shows the distribution of the 1,052 households with three or four hearths in Lady Day 1666. The entries in the transcript show some gentry and professionals with houses of four hearths, and more rarely three, and a significant number of more prosperous widows and unmarried women. Generally, however,

---

[116] At Lamesley and Fellside, Great Usworth and Hylton over 2 per cent of householders had over ten hearths, but no houses of between five and nine hearths are recorded in Lady Day 1666.

[117] Husbands in Schürer and Arkell, *Surveying the People*, pp.72-3; P. Styles, 'The Social Structure of Kineton Hundred in the Reign of Charles II' *Transactions of the Birmingham Archaeological Society* 78 (1962), pp. 96-117. See also M. Spufford, 'The Scope of Local History' and Pearson 'Kent Hearth Tax'.

[118] Levine and Wrightson, *Whickham*, p. 158.

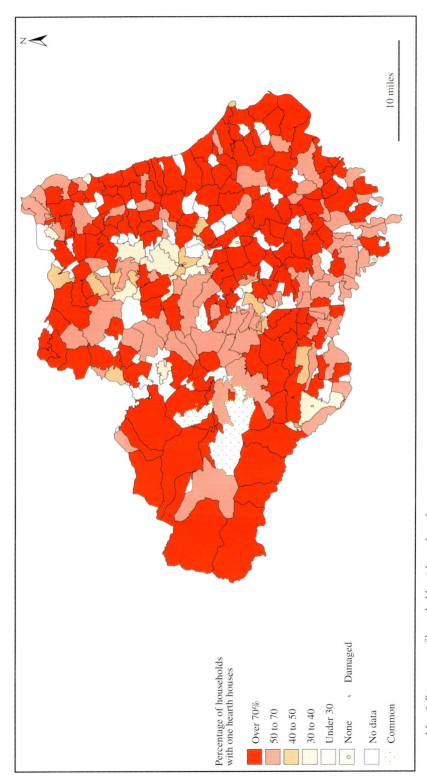

Map 9. Percentage of households with one hearth

the three and four-hearth category relates to the wealthier middling sort, particularly the more prosperous farmers, craftsmen and tradesmen. There were almost twice as many householders with four hearths than five (364 and 196 respectively), and a further 688 households had three hearths in 1666. These wealthier middling households should be compared with the distribution of two hearths, which generally contained the lower middling sections of society. Status and wealth was partly related to life-cycle, and there may be a generational element to the distinctions between houses with a different number of heated rooms. Some of the three or four hearth householders were middle-aged versions of their younger neighbours, perhaps newly weds who, if they prospered might upgrade their smaller house, or move to a larger one in middle age. However, the opportunities for accumulating sufficient wealth to fund a three or four-hearth house were limited, and wealth remained the key differential in relation to the number of heated rooms. The three and four-hearth households represent 14 per cent of paying households, and only just under nine per cent of all households. The relatively small upper middling element among Durham's population is highlighted by comparison with Kent, where nearly a fifth of the county's recorded households had three or four hearths, and in the well-off central parts of the county they accounted for a third of households, with the proportions only being comparable to Durham in the least prosperous eastern hundreds.[119]

The majority of places on Map 7 have less than ten per cent of households with three or four hearths, and their chimneys would have been all the more prominent for their rarity. Places with ten to twenty per cent are quite evenly spread across the county, while those places with over 20 per cent are mainly in and around the towns of Barnard Castle, Darlington, Bishop Auckland, Durham, Sunderland and South Shields. The few places with over 30 per cent of households with three or four hearths may represent peculiarly prosperous communities, but the map shows only the proportion of the recorded households, and not absolute numbers. The tables can indicate better how prominent middling houses were, by comparison with the number of smaller or larger houses (though this may be hazardous if the latter are under-assessed). Some forty places in 1666 have no entries with over four hearths, including Hartlepool, and middling villages such as Kirk Merrington, where there were one four-hearth and two three-hearth houses alongside forty-two with one or two hearths. In villages such as this, the three- and four-hearth householders invariably had the largest holdings and were usually regarded as the chief inhabitants of their communities. In Whickham, four-hearth households were occupied by the lesser gentry and principal farmers, whereas two to three-hearth households were occupied by lesser yeomen and better off craftsmen as well as the 'superior employees and semi-independent middlemen of the coal trade'.[120] The larger houses of this emergent managerial class in the coal field further distinguished them from their underlings.

[119] Pearson, 'Kent Hearth Tax', pp. xlv-xlvii.
[120] Levine and Wrightson, *Whickham*, pp. 159-60.

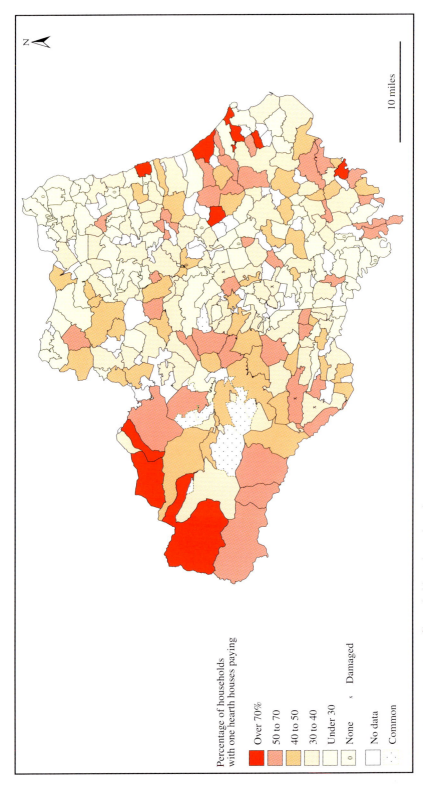

Percentage of households
with one hearth houses paying

Over 70%
50 to 70
40 to 50
30 to 40
Under 30
None   ×   Damaged
No data
Common

Map 10. Percentage of households with one hearth paying

10 miles

Households with One or Two Hearths

Rural communities in County Durham were characterised by a majority of single hearth-houses, some of which were occupied by those dependent on wage-labour. Most of these were exempt from the tax. Over 50 per cent of paying households were also single hearth, and husbandmen and craftsmen occupied houses with several rooms but only one hearth, while better-off husbandmen and some yeomen lived in two-hearth houses with several unheated rooms. The second hearth usually heated the parlour or a kitchen where cooking took place separately from in the hall. Both hearths were not always in domestic use: John Adamson had a shop with one hearth and a separate house with one hearth at West Auckland in March 1672.[121] Households paying on one or two hearths represent the more prosperous of the lower orders, with a secure household income. This group can be distinguished from those single-hearth households exempt from the tax, and although exemption does not represent a clear-cut poverty line it is possible that the material form of housing had some bearing on whether assessors regarded a household as up to paying.

Map 8 indicates that households with two hearths rarely amounted to more than a quarter of the population in 1666, and many places had fewer than 20 per cent. More prosperous lowland farming villages, with over 25 per cent of houses with two hearths, existed along the Rivers Tees and Wear, and only a few disparate places in the south and west of the county had over 40 per cent. Teesdale had a uniformly lower proportion of households with two hearths than Weardale, and Map 9 shows that all communities west of Barnard Castle had over 70 per cent of households with one hearth, while settlements along the river in Weardale had between 50 and 70 per cent with most of the remainder in two-hearth houses. This indicates greater prosperity and an earlier inclination to heat a second room in Weardale as a result of secure tenure, the quality of farmland and access to markets. There may also have been a cultural difference between the dales, with the adoption of a second hearth occuring somewhat later in upper Teesdale, where 50 to 70 per cent of recorded single-hearth households were prosperous enough to pay the tax. Not all single-hearth houses in Teesdale and Weardale were unimproved farmhouses, and the incidence of lead mining and other forms of waged employment account for those places where poorer single-hearth households predominated. The exemption criteria and degree of under-recording makes this difficult to quantify from the hearth tax, but something of the distinction between poorer households and unimproved farmhouses may be shown on Maps 10 and 11, showing the proportion of those who paid and did not pay on one hearth.

Two-hearth houses appear less prominent in the agrarian south-east of the county, where the majority of the population were in one-hearth houses. Maps 10 and 11 indicate the contrasts between neighbouring communities where a higher

---

[121] See Appendix III.

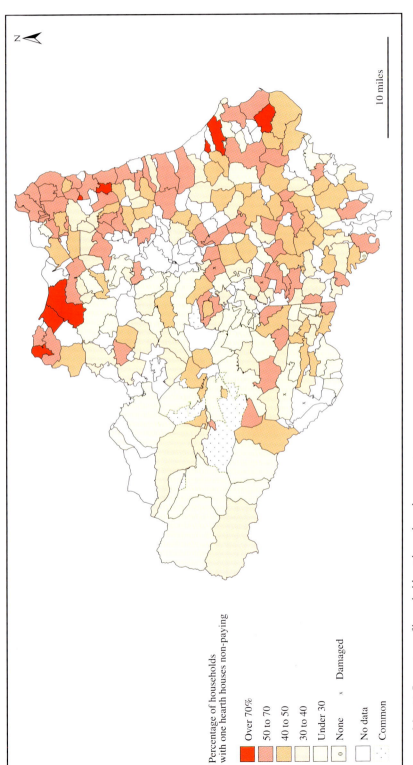

Map 11. Percentage of households with one hearth non-paying

Percentage of households
with one hearth houses non-paying

Over 70%
50 to 70
40 to 50
30 to 40
Under 30
None   ×   Damaged
No data
Common

10 miles

proportion of one-hearth houses did or did not pay, and the pattern largely relates to the progress of enclosure. Where smaller farmholdings remained in operation in 1666, husbandmen in single-hearth houses could presumably pay, whereas in those communities with larger farms and a greater demand for labourers a higher proportion of the population were in single-hearth cottages. These 'cottages' may previously have been husbandmen's farmhouses, even a decade before, and while some of these were sub-divided others were lost entirely as villages contracted. The east coast was particularly lacking in lower-middling houses of two hearths, but the port towns of Hartlepool, Sunderland and South Shields were both more prosperous and more middling by this measure (even accounting for the unusually high number of two-hearth exempt entries in Hartlepool). The social profile of Tyne-side is more in keeping with the agrarian parts of the county than is commonly assumed, as the proportion of lower middling households with two hearths was again generally under twenty per cent, except in Gateshead, and Winlaton West and Monkton, where pockets of middling prosperity were not engulfed by larger numbers of single-hearth households. The parishes around Chester-le-Street appear peculiarly affluent, with over 40 per cent of households in 1666 paying on two hearths; testimony to the prosperity generated at a lower middling level by the coal economy.

Map 9 shows the proportion of households with one hearth, and this naturally presents an inverse correlation to the distribution of wealthier households, most of which were along the Wear, in the Tees valley and in parts of the industrial districts in the north of the county. In all other places, single-hearth houses predominated to a degree unparalleled in many southern counties. The equivalent map for the Kent hearth tax does not even distinguish settlements with over 70 per cent of households in one-hearth houses (though similar maps for Wales and northern England would do).[122] In County Durham, communities had over 70 per cent of households with a single hearth throughout the watershed of the Tees, along the east coast, Tyne-side and on Derwent-side. This makes the industrial districts appear much less distinct from the rest of the county in terms of the proportion of the population with one hearth. Map 10, however, indicates that it was those areas with a lower proportion of two-hearth houses, especially in Teesdale and the south-east of the county, where a greater proportion of single-hearth houses paid. This implies that houses in these communities lacked a second heated room but were not necessarily impoverished or in drastically inferior accommodation. It is those places in Map 11 where a greater proportion of householders were exempt from the tax, which indicate more extreme poverty in proportional terms. The industrial patches of the north-east of the county emerge with over 50 or even 70 per cent of households with one hearth exempt, and a larger spread of non-paying single-hearth households along the coast and in the Tees lowlands. The uplands contained fewer non-paying single-hearth

---

[122] See histogram p. xcii.

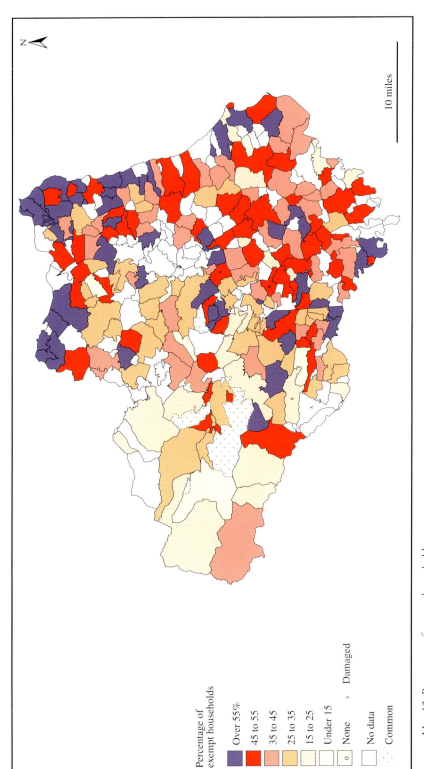

Map 12. Percentage of exempt households

households, except on the upland moor in Stanhope Quarter where over 70 per cent were exempt. Despite the likely under-recording of single-hearth households, and especially the patchy data for 1666, we can say that the mining communities on Tyne-side and Wear-side were not unique in the county in possessing a very high degree of relative poverty. Levine and Wrightson searched far and wide for published hearth tax returns which showed an equivalent level of exemption to Whickham, and found their closest parallel in Sandgate ward in Newcastle, but the Durham records reveal that the county generally was marked by very high levels of non-paying single-hearth households in both industrial and agricultural communities (see Map 12). These communities were very different from the Wear Valley, where more of the wealthier lived.

To comprehend the social relations of Durham's contrasting communities, we need to take notice of the incidence of households with over two hearths, as places without larger houses may have enjoyed community relations unmediated by upper middling or gentry interference. Places without any recorded three or four-hearth households occur throughout the county, especially on the high ground north of Weardale and in villages in the Tees valley and along the coast, but only twenty-four communities had no households assessed for over two hearths, with no particular correlation to agricultural or industrial activity. Neighbourhood life in these villages was possibly different from those places with no households with between three to nine hearths, but a gentry house of over ten. There was also no great homogeneity in what single-hearth households represented in terms of living standards, and they cannot all be equated with consistent poverty. The distinction between those that paid and those that did not represents one social difference. There were significant gradations within the seventeenth-century labouring class, and the richer among them could afford material possessions which would make their single-hearth homes different from their poorer neighbours.[123]

Exemptions

The maps showing where the exempt were have been discussed in relation to households with one and two hearths above, for the distribution of exemption should not be taken in isolation from their neighbours who paid the tax. Exemption from the hearth tax does not represent a real seventeenth-century poverty line, and the criteria for exemption was broader than other contemporary measures of poverty.[124] In comparison with other forms of taxation, the threshold for not-paying was set fairly low. This was in keeping with the spirit of a tax which aimed to maximise revenue for the exchequer, and recording the non-payers was intended to ensure that those eligible under the assessment criteria did pay. That the exemption lists do not enumerate the entire population, and omit the poorest,

---

[123] Arkell 'Incidence of Poverty'; A. Everitt, in Thirsk *Agrarian History*, pp. 396-465.
[124] Husbands in Schürer and Arkell, *Surveying the People*, pp. 65-77; Arkell, 'Incidence of Poverty', pp. 23-47.

reflects an ultimate lack of ability on the part of the state to record those who were never going to be able to contribute to the revenue, or who stood outside parish relief. Some may have been deliberately excluded at a local level. Receiving poor relief or contributing to taxation implied reciprocal obligations with the community, which they may not have been welcome in, or wanted to join. This is especially convincing for areas of County Durham where irregular industrial and maritime employment encouraged high levels of population mobility: people who appeared shiftless and faceless to the established householders. Similar strategies of deliberate social distancing presumably occured in agricultural villages as well. Non-payers in the hearth tax are best taken as recording the more stable sections of the population. Given the high degree of population mobility, the under-recording of the poorest and most transitory groups must have been considerable.

Many of those listed as non-payers were in reality little different in terms of wealth or material living conditions from some of those who did pay. Nationally, Wrightson suggests that wage earners could usually pay with only the destitute or near destitute exempted.[125] Destitution need not imply infirmity; Pollard and Crossley estimate that around half of those listed as non-payers were able bodied, and Husbands believes that the recorded exempt are generally the better-off of the seventeenth-century poor, with the poorest not listed at all.[126] We should not make casual assumptions about the poverty of the non-payers, and as Arkell has demonstrated, contemporary measures of taxation and poor relief indicate varying levels of poverty.[127] The poorest of the exempt were probably those in receipt of alms, the old, the ill and so forth, with some people regularly in receipt of relief, while others only received relief occasionally, including some able-bodied males. The next level of exempt were those who did not contribute to the poor rate but who received no relief themselves. The criteria for exemption from the hearth tax also extended to some who were deemed able to contribute to the local poor rate but who occupied houses or lands of low value (not more than twenty shillings per annum for houses and less than ten pounds for lands). The exemption rates in the hearth tax refer only to a broad level of relative poverty, which encompassed around a third of the population nationally. Highly localised employment and occupation patterns produced dramatic variations in local exemption rates. The mining districts on Tyne-side and Wear-side included some of the very highest levels of exemption identified nationally, though this is not so exceptional in the context of County Durham, and perhaps northern England generally.

By law, after the 1664 Act, no house with over two hearths could be exempted, and the vast majority of non-paying households in 1666 had only a single hearth (4,731 entries), while a further 229 housholders did not pay on two

---

[125] Wrightson, *English Society* 1580-1680, (London, 1982) p. 148.
[126] S. Pollard and D. Crossley, *The Wealth of Britain*, (London, 1968), p. 132; Husbands, 'Structure of the English Economy'.
[127] Arkell, 'Incidence of Poverty'.

hearths. In only two exceptional cases were three hearths exempt.[128] It is difficult to know whether there was much difference between the living accommodation of chargeable single-hearth households and those that were exempted. Indeed, those with fragile household economies may have slipped in and out of the exempt category. At a general level, a consistent level of exemption suggests a real difference in terms of housing between chargeable single-hearth households and the exempt. The nature of any such material difference is more difficult to ascertain. Possibly it was more apparent inside the house, where more goods could be afforded. Perhaps, there was a more striking difference, with those who paid the tax possessing a chimney stack, while many who did not pay may have had either an open hearth, or a flue which did not project above the roof line.

The listing of houses on commons was not systematically applied. Cottages on commons were specifically required to be listed in the printed instructions to hearth tax collectors of 1684, implying that they had not always been recorded previously.[129] The accretion of settlement on commons was significant in seventeenth-century Durham, where immigration exceeded the existing housing stock. In the north of the county, this involved new settlements near coal pits, as part of the industrialising landscape. Permanent housing also developed from squatting to infill on village greens, especially in market centres such as Sedgefield or Staindrop, but also in some farming villages, while areas of common moor at the periphery of townships were sites of squatter settlement.[130] It is unclear whether these semi-permanent households were included in the hearth tax. They may plausibly have been excluded if they lacked chimney stacks. Indeed, the established householders and office holders may well have been resistant to conferring any entitlement to settlement and excluded the transient population from poor relief.

The 1670s Exemption Certificates

One of the chief drawbacks of the Lady Day 1666 list is the number of places without lists of non-payers, including some notable omissions, such as Barnard Castle, Gateshead and Durham City. Fortunately most of these places do have exemption certificates surviving among the central records for the 1670s: the table in Appendix IV lists the places without non-payers in 1666 and the numbers recorded in the 1670s. Only the townships of Cold Hesledon, Dawdon, East and West Newbiggin in Bishopton parish, Thorpe Bulmer and Thrislington, have no data whatsoever in the records used for this volume. There may be entries in other years, unless they were always collected with other townships. Appendix IV prints the exemption certificates from 1672-4.[131] These were evidently copied from earlier certificates, as they closely match the number and sequence of names

---

[128] at Oxneyfield 'for ye new house', and John Collingwood at Haughton-le-Skerne.
[129] *Surveying the People*, pp. 39, 47-50.
[130] Roberts *Green Villages*.
[131] NA E179/327, part 2.

in the surviving 1671 certificates.[132] The later certificates have been printed here, as they provide slightly better coverage of the places with no data for non-payers in 1666. However, Pittington fell from twenty exempt in 1671 to ten in 1672-4, and Winlaton West Lordship is not included in the surviving 1672-4 certificates, but is present in 1671. Gateshead Bank Ward presents a further anomaly, with only a small portion of the exempt listed in 1674 included in the surviving 1670s certificates. The generally close correlation between the 1670s exemption certificates, indicates that there was a considerable amount of copying between hearth tax records, and an exact replication of the numbers in different records suggests that they do not accurately record the flows of population on the ground. While this means we must be circumspect about taking these exemption certificates as an accurate indicator of conditions in 1672-4, it does mean that they are more closely comparable chronologically to the 1666 assessment.

Empty Houses

Officially, empty houses were to be charged to their owners, whereas rented houses were charged to tenants. In practice, the liability of empty houses was not always clear or systematically applied and empty houses are likely to have been omitted from the records.[133] The recording of entries as empty occurs only spasmodically in the Exchequer lists: in 1666 only one empty house with one hearth is recorded as exempt, at Bishopwearmouth Panns. At Tudhoe in 1670, the constable's exceptionally thorough assessment records two houses as empty, one of which was 'empty and uninhabitable' by Michaelmas 1670, but had previously been occupied by Richard Haward and his infants, who were exempt in 1667. Houses vacated by the poorer members of the population could evidently deteriorate quickly, and were presumably of relatively poor construction. Mr Salvin was charged as the owner of the second empty house in 1670, but the tenant Harpers had paid on one hearth as occupier in previous years.[134] More substantial houses stood empty at West Auckland in the 1670s. In 1671 Mrs Ellin Eden was liable for Mr Robson's four-hearth house; in 1672 Mr Robson's house was empty, and in 1675 Elliner Eden was listed with an empty house. Robert Stothart junior was also listed with an empty property in 1675: he was liable for three hearths in 1671, had served as constable in 1663 and paid on one hearth in Lady Day 1666.[135] This limited evidence suggests that tenants were not always replaced very rapidly, and that houses could occasionally stand empty for long periods.

---

[132] NA E179/327, part 3, 15 January 1671.The close match between the certificates arose because the Exchequer mislaid them and declared the account for 1671-3 using the exemptions from 1670.
[133] *Surveying the People*, p.39.
[134] Appendix I.
[135] Appendix III.

Plate 1. *Low Woodifield Farm*, near Crook.
Unusual survival of a smaller seventeenth-century farmhouse, probably of one hearth. The
stepped chimney stack is characteristic of rural seventeenth-century houses.

Plate 2. *Slashpool Farm*, Hett.
Typical seventeenth-century farmhouse, of two or three hearths, in the Wear lowlands.
Two-and-a-half storeys, with rear stair turret. Possibly dating from the end of the seventeenth century, the cross-passage doorway is dated 1708 when the low-end service range (former byre) was rebuilt.

Plate 3. *Greystone Hall*.
Typical seventeenth-century farmhouse, of two or three hearths, in the Tees lowlands.
Originally a single-storey longhouse, rebuilt as two-and-a-half stories with rear stair turret, in the sevententh century. The low-end was rebuilt into two stories in the eighteenth century.

Plate 4. *Great Chilton Farm.*
A large late seventeenth-century farmhouse, assessed for three hearths in 1666.

Plate 5. *Great Chilton Farm*, seventeenth-century parlour fireplace.

Plate 6. *Great Chilton Farm*, seventeenth-century hall fireplace.

Plate 7. *Tudhoe Hall*, from the village green.
Assessed for eight hearths in 1666, for the Salvins. Originally a husbandman's farmhouse, remodelled into a gentry residence by the Salvins.

Plate 8. *West Auckland Old Hall*, from the village green.
Assessed for eight hearths in 1666. Originally a farmhouse, rebuilt in the early seventeenth century and further extended in the later seventeenth century. Almost every room, including the small chambers in the porch turret, have fireplaces.

Plate 9. *West Auckland Manor House.*
The home of the Eden family, possibly under-assessed for eight hearths in 1666, with seventeenth and eighteenth-century alterations to the sixteenth-century H-plan house.

Plate 10. *New House*, Ireshopeburn, upper Weardale.
An unusually large, and architecturally up-to-date, late seventeenth-century house in upper Weardale, built from the profits of lead mining.

Plate 11. *Bank House*, Wolsingham, Market Place.
Seventeenth-century corbelled chimney, heating first floor chamber.

Plate 12. *Abbey House*, Durham City, from Dun Cow Lane.
Late seventeenth-century brick chimney stack. Shaped gables such as this were a prominent feature of Durham's late seventeenth-century skyline.

Durham City

The population of seventeenth-century Durham is usually estimated to have been about 3,000 souls. A less conservative estimate, based on the 1674 hearth tax, suggests a population of 5,000.[136] This small cathedral city was characterised by gentry sociability and attendant service trades, and the presence of Newcastle and absence of a navigable river prevented it from developing into a more significant economic centre. In 1674 (a better guide than 1666 which includes no exempt for Durham city), the householders of Durham were recorded as 51 per-cent single hearth, 13 per-cent two hearths, and 4 per cent with over ten hearths. Durham was a less prosperous place than York, where 31 per cent had a single hearth, 22 per-cent two hearths and 4 per cent over ten hearths. Yet York and Durham, as gentry and ecclesiastical centres, contained an equivalent proportion of wealthy households, whereas in the mercantile metropolis of Newcastle, 62 per cent had single hearths, 13 per-cent two hearths and a mere 0.01 per cent had over ten hearths.[137] The low proportion of larger households reflects the comparatively small gentry presence in Newcastle, which the merchant élite failed to compensate for in house size relative to the total population. The exemption figures fit the pattern: York in 1672 had 20 per cent exempt, and Durham in 1674 had 27 per cent, while Newcastle is of a different order, with 43 per cent exempt in 1665.

Table 2: Durham City Hearth Ranges in 1674

	Exempt	1 hearth	2-4 hearths	5-9 hearths	10+ hearths
St. Nicholas	16%	28%	39%	42%	8%
High (North) Bailey	15%	6%	6%	9%	18%
Low (South) Bailey	0%	>1%	3%	9%	44%
St. Margaret Crossgate	15%	19%	13%	6%	5%
Framwellgate	14%	14%	14%	11%	5%
Elvet Borough	5%	2%	5%	11%	10%
Elvet Barony	17%	15%	7%	9%	5%
St. Giles	18%	16%	13%	3%	5%

Map 13 shows the divisions of Durham City used for the hearth tax. The peninsula presented an anomaly to the hearth tax collectors, as the Cathedral and Bishopric complex were extra-parochial. In 1666 the street names North and South Bailey were used to encompass these areas together with the parishes of St. Mary-le-Bow (in North Bailey) and St. Mary the Less (in South Bailey). In 1674, the use of the terms High and Low Bailey better accounted for the inclusion of the Castle, Palace Green and Cathedral. The peninsula was the most

[136] James, *Family, Lineage and Civil Society* p.11; D. Woodward, *Men at Work: Labourers and Building Craftsmen in the Towns of Northern England, 1450-1750*, (Cambridge, 1995) p.8. Revised estimate based on Durham City Ward except St. Gyles, using the same formula as for the county above.
[137] Figures for York from Hibbard in N. Alldridge, *The Hearth Tax: Problems and Possibilities* (Hull, 1983) and Newcastle, NA E179/158/109.

Figure 1. Durham drawn by Gregory King, from 'Durham Church notes' between ff. 10v. and 11.
Reproduced by kind permission of the College of Arms.

wealthy and high status area; the clerical and legal professions and many of the county gentry had town houses here. The South (or Low) Bailey was an almost exclusively élite area, dominated by the county gentry and clergy. South Bailey contained no exempt households in 1674, and only 0.4 per cent of Durham's single-hearth households. Even middling households were few, with only three per cent of Durham's two to four-hearth households and nine per cent of its five-to-nine-hearth households. Forty-four per cent of the largest households, with over ten hearths, were in the South Bailey. North (or High) Bailey was always a rather more complex area: whereas only fifteen households paid in 1674, forty-seven households (15 per cent) were exempt, and many of these were probably lawyers in lodgings or living-out clerks, who may have lacked £10 estate. Such exemption does not indicate poverty, and the North Bailey contained eighteen per cent of Durham's largest households, of over ten hearths, in 1674. The greater wealth of South Bailey is reflected in the collections for the relief of the Fire of London in 1666, when the North Bailey contributed 14s. and the South Bailey £1 1s. 4d.[138]

Durham's clerical élite are readily identifiable on the peninsula in 1666. The Lord Bishop, John Cosin, had twenty-two hearths; for the castle and possibly other buildings around Palace Green associated with the bishopric estate. The Dean of the Cathedral was Dr. John Sudbury between 1662 and 1684, and the twenty hearths for 'Mr Dean' must refer to an institutional assessment. Of the twelve major Cathedral canons, or prebendaries, five are assessed with South Bailey and six with North Bailey; all with between six and eleven hearths.[139] The missing twelfth prebend, is William Sancroft (9th Stall 1662-1674) who was Rector of Houghton-le-Spring from 1661 and elected Dean of St. Paul's Cathedral in 1664. The house belonging to the 9th Stall in the Cathedral College may have been rented out. Ms Rodgers, with three hearths, was also apparently dwelling within the cathedral precincts, and a number of genteel women occupied houses along the Bailey.

The peninsula was an élite space within the town, and the North and South Bailey were described in Bishop Cosin's correspondence as being 'no part of nor parcell of the City'.[140] Outside of the peninsula, Elvet Borough was the next wealthiest area, with 10 per cent of Durham's ten-plus households. The Barony of Elvet contained a higher proportion of poorer households, with 17 per cent of Durham's exempt and 15 per cent of its single-hearth households in 1674. St Nicholas parish covered the commercial centre of the town, including the Market Place, Silver Street, Saddler Street and Claypath. This was also the civic centre of the town and in Lady Day 1666 members of the civic élite are identified by their titles: Alderman Shives (five hearths) and Alderman Airson (nine

---

[138] *Correspondence of John Cosin*, II, p. 331.
[139] P. Mussett, *Lists of Deans and Major Canons of Durham 1541-1900* (Durham, 1974); M. Roberts, Durham, p. 80, shows the location of each stalls' house in the College; a list of alterations to prebendal houses is in J. T. Fowler (ed.) *Rites of Durham*, Surtees Society 107 (1902), pp. 159-60.
[140] *Correspondence of John Cosin*, II, pp. 385-6.

hearths). In common with most towns the central area was very mixed socially, and contained the greatest proportion of mid-range hearth numbers along with 16 per cent of Durham's exempt and 28 per cent of its single-hearth households in 1674. Most street-front properties had shops on the ground floor, with other households off passageways to the rear.[141] Behind the market place tenements, the poor were crowded together near the river banks. St. Margaret's Crossgate contained a similar but poorer profile to the Bishop's borough. In Framwellgate, traditionally the merchant district, households were more evenly spread across the hearth-ranges below five, with few houses over ten hearths but a prevalence of men designated Mr.

At the other end of the social spectrum from the clerical and genteel élite, were the building trade craftsmen. Several members of the mason's guild in 1657 can be traced in the hearth tax and probate records.[142] Christopher Scurroe 'late of Milbourne Gate' died in 1683, living in a house 'situate att Framwellgate Bridge end', and paid on two hearths in Crossgate in 1666.[143] In 1683, his house contained a 'fore house' (alias 'the low roome' in his will) and 'Middle Roome' on the ground floor, with a kitchen behind, and a 'fore chamber' (the main bedroom) and 'Kitchen Chamber' on the first floor with a 'Garrett Roome' above. Scurroe also held a 'farmhold and tenement call'd Garbitt' by lease from the Dean and Chapter, and while his inventoried goods amounted to just over ten pounds, he had £90 lent out in bonds. William Rowell was also assessed for two hearths in 1666, and at his death in 1684 had a house in Crossgate on a lease worth £25 'holden of the right Worshipful Dean and Chapter of Durham', containing moveable goods worth £2 9s. 4d.[144] The inventory only names one room, the fore house containing a close bed, and his limited household stuff (including kitchen utensils, a Bible, a red Mantle, and a seeing glasse) perhaps suggests he only occupied part of the house. His work gear included 'An iron, two Harcks A spaid and a shovell Gavelin ~~Three Wedges~~' 5s., as well as 'One Shop Chest' 2s. 6d. and 'one Ladder' 1s. More prosperous was John Taylor, Mason, whose 1680 will and inventory totalled £89 5s. (£50 of which was in bonds), and he may be the John Taylor at Witton Gilbert, assessed for 1 hearth in 1666.[145] His house at Bearpark consisted of a 'foar Roome', 'the other Roome' containing 'two beds, 3 chests, a chair and a kettle', and 'the Roome on the back of the Chimney' containing 'a Bed, 2 Chests, tubs, a Close presse and fatts and stand'. Far more prosperous, was Ralph Lee, rough mason, who died in 1666, leaving his wife Elizabeth their dwelling house and gardens in the South Bailey, where she paid for three hearths in 1666.[146] Their house comprised a brewhouse and cellar, with a forehouse and low parlour on the ground floor. On the first floor 'ye little fore Chamber'

[141] See Roberts *Durham*, pp. 130-9.
[142] Durham University Archive, Durham City Trade Guild Records; Durham Probate Registry.
[143] Christopher Scurroe 1683 will and inventory.
[144] William Rowell 1684 inventory.
[145] John Taylor 1680 will and inventory.
[146] Ralph Lee, 1666 will & Elizabeth Lee 1674 will and inventory.

was over the forehouse to the street front, and 'ye best room' provided a further reception room over the low parlour. In common with most seventeenth-century houses on the Bailey, the forehouse served as the main living room where cooking took place, towards the street, whereas the higher status reception rooms were at the garden side towards the river banks, and the Lees had a 'Garden house' overlooking the river. The garden house and second parlour signalled gentility, but Lee still practised his trade as mason: 'in ye Garth slates & flaggs 10s. 6d.'. In 1674 (the year of Elizabeth's death) only six households on the South Bailey had three hearths, and the Lees represent a dwindling continuity from the sixteenth century of tradesmen, and their widows, dwelling on the Baileys.

FURTHER ANALYSIS

Status in the Hearth Tax

Durham lacked a resident nobility in the late seventeenth century, aside from Lady Vane at Raby. Baronets, knights and esquires in 1666 mainly appear among the highest hearth ranges: most had over ten hearths, and some over twenty, but the threshold appears to be seven hearths or above. Together, the titled élite represent just six per cent of all those with status in Lady Day 1666, and the tiniest slither (0.08 per cent) of all recorded householders. Below the titled élite, genteel status was more fluid. Gregory King tried to get a handle on it by searching the hearth tax lists for householders of 'gentry' status, and reckoned that those with five hearths or more, might deserve the right to bear a coat of arms. In some counties he lowered his threshold to four hearths, and took note of the status designations mentioned in the hearth tax lists.[147] In Durham, the designation 'gentleman' in 1666 ranged from thirty-two hearths, in two cases, to three paying on one hearth. Forty-five per cent of 'gentlemen' paid on below five hearths, while 42 per cent had between five and nine hearths, and 13 per cent had ten hearths or more. The five-hearth threshold for gentry living was not therefore an absolute distinction in either the countryside or towns. Even a few baronets were assessed for four hearths — perhaps for secondary residences. Where individuals of status appear with low hearth assessments, perhaps especially for single hearths, then they are likely to be owners rather than occupiers. Alternatively, a small number of hearths can relate to high status individuals lodging in larger households.

Table 3 shows the average number of hearths among the different status groups among the gentry. Those designated 'gent.' or 'Mr' had on average seven hearths, which is comparable to Cooper's figures for Norfolk and not far off Oxfordshire or Surrey, and indicates greater prosperity among the lesser gentry than in Derbyshire, Dorset or Warwickshire. For the lesser élite in seventeenth-

---

[147] M. Spufford, 'The Scope of Local History', pp. 206-7; idem. and with J. Went, 'Poverty Portrayed: Gregory King and Eccleshall in Staffordshire in the 1690s'. *Staffordshire Studies*, 7 (1995), pp. 8-9.

century County Durham enjoyed a degree of prosperity comparable to the most 'advanced' parts of southern England, as the surviving gentry houses discussed below still demonstrate. The higher status gentry, those designated Esquire, Knight or Baronet, in the hearth tax, have a lower average number of hearths than their peers in most other English counties. The Durham average is closest to Warwickshire, and confirms the contemporary view that this was a 'middling rank' county.[148] The lack of very large gentry houses reflects the fact that a great deal of the wealth generated in the region, left it: witness Lord Baltimore's hearths in Whickham. The county's distance from London did little to encourage the highest flying families to reside here, while the extent of the church estates left little room for very large lay landowners, and some of the more prominent 'ancient' families in the county were unlikely to build very large houses as catholic recusancy limited their means and motivation. Halliday expected 'to find that the lesser gentry of Northumberland or Durham were occupying houses of four, or even three heaths', but cautions that house size is not a reliable indicator of authority, estate size or wealth.[149]

Those accorded status in the hearth tax were not evenly distributed across the county; half were in the towns, with Durham City including nearly a third of all those of status. Yet only Gateshead and Sunderland with Bishop Wearmouth had a significant number of householders of status; all other towns had ten such households or fewer. Outside of the towns, several communities contain notable clusters of households headed by individuals of status, and these twelve places alone account for 12 per cent of status households (Table 4). In the smaller of these communities, such as West Herrington, the four status households represent almost a quarter of all payers, and ten per cent of all households. Even in a large community like West Auckland, with over one hundred households in 1666, the four gentry households account for seven per cent of paying households, even if they only represent three per cent of all households. Paradoxically, those communities with fewer than four status households might have felt the gentry presence more strongly. Small communities with only one gentry household and landlord might well be regarded as gentry dominated, especially where most other households had only one or two hearths. In those few places where persons of status clustered together, the genteel presumably occupied a community of their own to some extent. Although there may have been no sharp cut off point between the householders accorded status by the hearth tax collectors, and their middling neighbours, social relations were presumably distinctive in communities with a significant concentration of genteel households and larger houses.

[148] Green, 'Houses and Households', p. 31.
[149] Halliday, 'Landed Élite', p. 51.

Table 3: Number and Average of Hearths for 'Gentry'[150]

No. of hearths Durham (1666)	Clergy / Dr.			Mr/Gent.			Esq.		Kt. & Bt.	
	County		City	County		City	County	City	County	City
	rural	urban		rural	urban					
20 +	0	1	2	4	0	0	1	0	3	1
10-19	1	0	3	20	6	10	5	0	10	2
5-9	6	2	11	75	38	58	5	0	4	0
4	0	0	0	30	12	12	0	0	1	0
3	0	0	0	27	9	11	0	0	1	0
2	0	0	0	37	4	15	0	0	0	0
1	1	0	0	12	7	6	0	0	0	0
Exempt	0	0	0	2	2	0	0	0	1	0
Total Hearths			279			2215		124		294
Durham Average			10.0			7.0		11.3		16.5
Kent						8.5		13.1		18.2
Norfolk						7.1		13.8		23.6
Oxfordshire						8.1		14.5		22.6
Derbyshire						4.8		12.7		19.0
Dorset						5.2		12.3		18.3
Surrey						8.0		14.9		18.8
Warwickshire						5.7		10.6		16.3
Westmorland								9.0		14.4

[150] Urban places in the county refer to Stanhope, Sedgefield, Chester-le-Street, Bishop Wearmouth, Darlington, Bishop Auckland, Stockton, Hartlepool, Barnard Castle, South Shields and Gateshead; other county averages are from Pearson 'Kent Hearth Tax', p. xli-xliii, and N. Cooper *Houses of the Gentry, 1480-1680*, (London, 1999), p. 6. Following Cooper, the county average for Knights and Baronets excludes entries with fewer than five hearths; the Kent figures only take entries with four hearths or more. The number of gentry in Cambridgeshire is given in Evans, *Cambridgeshire*, p. xxx.

Table 4: Places with Clusters of Status Households in 1666

Rural Places with 4 status households or more	All payers	All households	Status as % of payers	Status as % of all households
Lumley and Lambton (8)	70	(no exempt recorded)	11%	—
Brancepeth (6)	43	97	14%	6%
Witton-le-Wear (5)	55	80	9%	6%
West Auckland (4)	61	118	7%	3%
Egglescliffe (4)	37	44	11%	9%
Pittington (4)	18	(no exempt recorded)	22%	—
West Herrington (4)	18	41	22%	10%
Ryton Woodside (4)	31	127	13%	3%
Whickham Fellside (4)	25	108	16%	4%
Upper Heworth (4)	27	37	15%	11%
Nether Heworth (4)	53	114	8%	4%

Women and Families in the Hearth Tax

Seventeenth-century society projected itself as overwhelmingly patriarchal, yet a significant minority of women were independent of men and in charge of their own households. Around 15 per cent of the households recorded in 1666 were headed by women, and one in ten of those who paid were female. The very largest household, Raby Castle, was the responsibility of Lady Vane, but only 1 per cent of listed women had over ten hearths and the majority of female householders were poor. Between the five women with over ten hearths and the poor widows provided with house room by a relative, were a number of more prosperous and independent women. Around one in ten of both middling and smaller genteel households were paid for by women: 11 per cent of three and four hearth households, and two per cent of five to nine hearths. The significance of female-headed middling households is further underscored by the fact that 16 per cent of women listed in 1666 had three or four hearths, whereas seven per cent were in the higher status bracket of five to nine hearths. Although significant, prosperous women were a minority and 75 per cent of women who paid the tax did so on only one or two hearths, and a quarter of the exempt in 1666 were women.[151] Women paying on one hearth were probably little better off than their exempt neighbours, and most were presumably living in a small cottage

[151] A total of 1822 women identified in chargeable (706) and exempt (1116); 15% of households in 1666 were headed by women, with 10% of the payers identifiable as women and 22% of the recorded exempt.

or even a single room. Small dwelling spaces confirmed the low prominence of women in most communities, where they represented a minority of households, and women headed only five per cent of all one and two-per cent of all two-hearth households across the county.

One route for women to gain their own household was as a result of widowhood, and around a third of women in 1666 were listed as widows. Yet not all widows were identified as such in the hearth tax, and their apparent absence in some communities, especially among the exempt, probably relates to local variations in the customs for providing widows with accommodation — whether they occupied a separate household or were merely given house-room within a relative's house.[152] The degree to which a widow's house room was formally defined presumably determined whether it was assessed separately in the hearth tax. Widow Chilton with one hearth in Elwick and Hall, may have been under the same roof as Jonathon Chilton, the following entry, also with one hearth. More prosperous widowed women seem less likely to have been identitified as such in the hearth tax, and the label appears to have been applied more readily to lower status women. The vast majority of named widows had only one hearth, with about 40 per cent of non-paying women recorded as widows whereas only 27 per cent of paying women were identified as widow. This partly reflects the greater opportunity for propertied women to remarry, but also indicates that widows do not account for the majority of households not headed by men, and while some were doubtless estranged from living husbands, most were unmarried.[153]

A small number of women listed in 1666 were given the title Miss (Ms), with fifty-three entries among the payers. Only six individuals were identified as 'Mrs' (which was sometimes applied to older unmarried women). Both titles were used as status distinctions and were more common in towns, and do not provide an index of marriage. Rather, the prevalence of prosperous women in urban communities reflects a preference for urban residence. This applies both to those women who worked for their living and those with unearned or rentier income. At Chester-le-Street four women were recorded as Miss, from Ms Py with one hearth to Ms Maddison with six hearths. In Gateshead larger establishments are recorded: from Ms London with six hearths to Ms Ann Cole with twelve hearths, and some of these larger hearth numbers may have been inns. In Durham City nineteen householders were titled Ms. No doubt some of them were unmarried genteel women who enjoyed female sociability with their married and widowed neighbours in this 'leisure' town, and their demand for services created further opportunities for women to earn a livelihood. Women

[152] See M. Spufford, *Contrasting Communities: English Villagers in the Sixteenth and Seventeenth Centuries* (Cambridge, 1974). A. Erickson, *Women and Property in Early Modern England*, (London, 1993) p. 189, found that 'the legal splitting of even small houses, as opposed to the less formal granting of house room for life, appears to have been particularly common in Yorkshire'.

[153] L. Botelho and P. Thane, (eds.) *Women and Ageing in British Society since 1500*, (Harlow, 2000); C. Peters 'Single Women in Early Modern England: attitudes and expectations', *Continuity and Change* 12 (1997), pp. 325-45.

householders were a significant presence in the towns and marketing centres of the county and there were also a significant number in the industrial centres of Sunderland and Bishop Wearmouth, South Shields and Gateshead. In the coastal communities, some women householders may have been married to men engaged in maritime occupations, but generally we may assume they had independent lives and incomes.

Outside of the towns there are further clusters of women. In the Tyne-side townships of Ryton, Winlaton East and especially at Whickham, a significant number of non-paying women are recorded, mostly as widows. This may reflect higher male mortality in the most intensive coal mining parishes, as well as indicating that the Tyne-side economy generated a high degree of poverty for women as well as men. Among the more rural communities, several places have a concentration of women householders. Newbottle and Upper Heworth contain the highest proportions, with about 26 per cent of householders being female, while around a fifth of all householders were women in Brancepeth and Witton-le-Wear; a quarter at Greatham, and ten per cent or more across Stanhope parish. Of equal interest, are those places without women householders: at Quarrington, Wingate, Nesbitt, East and West Burdon, Dalton, Dawden, Eppleton, Cold Hesledon, East, Middle and West Herrington no chargeable women were listed, and at Quarrington and Dalton no non-chargeable either. Social relations and economic opportunities were evidently less restrictive for women in those places with a cluster of female households, and the uneven distribution of women in the hearth tax suggests that women moved to communities where they had greater opportunities of earning a livelihood, being provided with support in old age, and of enjoying female sociability. Living in neighbourhoods with other women of equivalent prosperity and status probably mattered to all independent women. Olwen Hufton and Amy Louise Erickson have observed 'spinster clustering' in both urban and rural areas, with women often living together in the same house. Such clusters included widows as well as single women, and 'often those who lived together were related by marriage or blood'.[154]

[154] Erickson, *Women and Property*, p. 191.

Table 5: Women in Lady Day 1666 Assessment

	Women payers	% of women payers	
1 hearth	371	52%	10% of all 1-hearth payers
2 hearths	164	23%	9% of all 2-hearth payers
3 hearths	81	11%	12% of all 3-hearth payers
4 hearths	37	5%	10% of all 4-hearth payers
5 hearths	15	2%	8% of all 5-hearth payers
6 hearths	15	2%	13% of all 6-hearth payers
7 hearths	8	1%	11% of all 7-hearth payers
8 hearths	5	1%	10% of all 8-hearth payers
9 hearths	5	1%	13% of all 9-hearth payers
5-9 hearths	48	7%	10% of all 5–9-hearth payers
10+ hearths	5	1%	6% of all 10+-hearth payers

Family names in the hearth tax allow further analysis of late seventeenth-century society, and as David Hey has shown, their distribution can illuminate issues of local identity.[155] There are a number of surnames related to place-names in the county, such as Chilton, Merrington and Hett, and Border surnames such as Armstrong. In addition, the Durham returns include a remarkable number of men named Cuthbert, which indicates a tradition of identification with the county's patrimonal saint, and may even suggest an adherence to catholicism in some communities. Further research into the distribution of names, especially in comparison to adjacent counties, would help to substantiate the relationship between patterns of population mobility and local or regional identities.

Within the county, clusters of family names might be expected to reflect strong kinship bonds and a preference to dwell near relatives. In St. John's Chapel (Stanhope Forest and Park Quarter), the surname Emmerson occurs some two dozen times among the payers, and several Emmerson women are among the non-payers in 1666. The name Fetherstone also occurs frequently in upper Weardale. Smaller clusters of family names can be found in the lowlands (for example, the three Hett and Armstrong households at Throston near Hartlepool). However, we cannot assume that family name clusters reflect close kinship, let alone longer-term generational continuity. Relatives distinguished as 'senior' and 'junior' are a firmer proof of kinship, and indicate the life-cycle dimension of households. Middle-aged fathers usually dwelt in larger houses than their sons, though the elderly may have fewer hearths, in or near the son's property.

[155] D. Hey '1997 Phillimore Lecture: The Local History of Family Names' *The Local Historian* vol. 27, no. 4 (November, 1997) pp. i-xx; D. Hey and G. Redmonds, *Yorkshire surnames and the hearth tax returns of 1672-73*, Borthwick Institute of Historical Research (York, 2002).

Close residential proximity is certainly suggested where 'senior' and 'junior' are consecutively listed, and residential propinquity of nuclear kin transcended wealth and status. In St. Nicholas, Durham City, Mr. Hall senior had five hearths, and Mr Hall junior four hearths. Very occasionally, two individuals are named for one property (at Dalton Piercy, William and James Shearton were assessed for two hearths) but house-sharing was not limited to family relatives (in Gateshead Pipewell Ward, Alexander Talior and Thomas Appleby were assessed for five hearths), and we might suspect that some of the unmarried women listed consecutively dwelt together.

The general pattern of kinship bonds across the county has been disputed. James claimed that by the mid seventeenth century there existed remarkably modern kinship relations in lowland areas (with nuclear families and more distant kinship ties disrupted by geographical mobility), and an even more modern social structure in northern, industrialised, County Durham (where colliers were marginal to the established social order, not owning land beyond plots for their cottages and difficult to incorporate into the parish organisation), whereas 'traditional' kinship obligations persisted in poorer and more isolated upland areas.[156] Issa's more systematic research (which makes use of the hearth tax), has demonstrated that seventeenth-century families in the large upland parish of Stanhope in Weardale followed very similar kinship patterns to those in the predominantly agricultural economy of lowland south-east County Durham, in Sedgefield parish, and that the industrialising society of north County Durham in Chester-le-Street parish was little different.[157] The implication of Issa's findings on the uniformity of family obligations across County Durham, is that household organisation was not radically dissimilar across the region or in relation to England as a whole. The varying socio-economic conditions of seventeenth-century County Durham did not apparently produce differences in family life at the level of kinship or household structure. The hearth tax indicates that it was the wealth, status and gender of households that varied between settlements and across the county. Wealth and poverty, indeed, are what distinguishes County Durham society within England as a whole.

---

[156] James *Family, Lineage and Civil Society*, pp. 19-29 and 93-6.
[157] C. Issa 'Obligation and Choice: Aspects of Family and Kinship in seventeenth-century County Durham' (unpublished University of St. Andrews PhD, 1987).

Houses and the Hearth Tax

Survival of Seventeenth-Century Houses

In Lady Day 1666 only one entry refers explicitly to building work, at Oxneyfield where the 'Old House' paid on four hearths while 'In Ye new house' three unused hearths were exempt. Other new houses went unremarked, but most of the entries refer to houses that were not so newly built. We need to consider the nature of the housing stock and its survival before considering the evidence of houses. Comparing the number of households recorded in 1674 with the number of houses listed as built before 1700, suggests that just 3 per cent of seventeenth-century houses, and 5 per cent excluding the exempt, survive. Although the listings do not provide a complete index of survival, these are very low figures compared with the 28 per cent survival in Suffolk and 30 per cent in central Kent.[158] Whereas in south-east England late medieval timber-framed houses were amenable to conversion in the sixteenth and seventeenth centuries, in stone regions such as the north-east the same alteration in living space was invariably achieved through rebuilding. House survival in Durham has also been affected by redevelopment through industrialisation in the centuries since 1700. Discounting single-hearth households as unlikely to be listed, perhaps 12 per cent of two hearth and larger houses survive. There are large differences in their survival across the county, with 38 per cent in Teesdale and the lowland Tees valley, 15 per cent in Weardale and the central Wear lowlands, and 10 per cent in Durham City, with just 1 per cent surviving in the area between Durham City and the Tyne. Many of these houses date from the last third of the seventeenth century, and post-date the 1666 hearth tax.

Only a minority of buildings in most communities had more than two hearths, and the remaining gentry halls and yeomen farmhouses in the countryside still retain their prominence in the landscape. In towns, seventeenth-century houses are somewhat less prominent, as most have been refaced in the eighteenth century. Yet the visible survival must not distort our view of housing conditions, and households with one or two hearths were not necessarily in less durable structures. It is factors of subsequent use which account for why certain houses have remained for over three centuries. Minor gentry halls and yeomen houses often survived through being converted for tenants. In other cases, yeomen farmhouses were preserved by families aspiring to genteel status in later centuries, and the name 'hall' or 'manor house' is often a misnomer for their seventeenth-century incarnation. In more cases the rebuilding of farms retained little outward sign of earlier buildings, and this process was begun in the seventeenth century by 'improving' landlords and tenants. The situation in towns

---

[158] Lists of Buildings of Special Architectural or Historic Interest are required to include all pre-1700 houses, but the Lists are not comprehensive and often omit smaller or disguised houses. Johnson, ' Traditional Architecture in Western Suffolk', pp. 27-38; Pearson 'Kent Hearth Tax', p. xc.

was similarly determined by patterns of redevelopment. Greater house survival in Durham City reflects some continuity in residential requirements, especially internally, as well as the absence of any great rebuilding in the nineteenth or twentieth centuries. In Sunderland, by contrast, even the most prestigious streets have been entirely redeveloped. These processes of redevelopment were continuous from the seventeenth century, and the degree to which older houses were retained or rebuilt was defined by whether they were appropriate to certain living requirements in particular locations.

The Hearth Tax and Surviving Buildings

Several of the largest houses in the Durham hearth tax had been adapted from medieval dwellings. The castles in the county are only the most obvious instances. A medieval courtyard house survives at Hunwick, remodelled in the early seventeenth century, with 'a sumptuous Jacobean fireplace'.[159] Crook Hall, near Durham, survives as an example of the medieval manor houses that skirted the city, with sixteenth- and seventeenth-century additions. In other cases seventeenth-century alterations almost completely disguised the medieval fabric. The Conyers were a leading county gentry family in the late medieval period, with a substantial residence at Horden, between Easington and the sea, remodelled in the early seventeenth century, complete with long gallery on the top floor accessed by a projecting stair turret, and a neo-classical façade. It was illustrated by James as an example of 'new-style gentry housing', typifying the civility of early seventeenth-century Durham's county élite; in 1666 Sir Christopher Conyers in Easington was assessed for fourteen hearths. The new clerical gentry of the seventeenth century also built architecturally innovative houses. Gainford Hall, built in c.1600 for the Rev. John Craddock (vicar of Gainford from 1594; died 1627), was of three storeys with the hall and parlour at a higher level to the kitchen and service rooms facing the road; this retained the traditional division of high and low status rooms in a compact square house. There was a great chamber over the hall, and a gallery was intended on the top floor, which was glazed but never completed internally. In 1666 Jno. Cradock was assessed for eleven hearths. Another clerical seventeenth-century gentry family were the Huttons at Houghton-le-Spring. Rev. Robert Hutton was Rector between 1589 and 1623 and built Houghton Hall as a rectangular stone house which like Gainford combines hall, parlours, and service rooms within a compact plan, with a great chamber over the hall and long gallery on the second floor. In 1666 Robert Hutton gent. was assessed for fifteen hearths. The 'parsonage' at Houghton-le-Spring was also assessed for fifteen hearths in 1666, following a substantial rebuild in c.1664: this house still retains a medieval core, battlements and late sixteenth- and seventeenth-century features, with a 'huge

---

[159] A. Emery, *Greater Medieval Houses of England and Wales 1300-1500*, Volume I Northern England (Cambridge, 1996) p. 106; N. Pevsner and E. Williamson, *The Buildings of England: County Durham*, (London, 1983), p. 335.

chimney' on the north side.[160]

The gentry halls at Horden, Gainford and Houghton, typify the architectural changes of the early-mid seventeenth century. These houses dispensed with the traditional linear arrangement of service and living spaces at either end of a central hall, although they maintained the status divisions in spatial terms, and all contained the requirement of early seventeenth-century higher status gentry houses to possess a hall, parlours, great chamber and long gallery. An extensive three-storey house of this type existed at Ramshaw Hall in Evenwood, as a 1631 inventory records,[161] but fire possibly necessitated rebuilding in the mid seventeenth century, when Ramshaw Hall became the property of Anthony Pearson. The Pearsons rebuilt Ramshaw as a somewhat more modest house, and in 1666 Ms Grace Pearson was assessed for eight hearths.[162] The accommodation at Ramshaw is comparable to Tudhoe Hall, remodelled in the 1660s for the Catholic Salvins to provide a T-plan house of two and a half storeys, with eight hearths but three unused in the 1670s.[163] These eight-hearth households are representative of minor gentry halls in the countryside.

The external appearance of larger late seventeenth-century houses, usually with between five and nine hearths, placed great emphasis on symmetrical façades with projecting porches and stair turrets running to two-and-a-half or three stories. Not all such houses were on the site of previously prestigious buildings, and some remodelled middling dwellings into imposing houses. West Auckland Hall (Plate 8) was remodelled from an early seventeenth-century farmhouse into an elaborate and exceptionally well-heated house in the later seventeenth century, which may be the eight hearth house assessed for Jno. Tongue in 1666. West Auckland Hall has a hearth in almost every room, including the small closet-like chambers over the porch on the first and second floors, and the chambers off the stair in the turret to the rear. Similarly, Tudhoe Hall (Plate 7) was remodelled from a husbandman's long-house in c.1600 into an eight hearth house by 1666. The enlargement of these houses is testimony to the prosperity and social prominence of the lesser gentry and upper middling sort in the seventeenth century.

Great Chilton Farm (Plate 4), on the northern edge of the lower Tees valley, presents an example of a larger seventeenth-century farmhouse, adjacent to Great Chilton Hall and the labouring village of Little Chilton. The 1674 hearth tax for Great and Little Chilton together, records twenty-four exempt households and eighteen chargeable households. In 1666, Lodowick Hall at Great Chilton Hall had eight hearths and Lawrence Brack had seven. Great Chilton Farm probably had three hearths (in the hall, parlour and chamber over the parlour), relating

[160] Pevsner and Williamson, *Durham*, p. 332.
[161] George Dixon 1631 inventory.
[162] Room names in her son Thomas Pearson's 1688 inventory tally with the surviving house: 'little parlour, great parlour, roome beyond ye dining room; dineing room; kitchin Chamber; Clossett above ye little parlour; Chamber garrett and Closett; kitchin; milkhouse; work tools in ye work house'.
[163] See Green, 'Tudhoe Hall and Byers Green Hall'.

in 1666 to Richard Grierson with three hearths. In 1666, Grierson was the most substantial middling member of the community, with the most substantial house, with only three neighbours with two hearths and a further twelve single hearth households among the payers. Grierson was linked to Lodowick Hall at Great Chilton Hall and may have been his steward.

Slashpool Farm, on the village green at Hett, between Ferry Hill and Durham, provides a good example of a yeoman farmhouse (Plate 2); similar in form but smaller than Great Chilton Farm. Both were marked out by their height, chimney stacks and external stair turrets, as the most substantial middling households in each community; each seemingly with three hearths. Both are two and a half storeys, with a hall and parlour and projecting stair turret to the rear. Whereas Great Chilton Farm has four-centred arched stone fireplaces to hall and parlour, of matching form but with the hall fireplace considerably larger (Plates 5 and 6), at Slashpool Farm only the parlour fireplace has a four-centred arch, and the vestiges of a smoke hood (rather than a full chimney) remain in the hall. In 1674, Hett contained twenty-four exempt and fifteen paying single-hearth households, with three two-hearth houses and one three-hearth house. In 1666, Thomas Wood occupied the three-hearth house, probably Slashpool Farm.[164] Greystone 'Hall', near Gainford, on the Tees, is a further surviving example of a seventeenth-century, two-and-a-half storey hall and parlour farmhouse, originally with a low end (presumably a byre) beyond the cross-passage behind the stack of the hall. This low-end was rebuilt as a kitchen with servant accommodation above in the early eighteenth century. Successive rebuilding of the main house and low end, at different times, is a common feature of these yeomen houses, and there appears to be a tendency for rebuilding kitchens after 1700, which may represent the first date at which cooking was removed from the hall. Two- as well as three-hearth houses in the hearth tax may therefore relate to such substantial farmhouses in the Tees and Wear lowlands.

The hearth-passage plan (where the cross passage runs behind the stack in the hall) is a common feature of surviving farmhouses, and indicates that they were usually the product of several phases of rebuilding. Grange Farm, Monkton, in Jarrow parish, was a Dean and Chapter holding of 132 acres in 1627, occupied by John Byres, clerk, worth £160, of which £111 11s. was livestock, which indicates the wealth of farmers on Tyneside. His house, of one and a half storeys, comprised a hall with chamber above, a parlour with a bed in it, and the kitchen had a loft for servant accommodation and storage. In 1661 the rent was doubled 'for improvements' by Richard Marshall, and the house became two full storeys.[165] Marshall's successor as tenant from 1665-1675, Ralph Burton, does not appear in the 1666 hearth tax, though a James Barton is exempt with two hearths. Not

---

164 Slashpool Farm is dated 1708 over the cross-passage, when the low-end was rebuilt as a kitchen. The plan and construction are late seventeenth century, though the absence of evidence for mullioned windows may indicate a date closer to 1700.

165 K. J. N. Fairless, 'Grange Farm – A Cross Passage House in Tyne and Wear', *Transactions of the Durham and Northumberland Architectural and Archaeological Society* 5, 1980, pp. 81-90.

all farmhouses, however, were of this standard linear arrangement. Byers Green Hall was rebuilt to a square plan for the yeomen Trotter family; William Trotter was assessed in 1666 for six hearths, but in 1674 the largest household recorded had three hearths (which may indicate that the 1666 assesment included hearths outside the main house).[166] The square form of Byers Green Hall represents the innovation of double-pile planning in the seventeenth century at a middling level, in parallel with the rectilinear gentry houses discussed above.

In Teesdale and Weardale houses underwent a parallel process of rebuilding as in the lowlands. A number of seventeenth-century houses with a hearth-passage plan, smoke hood in the hall and stone fireplace in the parlour (as at Slashpool Farm, Hett), survive in Weardale,[167] and several underwent the same development as Grange Farm, Monkton, being rebuilt from one-and-a-half to two storeys, with the black thatch roof replaced with stone slates. In Teesdale, Harrison and Hutton observed the prevalence of the hearth-passage plan, and while long houses were rarely built after the mid-seventeenth century many continued in use for much longer.[168] The occupation of long houses, with a single hearth in the open hall, and perhaps only a small service room and parlour, or even no additional room at all beyond the main living room, were probably quite common in both upland and lowland County Durham in 1666. As in North Yorkshire many of these were rebuilt in stone with the addition of an upper storey and a rear stair turret, in the decades after 1670.[169] Others survived in lower status occupation, and were probably comparable to the single-hearth long houses originally of cruck construction still standing on the North York Moors.[170] In Weardale, the surviving stone farmhouses (and incidence of two-to-four-hearth houses in 1666) suggest a greater degree of rebuilding in the seventeenth century though survival in Teesdale is distorted by the more widespread remodelling of tenant farms in the eighteenth and nineteenth centuries. The predominance of the bishop's estate in Weardale already enabled householders to operate more like freeholders in the seventeenth century, as secure lease-holding tenure encouraged farmers to rebuild their houses.[171] At Westernhopeburn, in central Weardale, a long farmhouse of two storeys with a stone slate roof, is dated 1606 above the door. For smaller holdings, houses only survive in substantial numbers from the 1670s, while stone cottages mainly date from the mid eighteenth century.[172] The

[166] Green, 'Tudhoe Hall and Byers Green Hall'.
[167] For example, at Linnew, Wolsingham and Peakfield, Frosterley.
[168] B. Harrison and B. Hutton, *Vernacular Houses in North Yorkshire and Cleveland* (Edinburgh, 1984), pp. 42-73; V. Chapman, 'The Aukside estate of Anthony Todd, freeholder, of Middleton-in-Teesdale', *Trans. Archit. Archaeol. Soc. Durham Northumberland*, new ser. 3 (1974), pp. 75-86.
[169] M. Barley, *The English Farmhouse and Cottage* (London, 1961); R. W. Brunskill, 'The Vernacular Architecture of the Northern Pennines', *Northern History* XI 2 (1975), pp. 107-142.
[170] RCHME, I (London, 1987); V. Chapman, 'Cruck-framed buildings in the Vale of Tees' *Transactions of the Durham and Northumberland Architectural and Archaeological Society* 4 (1978), pp. 35-42.
[171] P. Bowes, *Weardale: Clearing the Forest* (Bishop Auckland, 1990); J. L. Drury, 'More stout than wise: tenant right in Weardale in the Tudor period' in *The Last Principality: Politics, Religion and Society in the Bishopric of Durham 1494-1660* ed. by D. Marcombe (Nottingham, 1987).
[172] Brunskill, 'Northern Pennines'.

limited evidence for pre-1670 smaller houses, should not lead us to dismiss the earlier houses (still standing in 1666) as inferior, and many had probably been altered in the preceding sixty years. The bastle houses of Northumberland and Cumberland are testimony to rebuilding in upland areas between 1570 and 1640, and there are occasional examples in upper Weardale.[173] At the opposite end of Weardale, towards the lowlands, Low Woodifield Farm near Crook survives as an example of a probably single-hearth farmhouse from the late seventeenth century, with a substantial stepped stack (see Plate 1).

Seventeenth-century stepped stacks survive on a number of stone houses whose age has often otherwise been disguised by extensive alteration: as at Needless Hall, Toronto, which may be one of the houses depicted in the countryside around Bishop Auckland on Gregory King's drawing (Frontispiece). Newfield farmhouse, also near Bishop Auckland, is a further example, as is the smaller farmhouse at Nafferton near Brancepeth, and the large farmhouse at Great Chilton with stepped stacks to both hall and parlour chimneys (Plate 4). These stepped stacks indicate the importance of chimneys as a marker of status and wealth; signalling the substance of the household to those outside the house; including chimney money collectors, and those in less substantial houses.

The hearth tax falls mid-way through a protracted period of change in the provision and heating of space in houses. The relatively high social status of most standing buildings built before 1700 has tended to obscure the degree to which people continued to occupy houses which did not comply with the requirements of their more wealthy and increasingly socially distant neighbours. Only for the more successful middling households, usually based on married couples with secure incomes, can we posit the replacement of an open-hall house (with an inner reception or sleeping room to the high end and service rooms to the low end, both of which may be floored) by a hall and parlour house with a full upper storey linking the high and low status ends of the house, and a greater number of service rooms, including a kitchen for cooking in, and work spaces in or about the house. The desire to heat some of these rooms, primarily the hall and kitchen, but also the parlour, and sometimes upstairs chambers, determined the number of hearths such a house might have. While much attention has been given to the changing social relations involved with enclosing the open hall, the increased use of upper floors was equally important and helps explain the introduction of chimneys. Chimney stacks provided a means of heating rooms on upper floors, and while this usually refers to houses with three hearths or more, many houses with one or two hearths on the ground floor had unheated rooms above, and required the smoke from their hearths to be evacuated by a flue. The increasing use of coal, especially prevalent in County Durham, provided a further motivation for the cultural preference of containing smoke within a flue.

[173] H. G. Ramm, *et. al. Shielings and bastles* (Royal Commission on Historical Monuments, 1970); P. Ryder, 'Fortified medieval and sub-medieval buildings in the north-east of England' in *Medieval Rural Settlement in North-East England* ed. by B. Vyner (Durham, 1990), pp. 127-39.

By the late seventeenth century, the adoption of chimneys was so widespread as to provide a basis for taxing as broad a section of the population as the governing classes could countenance.

For County Durham, 1666 may be slightly too early for many of the houses which were rebuilt in the later seventeenth century. Some were provided with additional hearths through rebuilding, while many were being rebuilt in stone with only one hearth. Newhouses, Hunderthwaite, for instance, is a small stone farmhouse of 1668. Comparison of Lady Day 1666 with 1674 suggests a greater degree of rebuilding for houses of over two hearths (see Table 1). There were two hundred fewer two-hearth houses assessed in 1674 than eight years previously, and a proportion of these had acquired more heated rooms. The enlargement of what were two-hearth houses in 1666 becomes even more likely when we consider that some of those assessed for two hearths in 1674 presumably had only one in 1666. The difference between three and four-hearth houses in 1666 and 1674 is not great, and the increase in the number of households with between five and nine-hearth houses is more impressive. This confirms our picture of increasing prosperity for those of more than moderate wealth in the 1660s and 1670s, while the bulk of the population remained in smaller dwellings with only one hearth. This occurred in a culture which generally placed great importance on 'improvement', and while remodelling houses was only one aspect of this, there was a marked preference for investing surplus income in house improvements, which encompassed even the most modestly prosperous households. Yet the decision to heat additional rooms was not uniformly related to wealth or social status, and had much to do with whether the existing house was otherwise adequate. Individuals in older houses may not have felt compelled to rebuild if they had sufficient space. As Pearson has emphasised 'it was not so much the style, or even plan form, as the age of the building and the form and physical structure of its hearths and chimney stacks which influenced the number of hearths a building may have'.[174] Recently rebuilt houses usually contained a greater number of hearths than older buildings, and occupants of rebuilt houses with two, three or four hearths, could be of comparatively lower status or wealth, and in smaller houses, than those occupying older houses with fewer hearths.

The limitations of survival make it difficult to gauge the degree and exact chronology of changes in the use of hearths in County Durham. It is precisely those single-hearth houses which were least likely to survive later housing developments that would have contained open hearths in an unceilinged hall or plaster and timber smoke stacks rather than brick or stone chimneys in the 1660s and 1670s. We should not dismiss these houses as inadequate. A single hearth in the open hall, with its smoke rising to a thatched roof was more than serviceable, not least because it kept thatch free of infestation. Chimneys were less hygienic in this regard, and their introduction presumably encouraged the adoption of

---

[174] Pearson, 'Kent Hearth Tax', p. ci.

tiled roofs (though thatch remained a prevalent roofing material across County Durham, and especially in the uplands until the twentieth century).[175]

Surviving seventeenth-century houses and inventories indicate that many two-hearth households in Durham contained a heated hall (or forehouse), with the second fire in a parlour or kitchen, with a number of unheated service rooms and upstairs chambers. Others, however, could have a similar range of rooms with only one hearth in the hall (or firehouse). These households need not have been of dramatically lower wealth or status than their neighbours with two hearths. Recently modified houses were most likely to contain two hearths, and were usually provided with a greater number of upstairs rooms. As in Kent, rebuilt houses at lower social levels could have greater provision of hearths than older houses with occupants of higher status and wealth.[176] Whereas most pre-1600 houses were of one-storey, with some loft space either side of the open hall, rebuilding in the seventeenth century could include the provision of a full second storey, or a half-storey with lofts for sleeping and storage. Chimney stacks enabled these houses to have hearths on their upper floor, though the provision of stacks with more than one flue may have entailed extra cost or complications of craftsmanship that not every householder or mason was prepared to countenance for the small benefit of lugging coals up stairs. Lofts remained important for storage and sleeping, and most middling houses were either of one-and-a-half or two-and-a-half storeys. Neither goods in storage nor the lower status members of the household who slept here were regarded as requiring direct heat, and both might even have been thought to be spoilt by it.

The range of accommodation that a single-hearth household could comprise is clear where probate inventories can be matched to individuals in the hearth tax. Christopher Dodds, thatcher, paid on a single hearth in 1666 in Sedgefield, seemingly for a two-room dwelling: in 1670 his moveable goods were worth £7 'in the Roome where he dyed', with provision for sleeping and storage 'in one Chamber', and 'the instruments belonging to his trade'.[177] John Bunting, yeoman, of Stockton, also paid on one hearth in 1666, but his probate inventory of 1667 itemises six rooms in a more substantial middling farm, with goods 'in the barne at home', 'in another barne', 'in the kitching', 'in the fore house', 'in another little room called the butterey', 'in the loft over ye fore house', 'in another loft', and 'in another roome'.[178] The lofts imply a one-and-a-half storey house.

At the time of the hearth tax, cooking still took place in the hall in some households, and even where kitchens are recorded in inventories, they might be unheated spaces for the cool storage of food and utensils. Before 1700,

---

[175] V. Chapman, 'Heather-thatched buildings in the northern Pennines' *Transactions of the Durham and Northumberland Architectural and Archaeological Society* 6 (1982), pp. 9-12; N. Emery 'Materials and Methods: some aspects of building in County Durham, 1600-1930' *Durham Archaeological Journal* 2 (1986), pp. 113-120.
[176] Pearson, 'Kent Hearth Tax', p. ci.
[177] Chistopher Dodds, thatcher, Sedgefield, 1670 probate inventory.
[178] John Bunting, yeoman, Stockton, 1667 probate inventory.

a kitchen for cooking may largely have been the preserve of more prosperous households with servants who were not regarded as part of the family. While cooking and household tasks took place in the hall, the provision of a parlour provided an alternative space for retirement and receiving guests. Inventories indicate that in many middling households the best bed was in the parlour in the late seventeenth century, and a lit fireplace in this room provided a focus for activities as diverse as dressing, reading, needlework and conversation. Surviving seventeenth-century parlour fireplaces, invariably of stone with a four-centred arch and decorated chamfered mouldings which may have been painted, convey the importance of this hearth to the household. At East Oakley House in West Auckland, the parlour fireplace was inscribed with the date and initials of the householder and his wife: IKK 1651. This, very probably, was John Kay's house, and records the Kays moving in shortly after their marriage in 1650.[179] Surviving houses in towns indicate the provision of similar fireplaces on the first floor, in the living rooms above the shop. Examples are Old Bank House, Front Street, Wolsingham, where the stack is corbelled out at first-floor level externally (Plate 11), or at houses along The Bank, Barnard Castle.

The one and two-hearth entries in the hearth tax relate to a wide variety of accommodation, and neither the distinction between payers and non-payers nor between one and two hearths represents a constant dividing line. Even among the exempt we can not assume that all were in single-room cottages, temporary shelters on commons, or in 'hovels' around the coal pits, though many were. Not all of these entries even relate to houses: a few institutional buildings are named in 1666 among the exempt, such as Hartlepool Town Hall, and the school houses at Darlington Bondgate, Ingleton, Piercebridge and Westwick, all with one hearth. The occupants of commercial lodgings may also appear as single-hearth households, as may those dwelling with relatives, especially the elderly. Houses and cottages similarly entailed a variety of accommodation, and most of those who paid the tax on one or two hearths occupied permanent and well furnished homes. A house with a main living room used for cooking and eating could also have an unheated parlour, service rooms and chambers.

Non-surviving houses
Over 95 per cent of the dwellings documented in the Durham hearth tax no longer survive. Some of these would have been comparable to the surviving houses discussed above. What we have largely lost through rebuilding after 1670 is standing evidence for the smaller houses, the variety of houses and lodgings in towns, especially on the coast, the highly variegated settlements of Tyne-side and Wear-side, and the accommodation of labourers and industrial workers. While the limitations of survival make it difficult to pursue village case studies for Durham houses, documentary sources present an embarrassment of riches,

---

[179] I am grateful to Martin Roberts for observing the link between East Oakley House and John Kay.

especially in probate and estate records, which are best understood in the context of the available archaeological evidence. Reid has done just this for Long Newton in Teesdale. A map of the village in c.1616 depicts the houses and their chimneys in three-dimensions, and their 'comparatively high walls and medium pitched roofs' suggest that 'they were of fairly recent construction' when compared with the excavated evidence of houses at West Hartburn or the plan of Whessoe of 1594 'where the houses are represented as having walls of minimum height and steeply pitched roofs'. In 1666, seventeen households in Long Newton paid on one hearth, in houses that were presumably similar to those depicted fifty years earlier, while five had two hearths, and a further three households had five hearths or more. The largest was Sir George Vane's newly built seven-hearth house, while the six-hearth house of the bailiff Christopher Hall, gent., contained a hall, parlour, kitchen, buttery and milkhouse, with chambers over the hall and parlour (a range of rooms no more elaborate than some yeomen, but more extensively heated). Reid's analysis of the inventories suggests that the single-hearth houses in Long Newton contained 'a hall or forehouse (or firehouse) with one other room usually designated chamber or occasionally parlour. A few houses had one or two chambers above and, as a rule, only a few people of standing had the addition of a kitchen, buttery or milkhouse'.[180] This summary can stand for much of the rural housing in County Durham; especially since the inventory room names are common to the uplands and lowlands, and in market towns. Further research might indicate a correlation between social status, the form of building, and the nomenclature of firehouse, forehouse and hall. Reid's study of Long Newton corroborates the archaeological evidence of standing buildings, that houses were being rebuilt at a neighbourhood level from c.1600 in most communities, and that only the larger examples have survived unaltered to the present day.

From the limited excavated evidence available, we can gauge to some degree the nature of smaller houses. Houses in West Whelpington, Northumberland, were being altered in the centuries before its desertion sometime before 1715, and German and Dutch ceramics show that the seventeenth-century inhabitants were not living at or near subsistence level.[181] These houses have been interpreted as less substantial than those documented in the inventories of Leicestershire yeomen and husbandmen in the sixteenth and seventeenth century.[182] This may be an unfair comparison, as Leicestershire 'peasants' with insufficient wealth to warrant an inventory, may well have occupied houses similar to West Whelpington, if only we could excavate them. At least one house in West Whelpington had glazed windows and coal fires, and was probably lit by candles. Unlike Wharram Percy, Yorkshire, houses in West Whelpington were not rebuilt successively above each

[180] D. S. Reid, *The Durham Crown Lordships* (Durham Local History Society, 1990), p. 91.
[181] M. Jarratt, 'The deserted village of West Whelpington, Northumberland' *Archaeologia Aeliana* 4th series, XL 1964, pp. 189-225.
[182] W. G. Hoskins, *The Midland Peasant: The Economic and Social History of a Leicestershire Village*, (London, 1957).

other. The West Whelpington houses have been interpeted as representing a type of rural housing which preceded the 'permanence' of the Great Rebuilding; requiring regular maintenance to their thatched and stone slate roofs, and clay walls footed by undressed river boulders. Housing conditions and the need for regular repair was comparable at West Hartburn, County Durham, a village in the lower Tees valley depopulated by the late sixteenth century. West Hartburn houses were being remodelled in the late sixteenth century, when the open hearth in the centre of the room was replaced at House A by a new hearth to the side of the room, possibly in a projecting chimney stack.[183] At neighbouring East Hartburn, a century after West Hartburn was deserted, nine single hearth, eight two hearth, and one three hearth households, were assessed in the 1674 Hearth Tax, with twenty-one households exempt. Many of these must have experienced similar, and subsequent, post-medieval remodelling to that uncovered in West Hartburn, before 1600. In the seventeenth century, rural settlements across the county probably contained comparable buildings to West Whelpington and West Hartburn which do not survive today.

   Excavated evidence indicates that moderately sized rural houses built in the fifteenth and sixteenth centuries were well constructed, even if they required regular repair before desertion in the seventeenth and eighteenth centuries.[184] Virtually no houses of timber-framed construction survive in rural County Durham, but examples from North Yorkshire may indicate what some houses were like in the southern parts of the county.[185] For workers' housing in the north of the county, we have documentary sources to compensate for the lack of archaeological survival or investigation; but we should not take the élite descriptions of 'hovels' at face value. Although the prevalence of single-hearth households is exceptionally high by national standards, this does not necessarily indicate absolute poverty or widespread impermanent housing. Pitmen were often provided with accommodation by their employers, sometimes in lodgings (which may have contained one hearth) and more often in temporary shelters near the coal pits and spoil heaps.[186] These workers, especially those without wives and families, were often living away from the established areas of settlement, and it is likely that these were the kind of people who were not always included among the exempt and did not appear in the hearth tax returns at all. More securely employed workers in the coal trade had commensurately more permanent housing, and the late seventeenth century witnessed the beginnings of pit-men 'rows', with each household in a single room with one hearth. Managerial and better paid skilled workers occupied houses with several rooms and often had more than one hearth. Workers employed in glass and metal manufacture, and

---

[183] A. Pallister & S. Wrathmell 'West Hartburn, Third Report'.

[184] A. Pallister and S. Wrathmell, 'The Deserted Village of West Hartburn, Third Report: Excavation of Site D and Discussion' in *Medieval Rural Settlement in North East England*, pp. 59-75.

[185] B. Harrison, 'Longhouses in the Vale of York', *Vernacular Architecture* 22 (1991), pp. 31-39; RCHME, *Houses of the North York Moors*.

[186] See Green, 'Houses and Landscape in Early Industrial County Durham'.

salt panning, occupied a similar range of accommodation. The concentration of these industries, along with ship building and rope making, encouraged the development of terraced housing. Salt-pan workers in South Shields were housed in 'rows' of cottages, as were labouring families in Sunderland by at least the 1690s.[187]

On Tyne-side and Wear-side, the more securely employed workers with families to augment their household income, were probably better accommodated than is normally imagined. They may indeed have been better housed than agricultural labouring families, who were usually on a lower income. Yet the relationship between wages and prices benefited labourers of all sorts in the later seventeenth century. Partly for this reason, Margaret Spufford has suggested that there was a 'great rebuilding' of cottages in the late seventeenth century, which was the corollary of earlier rebuilding by yeoman farmers (who prospered most when wages were low and prices high in the decades before 1640). Spufford notes a case in the 1664 Cambridgeshire hearth tax of 'the house blowne away' since the 1662 assessment, but suggests that 'fewer seventeenth-century cottages, judging by the number of survivals, blew away than their predecessors'.[188] The fragmentary survival of cottages in County Durham would tend to confirm her observation, as only from the later seventeenth century do we have smaller houses and surviving examples of single-room cottages built in rows, later incorporated into one house. These undoubtedly housed the better off of the seventeenth-century poor.

Equating rebuilding with increased permanence is, however, problematic; frequent and piecemeal repair is necessary for almost all houses to remain habitable, and we simply lack the evidence to say how many people occupied houses which were not constructed of stone or durable timber-frames before 1700. Furthermore, we must take account of the increasing dependency on wage-labour of a growing proportion of the population in County Durham, as elsewhere in England, between the late sixteenth and late seventeenth centuries. Those families occupying single-room cottages, when in work, in the later seventeenth century may well have had great grandparents in long houses, who raised their own food, a hundred years before. We should not romanticise the pre-industrial past, and nor should we project later social attitudes onto the seventeenth century, but given that this was a period of early industrialisation, it may be instructive to glance at reports of housing conditions in the nineteenth century. Machin's unpublished study of nineteenth-century poor housing, documented in Parliamentary Commission reports, demonstrates the extreme poverty of rural southern England, where the poor housed themselves in 'cottages' which their social superiors described as 'hovels'.[189] Many of these

---

[187] See Newman, C. and M. Meikle, *The Origins of Sunderland*, (VCH, forthcoming).

[188] M. Spufford *The Great Reclothing of Rural England*, (Cambridge, 1984), p. 3 n. 11, and see W. G. Hoskins, 'The Rebuilding of Rural England, 1570-1640', *Past and Present* 4 (1953), pp. 44-59.

[189] R. Machin, ''The Lost Cottages of England: An essay on impermanent building in post-medieval England', unpublished paper.

houses were constructed of 'impermanent' materials, requiring regular repair: mud, turf, wattle and daub, and perhaps earth-fast timber framing. It is unclear to what extent such housing existed in seventeenth-century England. Arguably, the poverty which prompted parliamentary commissions was a creation of industrialisation and agricultural change in southern England in the eighteenth century. Similar reports exist for the north of England, and Sir John Walsham published in 1840 *Three Reports on the state of the dwellings of the labouring classes in Cumberland, Durham and Westmoreland*, based upon the Poor Law Commission: 'In the rural districts, the cottages on the estates of the largest proprietors have rarely more than one single room for every purpose. In the pit-rows and in towns they have nominally two rooms, but even there the inhabitants are accustomed to live and sleep (irrespective of sexes) in the same room; and of conveniences for cleanliness, to say nothing of improvements for the more economical management of fuel and household resources, there are scarce any instances'.[190] Despite early industrialisation and agricultural change in County Durham, we cannot project these moralising nineteenth-century views of wretched housing conditions back onto the seventeenth century. The households of seventeenth-century Durham had more self-respect. Yet the hearth tax does demonstrate the relative poverty of the population of County Durham and demonstrates high turnover in household occupancy, with severe implications for housing conditions. Despite the presumably low standard of housing in the sixteenth-century north east, compared to southern England, the seventeenth century witnessed a worsening of housing conditions for the majority of the poor and wage-labourers of County Durham. Conversely, the prosperous craftsmen, skilled labourers, and farmers with sufficient size holdings to exploit the market for agricultural produce created by the burgeoning wage-labour population in the coal field, experienced a dramatic improvement in housing conditions. Industrialisation and agricultural change apparantly pauperised the majority of the population, perhaps in a manner analogous to the social polarisation witnessed in late eighteenth and early nineteenth century southern England. Whereas those prospering from economic change, the middling sort and above, experienced a 'great rebuilding' from c.1600, more in line with housing change in southern England.

[190] Sir John Walsham *Three reports on the state of the dwellings of the labouring classes in Cumberland, Durham and Westmoreland* (London, William Cowes, 1840), p. 6.

CONCLUSION

Houses and chimneys presented an index of wealth and poverty to contemporaries, and the hearth tax enables us to establish the socio-economic profile of seventeenth-century communities. Yet it has not always been regarded as a blessing. Whig historians claimed it offended English liberty by intruding upon property,[191] and contemporaries were certainly aggravated by tax collectors entering their homes, and hostile to what was effectively an income tax. Despite the difficulties of introducing any form of permanent taxation on wealth, Sir William Petty conceived of the hearth tax as a form of excise and believed the number of hearths in a house were a measure of an individual's purchasing power.[192] In the 1690s the window tax aimed at a similar means of raising funds and was also unpopular, but the fiscal arrangements introduced with the Bank of England in 1694 secured the finances of the state to such an extent that direct income tax was not introduced until the end of the eighteenth century. Permanent taxation of wealth was widely regarded as unjust and this partly explains contemporary resistance to the hearth tax. In Durham, evidence of resistence is remarkably muted. Despite some initial refusal by constables and parochial officials to co-operate in 1662, 1663 and 1664, no disorderly resistance is known to have occurred, and 1666 was remarkably quiet in comparison with some other counties. This might suggest some accommodation between ordinary householders and those in authority, and the context of tax collection certainly warrants considerable caution over under-recording. The Tudhoe evidence indicates that perhaps 40 per cent of households were omitted from the Lady Day 1674 Exchequer Return for County Durham, excluding the poorer third of the population. The Tudhoe lists also reveal significant under-recording among the chargeable population, of between ten and twenty per cent of both householders and hearths. Under-recording also reveals a larger truth: that a significant proportion of the population were beyond the reach of state authority.

County Durham had an exceptionally high level of relative poverty, with around four in ten recorded households exempted from the tax in 1666 and 1674. Rural settlements were characterised by a majority of single hearth households, of cottagers and wage labourers, most of which were exempt from the tax. Over half of charged households had single hearths, with over a third in the middling bracket of two to four hearths. Lesser craftsmen and husbandmen, along with better paid specialist workers in industrial employment had one or two hearths, and a smaller number of more wealthy yeomen farmers, and middling tradesmen in towns, occupied houses of three or four hearths. A generally sparsely spread gentry, clustered in certain towns and villages, as well as wealthy tradesmen and professionals in towns, usually lived in houses of over five hearths. This broad élite, represents less than ten per cent of charged households, and around five

---

[191] Lord Macaulay, *The History of England* (London, 1873), Vol. I pp. 471 and 673.
[192] Evans, *Cambridgeshire*, pp. xiii & xv.

per cent of the recorded population. There were only a few great houses of over twenty hearths in the county, chiefly the medieval castles occupied by a new élite in the seventeenth century.

County Durham presents a complex picture of prosperity for the lesser élite and middling sort in the late seventeenth century, clearly occupying larger houses. This prosperity rested on the coal trade, related commercial enterprises and associated agricultural change; processes which had pauperised a proportion of small farmers and cottagers during the seventeenth century while allowing others more stable employment. The high proportion of single hearth households in the county reflects the wide base of County Durham's social pyramid. The incomes of many of these households were probably higher than might be imagined. The houses of at least the most securely employed and those with household incomes enhanced by working dependents, were very probably better constructed and entailed a wider variation in accommodation than has usually been assumed. The massive levels of exemption, and the indications of considerable under-recording, suggests that the foundations of the social pyramid are not documented. If they are not, and considerable sub-strata lie under the records we have, this, of course, makes the dramatic figures we already have for cottagers and industrial workers only more dramatic.[193] Only excavation would enable us to see more clearly the houses of these social groups. The hearth tax remains our most comprehensive documentary guide to housing, wealth and society before 1700.

[193] See histogram p. xciii.

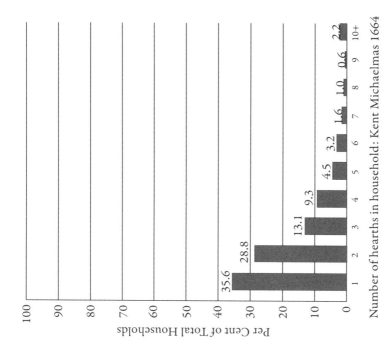

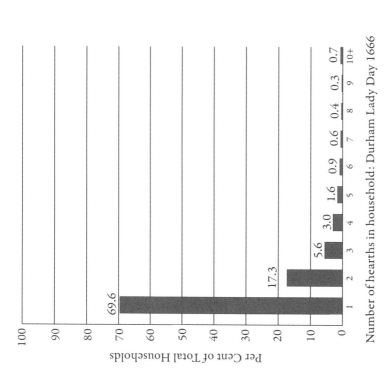

Figure 2: Distribution of Households assessed on differing numbers of hearths in Durham and Kent.

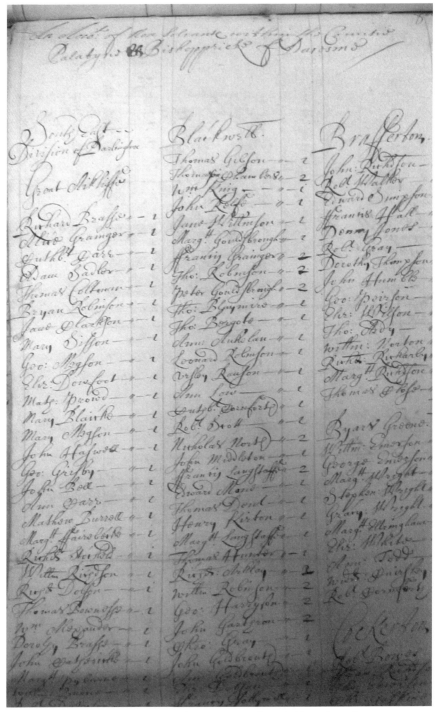

Figure 3. Opening membrane of the non-paying households in the Lady Day 1666 Assessment, covering parts of the townships of Great Aycliffe, Blackwell, Brafferton and Byers Green. TNA E179/106/28 m.18, transcript pp.106–7.

Table 6. Lady Day 1666. Totals of Households and Hearths in the Lady Day 1666 Assessment.

This table is arranged by townships within parishes, and for convenience of reference the parish map from the front end-paper is repeated overleaf. All the data from the 1666 assessment is also displayed in the form of maps 2–12, distributed in the Introduction. A more detailed map of the Durham City parishes will be found on p. cii. A township map will be found on the back end paper.

As explained on pp. xxxvi–xxxvii above, the chargeable were assessed by the civil area in which they lived; those exempted by certificate were listed by their ecclesiastical area. The actual record is therefore divided in two parts. Pages 1–105 list the paying, by township within divisions of wards, and pp. 106–177 record the certified exempt. In this table we have striven to co-ordinate payers and non-payers. Although the exemption certificates show that non-payers were identified by churchwardens and clergy working in terms of ecclesiastical parishes and chapelries, they appear in this table under townships within civil parishes.

Explanatory Note

Whereas the figures in the columns of hearth numbers 1 to 9 record the actual number of households, the figures in the **10+** column show the actual hearth number in square brackets.

Where damage is noted (*dm*) the resulting figures only include legible data so that only approximate figures can be given for the analyses.

? signifies a similar approximation.

* is used where the data includes one or more names without a hearth number or where the total hearth number in the document appears to be incorrect.

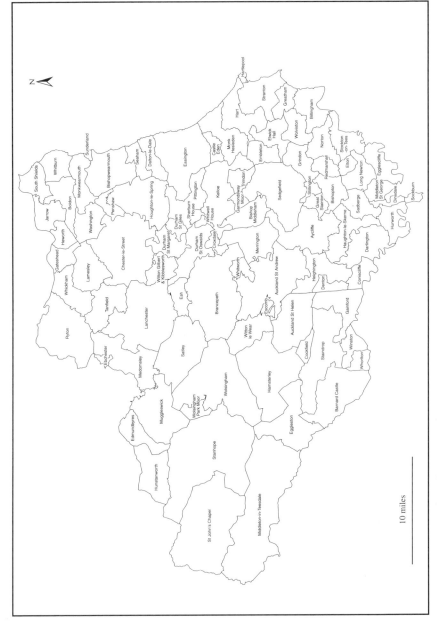

Map 13. Durham County Parishes

		\multicolumn{Number of hearths:}										Total Households	Total Hearths
		1	2	3	4	5	6	7	8	9	10+		
AUCKLAND ST ANDREW, Darlington North West Division													
Some townships Darlington South East													
Bishopley	Paying	5	1	1								7	10
	Non-paying	7										7	7
	TOTAL	12	1	1								14	17
Coundon	Paying	15	7	1								23	32
	Non-paying	15										15	15
	TOTAL	30	7	1								38	47
Eldon *DSE*	Paying *dm*	13	5									21	29
	Non-paying	21										21	21
	TOTAL	34	5									42	50
Hunwick	Paying	14	8	1				1		1		25	49
	Non-paying	7										7	7
	TOTAL	21	8	1				1		1		32	56
Middlestone *DSE*	Paying	5	1	1		2						9	20
	Non-paying	3										3	3
	TOTAL	8	1	1		2						12	23
Middridge *DSE*	Paying	12	7									19	26
	Non-paying	22										22	22
	TOTAL	34	7									41	48
Newton Cap	Paying*	8	5	1	1	1	1					17	36
	Non-paying	3	1									4	5
	TOTAL	11	6	1	1	1	1					21	41
Shildon	Paying	3	4		2							9	19
	Non-paying	5										5	5
	TOTAL	8	4		2							14	24
St Andrew Auckland	Paying	7	3	2	1						1	14	32
	Non-paying	7										7	7
	TOTAL	14	3	2	1						1	21	39
Westerton	Paying	1	1	5								7	18
	Non-paying					*No data*							
AUCKLAND ST ANDREW		173?	43?	12?	4?	3?	1	1			2	242	363

		Number of hearths:										Total Households	Total Hearths
		1	2	3	4	5	6	7	8	9	10+		
AUCKLAND ST HELEN, Darlington North West Division													
Evenwood	Paying	12	5	1								18	25
	Non-paying	26	1									27	28
	TOTAL	38	6	1								45	53
Evenwood Barony	Paying	24	6		1		1		1			33	54
	Non-paying	14										14	14
	TOTAL	38	6		1		1		1			47	68
St Helen Auckland	Paying	6	4	3	1						1 [13]	15	40
	Non-paying	26	1									27	28
	TOTAL	32	5	3	1						1	42	68
West Auckland	Paying	37	13	5	3	1			2			61	111
	Non-paying	55	2									57	59
	TOTAL	92	15	5	3	1			2			118	170
AUCKLAND ST HELEN		**200**	**32**	**9**	**5**	**1**	**1**		**3**		**1**	**252**	**359**
AYCLIFFE, Darlington South East Division													
Brafferton	Paying	9	4	2	1			2				18	41
	Non-paying	15										15	15
	TOTAL	24	4	2	1			2				33	56
Great Aycliffe	Paying	30	14	4	2	1						51	83
	Non-paying	43	2									45	47
	TOTAL	73	16	4	2	1						96	130
Preston-le-Skerne	Paying	17	3	1		1						22	31
	Non-paying	15										15	15
	TOTAL	32	3	1		1						37	46
Woodham	Paying	12	3	2	1							18	28
	Non-paying	4										4	4
	TOTAL	16	3	2	1							22	32
AYCLIFFE		**145**	**26**	**9**	**4**	**2**		**2**				**188**	**264**
BARNARD CASTLE, Darlington South West Division													
Barnard Castle	Paying *dm*	53	35	19	8	8	3					*133*	*291*
	Non-paying					*No data*							
BILLINGHAM, Stockton North East Division													
Billingham	Paying	27	6		2							35	47
	Non-paying	27										27	27
	TOTAL	54	6		2							62	74
Cowpen Bewley	Paying	17	6	2								25	35
	Non-paying	18										18	18
	TOTAL	35	6	2								43	53

Table 6. Totals of Households and Hearths, Lady Day 1666   xcix

		\multicolumn{10}{c}{Number of hearths:}	Total Households	Total Hearths
		1	2	3	4	5	6	7	8	9	10+		
Newton Bewley	Paying	8	9	1								18	29
	Non-paying	12										12	12
	Total	20	9	1								30	41
Billingham		**109**	**21**	**3**	**2**							**135**	**168**
BISHOP MIDDLEHAM, Stockton North East Division													
Bishop Middleham	Paying	18	6	3	2							29	47
	Non-paying	32										32	32
	Total	50	6	3	2							61	79
Cornforth	Paying	10	8	2								20	32
	Non-paying	24										24	24
	Total	34	8	2								44	56
Mainsforth	Paying	5			1	1						7	14
	Non-paying	2										2	2
	Total	7			1	1						9	16
Thrislington	Paying		1									2	6
	Non-paying				\multicolumn{6}{c}{No data}			
BISHOP MIDDLEHAM		**91**	**15**	**5**	**4**	**1**						**116**	**157**
BISHOPTON, Stockton South West Division													
Bishopton	Paying	21	9	5				1				36	61
	Non-paying	29										29	29
	Total	50	9	5				1				65	90
East & West Newbiggin	Paying	4	2									6	8
	Non-paying				\multicolumn{6}{c}{No data}			
Little Stainton	Paying	6	2		1							9	14
	Non-paying	8										8	8
	Total	14	2		1							17	22
BISHOPTON		**68**	**13**	**5**	**1**			**1**				**88**	**120**
BISHOPWEARMOUTH, Easington North Division													
Bishopwearmouth	Paying	78	21	5	1	2			1	1		109	166
	Non-paying	124	3									127	130
	Total	202	24	5	1	2			1	1		236	296
Bishopwearmouth Panns	Paying	9	5		2	1	2			1		20	53
	Non-paying	63	2									65	67
	Total	72	7		2	1	2			1		85	120
Burdon	Paying	5	4									9	13
	Non-paying	7										7	7
	Total	12	4									16	20

		Number of hearths:											Total Households	Total Hearths
		1	2	3	4	5	6	7	8	9	10+			
Ryhope	Paying	12	5	1									18	25
	Non-paying	22											22	22
	TOTAL	34	5	1									40	47
Silksworth	Paying	5	3		1	2							11	25
	Non-paying	14											14	14
	TOTAL	19	3		1	2							25	39
Tunstall	Paying		2	1				1					4	14
	Non-paying	14											14	14
	TOTAL	14	2	1				1					18	28
BISHOPWEARMOUTH		**353**	**45**	**7**	**4**	**5**	**2**	**1**	**1**		**2**		**420**	**550**
BOLDON, Chester East Division														
East Boldon	Paying	5	3	1	1		1						11	24
	Non-paying	16	1										17	18
	TOTAL	21	4	1	1		1						28	42
West Boldon	Paying	13	5				1						19	29
	Non-paying	14	1										15	16
	TOTAL	27	6				1						34	45
BOLDON		**48**	**10**	**1**	**1**		**2**						**62**	**87**
BRANCEPETH, Darlington North West Division. *Some townships Darlington South East*														
Brancepeth (with Castle)	Paying	12	14	9	2	2			1	1	2 [11] [17]		43	130
	Non-paying	44	10										54	64
	TOTAL	56	24	9	2	2			1	1	2		97	194
Brandon	Paying	7	6	1		1	1	1					17	40
	Non-paying	12											12	12
	TOTAL	19	6	1		1	1	1					29	52
Byshottles	Paying	7	9	3	1	1	1					1 [12]	23	61
	Non-paying	3	1										4	5
	TOTAL	10	10	3	1	1	1					1	27	66
Crook & Billy Row	Paying	9	5	2		1							17	30
	Non-paying						*No data*							
Helmington Row	Paying	12	6	1									19	27
	Non-paying	12	4										16	20
	TOTAL	24	10	1									35	47
Stockley	Paying	16	6	1		1	1						25	42
	Non-paying	25											25	25
	TOTAL	41	6	1		1	1						50	67

		Number of hearths:										Total Households	Total Hearths
		1	2	3	4	5	6	7	8	9	10+		
Willington *DSE*	Paying	16	3	1								20	25
	Non-paying	23	3									26	29
	TOTAL	39	6	1								46	54
BRANCEPETH		**198**	**67**	**18**	**3**	**6**	**3**	**1**	**1**	**1**	**3**	**301**	**510**
CASTLE EDEN, Easington South Division													
Castle Eden	Paying	10			1							11	14
	Non-paying	7										7	7
	TOTAL	17			1							18	21
CHESTER-LE-STREET, Chester Middle Division. *Some townships Easington North*													
Birtley	Paying	8	5		2							15	26
	Non-paying	8										8	8
	TOTAL	16	5		2							23	34
Chester-le-Street	Paying	29	21	15	10	3	4	1				83	202
	Non-paying	32										32	32
	TOTAL	61	21	15	10	3	4	1				115	234
Edmondsley	Paying	5	6	1	1	1						14	30
	Non-paying				*No data*								
Harraton	Paying	5	4	1	2					1		13	33
	Non-paying	25										25	25
	TOTAL	30	4	1	2					1		38	58
Lumley and Lambton *EN*	Paying	26	22	8	6	1	2	1	2		2 [11] [32]	70	201
	Non-paying				*No data*								
Pelton	Paying	4	6	2	3							15	34
	Non-paying	4	1									5	6
	TOTAL	8	7	2	3							20	40
Plawsworth	Paying	8	6				1	1			1 [11]	17	44
	Non-paying	21										21	21
	TOTAL	29	6				1	1			1	38	65
Urpeth	Paying	1	9		1							11	23
	Non-paying	11	1									12	13
	TOTAL	12	10		1							23	36
Waldridge	Paying	1	5	2								8	17
	Non-paying	5										5	5
	TOTAL	6	5	2								13	22
CHESTER-LE-STREET		**193**	**86**	**29**	**25**	**4**	**8**	**3**	**2**	**1**	**3**	**354**	**720**

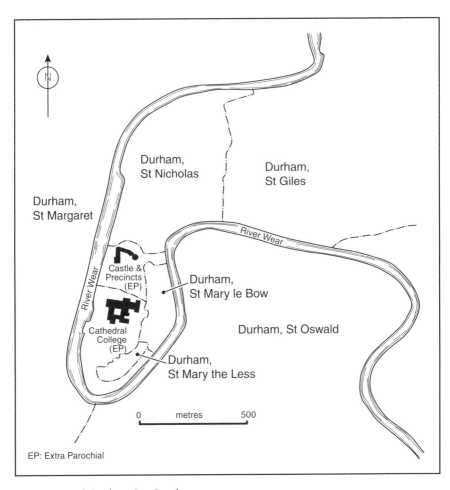

Map 14. Durham City Parishes.

					Number of hearths:							Total Households	Total Hearths
		1	2	3	4	5	6	7	8	9	10+		
COCKFIELD, Darlington South West Division														
Cockfield	Paying	26	13	3		1							43	66
	Non-paying	20	2										22	24
	TOTAL	46	15	3		1							65	90
CONISCLIFFE, Darlington South East Division														
High Coniscliffe	Paying	13	9	4	1	1		2			1 [12]		31	78
	Non-paying	21	1										22	23
	TOTAL	34	10	4	1	1		2			1		53	101
Low Coniscliffe	Paying	4	5	2	1								12	24
	Non-paying	13	1										14	15
	TOTAL	17	6	2	1								26	39
CONISCLIFFE		51	16	6	2	1		2			1		79	140
CROXDALE, Easington South Division														
Croxdale and Butterby	Paying	6	8	1	2						3 [10] [11] [15]		20	69
	Non-paying					*No data*								
Sunderland Bridge	Paying	2	4				1						7	16
	Non-paying	4											4	4
	TOTAL	6	4				1						11	20
CROXDALE		12	12	1	2		1				3		31	89
DALTON-LE-DALE, Easington North Division														
Cold Hesledon	Paying	9			2								11	17
	Non-paying					*No data*								
Dalton	Paying		3	2	1								6	16
	Non-paying	9											9	9
	TOTAL	9	3	2	1								15	25
Dawdon	Paying	6	1								1 [17]		8	25
	Non-paying					*No data*								
East Murton	Paying	6	2	2									10	16
	Non-paying	7											7	7
	TOTAL	13	2	2									17	23
DALTON-LE-DALE		37	6	4	3						1		51	90
DARLINGTON, Darlington South East Division														
Archdeacon Newton	Paying	9	3								1 [12]		13	27
	Non-paying					*No data*								
Blackwell	Paying	7	13	3	2		1						26	56
	Non-paying	25	10										34	44
	TOTAL	32	23	3	2		1						60	100

		Number of hearths:										Total Households	Total Hearths
		1	2	3	4	5	6	7	8	9	10+		
Cockerton	Paying	19	9	5								33	52
	Non-paying	30	1									31	32
	TOTAL	49	10	5								64	84
Darlington Bondgate	Paying	30	9	3	3	1	2			1		49	95
	Non-paying	65	9									74	83
	TOTAL	95	18	3	3	1	2			1		123	178
Darlington Borough*	Paying	35	40	29	15	1	2	1			1 [10]	124	296
	Non-paying	14	1									15	16
	TOTAL	49	41	29	15	1	2	1	1	139	312	139	312
Darlington Prebend Row	Paying	2	2	2	1							7	16
	Non-paying	6										6	6
	TOTAL	8	2	2	1							13	22
Oxneyfield	Paying				1							1	4
	Non-paying			1								1	3
	TOTAL			1	1							2	7
DARLINGTON		242	97	43	22	2	5	1		1	2	414	730
DENTON, Darlington South East Division													
Denton	Paying	4	3	2	1	1			1			12	33
	Non-paying	19										19	19
	TOTAL	23	3	2	1	1			1			31	52
Houghton le Side	Paying	8	5		2							15	26
	Non-paying	11	2									13	15
	TOTAL	19	7		2							28	41
DENTON		42	10	2	3	1			1			59	93
DINSDALE, Stockton South West Division													
Dinsdale	Paying	8	2	2					1			13	26
	Non-paying					*No data*								
DURHAM ST. GILES, Durham Division													
Durham St. Giles	Paying	26	21	9	4	2			2		2 [13] [25]	66	175
	Non-paying					*No data*								
DURHAM ST. MARGARET, Durham Division													
Crossgate	Paying	51	32	11	4	4	3	2	1		1 [12]	109	236
	Non-paying					*No data*								
Framwellgate	Paying	32	24	13	7	3	2	2	2	1	2[10] [10]	88	233
	Non-paying					*No data*								
DURHAM ST. MARGARET		83	56	24	11	7	5	4	3	1	3	197	469

Table 6. Totals of Households and Hearths, Lady Day 1666　　　cv

		\ Number of hearths:										Total Households	Total Hearths
		1	2	3	4	5	6	7	8	9	10+		
DURHAM ST. MARY THE LESS, Durham Division													
South Bailey	Paying		1	3		3	3	3	1	1	4[10] [10] [10] [11]	19	123
	Non-paying					*No data*							
DURHAM ST. MARY-LE-BOW, Durham Division													
North Bailey*	Paying	4	5	7	5	6	3	4	8	5	6[10] [10] [11] [11] [20] [22]	53	324
	Non-paying					*No data*							
DURHAM ST. NICHOLAS, Durham Division													
Durham St. Nicholas	Paying	55	60	24	17	18	6	5	3	4	3[10] [12] [12]	195	570
	Non-paying					*No data*							
DURHAM ST. OSWALD, Durham City Division. *Some townships Chester Middle*													
Broom *CM*	Paying	7	5	2	1							15	27
	Non-paying	5	1									6	7
	TOTAL	12	6	2	1							21	34
Elvet, Barony	Paying	32	17	9	2	3		1		1	2[10] [11]	67	153
	Non-paying					*No data*							
Elvet, Borough	Paying	6	8	7	9	5	2	4		2	3[10] [11] [12]	46	195
	Non-paying					*No data*							
DURHAM ST. OSWALD		50	31	18	12	8	2	5		3	5	134	382
EASINGTON, Easington South Division													
Easington	Paying	32	11	1			1				1 [14]	46	77
	Non-paying	54	1									55	56
	TOTAL	86	12	1			1				1	101	133
Haswell	Paying	14						1				15	21
	Non-paying	16										16	16
	TOTAL	30						1				31	37
Hawthorn	Paying	20	5			1						26	35
	Non-paying	17										17	17
	TOTAL	37	5			1						43	52

		Number of hearths:										Total Households	Total Hearths
		1	2	3	4	5	6	7	8	9	10+		
Shotton	Paying	14	8	1			1					24	39
	Non-paying	28										28	28
	TOTAL	42	8	1			1					52	67
EASINGTON		**195**	**25**	**2**		**1**	**2**	**1**			**1**	**227**	**289**
EBCHESTER, Chester West Division													
Ebchester	Paying	7	7	1								15	24
	Non-paying	9										9	9
	TOTAL	16	7	1								24	33
EDMONBYERS, Chester West Division													
Edmond Byers	Paying	12	1									13	14
	Non-paying					*No data*								
EGGLESCLIFFE, Stockton South West Division													
Aislaby	Paying	15		1	1		1	1				19	35
	Non-paying	17										17	17
	TOTAL	32		1	1		1	1				36	52
Egglescliffe	Paying	22	11	2	1			1				37	61
	Non-paying	7										7	7
	TOTAL	29	11	2	1			1				44	68
EGGLESCLIFFE		**61**	**11**	**3**	**2**		**1**	**2**				**80**	**120**
EGGLESTON, Darlington South West Division													
Eggleston	Paying	26	1	1				1				29	38
	Non-paying	31	3									34	37
	TOTAL	57	4	1				1				63	75
ELTON, Stockton South West Division													
ELTON	Paying	6	3									9	12
	Non-paying	6										6	6
	TOTAL	12	3									15	18
ELWICK HALL, Stockton North East Division													
Elwick Hall	Paying	17	1	1	1	1		1				22	38
	Non-paying	23	1									24	25
	TOTAL	40	2	1	1	1		1				46	63
EMBLETON, Stockton North East Division													
Embleton	Paying	9	2	2			1		1			15	31
	Non-paying	3										3	3
	TOTAL	12	2	2			1		1			18	34

		Number of hearths:										Total Households	Total Hearths
		1	2	3	4	5	6	7	8	9	10+		
ESCOMB, Darlington North West Division													
Bondgate in Bishop Auckland	Paying	13	13	9	4	2	2					43	104
	Non-paying	60										60	60
	TOTAL	73	13	9	4	2	2					103	164
Borough of Auckland	Paying	19	17	12	12	11	3				2 [18] [35]	76	263
	Non-paying	28										28	28
	TOTAL	47	17	12	12	11	3				2	104	291
Escomb	Paying	12	5	7								24	43
	Non-paying	7	1									8	9
	TOTAL	19	6	7								32	52
Newgate in Bishop Auckland	Paying	14	15	10	4	3				1		47	114
	Non-paying	53	4									57	61
	TOTAL	67	19	10	4	3				1		104	175
ESCOMB		**206**	**55**	**38**	**20**	**16**	**5**			**1**	**2**	**343**	**682**
ESH, Chester West Division													
Burnhope & Hamsteels	Paying	12	2	4	1							19	32
	Non-paying	6	1									7	8
	TOTAL	18	3	4	1							26	40
Esh	Paying	13	7	1		1					1 [22]	23	57
	Non-paying	16										16	16
	TOTAL	29	7	1		1					1	39	73
ESH		**47**	**10**	**5**	**1**	**1**					**1**	**65**	**113**
GAINFORD, Darlington South West Division													
Bolam	Paying	21	5			1						27	36
	Non-paying	10	1									11	12
	TOTAL	31	6			1						38	48
Cleatlam	Paying	15	3	2						1		21	36
	Non-paying	15	1									16	17
	TOTAL	30	4	2						1		37	53
Gainford	Paying	8	9	4	1		1				2 [11] [21]	25	80
	Non-paying*	23	8									31	39
	TOTAL	31	17	4	1		1				2	56	119
Headlam	Paying	8	3	2			1		1			15	34
	Non-paying	8	1									9	10
	TOTAL	16	4	2			1		1			24	44

		Number of hearths:										Total Households	Total Hearths
		1	2	3	4	5	6	7	8	9	10+		
Langton	Paying	16	5	1								22	29
	Non-paying	13	4									17	21
	Total	29	9	1								39	50
Marwood	Paying *dm*	13	5	4	1							25	43
	Non-paying					*No data*							
Morton Tinmouth	Paying	4	1						1			6	14
	Non-paying	3										3	3
	Total	7	1						1			9	17
Piercebridge	Paying	6	8				1					15	28
	Non-paying	34	4									38	42
	Total	40	12				1					53	70
Streatlam	Paying	36	9								1 [12]	46	66
	Non-paying	21	3									24	27
	Total	57	12								1	70	93
Summerhouse	Paying	6	5	1	1							13	23
	Non-paying	6										6	6
	Total	12	5	1	1							19	29
Westwick	Paying	10	5	1	1		1					18	33
	Non-paying	5										5	5
	Total	15	5	1	1		1					23	38
Gainford		281?	80?	15?	4	1	4		2	1	3	393	604
Gateshead, Chester Middle Division													
Bank Ward	Paying	21	32	13	14	10	6	2	4	1		103	321
	Non-paying					*No data*							
High Ward	Paying	81	21	11	5	3	4	3		2	2 [10] [17]	132	281
	Non-paying					*No data*							
Pant Ward	Paying*	80	26	12	7	7	6	2	1	1	1 [12]	143	310
	Non-paying					*No data*							
Pipewell Ward	Paying	44	41	12	12	4	3	2	1		2 [10] [11]	121	291
	Non-paying					*No data*							
Gateshead		226	120	48	38	24	19	9	6	4	5	499	1203
Great Stainton, Stockton North East Division													
Great Stainton	Paying	3	4	4	1			1				13	34
	Non-paying	18	1									19	20
	Total	21	5	4	1			1				32	54

		Number of hearths:										Total Households	Total Hearths
		1	2	3	4	5	6	7	8	9	10+		
GREATHAM, Stockton North East Division													
Greatham	Paying	11	7	2		1	1				1 [13]	23	55
	Non-paying	69										69	69
	TOTAL	80	7	2		1	1				1	92	124
GRINDON, Stockton North East Division													
Whitton	Paying	2	4	2								8	16
	Non-paying	9										9	9
	TOTAL	11	4	2								17	25
HAMSTERLEY, Darlington North West Division													
Hamsterley	Paying	27	10	1	3							41	62
	Non-paying	26										26	26
	TOTAL	53	10	1	3							67	88
Lynesack & Softley	Paying	25	5	1								31	38
	Non-paying	40										40	40
	TOTAL	65	5	1								71	78
South Bedburn	Paying	22	10	2	2	1		1				38	68
	Non-paying	7										7	7
	TOTAL	29	10	2	2	1		1				45	75
HAMSTERLEY		**147**	**25**	**4**	**5**	**1**		**1**				**183**	**241**
HART, Stockton North East Division. *Some townships Easington South*													
Dalton Piercy	Paying	9	1		1	1						12	20
	Non-paying	2										2	2
	TOTAL	11	1		1	1						14	22
Hart Town	Paying	11	7	1								19	28
	Non-paying	54	2									56	58
	TOTAL	65	9	1								75	86
Nesbitt *ES*	Paying	1			1							2	5
	Non-paying	13										13	13
	TOTAL	14			1							15	18
Thorpe Bulmer *ES*	Paying	1							1			2	9
	Non-paying						*No data*						
Thorpe Thewles	Paying	25	5					1				31	42
	Non-paying	23										23	23
	TOTAL	48	5					1				54	65
Throston	Paying	13	2									15	17
	Non-paying	3										3	3
	TOTAL	16	2									18	20
HART		**155**	**17**	**1**	**2**	**1**		**1**	**1**			**178**	**220**

		Number of hearths:										Total Households	Total Hearths
		1	2	3	4	5	6	7	8	9	10+		
HARTLEPOOL, Stockton North East Division														
Hartlepool	Paying	10	12	9	3	2	1	2				39	103
	Non-paying	30	12									42	54
	TOTAL	40	24	9	3	2	1	2				81	157
HAUGHTON-LE-SKERNE, Darlington South East Division. *Some townships Stockton South West Division*														
Barmpton	Paying	9	3	1	1							14	22
	Non-paying	12										12	12
	TOTAL	21	3	1	1							26	34
Coatham Mundeville *SSW*	Paying	5	2	5	1							13	28
	Non-paying	7										7	7
	TOTAL	12	2	5	1							20	35
Great Burdon	Paying	1	1	4								6	15
	Non-paying	6	1									7	8
	TOTAL	7	2	4								13	23
Haughton	Paying	16	12	1	1	1		1	1			33	67
	Non-paying	19	1	1								21	24
	TOTAL	35	13	2	1	1		1	1			54	91
HAUGHTON-LE-SKERNE		75	20	12	3	1		1	1			113	183
HEIGHINGTON, Darlington South East Division														
Heighington & Old Park	Paying	13	18		2		1					34	63
	Non-paying	46	8									54	62
	TOTAL	59	26		2		1					88	125
Killerby	Paying	9	6	3								18	30
	Non-paying	7										7	7
	TOTAL	16	6	3								25	37
Redworth	Paying	9	6	3	3	1					1 [11]	23	58
	Non-paying	28										28	28
	TOTAL	37	6	3	3	1					1	51	86
School Aycliffe	Paying	9	4		1	1	1					16	32
	Non-paying	4	1									5	6
	TOTAL	13	5		1	1	1					21	38
Walworth	Paying	8	4	2							1 [23]	15	45
	Non-paying	7										7	7
	TOTAL	15	4	2							1	22	52
HEIGHINGTON		140	47	8	6	2	2				2	207	338

		Number of hearths:										Total Households	Total Hearths
		1	2	3	4	5	6	7	8	9	10+		
HEWORTH, Chester East Division													
Nether Heworth	Paying	29	17	2	3	1				1		53	95
	Non-paying	61										61	61
	TOTAL	90	17	2	3	1				1		114	156
Upper Heyworth	Paying	19	5	1	1		1					27	42
	Non-paying	10										10	10
	TOTAL	29	5	1	1		1					37	52
Heworth		119	22	3	4	1	1			1		151	208
HOUGHTON-LE-SPRING, Easington North Division													
East & Middle Herrington	Paying	9	10	1								20	32
	Non-paying	18	1									19	20
	TOTAL	27	11	1								39	52
East Rainton	Paying	10	5	1								16	23
	Non-paying	10										10	10
	TOTAL	20	5	1								26	33
Eppleton	Paying	3	1	1							1 [13]	6	21
	Non-paying	3										3	3
	TOTAL	6	1	1							1	9	24
Hetton-le-Hole	Paying	16	7		1						1 [10]	25	44
	Non-paying	21										21	21
	TOTAL	37	7		1						1	46	65
Houghton-le-Spring	Paying*	21	9	5							2 [15] [15]	37	84
	Non-paying	31	1									32	33
	TOTAL	52	10	5							2	69	117
Moorsley	Paying	6	4									10	14
	Non-paying					*No data*							
Newbottle	Paying	22	7	1	1							31	43
	Non-paying	37										37	37
	TOTAL	59	7	1	1							68	80
West Herrington	Paying	12	1	1		2	1	1				18	40
	Non-paying	23										23	23
	TOTAL	35	1	1		2	1	1				41	63
West Rainton	Paying	7	11	2	1	1	1	1				24	57
	Non-paying	54	2									56	58
	TOTAL	61	13	2	1	1	1	1				80	115
HOUGHTON-LE-SPRING		303	59	12	3	3	2	2			4	388	563

		Number of hearths:										Total Households	Total Hearths
		1	2	3	4	5	6	7	8	9	10+		
HUNSTANWORTH, Chester West Division													
Hunstanworth	Paying	23		1									24	26
	Non-paying						*No data*							
HURWORTH, Stockton South West Division													
Hurworth	Paying	11	2	5	3	1							22	47
	Non-paying	53	5										58	63
	TOTAL	64	7	5	3	1							80	110
Neasham	Paying	14	9	2	1								26	42
	Non-paying						*No data*							
HURWORTH		78	16	7	4	1							106	152
JARROW, Chester East Division													
Harton	Paying		3	3	1	1							8	24
	Non-paying	11											11	11
	TOTAL	11	3	3	1	1							19	35
Hedworth	Paying	3	2	3									8	16
	Non-paying	10	1										11	12
	TOTAL	13	3	3									19	28
Monkton	Paying	7	7	3	3							1 [22]	21	64
	Non-paying	3	5										8	13
	TOTAL	10	12	3	3							1	29	77
JARROW		34	18	9	4	1						1	67	140
KELLOE, Easington South Division													
Cassop	Paying		3	2	1							2 [10] [11]	8	37
	Non-paying	7											7	7
	TOTAL	7	3	2	1							2	15	44
Kelloe	Paying	15	2		1		1	1				1 [14]	21	50
	Non-paying						*No data*							
Quarrington	Paying	7	1										8	9
	Non-paying	14											14	14
	TOTAL	21	1										22	23
Wingate	Paying	25	1			1							27	32
	Non-paying	14											14	14
	TOTAL	39	1			1							41	46
KELLOE		82	7	2	2	1	1	1				3	99	163

		Number of hearths:											Total Households	Total Hearths
		1	2	3	4	5	6	7	8	9	10+		
LAMESLEY, Chester Middle Division														
Hedley	Paying	4	2	1									7	11
	Non-paying	3											3	3
	TOTAL	7	2	1									10	14
Kibblesworth	Paying	9	10	1		1				1			22	46
	Non-paying	3											3	3
	TOTAL	12	10	1		1				1			25	49
Lamesley & Fellside	Paying	8	6	4	2							1 [28]	21	68
	Non-paying	23											23	23
	TOTAL	31	6	4	2							1	44	91
Ravensworth	Paying	11	3	2									16	23
	Non-paying	8											8	8
	TOTAL	19	3	2									24	31
LAMESLEY		69	21	8	2	1				1		1	103	185
LANCHESTER, Chester West Division														
Greencroft	Paying	2	4	2	2	1							11	29
	Non-paying	9											9	9
	TOTAL	11	4	2	2	1							20	38
Iveston	Paying	12	2					1					15	22
	Non-paying	20											20	20
	TOTAL	32	2					1					35	42
Kyo	Paying	11	5			2	1						19	34
	Non-paying	8											8	8
	TOTAL	19	5			2	1						27	42
Lanchester	Paying	20	8	5	1	2							36	65
	Non-paying	16											16	16
	TOTAL	36	8	5	1	2							52	81
Langley	Paying	11	3										14	17
	Non-paying	7											7	7
	TOTAL	18	3										21	24
LANCHESTER		116	22	7	5	4	1						155	227
LONG NEWTON, Stockton South West Division														
Long Newton	Paying	17	5				1	1	1				25	45
	Non-paying	24											24	24
	TOTAL	41	5				1	1	1				49	69

		Number of hearths:										Total Households	Total Hearths
		1	2	3	4	5	6	7	8	9	10+		
Medomsley, Chester West Division													
Benfieldside	Paying	7	5	2	1							15	27
	Non-paying					*No data*								
Consett	Paying	8	4	1								13	19
	Non-paying	6										6	6
	Total	14	4	1								19	25
Medomsley	Paying	14	6	1	1	1						23	38
	Non-paying	14										14	14
	Total	28	6	1	1	1						37	52
Rowley & Roughside	Paying	8	9									17	26
	Non-paying	5										5	5
	Total	13	9									22	31
Medomsley		62	24	4	2	1						93	135
Merrington, Darlington South East Division													
Ferryhill	Paying	10	6		2	2	1					21	46
	Non-paying	16										16	16
	Total	26	6		2	2	1					37	62
Great Chilton	Paying	12	3	1				1	1			18	36
	Non-paying	18	2									20	22
	Total	30	5	1				1	1			38	58
Hett	Paying	11	4	1								16	22
	Non-paying	23	1									24	25
	Total	34	5	1								40	47
Kirk Merrington	Paying	17	10	2	1							30	47
	Non-paying	17										17	17
	Total	34	10	2	1							47	64
Merrington		124	26	4	3	2	1	1	1			162	231
Middleton St. George, Stockton South West Division													
Middleton One Row	Paying	3	4	1		1						9	19
	Non-paying	22										22	22
	Total	25	4	1		1						31	41
Middleton St. George	Paying	9	3		1						1 [10]	14	29
	Non-paying	2										2	2
	Total	11	3		1						1	16	31
Middleton St. George		36	7	1	1	1					1	47	72

		\multicolumn{10}{c}{Number of hearths:}			Total Households	Total Hearths
		1	2	3	4	5	6	7	8	9	10+		
MIDDLETON-IN-TEESDALE, Darlington South West Division													
Middleton Bounds	Paying	40	6	1	1	2						50	69
	Non-paying	12	3									15	18
	TOTAL	52	9	1	1	2						65	87
Newbiggin on Tees	Paying	24	1	1								26	29
	Non-paying	8										8	8
	TOTAL	32	1	1								34	37
MIDDLETON-IN-TEESDALE		**84**	**10**	**2**	**1**	**2**						**99**	**124**
MONK HESLEDEN, Easington South Division													
Hesleden	Paying	6	5	1				1				13	26
	Non-paying	20										20	20
	TOTAL	26	5	1				1				33	46
Hutton Henry	Paying	18	4	1								23	29
	Non-paying	18										18	18
	TOTAL	36	4	1								41	47
Sheraton	Paying	15	2									17	19
	Non-paying	13										13	13
	TOTAL	28	2									30	32
MONK HESLEDEN		**90**	**11**	**2**				**1**				**104**	**125**
MONKWEARMOUTH, Chester East Division													
Fulwell	Paying	4	2	2								8	14
	Non-paying	7										7	7
	TOTAL	11	2	2								15	21
Hylton	Paying	6	8	4							1 [10]	19	44
	Non-paying	10										10	10
	TOTAL	16	8	4							1	29	54
Monkwearmouth	Paying	5	8	8	4	1						26	66
	Non-paying	46	10									56	66
	TOTAL	51	18	8	4	1						82	132
Southwick	Paying	3	4	1				1				9	21
	Non-paying	16										16	16
	TOTAL	19	4	1				1				25	37
MONKWEARMOUTH		**97**	**32**	**15**	**4**	**1**		**1**			**1**	**151**	**244**
MUGGLESWICK, Chester West Division													
Muggleswick	Paying	22	12									34	46
	Non-paying	8										8	8
	TOTAL	30	12									42	54

		Number of hearths:										Total Households	Total Hearths
		1	2	3	4	5	6	7	8	9	10+		
NORTON, Stockton South West Division													
Hartburn	Paying	8	2	1								11	15
	Non-paying	13										13	13
	Total	21	2	1								24	28
Norton	Paying	40	16	9	1	1		1			1 [17]	69	132
	Non-paying					*No data*							
NORTON		**61**	**18**	**10**	**1**	**1**		**1**			**1**	**93**	**160**
PENSHAW, Easington North Division													
Offerton	Paying	23	2			1	1					27	38
	Non-paying	16										16	16
	Total	39	2			1	1					43	54
Penshaw	Paying	11	2	1	2		1				1 [15]	18	47
	Non-paying	20										20	20
	Total	31	2	1	2		1				1	38	67
PENSHAW		**70**	**4**	**1**	**2**	**1**	**2**				**1**	**81**	**121**
PITTINGTON, Easington South Division													
Pittington	Paying	10	3	1	1		1	1	1			18	44
	Non-paying					*No data*							
Shadforth	Paying	12	5	1	1							19	29
	Non-paying	13										13	13
	Total	25	5	1	1							32	42
PITTINGTON		**35**	**8**	**2**	**2**		**1**	**1**	**1**			**50**	**86**
REDMARSHALL, Stockton South West Division													
Carlton	Paying	12	11									23	34
	Non-paying	13										13	13
	Total	25	11									36	47
Redmarshall	Paying	5	1		1							7	11
	Non-paying	4	1									5	6
	Total	9	2		1							12	17
REDMARSHALL		**34**	**13**		**1**							**48**	**64**
RYTON, Chester West Division													
Chopwell	Paying	16	3	2							1 [11]	22	39
	Non-paying	18										18	18
	Total	34	3	2							1	40	57
Crawcrook	Paying	12	2	1	2			1				18	34
	Non-paying	45										45	45
	Total	57	2	1	2			1				63	79

		Number of hearths:											Total Households	Total Hearths
		1	2	3	4	5	6	7	8	9	10+		
Ryton	Paying	10	8	3					1			22	43
	Non-paying	27										27	27
	TOTAL	37	8	3					1			49	70
Ryton Woodside	Paying	14	11	4	1						1 [22]	31	74
	Non-paying	85	11									96	107
	TOTAL	99	22	4	1						1	127	181
Winlaton East	Paying	15	10	3			1				3 [12] [13] [14]	32	89
	Non-paying	124										124	124
	TOTAL	139	10	3			1				3	156	213
Winlaton West	Paying	10	7	1			1					19	33
	Non-paying					*No data*							
RYTON		376	52	14	3		2	1	1		5	454	633
SADBERGE, Stockton South West Division													
Sadberge	Paying	18	15				1					34	53
	Non-paying	17	1									18	19
	TOTAL	35	16				1					52	72
SATLEY, Chester West Division. *Some townships Darlington North West*													
Butsfield	Paying	9	11	3								23	40
	Non-paying					*No data*							
Cornsay	Paying	9	6	2	1							18	31
	Non-paying	9	2									11	13
	TOTAL	18	8	2	1							29	44
Hedley & Cornsay *DNW*	Paying	11	6						1			18	32
	Non-paying	2										2	2
	TOTAL	13	6						1			20	34
SATLEY		40	25	5	1				1			72	118
SEAHAM, Easington North Division													
Seaham	Paying	9	2		2							13	21
	Non-paying	17	1									18	19
	TOTAL	26	3		2							31	40
Seaton	Paying*	8	2	2								12	18
	Non-paying	6										6	6
	TOTAL	14	2	2								18	24
SEAHAM		40	5	2	2							49	64

		\multicolumn{10}{c}{Number of hearths:}	Total Households	Total Hearths
		1	2	3	4	5	6	7	8	9	10+		
Sedgefield, Stockton North East Division													
Bradbury	Paying	8	3									11	14
	Non-paying	6										6	6
	Total	14	3									17	20
Butterwick	Paying	3	1	1					1			6	16
	Non-paying	4										4	4
	Total	7	1	1					1			10	20
Fishburn	Paying	13	6	2	2							23	39
	Non-paying	17	6									23	29
	Total	30	12	2	2							46	68
Foxton & Shotton	Paying	8	1			1						10	15
	Non-paying	7										7	7
	Total	15	1			1						17	22
Mordon	Paying	6	5	1								12	19
	Non-paying	24	1									25	26
	Total	30	6	1								37	45
Sedgefield	Paying	53	17	10		1	1				1	2 [11] [14]	85	162
	Non-paying	78										78	78
	Total	131	17	10		1	1				1	2	163	240
Sedgefield		227	40	14	2	2	1		1		1	2	290	415
Sherburn House, Easington South Division													
Sherburn House	Paying	13	6	2					1			22	39
	Non-paying	13										13	13
	Total	26	6	2					1			35	52
Sockburn, Stockton South West Division													
Sockburn	Paying	3	1						1			5	13
	Non-paying	\multicolumn{10}{c}{*No data*}		
South Shields, Chester East Division													
South Shields	Paying	28	51	18	22	12	11	1	1			2 [10] [10]	146	433
	Non-paying	209	7									216	223
	Total	237	58	18	22	12	11	1	1			2	362	656
Westoe	Paying	1	4	3	5							13	38
	Non-paying	16	3									19	22
	Total	17	7	3	5							32	60
South Shields		254	65	21	27	12	11	1	1			2	394	716

		Number of hearths:										Total Households	Total Hearths
		1	2	3	4	5	6	7	8	9	10+		
STAINDROP, Darlington South West Division													
Hilton	Paying	12	1			1						14	19
	Non-paying	8										8	8
	Total	20	1			1						22	27
Ingleton	Paying	8	4	4								16	28
	Non-paying	13	2									15	17
	Total	21	6	4								31	45
Langleydale	Paying *dm*	32	8	4	*1*							45	64
	Non-paying	10										10	10
	Total	42	8	4	1							55	74
Raby With Keverstone	Paying	15	18	2	1						1 [47]	37	108
	Non-paying	3	1									4	5
	Total	18	19	2	1						1	41	113
Shotton Teesdale Forest	Paying	27	2									29	31
	Non-paying	18	1									19	20
	Total	45	3									48	51
Staindrop	Paying	26	12	9	3	4	1					55	115
	Non-paying	51	11	1								63	76
	Total	77	23	10	3	4	1					118	191
Wackerfield	Paying	10	3									13	16
	Non-paying	12	1									13	14
	Total	22	4									26	30
STAINDROP		245?	64?	20?	5	5	1				1	341	531
STANHOPE, Darlington North West Division													
Frosterley	Paying	11	2	2								15	21
	Non-paying	13										13	13
	Total	24	2	2								28	34
Stanhope Forest	Paying	79	4	1								84	90
	Non-paying	26	1									27	28
	Total	105	5	1								111	118
Stanhope Newlandside and Stanhope Baileywick[†]	Paying	60	26	3	2	2	2				1	2 [10] [14]	98	184
	Non-paying	46										46	46
	Total	106	26	3	2	2	2				1	2	144	230

[†] Note: In the document the paying are combined under this heading. The non-paying are put under the headings 'Stanhope Quarter', which must be the same as 'Stanhope Baileywick', and 'Stanhope', which by deduction must be 'Stanhope Newlandside'.

		1	2	3	4	5	6	7	8	9	10+	Total Households	Total Hearths
Stanhope Park	Paying	15	11	3	3		1					33	64
	Non-paying	5										5	5
	Total	20	11	3	3		1					38	69
STANHOPE		**255**	**44**	**9**	**5**	**2**	**3**			**1**	**2**	**321**	**451**
STILLINGTON, Stockton South West Division													
Stillington	Paying	4	1					1	1			7	21
	Non-paying	14										14	14
	Total	18	1					1	1			21	35
STOCKTON ON TEES, Stockton South West Division													
Preston on Tees	Paying	4	1									5	6
	Non-paying					*No data*							
Stockton Borough	Paying	37	7	4	3	2	1	1				55	98
	Non-paying	33										33	33
	Total	70	7	4	3	2	1	1				88	131
Stockton Town	Paying	30	7	2	2	1						42	63
	Non-paying	12										12	12
	Total	42	7	2	2	1						54	75
STOCKTON ON TEES		**116**	**15**	**6**	**5**	**3**	**1**	**1**				**147**	**212**
STRANTON, Stockton North East Division													
Brierton	Paying	7										7	7
	Non-paying					*No data*							
Seaton Carew	Paying	18	5	1				1				25	38
	Non-paying	30										30	30
	Total	48	5	1				1				55	68
Stranton	Paying	18	4			1		1			1 [10]	25	48
	Non-paying	44										44	44
	Total	62	4			1		1			1	69	92
STRANTON		**117**	**9**	**1**		**1**		**2**			**1**	**131**	**167**
SUNDERLAND, Easington North Division													
Sunderland	Paying	23	40	25	17	5	2		2	1		115	308
	Non-paying					*No data*							
TANFIELD, Chester Middle Division													
Lintz Green	Paying	12	4	2	2			1		1		22	50
	Non-paying	8										8	8
	Total	20	4	2	2			1		1		30	58

Table 6. Totals of Households and Hearths, Lady Day 1666   cxxi

		Number of hearths:										Total Households	Total Hearths
		1	2	3	4	5	6	7	8	9	10+		
TRIMDON, Easington South Division													
Trimdon	Paying	27	4	1		1						33	43
	Non-paying	25	2									27	29
	TOTAL	52	6	1		1						60	72
WASHINGTON, Chester East Division													
Barmston	Paying	9	5									14	19
	Non-paying	9										9	9
	TOTAL	18	5									23	28
Usworth (Great)	Paying	9	5	2							1 [10]	17	35
	Non-paying	14										14	14
	TOTAL	23	5	2							1	31	49
Washington	Paying	17	6	1		1					1 [10]	26	47
	Non-paying	17										17	17
	TOTAL	34	6	1		1					1	43	64
WASHINGTON		**75**	**16**	**3**		**1**					**2**	**97**	**141**
WHICKHAM, Chester West Division													
Swalwell	Paying	12	10	1	1							24	39
	Non-paying	30	3									33	36
	TOTAL	42	13	1	1							57	75
Whickham	Paying	2	8	5	7	4	2	1		1		30	109
	Non-paying	70										70	70
	TOTAL	72	8	5	7	4	2	1		1		100	179
Whickham Fellside	Paying	6	9	4	2			1			3 [10] [10] [11]	25	82
	Non-paying	72	11									83	94
	TOTAL	78	20	4	2			1			3	108	176
Whickham Lowhand	Paying	9	7	2					1	1		20	46
	Non-paying	102	3									105	108
	TOTAL	111	10	2					1	1		125	154
WHICKHAM		**303**	**51**	**12**	**10**	**4**	**2**	**2**	**1**	**2**	**3**	**390**	**584**
WHITBURN, Chester East Division													
Cleadon	Paying	4		5							1	10	28
	Non-paying	11										11	11
	TOTAL	15		5							1	21	39

		1	2	3	4	5	6	7	8	9	10+	Total Households	Total Hearths
Whitburn	Paying	2	14	4			1		1			22	56
	Non-paying	41										41	41
	TOTAL	43	14	4			1		1			63	97
WHITBURN		**58**	**14**	**9**			**1**		**1**	**1**		**84**	**136**
WHITWORTH, Darlington South East Division													
Byers Green	Paying	12	4		2		1					19	34
	Non-paying	10										10	10
	TOTAL	22	4		2		1					29	44
Tudhoe	Paying *dm*	*19*	*7*	*2*								*30*	*43*
	Non-paying	32										32	32
	TOTAL	51	7	2								62	75
Whitworth	Paying	15	1	3	1						1 [15]	21	45
	Non-paying	7	1									8	9
	TOTAL	22	2	3	1						1	29	54
WHITWORTH		**95?**	**13?**	**5?**	**3**		**1**				**1**	**120**	**173**
WHORLTON, Darlington South West Division													
Whorlton	Paying	16	7			1					1 [10]	25	45
	Non-paying	11	1									12	13
	TOTAL	27	8			1					1	37	58
WINSTON, Darlington South West Division													
Winston	Paying	23	14	5	4							46	82
	Non-paying	17	3									20	23
	TOTAL	40	17	5	4							66	105
WITTON GILBERT AND KIMBLESWORTH, Chester West Division													
Kimblesworth	Paying	2		1								3	5
	Non-paying					*No data*							
Witton Gilbert	Paying*	33	12	4	1	1		2				53	92
	Non-paying	19										19	19
	TOTAL	52	12	4	1	1		2				72	111
WITTON GILBERT AND KIMBLESWORTH		**54**	**12**	**5**	**1**	**1**		**2**				**75**	**116**
WITTON-LE-WEAR, Darlington North West Division													
North Bedburn	Paying	24	9	4	1	1						39	63
	Non-paying	8										8	8
	TOTAL	32	9	4	1	1						47	71

		Number of hearths:										Total Households	Total Hearths
		1	2	3	4	5	6	7	8	9	10+		
Witton-le-Wear	Paying	32	20	1		1					1 [16]	55	96
	Non-paying	23	2									25	27
	Total	55	22	1		1					1	80	123
Witton-le-Wear		**87**	**31**	**5**	**1**	**2**					**1**	**127**	**194**
Wolsingham, Darlington North West Division													
Thornley & Helm Park	Paying	17	1	1								19	22
	Non-paying	18	1									19	20
	Total	35	2	1								38	42
Wolsingham East	Paying	19	8	1	2	1		1				32	58
	Non-paying	25										25	25
	Total	44	8	1	2	1		1				57	83
Wolsingham South	Paying	11	6	2	2							21	37
	Non-paying	7										7	7
	Total	18	6	2	2							28	44
Wolsingham Town	Paying	26	19	2	2					1		50	87
	Non-paying	48										48	48
	Total	74	19	2	2					1		98	135
Wolsingham		**171**	**35**	**6**	**6**	**1**		**1**		**1**		**221**	**304**
Wolsingham Park Moor, Darlington North West Division													
Wolsingham Park	Paying	10	5									15	20
	Non-paying	4										4	4
	Total	14	5									19	24
Wolviston, Stockton North East Division													
Wolviston	Paying	24	8	5								37	55
	Non-paying	37										37	37
	Total	61	8	5								74	92
County Durham		**8558**	**2132**	**688**	**364**	**196**	**115**	**75**	**48**	**38**	**86**	**12313**	**20494**

Table 7. Totals of Households and Hearths in the Lady Day 1674 Assessment. Households by ward and township and number of hearths.

This table is arranged, like the original document, by townships within wards. A map of townships will be found on the back end paper, with a key in the final pages of the volume. A map showing the wards can be found on the next page. Unfortunately the collection units used in 1674 do not correlate with those used in 1666, so comparisons cannot always easily be made. For this assessment the number of non-paying householders cannot be broken down by the number of their hearths, so we can only give the total number of households, not of hearths.

Explanatory Note

The figures in square brackets in the **10+** column give the actual number of hearths per household. The 'illegible entries' column gives an estimate of the number of illegible chargeable entries.

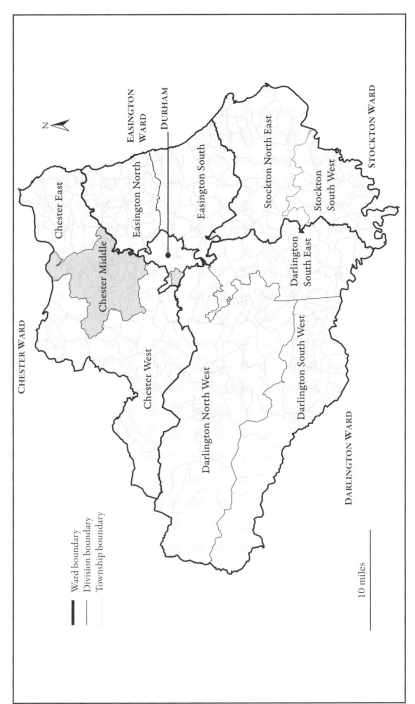

Map 15. Ward and Township boundaries.

CHESTER WARD East Division	Number of hearths (paying)									10+	Illegible entries	Total paying households	Total non-paying households	Total households
	1	2	3	4	5	6	7	8	9					
Barmston	10	1	1	0	0	0	0	0	0			12	29	41
"Bolden, East and West"	21	8	2	0	1	1	1	0	0			34	56	90
Cleadon	4	3	3	0	0	0	1	0	0			11	61	72
Fulwell and Southwick	6	7	1	0	0	1	0	0	0			15	28	43
Gateshead Bank Ward	35	21	13	11	13	11	5	3	0	1x[10]		113	151	264
Gateshead High Ward	73	27	13	8	8	4	2	3	0	1x[10]1x[17]		140		140
Gateshead Pant Ward	37	17	6	14	8	9	1	2	1	1x[10]1x[11] 1x[12]1x[15]		99	46	145
Gateshead Pipewell Ward	55	37	20	16	9	5	2	2	2	1x[11]		149	29	178
Harton	1	6	0	0	1	0	0	0	0			8		8
Hedworth	15	2	1	0	0	0	0	0	0			18	34	52
"Heworth, Nether and Upper"	15	14	6	2	3	1	1	0	0			42	34	76
Hylton	21	11	0	0	0	0	0	0	1			33	22	55
Monkwearmouth	9	13	4	4	1	0	0	0	0			31	40	71
Monkton	9	7	2	1	1	0	0	0	0	1x[20]		21		21
South Shields 1st Const	13	16	7	3	5	0	0	1	0			45		45
South Shields 2nd Const	69	13	5	7	3	2	1	0	0			100		100
South Shields East Panns 1st Const	31	12	9	5	5	7	1	0	0	1x[11]		71	143	214
South Shields West Panns 2nd Const	6	5	0	5	4	4	1	2	0			27	61	88
"Usworth, Great and Little"	12	8	0	0	0	0	1	0	0	1x[11]		22		22
Washington	14	6	0	0	1	0	0	0	0	1x[11]		22	29	51
Westoe	1	8	3	2	0	0	0	0	0			14	31	45
Whitburn	17	8	2	0	0	0	1	1	0			29		29
Total Chester East	474	250	98	78	63	45	18	14	4	12		1056	794	1850

Table 7. Lady Day 1674. Households by ward, township and number of hearths.

CHESTER WARD Middle Division	Number of hearths (paying)										Illegible entries	Total paying households	Total non-paying households	Total households
	1	2	3	4	5	6	7	8	9	10+				
Birtley and Waldridge	8	8	3	1	0	1	0	0	0			21	5	26
Chester-le-Street Town	56	11	16	7	1	4	1	0	2			98	84	182
Edmondsley	3	8	1	1	1	0	0	0	0			14	14	28
Harraton and Urpeth	15	7	3	4	1	0	0	0	0	1x[11]		31	39	70
Hedley and Tanfield	20	5	2	0	0	1	0	0	1			29	36	65
Kibblesworth	12	9	2	1	0	0	0	0	0			24	4	28
Lintz Green	11	2	3	0	1	1	0	0	0			18	20	38
Pelton	11	4	3	2	0	0	0	0	0			20	36	56
Plawsworth	14	2	0	0	0	1	1	1	0	1x[11]		19		19
Ravensworth	17	15	4	0	1	0	0	0	0			37	74	111
Total Chester Middle	**167**	**71**	**37**	**16**	**5**	**8**	**2**	**0**	**3**	**2**		**311**	**312**	**623**

CHESTER WARD West Division	Number of hearths (paying)										Illegible entries	Total paying households	Total non-paying households	Total households
	1	2	3	4	5	6	7	8	9	10+				
Burnhope and Hamsteels	14	2	3	0	0	0	0	0	0			19		19
Butsfield	17	8	2	0	0	0	0	0	0			27		27
Chopwell Constabulary	19	3	2	1	0	0	0	1	0	1x[10]		27		27
Consett	8	1	1	0	0	0	0	0	0			10		10
Crawcrook	21	1	1	0	0	0	0	0	0			23	14	37
Ebchester and Benfieldside	19	3	2	0	0	0	0	0	0			24	20	44
Edmondbyers	12	0	0	0	0	0	0	0	0			12		12
Esh	10	5	3	0	2	0	0	0	0	1x[20]		21	14	35
Greencroft	7	3	2	2	1	0	0	0	0			15		15
Hunstanworth	22	0	1	0	0	0	0	0	0			23	2	25
Iveston	13	0	0	0	0	1	0	0	0			14	19	33

CHESTER WARD West Division *continued*	Number of hearths (paying)										Illegible entries	Total paying households	Total non-paying households	Total households
	1	2	3	4	5	6	7	8	9	10+				
Kyo	12	4	3	2	0	0	0	0	0			21		21
Lanchester	15	7	4	0	1	0	0	0	0			27	43	70
Langley	15	1	1	0	0	0	0	0	0			17	12	29
Medomsley	10	6	1	2	0	0	0	0	0			19	26	45
Muggleswick	21	9	0	0	0	0	0	0	0			30		30
Roughside and Rowley	10	7	0	0	0	0	0	0	0			17		17
Ryton Town	13	9	1	0	0	0	1	0	0			24	35	59
Ryton Woodside	13	7	9	3	1	0	0	0	2			35	67	102
Swalwell	6	5	2	3	0	0	0	0	0			16	27	43
Whickham	20	15	10	5	2	1	0	1	0			54		54
Whickham Fellside	10	9	1	2	0	0	0	0	0	2x[10] 1x[15]1x[18]		26		26
Whickham Lowhand	6	9	1	0	0	0	0	0	0	1x[16]		17		17
Winlaton East Lordship	20	10	3	2	0	1	0	0	0	1x[12]		39	130	169
Winlaton West Lordship	13	2	1	0	0	1	0	0	0	1x[13]1x[14]		17		17
Witton Gilbert	26	11	3	1	1	1	1	0	0			44	24	68
Total Chester West	372	137	57	23	8	5	2	2	2	10		618	433	1051

Table 7. Lady Day 1674. Households by ward, township and number of hearths.

DARLINGTON WARD North West Division	Number of hearths (paying)										Illegible entries	Total paying households	Total non-paying households	Total households
	1	2	3	4	5	6	7	8	9	10+				
Auckland St Helen	5	4	4	0	0	1	0	0	0	1x[13]		15	27	42
Bishop Auckland Bondgate	29	16	4	5	0	2	0	0	0	1x[16] 1x[26]		58	75	133
Bishop Auckland Borough	17	20	6	13	5	4	0	0	0			65	42	107
Bishop Auckland Newgate	25	17	4	5	3	2	0	0	1			57	31	88
Bishopley	5	1	0	0	0	0	0	0	0			6	4	10
Brandon and Byshottles	20	6	1	4	0	3	1	0	0	1x[12]		36		36
Brancepeth and Park	24	15	5	5	0	0	1	0	0	1x[14]	3	54	42	96
Coundon	11	7	1	0	0	0	0	0	0			19	18	37
Crook and Billy Row	10	5	4	0	0	1	0	0	0			20	1	21
Escomb	8	3	7	1	2	0	0	0	0			21	12	33
Evenwood and Barony	34	10	1	0	0	2	0	1	0			48	58	106
Frosterley	6	3	1	1	0	0	0	0	0			11	14	25
Hamsterley	22	4	0	3	0	0	0	0	0			29	26	55
Hedley and Cornsay	21	11	2	0	1	0	0	1	0			36	14	50
Helmington Row	12	7	2	0	0	0	0	0	0			21	7	28
Hunwick	6	6	0	2	0	0	1	0	0			15	19	34
Lynesack	25	7	2	0	0	0	0	0	0			34	31	65
Newton Cap	10	3	1	0	0	1	0	0	0		1	16	5	21
Shildon	5	4	0	0	0	0	0	0	0			9	14	23

DARLINGTON WARD North West Division *continued*	Number of hearths (paying)										Illegible entries	Total paying households	Total non-paying households	Total households
	1	2	3	4	5	6	7	8	9	10+				
South Bedburn	24	12	2	3	1	0	0	0	0			42	4	46
Stanhope Forest	66	4	0	0	0	0	0	0	0			70	3	73
Stanhope Newlandside Quarter	11	11	3	1	1	0	0	0		1x[14]	1	29	3	32
Stanhope Park Quarter	20	6	3	1	1	1	0	1	0			33	10	43
Stanhope Town	39	9	4	0	2	1	1	0	0	1x[10] 1x[11]		58	40	98
Stockley	16	6	1	0	1	0	1	0	0			25	28	53
Thornley and Helm Park	8	1	1	0	0	0	0	0	0			10	13	23
West Auckland	22	12	4	3	1	0	0	1	1			44	57	101
Willington	17	6	2	0	0	0	0	0	0			25	15	40
Witton-le-Wear	29	13	5	1	2	0	1	0	0		5	56	38	94
Wolsingham	14	9	5	3	0	0	0	0	1			32	97	129
Wolsingham East Side Quarter	17	5	6	1	1	0	0	0	0		2	32	35	67
Wolsingham Park	9	4	0	0	0	0	0	0	0			13	6	19
Wolsingham South Side Quarter	17	7	3	2	4	0	0	0	0			33	7	40
Total Darlington North West	604	254	84	54	25	18	6	4	3	8	12	1072	796	1868

Table 7. Lady Day 1674. Households by ward, township and number of hearths.

DARLINGTON WARD South East Division	Number of hearths (paying)										Illegible entries	Total paying households	Total non-paying households	Total households
	1	2	3	4	5	6	7	8	9	10+				
Archdeacon Newton	7	2	0	0	0	0	0	0	0	1x[12]		10	3	13
Barmston	8	4	0	0	0	0	0	0	0			12	8	20
Blackwell	10	11	6	0	0	0	0	0	0			27	29	56
Brafferton	11	6	1	1	0	1	1	0	0			21	10	31
Byers Green	12	2	0	1	0	0	0	0	0			15	14	29
"Chilton, Great and Little"	12	3	1	0	0	1	1	0	0			18	24	42
Cockerton	24	10	5	1	0	0	0	0	0			40	20	60
"Coniscliffe, High"	12	14	1	4	0	0	1	1	0	1x[10]		34	23	57
"Coniscliffe, Low"	5	6	1	1	0	0	0	0	0			13	14	27
Darlington Borough	54	30	18	10	2	0	1	1	1	1x[10]		121	63	184
Darlington Bondgate	25	8	3	4	2	1	0	0	1			44	64	108
Darlington Prebend Row	1	1	1	1	0	1	0	0	0			5	4	9
Denton	5	3	1	1	0	0	0	1	0			11	21	32
Eldon	13	3	1	0	1	0	0	0	0			18	23	41
Ferryhill	13	4	1	2	2	1	0	0	0			23	20	43
Great Aycliffe	28	15	6	1	1	0	0	0	0			51		51
Great Burdon	2	4	3	0	0	0	0	0	0			9	3	12
Haughton-le-Skerne	18	9	3	1	1	1	2	0	0			35	29	64
Heighington	12	15	1	2	0	2	0	0	0			32	57	89
Hett	15	3	1	0	0	0	0	0	0			19	24	43
Houghton le Side	9	6	1	1	0	0	0	0	0			17	6	23

DARLINGTON WARD South East Division *continued*	Number of hearths (paying)										Illegible entries	Total paying households	Total non-paying households	Total households
	1	2	3	4	5	6	7	8	9	10+				
Killerby	4	7	2	0	0	0	0	0	0			13	10	23
Kirk Merrington	11	10	1	1	0	0	0	0	0			23	16	39
Middridge	9	8	0	0	0	0	0	0	0			17	35	52
Oxneyfield	0	0	1	1	0	0	0	0	0			2	1	3
Preston-le-Skerne	11	5	2	1	0	0	0	0	0			19	8	27
"Redworth, Newbiggin and Middridge"	15	6	4	0	1	0	0	0	0	1x[12]		27	21	48
School Aycliffe	7	3	1	0	1	1	0	0	0			13	38	51
Sunderland Bridge	2	4	0	1	0	0	0	0	0			7	16	23
Tudhoe	15	4	2	0	1	1	0	0	0			23	34	57
Walworth	7	2	3	0	0	0	0	0	0	1x[23]		13	6	19
Whitworth	10	2	1	1	0	0	0	0	0	1x[15]		15	19	34
Windlestone and Westerton	17	5	2	1	0	0	0	1	0			26	4	30
Woodham	14	5	2	1	0	0	0	0	0			22	2	24
Total Darlington South East	418	220	76	38	12	13	6	4	2	6		795	669	1464

Table 7. Lady Day 1674. Households by ward, township and number of hearths.

DARLINGTON WARD South West Division	Number of hearths (paying)										Illegible entries	Total paying households	Total non-paying households	Total households
	1	2	3	4	5	6	7	8	9	10+				
Barnard Castle	47	42	22	19	8	5	2	0	0		5	150	131	281
Bolam	20	4	1	0	0	0	0	0	0			25	10	35
Cleatlam	11	2	0	2	0	0	0	0	1			16	13	29
Cockfield	18	13	5	0	1	0	0	0	0			37	10	47
Eggleston	38	1	0	0	0	0	1	0	0			40	8	48
Gainford	9	6	2	4	1	1	0	0	0	1x[11]1x[12]		25	31	56
Headlam	2	1	0	1	1	1	0	0	0	1x[10]		7	7	14
Hilton	12	1	0	0	1	0	0	0	0			14	9	23
Ingleton	8	2	2	1	1	0	0	0	0			14	14	28
Langleydale Forest	25	13	2	0	0	0	0	0	0			40	15	55
Langton	15	5	1	0	0	0	0	0	0			21	16	37
Marwood	20	8	3	0	0	0	0	0	0			31	1	32
Middleton-in-Teesdale	42	4	2	2	1	0	0	1	0			51	15	66
Morton Tinmouth	3	2	0	0	0	0	0	0	0			6		6
Newbiggin	17	2	1	0	0	0	0	0	0			20	11	31
Piercebridge	9	8	3	1	0	0	0	1	1			22	30	52
Raby	16	13	3	0	1	0	0	0	0			33	38	71
Staindrop	28	10	10	6	3	0	0	0	0			57	65	122
Stainton	16	5	0	0	0	0	0	0	0			21	25	46
Streatlam	14	4	0	0	0	0	0	0	0			18	4	22
Summerhouse	6	4	1	0	0	1	0	0	0			12	7	19

DARLINGTON WARD
South West Division continued

	Number of hearths (paying)										Illegible entries	Total paying households	Total non-paying households	Total households
	1	2	3	4	5	6	7	8	9	10+				
Shotton Teesdale Forest	26	1	0	0	0	0	0	0	0			27	11	38
Wackerfield	8	4	0	0	0	0	0	0	0			12	11	23
Westwick	11	4	2	0	0	1	0	0	0			18		18
Whorlton	15	8	0	1	0	0	0	0	0	1x[11]		25	15	40
Winston	17	15	2	4	0	1	0	0	0			39	22	61
Total Darlington South West	453	182	62	41	18	10	3	2	1	4	5	781	519	1300

DURHAM CITY

	Number of hearths (paying)										Illegible entries	Total paying households	Total non-paying households	Total households
	1	2	3	4	5	6	7	8	9	10+				
Crossgate St Margarets	51	19	15	10	3	2	4	0	1	2x[12]		107	47	154
Elvet Barony	39	11	6	7	9	2	3	1	0	1x[10]1x[11]		80	50	130
Elvet Borough	6	8	3	6	10	2	4	1	2	2x[10]1x[12] 1x[13]1x[14]		47	15	62
Framwellgate	37	16	19	11	9	5	2	2	0	1x[10]1x[11]	4	107	43	150
High Bailey	15	8	3	7	5	6	1	2	3	2x[10]2x[11] 2x[12]1x[28]	3	60	47	107
Low Bailey	1	1	6	2	1	2	1	2	9	8x[10]7x[11] 1x[12]1x[18]		42		42
St Giles	43	24	14	5	2	1	0	1	1	1x[19]1x[27]		93	54	147
St Nicholas	75	59	48	21	21	16	4	6	3	3x[10]	10	266	48	314
Total Durham City	267	146	114	69	60	36	19	15	19	40	17	802	304	1106

Table 7. Lady Day 1674. Households by ward, township and number of hearths.

EASINGTON WARD North Division	Number of hearths (paying)										Illegible entries	Total paying households	Total non-paying households	Total households
	1	2	3	4	5	6	7	8	9	10+				
Bishopwearmouth Panns and Offerton	20	7	1	2	0	2	2	0	1			35	75	110
Burdon and Silksworth	8	5	0	1	1	0	0	1	0			16	21	37
Cold Hesledon and Dalton-le-Dale	9	6	1	2	0	0	0	0	0	1x[25]		19	19	19
East Murton	7	1	1	0	1	0	0	0	0			10	19	29
"Herrington, East and Middle"	12	2	0	1	0	0	0	0	0			15	19	34
"Herrington, West"	4	1	1	0	0	1	2	0	0			9	16	25
Hetton-le-Hole and Eppleton	20	8	1	0	0	1	0	0	2			32	13	45
Houghton-le-Spring	21	13	2	2	0	0	0	0	0	2x[15]		40	35	75
Lumley and Lambton	17	8	12	5	2	1	1	1	1	1x[12]1x[32]		50	191	241
Moorsley	4	5	0	1	0	0	0	0	0			10	61	71
Newbottle and Penshaw	14	13	4	0	0	1	1	0	0	1x[12]1x[17]		35	65	100
"Rainton, East and West"	11	10	2	1	3	1	0	1	0			29	57	86
Ryhope and Bishopwearmouth	51	18	4	3	3	1	1	0	2		3	86	129	215
Seaham	9	3	0	1	1	0	0	0	0			14	15	29
Seaton and Slingley	5	1	4	0	0	0	0	0	0			10	5	15
Sunderland by Sea	43	62	37	17	11	8	2	2	3			185	101	286
Tunstall	1	2	1	0	0	1	0	0	0			5	29	34
Total Easington North	256	165	71	36	22	17	9	5	9	7	3	600	851	1451

EASINGTON WARD South Division	Number of hearths (paying)										Illegible entries	Total paying households	Total non-paying households	Total households
	1	2	3	4	5	6	7	8	9	10+				
Butterby and Quarrington	12	0	1	0	0	0	0	2	0	1x[16]		16		16
Cassop	0	2	3	2	0	0	0	0	0	1x[10]1x[11]		9	19	28
Castle Eden and Shotton	23	5	3	2	0	0	0	0	0		1	34	26	60
Easington	27	7	2	1	1	0	1	0	0	1x[13]	1	41	40	81
Haswell and Shadforth	21	9	2	0	0	0	1	0	0			33	64	97
Hawthorn and Haswell													17	17
Hutton Henry	12	3	0	0	1	0	0	0	0			16	18	34
Kelloe	12	3	0	1	0	1	0	1	0	1x[13]		19	30	49
Sheraton and Monk Hesleden	23	7	3	0	0	1	0	0	0			33	22	55
Sherburne and Pittington	21	11	3	0	1	1	1	1	0	1x[14]		40	18	58
Shincliffe	4	6	3	2	0	0	0	0	0	1x[11]1x[12]		17	24	41
Trimdon	17	3	2	0	1	0	0	0	0			23	13	36
Wingate and Wheatley Hill	18	4	1	0	1	0	0	0	0			24		24
Total Easington South	190	60	23	8	5	2	3	4	0	8	2	305	291	596

Table 7. Lady Day 1674. Households by ward, township and number of hearths.

STOCKTON WARD North East Division	Number of hearths (paying)										Illegible entries	Total paying households	Total non-paying households	Total households
	1	2	3	4	5	6	7	8	9	10+				
Billingham	19	9	2	0	0	0	0	0	0			30	54	84
Bishop Middleham	13	5	3	0	0	0	0	0	0			21	28	49
Bradbury and Great Stainton	9	4	6	1	0	1	0	0	0			21		21
Brierton and Burntoft	19	3	2	0	0	1	1	0	0			26		26
Butterwick and Embleton	13	5	3	0	0	0	1	0	0			22		22
Cowpen Bewley and Newton Bewley	9	8	1	1	0	0	0	0	0		2	21	15	36
Dalton Piercy	6	3	1	0	0	0	0	0	0			10	18	28
Elwick	20	4	2	0	0	0	0	0	0			26	17	43
Fishburn	9	5	2	2	0	0	0	0	0			18		18
Foxton and Mordon	14	4	2	0	2	0	0	0	0			22		22
Greatham	32	4	3	0	1	0	0	0	0	1x[13]		41	68	109
Hartlepool	13	9	7	4	2	3	0	0	0			38	51	89
Mainsforth and Cornforth	16	5	3	0	0	1	0	1	0			26	16	42
Seaton Carew	15	4	0	0	0	0	0	0	1			20	28	48
Sedgefield	56	18	9	4	2	1	0	0	1	1x[12]1x[14]		93	66	159
Stranton	21	4	1	0	0	1	1	0	0			29	30	59
Throston and Hart Town	30	9	0	4	0	0	0	0	0	1x[13]		43	47	90
Whitton and Thorpe Thewles	20	10	2	1	0	0	1	0	0	1x[12]		35	28	63
Wolviston	17	10	8	0	0	0	0	0	0			35	30	65
Total Stockton North East	351	123	57	17	7	8	4	1	2	5	2	577	496	1073

STOCKTON WARD South West Division	Number of hearths (paying)										Illegible entries	Total paying households	Total non-paying households	Total households
	1	2	3	4	5	6	7	8	9	10+				
Aislaby	10	0	0	1	1	1	1	1	0			15		15
Bishopton	24	14	5	0	0	0	1	0	0			44	5	49
Coatham Mundeville	5	3	2	3	0	0	0	0	0			13	23	36
Dinsdale and Sockburn	14	0	2	0	0	0	1	0	1			18	21	39
East Hartburn and Elton	9	8	1	0	0	0	0	0	0			18	21	39
Hurworth	6	7	2	2	1	0	0	0	0			18	49	67
Long Newton	23	3	0	1	1	1	1	0	0			30	30	60
Middleton One Row	15	5	1	0	1	0	0	0	0	1x[10]		23	36	59
Neasham	16	7	4	0	1	0	0	0	0			28		28
Norton	36	11	11	1	1	0	1	0	0	1x[17]		62	72	134
Preston on Tees	25	7	3	2	0	0	0	1	1			39	33	72
Redmarshall and Little Stainton	11	5	1	1	0	0	0	0	0			18	4	22
Sadberge and Newbiggin	19	12	1	0	1	0	0	0	0			33	20	53
Stillington and Carlton	14	9	2	2	0	0	1	1	0			28	24	52
Stockton Borough	33	7	3	3	2	2	0	0	0			50	32	82
Stockton Town	46	5	2	1	1	2	0	0	0			57	35	92
Total Stockton South West	**306**	**103**	**40**	**17**	**10**	**6**	**6**	**2**	**2**	**2**		**494**	**405**	**899**

Table 7. Lady Day 1674. Households by ward, township and number of hearths.

DURHAM COUNTY WARDS	Number of hearths (paying)										Illegible entries	Total paying households	Total non-paying households	Total households
	1	2	3	4	5	6	7	8	9	10+				
Chester Ward East Division	474	250	98	78	63	45	18	14	4	12	0	1056	794	1850
Chester Ward Middle Division	167	71	37	16	5	8	2	0	3	2	0	311	312	623
Chester Ward West Division	372	137	57	23	8	5	2	2	2	10	0	618	433	1051
Darlington Ward North West Division	604	254	84	54	25	18	6	4	3	8	12	1072	796	1868
Darlington Ward South East Division	418	220	76	38	12	13	6	4	2	6	0	795	669	1464
Darlington Ward South West Division	453	182	62	41	18	10	3	2	1	4	5	781	519	1300
Durham City	267	146	114	69	60	36	19	15	19	40	17	802	304	1106
Easington Ward North Division	256	165	71	36	22	17	9	5	9	7	3	600	851	1451
Easington Ward South Division	190	60	23	8	5	2	3	4	0	8	2	305	291	596
Stockton Ward North East Division	351	123	57	17	7	8	4	1	2	5	2	577	496	1073
Stockton Ward South West Division	306	103	40	17	10	6	6	2	2	2	0	494	405	899
Total Durham County	3858	1711	719	397	235	168	78	53	47	104	41	7411	5870	13281

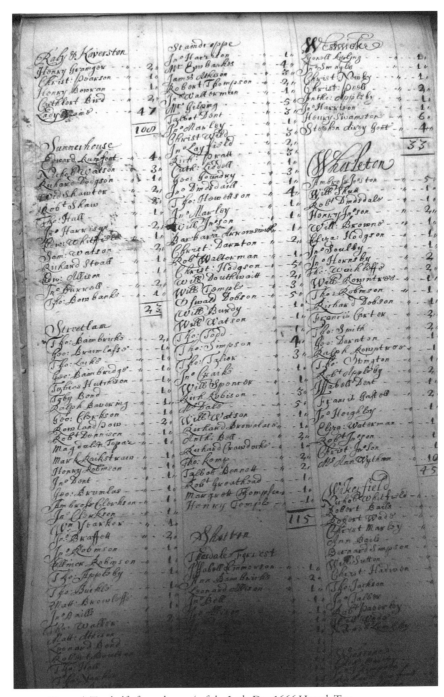

Figure 4. Top half of membrane 4 of the Lady Day 1666 Hearth Tax Assessment, TNA E179/106/28. Part of those assessed to pay in Darlington Ward, south west division, transcribed on pp.18–20. Amongst the ordinary entries for Raby and Keverstone, in a completely unassuming way, is Lady Vane's house, Raby Castle, the largest in the county, with 47 hearths.

Editorial Method

The transcript published here follows the order of the original, that is to say, alphabetically by township within the divisions of the wards. For convenience of reference a map of the wards and their divisions will be found on p. cxxv, before Table 7, derived from the Lady Day 1674 assessment which was also arranged by wards. In the original the text was written in three columns. Here it is printed in two columns. The text should be read down the left hand column and then across to the right hand column and down. The original membrane and column numbers are given in italics at the appropriate place in the text. Italics are also used for those entries and hearth numbers noted as errors in the text. There are a few places where a seventeenth-century clerk has added a corrected total with the letters es – possibly an abbreviated form of the Latin *estimatio* meaning estimate (see p. 40). In these instances the original incorrect total is written in italics (see p. 54)

Square brackets enclose editorial comments written in italics such as [*about seven entries missing*]. Square brackets are also used to denote a modern corrected hearth total where the original arithmetic appears to be incorrect (see p. 5).

Names and numbers illegible due to membrane damage are represented by ... Unreadable names and numbers are represented by [?] and uncertain names and numbers are followed by [?] . The original punctuation has not been retained because of the difficulties of interpretation and the problems of distinguishing between a mark and ink showing through.

Place names
The place names are written in bold. Where the modern version is different from the original it has been added in square brackets.

Personal names
It has not been posssible to replicate the seventeenth-century script, superscript or some of the abbreviations. The contemporary standard abbreviation of a line above a letter to indicate an omission has been extended as in Summers. The names are written as found whether they are in an abbreviated form or variant spellings. For certain letters it is not always easy to distinguish between a 'u' and 'v' and in these instances, the modern version such as in David has been used.

Status
Abbreviations giving title or status are also written as found. Many of them have several variations such as widdow which appears as widd, wid and the Latin form of *vid*.

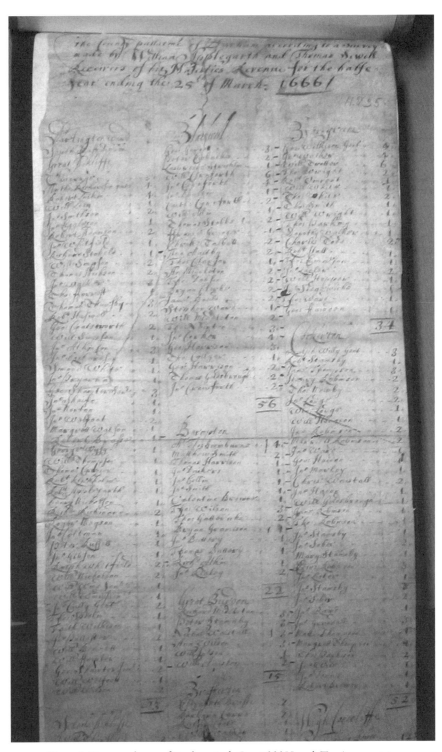

Figure 5. First membrane of Durham Lady Day 1666 Hearth Tax Assessment, National Archives E179/106/28

m. 1

The Number of Firehearths and Stoves within the County pallatine of Durham according to a Survey made by William Applegarth and Thomas Sewell Receivers of his Majesties Revenue for the halfe year ending the 25th of March 1666

c. 1

Darlington Ward
South East Division

Great Aikliffe		Thomas Crozier	1
[Great Aycliffe]		Robt Kirkholm	1
Viccorage	5	Robt Applegarth	1
Antho Richardson gent	4	Henry Nicholson	1
Robert Laikin	4	Richd Richmond	2
Will Long	1	Roger Megson	1
Jno Smithson	2	Jno Coltman	1
Jno Eggleson	1	Peter Russell	1
Robert Adamson	2	Jno Gibson	1
Jno Whitfield	1	Ralph Whitfield	2
Richard Stokeld	1	Will Nicholson	2
Will Simpson	2	Will Wind senr	1
Thomas Hickson	2	Will Wind junr	1
Jno Walker	3	Jno Cully Gent	2
Tho Forrest	1	Tho Spedlin	1
Thomas Thursby	3	Faith Wilkison	1
Robt Haswell	2	Jno Pallaster	2
Geo Coatsworth	2	Will Bennett	1
Will Simpson	1	Will Fowler	1
Jno Atkinson	3	Geo Shawter junr	2
Jno Richardson	1	Will Welfoott	1
Simond White	1	Will Wilson	2
Jno Pryarman	1		83
Geo Shawter senr	3		
Jno Skaife	1	**Schoole Aikliffe**	
Jno Norton	1	**[School Aycliffe]**	
Jno Welfoot	2	Will Thursby	2
Margrett Watson	1	Francis Wildbore Gent	6
Robt Brasse	1	Edward Rumfoott	1
Geo Wysy	1	William Walton	1
Will Thompson	1	Will Fell	1

Robert Stobbs	1
John Thursby	1
Geo Wright	4
Rich Ranson	1
Nichol Lazenby	5
Robert Peacocke	2
George Archelme	2
John Atkinson	2
Cuthbert Dawson	1
Thomas Browne	1
George Peacocke	1
	32

m. 1, c. 2

Blackwell

Geo Garrett	3
Peter Ewbankes	2
Lawrence Stricklin	1
Will Cornforth	6
Jno Cornforth	4
Jno Boultin	1
Cuth Cornforth	2
Will Allin	1
Thomas Stobbs	2
Francis Granger	1
Christ Talbott	2
Ann Maltby	2
Tho Claxson	1
An Middleton	2
Tho Dobson	2
Bryan Clerke	2
James Bould	2
Stephen Ward	1
Will Middleton	2
Tho Newton	3
Jno Corker	4
Geo Harrison	3
Thomas Collyer	1
George Harrison	2
Thomas Goldsbrough	2
Jno Crawforth	2
	56

Barmpton

Mr Tho Swinburne	4
Matthew Smith	2
Thomas Harrison	1
Jno Daikers	1
Jno Collin	1
Jno Smith	1
Valentine Browne	1
Tho Wilson	3
Tho Gattericke	2
Bryan Gramison	1
Jno Buttery	1
Thomas Buttery	1
Richd Atkin	1
Jno Ridley	2
	22

Great Burdon

Richard Middleton	3
Peter Stainsby	3
Nichol Waistall	3
Ann Wilson	3
Will Jnoson	1
Will Anisley	2
	15

Brafferton

Elizabeth Brasse	7
Barbara Carre	7
Richard Coale	1
Will Walker	1
Geo Heighington	2
Tho Wilson	2
Tho Norton	1
Henry Norton	1
Jno Atkin	1
Richard Thursby	4
Edw Earle	2
Henry Russell	3
Robert Gibson	1
Tho Read	2
Will Addy	1
Ralph Sowrby	1
Tho Wilson junr	3
Jno Lawson	1
	41

m. 1, c. 3

Byarsgreene
[Byers Green]

Geo Wilkison Gent	4
Jno Walker	4
Will Trotter	6
Tho Wright	2
Robt Vincent	1
Will White	1
Tho White	2
Tho Smith	1
Will Wright	1
Tho Parking	1
Dorothy Walker	1
Charles Todd	2
Robt Hall	1
Tho Emmrson	1
Jno Ladler	2
Will Hopper	1
Jno Sidgewicke	1
Tho Ward	1
Geo Fawden	1
	34

Cockerton

Ralph Willy Gent	3
Robt Stainsby	1
Jane Thompson	3
Henry Robinson	2
Tho Newby	2
Jno Lodge	2
Wid Lodge	1
Will Hodgson	1
Jno Robinson	2
Mirriell Robinson	2
Jno Ward	1
Geo Haidon	1
Jno Morley	1
Chris Waistall	2
Jno Hadon	1
Will Goldsbrough	1
Jane Robinson	1
Tho Robinson	1
Jno Stainsby	1
Jno Sober	2
Mary Stainsby	1

Edw Robinson	3
Jno Lister	1
Jno Stainsby	3
Jno Sober	2
Jno Raine	1
Jno Grundall	3
Matt Thompson	1
Margrett Thompson	1
Tho Parkison	2
Jno Wild	1
Jno Dennis	1
Robert Brewer	1
	52

High Conscliffe
[High Coniscliffe]

Sr Francis Bowes	12
Nichol Salkeld Gent	7
Tho Robinson	1
Tho Tifman	1
Jno Scott	1
Cuth Potter	2
Jno Greathead	1
Henry Robinson	2
Widd Dockley	2
Christ Vazy	5
Peter Wilson	2
Oswald Swainston	3
Andrew Cuthbertson	1
Joseph Salkeld Gent	3
Will Gibson	2
Jno Atkinson	2

m. 1v, c. 1

Matt Hudson	2
Jno Bell	1
Richard Bell	1
Wid Greathead	1
Ann Jackson	1
Will Vazie	1
Rowland Haddocke	3
Tho Allison	1
Matt Dent	7
Jno Robinson	2
Ralph Robinson	4
Geo Cleaton	3

Phillip Dickinson	1
Tho Dowing	2
Tho Stott	1
	78

Low Conscliffe
[Low Coniscliffe]

Jno Richardson	4
Jno Cooke	2
Jno Counden	2
Peter Robinson	1
Geo Robinson	1
Jno Simpson	3
Jno Robson	2
Francis Oswald	1
Richard Oswald	2
Tho Robinson	2
Anthony Short	1
Will Barnes Gent	3
	24

Great Chilton

Robt Hutchinson	1
Lodowick Hall Esqr	8
Robert Rickerby	2
Robt Wall	2
Jno Jefferson	1
Christ Pearson	2
Geo Chandler	1
Jno Hickson	1
Richard Hickson	1
Richard Greirson	3
Robt Buckle	1
Humphrey Moorley	1
Jno Stephenson	1
Lowrence Bracke	7
Robt Hutchinson	1
Geo Ellingson	1
Jno Buckle	1
Mich Munday	1
	36

Darlington Brough
[Darlington Borough]

Cuth Hodgson	2
Geo Hodgson	2

Robt Jeckell	1
Jno Rippon	2
Robt Shaw	3
Jno Richardson	2
Margrett Harrison	3
Jno Lainge senr	3
Jno Welbanke	2
Margery Stainsby	1
Robt Kidd	2
Robt Shearburne	2
Jno Laing junr	1
Rodger Fewler	3
Matt Talior	3
Richard Jnoson	2
Henry Booth Gent	1
Will Baitts	2
Edward Hall	2
Christ Raine	4
Robert Fossicke	2
Anthony Eastgate	6
Will Sidgwicke	3
Robert Fossicke	3
Mary Hills	3
Thomas Bell	2
Katharin Colling	1
Robert Newton	1
Eliza Kidd	1
Siscilly Lodg	4
Edward Fisher	3
Anthony Appleby	1
Christ Nicholson	3
Simon Becke	1

m. 1v, c. 2

Wid Catteran	3
Tho Brantingham	1
Jno Marshall	4
Ralph Coates	2
Edward Dunnell Gent	3
Jno Coulson	2
Thom Finley	5
Henry Shaw	4
Jno Jnoson	2
Jno Gregory	3
Christ Ward	3
Tho Hall Gent	3

Robert Bolton	3	Tho Willson	2
Robt Coarson	4	Henry Kendall	3
Jane Oswald	4	Rich Forrest	2
Cuth Bower	3	Mr Farwood	3
Ms Glover	2	Ralph Hall	1
Stephen Robison	6	Jno Wood	2
Robt Nicholson	4	Mich Colling	2
Barbara Allenson	2	Tho Branson	1
Henry Richardson	4	Eliza Tewart	1
Margrett Surties	4	Jayne Pearson	1
Richard Skaife	3	Rich Belwood	2
Mr Thomas Inglethorne	3	Geo Bailey	2
Christ Ward	4	Will Chatter	1
Christ Newton	4	Bartho Story	1
Francis Readman	4	Tho Tweedy	1
Robert Summerwhaitt	3	Widd Pristott	1
Phill Tinkler	4	Jno Davieson	2
Richard Lumbley	1	Francis Jackson	2
Bartho Hannah	1	Jno Hall	3
Henry Shawes	2	Robt Cockerill	3
Michaell Shaw	1	Will Priscott	2
Jno Harrison	3	Rich Sober	2
Robert Wilson	4	Rich Parkinson	2
Robt Tinkler	2	Mr Place	7
Thomas Thompson	3	Mr Middleton	10
Widd Wilson	2	Edward Browne	2
Will Belwood	1	Wid Heighley	1
Alice Woodhall	3	Ralph Hilton	2
Jno Scott	3	Robert Thompson	4
Luke Calbert	1		
Jane Girlington	1	*m. 1v, c. 3*	
Will Robinson	1	James Kirkby	2
Eliza Stephenson	1	Widd Coopper	2
Mich Middleton	1	Francis Newton	2
Tho Justus	1		295
Tho Wright	1		[296]
Jno Harvey	2		
Henry Jnoson	3	**Darlington Prebend Row**	
Tho Talior	2	Phillip Reine	1
James Crawforth	1	Leonard Pilkington	3
Martin Green	1	Robt Cuthbert	3
Jno Pearson	2	Will Samses	2
Tho Garth Gent	2	Rowland Wilson	4
Nichol Short	1	Dorothy Jefferson	2
Will Leacklman	1	Jane Parkison	1
Eliz Miller	1		16

Darlington Bondgate

Mrs Gerrard	9
Mr Tho Bell	4
Mr Colthirst	5
Ralph Colling	6
Richard Charlesworth	1
Mr Fearnley	1
Will Newton	2
Will Butterwicke	1
Will Eastate	1
Tho Wilkison	1
Robert Sober	4
Geo Wasall	2
Thomas Emmerson	6
Antho Elgy	3
Christ Hodgson	2
Mary Vickson	1
Christ Lumbley	1
Lawrence Emmrson	2
Robt Smurfoot	2[?]
Jno Balmbrough	1[?]
Jno Dunn	1
Mich Wilson	1
Edward Sober	1
Jno Bradforth	2
Robt Ward	3
Francis Boyes	1
Jno Wright	1
Henry Wright	2
Mr Tocketts	4
Ralph Becke	2
Robt King	3
Robt Whorton	1
Will Ladley	1
Tho Robinson	1
Robt Nicholson	1
Jno Dent	1
Will Harperley	1
An Pain	1
Tho Bell	1
Jno Coulson	1
Jno Watson	2
Ann Earthy	1
James Leadman	1
Tho Busby	1
Henry Shaw	1

Will Tindale	1
Mich Browne	1
Will Wastall	1
Francis Thorp	1
	95

Denton

Antho Byerley Gent	8
Will Hutton Gent	3
Jno Simpson	5
Richard Stobson	2
Jno Todd	1
Will Coall	4
Matthew Coats	1
Tho Simpson	2
Jno Steamson	1
Jno Hutchinson	3
Richard Morton	1
Jno Howden	2
	33

m. 2, c. 1

…[Eldon]

[*about seven entries missing*]

Thomas S…	…
Richard Big…man	…
Richard Corner	2
Robert Appleby	1
Rich Hopper	2
Will Harrison	2
Tho Foster	1
Henry Smith	1
Will Harrison	2
Joseph Hopper	2
Richard Harrison	1
Tho Watson	1
George Slater	1
Antho Harrison	1
	29

Ferryhill

Robert Hearon	1
Jno Shaw Gent	6
Jno Dunn	2
Bryan Heavyside	1
Robt Dun senr	1

Robt Dun junr	1
Henry Lax	2
Eliza Rose	1
Ann Pearson	1
Robt Richardson	5
Jno Ferry	1
Jno Pearson	1
Jno Lax	5
Thom Foster	1
Ralph Tattum	4
Jno Bracke	1
Jane Kirkhouse	2
Jno Brasse	2
Ralph Darnton	2
Robt Hickson	4
John Vacy	2
	46

Houghton in ye Side
[Houghton le Side]

Jno Hobson	4
Richard Darnton	2
Will Darnton	4
Geo Lodge	1
Margret Lodge	1
Jno Lawson	2
Jno Whitfield	1
Christ Burden	1
Richard Simpson	1
Jno Deanham	2
Geo Rumford	1
Marmaduke Robison	2
Will Deanham	2
Robt Burden	1
Geo Simpson	1
	26

Haughton
[Haughton-le-Skerne]

Jno March	8
Tobias Midcalfe	3
Tho Harrison	2
Thomas Dickin	1
Jno Hanson	1
Jno Cully	7
Robt Shepherd	5

Francis Parker	1
Will Wreay	1
James Wastall	2
Jno Hunter	1
Geo Glover	1
Will Waistall	1
Christ Smurfoot	1
Jno Hull	2
Jno Dicking	2
Robert Robinson	1

m. 2, c. 2

…st Harrison	1
… Newton	2
Robt Wilson	2
Will Kitching	2
Wid Dicking	1
Christ Justus	2
James Burton	1
Richard Simpson	2
Robt Simpson	4
Thomas Simpson	2
Daniell Gill	2
Tho Youll	1
Richard Wall	1
Ralph Hickson	1
Jno Blaixton	2
Robert Cuthbert	1
	67

Heighington and Old Parke
[Heighington and Old Park]

Jno Wood	6
Henry Atkinson	2
Antho Atkinson	1
Lamericke Toward	2
Gilbt Robinson	2
Jno Raine	2
Will Dobson	2
Jno North	1
Jno Wilkison	2
Will Wilkison	1
Will Cooke	2
Francis Tyewhatt	2
Jno Richmond	4
Christ Richmond	4

Will Morley	1
Edw Fewler	2
Percivall Taitt	2
Jno Mason	2
Will Stephenson	1
Geo Morley	1
Edw Fuiller	2
Francis Peachy	1
Robt Wilkisonn	2
Thomas Dobson	2
Henry Lawson	2
Jno Oliver	1
Will Rumfoott	1
Christ Rumfoott	1
Will Richmond	2
Thom Richmond	1
Cuth Allison	2
Robert Russell	2
Stephen Bellasis	1
Francis Fawell	1
	63

Hett

Thomas Wood	3
Jno Watson	2
Will Cheswicke	1
Ralph Jackson	1
Jno Meaburne	2
Ralph Adamson	2
Nichol Wood	1
Jno Rea	1
Robt Midfield	1
Will Gelson	1
Jno Hobson	2
Jno Steall	1
Ralph Suddicke	1
Geo Wyly	1
Jno Lax	1
Jno Meaburne	1
	22

Killerby

Lawr Hillton	3
Lawr Chatter	1
Ann Hutchison	1
Robert Woodhouse	2

Jno Marley	2
Cuth Crawford	2
Ellinor Hall	1

m. 2, c. 3

Robert Smith	2
Peter Murton	1
Rich Easterby	3
Cuth Nicholson	3
Thom Thompson	2
James Richardson	1
Jno Wardall	1
Jno Clerke	1
Nichol Leizure	1
Robt Newton	1
Tho Trotter	2
	30

Middlestone

Christ Downes Gent	5
Mr Carre	5
Jno Stelling	3
Rich Liddell	1
Tho Thompson	1
Will Hickson	2
Jno Elstobb	1
Jno Richardson	1
Widd Harrison	1
	20

Kirkmerrington
[Kirk Merrington]

Robt Hickson	4
Jno Wood	2
Jno Dodgson	2
Ralph Richardson	1
Ann Richardson	1
James Dunne	2
James Thompson	3
Martin White	2
Thom Wyly	1
Ralph Wyly	2
Mary Wood	3
Will Airey	1
Jno Maxwell	1
Rich Binley	1

Jno Hickson	2
Geo Smurthwaitt	1
Tho Hickson	2
Geo Lindsey	1
Will Wood	2
Francis Meaburne	2
Robt Wood	1
Geo Widdgfield	2
Jno Lindsey	1
Robert Hickson	1
Tho Fleatham	1
Hugh Dods	1
Mary Masterman	1
Antho Richardson	1
Jno Richardson	1
Christ Smith	1
	47

Midridge
[Middridge]

Jno Bainbridge	2
Jno Hunter	2
Richard Dobbin	2
Rich Lowson	1
Robt Clayton	1
Jno Craigs	2
James Tower	1
Rich Palleser	1
Richard Craiges	1
Humphrey Hunter	1
Jno Watson	1
Jno Stabler	1
Jno Jackson senr	2
Richard Croft	1
Jno Jackson junr	2
Geo Jackson	2
Edw Harden	1
Cuth Goundry	1
Jno Sunkbanke	1
	26

Archdeacon Newton

Sr Will Blaixton	12
Antho Harrison	1
Sam Kipling	1
Tho Robinson	2
Jno Billton	1

m. 2v, c. 1

Tho Chapman	1
Tho Harrison	1
Jno Coopland	1
Geo Chapman	1
Jno Hollcatt	1
Geo Memphas	1
Jno Parkin	2
Geo Chapman	2
	27

Oxnetfield
[Oxneyfield]

Old House	4

Preston upon Skerne
[Preston-le-Skerne]

Richard Byars	2
Geo Thompson	1
Margrett Emmrson	1
Christ Hickson	1
Rob Pearson	2
Richd Parkin	1
Ms Wyklife	3
Richard Collin	1
Richard Stephenson	5
Rich Adamson	1
Matt Longstaffe	2
James Clement	1
Jno Bownas senr	1
Robt Pallister	1
Nichol Steadman	1
Richard Kirkhouse	1
Jane Middleton	1
Margrett Young	1
Geo Moody	1
Richard Gyles	1
Jno Bownas	1
Robt Newton	1
	31

Redworth

Antho Byarley Esqr	11
Geo Trotter	3
Christ Raine	4
Christ Todd	3

Jno Watson	1
James Trotter	2
Will Garth	4
Issabell Greathead	1
Ralph Baimbridge	5
Geo Swinburne	1
Robt Todd	2
Tho White	2
Tho Dobson	2
Will Greathead	1
James Richmond	3
Jno Swinbanke	1
Marmad Blackett	2
Ralph Swinbanke	2
Tho Crozier	4
Robt Lax	1
Tho Hall	1
Ellinor Seamer	1
Eliza Trotter	1
	58

Tuddoe
[**Tudhoe**]

Will Readhead	1
Jno Braike	1
Francis Heighington	1
Henry Trewhitt	3
Henry Sidgewicke	2
Richard Wilson	…
Ellinor …	
[about four entries missing]	
Will Bell	1
Roger Turping	1
Jno Richardson	2
Sarah Briggs	1
John Atchinson	2
Will Byerley	3

m. 2v, c. 2

Will Byerley	2
Ellinor Jackson	2
Jno Sparke	1
Jno Sparke	1
Tho Pickering	1
Nichol Fishburn	1
Geo Isle	1

Tho Walker	1
Henry Jackson	1
Jno Wheatley	1
Geo Richardson	1
Ralph Dunn	2
Ralph Salvin Gent	2
	43

Walworth

Jno Jennison Esqr	23
Jame Crawford	2
Jno Harrison	3
Wid Simpson	1
Geo Emmrson	1
Jno Emmerson	1
Jno Bilton	1
Geo Bilton	1
Henry Lister	2
Geo Mawer	3
Jno Bowfoott	1
Jno Richardson	1
Margrett Grinshaw	2
Ann Harrison	1
Tho Smith	2
	45

Woodholme
[**Woodham**]

Will Suddicke	1
Geo Hickson	3
Henry Nateby	1
Thomas Heightley	2
Robt Greireson	3
Eliza Haswell	1
Jno Jobling	1
James Croft	1
Jno Blackett	1
Geo Clement	2
Will Clement	2
Will Parkin	1
Geo Jackson	1
Will Jackson	1
Jno Stoddart	1
Mr Hutton	4
Hugh Robinson	1

Ralph Emmrson	1
	28

Willington

Ralph Douthwaitt	1
Henry Foster	1
Widd Dinall	2
Widd Brackes	1
Humphrey Wall	2
Jane Hall	1
Nichol Bracke	1
Antho Cuming	1
Robert Thornton	1
Luke Dunn	1
Thomas Trotter	1
Charles Pickering	1
Robert Smith	1
Martin Nicolson	1
Jno Robinson	2
Richard Smith	1
Charles Pickering	3
... Clayton	1
... Atchinson	1
William Pickering	1
	25

Whittworth
[Whitworth]

Robt Shaftoe Gent	15
Tho Grinwell	3
Ralph Wright	1
Jno Middleton	1

m. 2v, c. 3

Tho Knaggs	3
Jno Adamson	1
Will Hardy	1
Geo Emmerson	2
Geo Pickering	1
Antho Dowens	1
Jno Carter	1
Will Mallam	1
Cuth Nicolson	1
Ellinor Wilson	1
Mr Dickinson	4
Will Adamson	3

Will Farrow	1
Geo White	1
Ralph Douthwaitt	1
Charles Liddell	1
Henry Wilson	1
	45

Westerton

Robert Sharp	3
Geo Lax	3
Jno Lax	3
Ralph Weddall	3
Widd Lax	2
Will Parkin	1
Henry Lax	3
	18

Darlington Ward
South West Division

Bealam
[Bolam]

Oliver Trotter	1
Jane Wetherall	1
Martin Weddell	1
Will Southerin	2
Richard Crawforth	1
Francis Hoggart	1
Jno Garth	2
Jane Talior	1
Will Garth	5
Edw Wrangham	1
Jno Martin	1
Rowland Bell	1
Jno Jobling	1
Jno Goundry junr	2
Will Hammers	1
Ralph Lawson	1
Jno Goundry senr	1
Jno Sigsworth	1
Eliza Goundry	1
Ann Wrangham	1
Francis Garth	1
Richard Musgrave	1
Francis Hoggart	1

Rodger Talior	2	… Lightly	3
Geo Lindsey	1	…chely[?]	1
Cuth Wrangham	2	…	2
Francis Gartherin	1	…	5
	35	…	1
[*corrected total*]　　es[?]	36	…	…
		…	…
		[*about ten entries missing*]	
Bernardcastle		…elling house	3
[Barnard Castle]		Jane Cooper	2
Sam Mckendale	5	Henry Sinkson	2
Tho Shellen	5	Margt Stobbs	3
Tho Heslop	5	Tho Fothergaill	2
Will Pinkney	4	Phillis Sourby	3
Matthew Sowrby	5	Mary Hutton	3
Jno Briggs	2	Mr Pudsey	1
Nichol Baxter	4	Cuth Baills	2
Phillis Sanderson	4	Tho Wastall	2
Bartho Lonesdale	4	Tho Lodman	1
Tho Simpson senr	1	Christ Robinson	1
Ambrose Toward senr	1	Ralph Coulton	1
Jno Edwards	2	Mr Crawdocke	3
Robt Boulton	2	Tho Blaclocke	2
Arthur Emmerson	6	Phillis Baill	1
Robt Dent	1	Robert Pell	1
Jno Bails	2	Stephen Hardy	1
Geo Peacocke	4	Ms Totall	3
Tho Peacocke	1	Ms Buckerton	3
Bartho Harwood	1	Tho Bull	3
Robt Dent	3	Tho Baills	3
Jno Wilson	1	Geo Smith	3
Cuth Raine	2	Tho Horne	2
Christ Hornsby	1	Tho Vint	1
Samuell Hinde	1	Tho Newby	1
Tho Blakeburne	2	Henry Raine	2
		Robt Tod junr	2
m. 3, c.1		Robt Todd senr	2
Will Sanderson	2	Tho Chator	1
Robert Glover	1	Will Peacocke	1
Jno Percivall	5	Matt Binkes	6
Jno Westwicke	1	Geo Green	1
Will Hutchinson	1	Peter Orange	1
Jno Hutchinson	1	Tho Shepherd	1
Jno Carther	1	Will Vint	1
… Richmond	4	Will Hatton	5
… …derson	2	Ambrose Barnes	2
Will Dobson	4	Geo Brownlas	1

Jno Wild	1
Henry Abron	1
Wid Blaclocke	2
Tho Coats	1
Will Allison	2
Marke Coats	2
Jno Hornes	1
Jno Glover	1
Franc Hutchinson	5
James Fothergaill	2
Jno Horne	1
Tho Shaw	2
Robt Kipling	1
Antho Blenkisop	2
Christ Pinkney	2
Ralph Atchison	2
Margt. Blenkisop	2
Lance Newby junr	1
Jno Story	1
Antho Dinsdale	1
Jno Lordman	2
Jno Tinkeler	1
Jon Fothergall	1
Will Smith	1
Bryan Chater	2
Thomas Robinson	1
Matthew Stoddart	6

m. 3, c. 2

Ann Newton	2
Jno Granger	1
Jno Blaclocke	1
Tho Bell	1
Phillip Bell	2
Robert Hutton	3
Richard Anderson	3
Wid Peacocke	2
Christ Eyon	3
Wid Adington	3
Lance Newby	1
Wid Dobson	4
Tho Wind	3
Jno Newby	3
Antho McKendall	3

George Aud		2
		285
[*corrected total*]	es[?]	291

Cleatlam

Jno Witingham	3
Geo Winter	1
Jane Kipling	1
Edward Peverall	1
Will Suddren	1
Phillis Wrangham	1
Jno Bell	2
Robert Elrins	1
Christ Wilson	1
Tho Garmison	1
Gregory Viccars	3
Jno Sidgewicke	1
Tho Barnes	1
Jno Compton	2
Jno Dunn	1
Jno Bell	1
An Yearle	1
Will Urre	2
Francis Southerin	1
Mary Douthwaitt	1
Tho Hall	9

		33
[*corrected total*]	es[?]	36

Cockfield

Ralph Shaw senr	1
Ralph Shaw junr	1
Richard Percivall	1
Ann Lodge	2
Richd Douthwaitt	1
Barnard Douthwaitt	1
Geo Alderson	1
Cuth Appleby	2
Will Burden	1
Tho Burden	1
Geo Pattison	1
Christ Todd	1
Ralph Walker	1
Tho Watt	1
Richard McKreith	1
Katharin Stanford	2

Will Led	1	Tho Hodgson	1
Robert Lodge	2	Charles Coltsworth	1
Leonard Hodgson	1	Francis Gregsworth	2
Will Rand	2	Jno Raine	1
Peter Fairbanke	3	Lyonell Kipling	1
Nichol Arrowsmith	2	Henry Richardson	1
Margrett Lodge	2	Will Dawson	1
Jno Sidgewicke	2	Jacob Sowrby	1
Geo Arrowsmith	1	Christ Bland	1
Will Maddison	1	Henry Ewbankes	1
Matt Hodgson	1	Antho Lockey junr	1
Will Viccars	1	Charles Pinkney	1
Edw Gargrave	2	Jno Bell	3
Tobias Sidgewicke	3	Ralph Dawson	1
Henry Stephenson	1	Christ Dixson	1
Ralph Stamford	1		**38**
Robert Gorden	1		
Christ Jefferson	1	**Gainsford**	
Mr Watson	5	**[Gainford]**	
Tho Noble	2	Edmond Fotherley	6
Ralph Lodge senr	1	Jno Brackenbury	4
Geo Goundry	2	Jno Crawdocks Esqr	11
Elizabeth Lambert	1	Robert Stoddart	2
Ralph Ayd	1	Edw Raine	3
James Watt	2	Will Crawforth	3
Jno Claper	3	Francis Blaixton	2
Henry Bramley	2	Robt Ray	1
	66	Gilbt Marshall gent	21
		Geo Goundry	3
m. 3, c. 3		Geo Fleett	1
Egglestone		Edward Tinkler	2
[Eggleston]		Jno Swainston	2
Tho Sanderson Esqr	7	Ann Welbanke	1
Antho Headlam	1	Will Thackwray	2
Jno Addison	1	Henry Abbott	1
Will Addison	1	Will Middleton	1
Antho Lockey senr	1	Robt Swainston	2
Will Harrison	1	Jane Simpson	2
Nichol Lockey	1	Jno Burrell	2
Antho Stephenson	1	Margrett Joyner	1
Nichol Headlam	1	Jno Hood	1
Will Stephenson	1	Ann Eden	3
Richard Pinkney	1	Will Joyner	1
Tho Baills	1	Cuth Reenald	2
Mary Dawson	1		**80**
Christ Pinkney junr	1		

Headlam

Henry Draper	8
Grace Pearson	2
Eliza Garth	6
Will Garth	3
Jno Bowbankes	2
Jno Ratclife	1
Jno Winkle	1
Robt Burrell	1
Jno Atkinson	1
Will Garth senr	3
Geo Burrell	2
Rowland Goodburne	1
Will Errington	1
Tho Errington	1
Tho Elivan	1
	34

Hiltonn
[Hilton]

Henry Marley	5
Peter Marley	1
Mr Hilton	2
Jno Firchall	1
Jno Hutchinson	1
Henry Marley	1
Jno Dawson	1[?]
Tho Hugh	1[?]
Jno Reads	1[?]

m. 3v, c. 1

Henry Hadwen	1
Rodger Shaw	1
William Hall	1
Ralph Swinbanke	1
Luke Robinson	1
	19

Ingleton

Jno Shaw	3
Christ Shaw	3
Ann Shaw	1
Robt Peverall	3
Jno Middleton	1
Dorothy Marley	2
Isabell Marley	3

Jno Peverell	2
Edw Huntington	1
Geo Dunwell	1
Geo Waid	2
Jno Horne	1
Will Watson	2
Geo Marley	1
Eliza Marley	1
Eliza Shawter	1
	28

Langton

Richard Simpson	1
Jno Fairlasse	2
Jno Mason	1
Geo Cockfield	1
Robert Spencer	3
Ralph Stoddart	1
Ralph Spencer	1
Jno Grahame	1
Cuth Spencer	1
Will Elwaitt	1
Jno Spencer	2
Jno Thompson	1
Henry Singleton	1
Will Simpson	1
Ralph Singleton	1
Ann Gastell	2
Peter Grasham	1
Chris Elwaitt	1
Widd Ovington	2
Cuth Talior	2
Lanc Stoddart	1
Will Worthy	1
	29

Langley Forrest
[Langleydale]

Tho Sidgewicke	1
Will Raine	1
Ralph Sidgewicke	2
Will Raine senr	4
Ralph Shaw	2
Cuth Robison	1
Dorothy Hodgson	2
Arthur Watson	1

Christ Sidgewicke	2	Richard Jnoson	1
Ralph Hodgson	1	Jno Dent	1
Wid Martindale	1	Ralph Johnson	1
Francis Martindale	1	Jno Jnoson	1
Wid Bankes	1	Henry Baimbricke	2
John Dobson[?]	1	Will Kind	1
… Atkinson	1	Ralph Colepitts	1
…field	1	Jno Wilson senr	1
[about six entries missing]		Leonard Wilson	1
…	1	Henry Kipling	1
…	2	Issabell Gibson	1
…	1	Antho Rutter	1
…	1	Tho Jnoson	2
…ward Railston	1	Jno Rytton junr	1
Eliza Coats	1	Will Lind	2
Charles Robison	3	Will Tinkler	1
Matthew Yearker	1	Rodger Bainbrigg	1
Margrett Willis	1	Tho Allenson	1
Will Sidgewicke	1	Jno Robison	3
Gabriell Sidgewicke	3	Rodger Colepitts	2
Jno Willis	2	Ann Gibson	1
Geo Sidgewicke	3	Ambrose Winter	1
Eliza Talior	1	Tho Lind	1
		Peter Wilson	1
m. 3v, c. 2		Christ Parking	1
Ralph Sidgewicke	2	Will Gibson	1
Gerrard Stokeld	1	Richard Holmes	2
Tho Watson	1	Tho Allenson	1
Andrew Mordy	1	Jane Gibson	1
Jno Baines	1	Eliza Baimbricke	1
Jno Walton	1	Will Gibson	1
James Atkinson	1	Antho Gastell	1
Ellinor Harrison	3	Michaell Dent	2
Tobias Hutton	1	Cuth Lind	1
	64	Tim Tully Gent	4
		Tho Kentish	1
Middleton Bounds		Henry Baimbridge	1
Will Lee	1	Tho Jnoson	1
Tho Myres	1	Jno Baimbridge Gent	5
Will Gastell	5	Rodger Baimbridge	1
Robt Myres	1	Lowrence Tinkler	1
Richd Richdson	1		69
Hugh Glenton	1		
Nichol Branton	1	**Murton Tinmouth**	
Jno Walton	1	**[Morton Tinmouth]**	
Rodger Gibson	1	Mr Burbeck	8

Francis Goundrie	2
Tho Trotter	1
Henry Baimbricke	1
Henry Earle	1
Richd Musgrave	1
	14

Marwood

Mr Thursby	3
Jno Glenton	1
Jno Wilson	1
Phillip Emrson	1
Henry Newby	1
Jno Addison	2
Ambrose Simpson	2
Cuth Midcalfe	1
Bartho Midcalfe	1
Will Garford	2
Will Barnes	2
Robt Errington	3
Ralph Hodgson	1
Jno Mitchell	3
Tho Peacke	1
Christ Dent	1
Jno Stokes	1

m. 3v, c. 3

Cuthbert Stokes	…
Jane Raine	…
John Pickering	1
Anthony Vazy	2
Richard Dawson	3
Ralph Simpson	4
Will Walton	1
Robt Raine	1
	43

Newbiggin upon Tease
[Newbiggin on Tees]

James Peacke	1
Christ Parking	1
Mr Arthur Baimbricke	1
Robt Teasdale	1
Jno Bell	1
Cuth Allison	1
Lanc Coatsworth	1

Will Hunter	1
Christ Parkin senr	1
Jno Allison	1
Jno Gibson	1
Christ Allison	1
Rodger Gastell	1
Geo Allison	1
Christ Allison	1
Jno Natris	1
Jno Allison	1
Tho Parkin	2
Will Allison senr	1
Will Allison	1
Richd Robinson	1
Geo Race	1
Tho Baimbrig	1
Christ Bainbrig	1
Cuth Bainbrig Gent	3
Jeffray Gibson	1
	29

Pearcebridge
[Piercebridge]

James White	2
Nichol Holdrist	2
Will Mann	6
Francis Gibson	1
Leonard Ewbanke	2
Marke Stobbs	2
Geo Boulton	1
Tho Fell	1
Tho Hildridge	1
Will Carter	2
Thomas Coole	2
Edward Berry	1
Jno Docke	2
Tho Welbanke	2
Rich White	1
	28

Raby & Kaverstone
[Raby with Keverstone]

Tho Ewards Gent	4
Cuth Bird	2
James Robison	1
Jno Todd	2

Tobias Ewbanke	2
Tho Viccars	2
Henry Bowran	1
James Thompson	2
Tobias Thompson	1
Christ Crawford	3
Tho Watson	1
Rich Pickering	1
Geo Pickering	2
Will Bails senr	2
Will Baills junr	1
Jno Batty	2
Cuth Lowrance	2
Christ Pickering	2
Henry Elgy	1
Francis Temple	2
Robt Richardson	1
Jno Elgy	2
Will Lawrence	1
James Wrey	2
Geo Longstaffe	2
James Richardson	1
James Viccars	1
James Grainger	3
James Atkinson	2
Tho Wild	2
Geo Dickson	1
Daniell Carmichaell	1

m. 4, c. 1

Henry Grainger	2
Christ Pearson	1
Henry Bowman	1
Cuthbert Bird	2
Lady Vaine	47
	108

Summerhouse

Edward Rumfoot	4
Nichol Watson	3
Richard Dodgson	1
Wid Shawter	2
Robt Shaw	2
Tho Hall	1
Jno Harrison	2
Edw Whitfield	1

Sam Watson	2
Richard Steall	1
Edw Allison	1
Jno Burrell	2
Tho Bowbanke	1
	23

Streetlam
[Streatlam]

Tho Baimbricke	2
Geo Brumlasse	1
Tho Lacke	1
Geo Baimbridge	1
Tobias Hutchison	1
Toby Bend	1
Ralph Bavering	1
Geo Clerkson	1
Rowland Pow	2
Robt Dennison	1
Magdalen Topaz	1
Mark Raikstraw	1
Henry Robinson	1
Jno Dent	1
Geo Brumlas	1
Ambrose Clerkson	1
Jno Clerkson	1
Wm Yearker	1
Jno Braffett	2
Jno Robinson	1
Ellinor Robinson	1
Tho Appleby	1
Tho Buckle	1
Matt Browlesse	1
Jno Baills	1
Tho Walker	2
Matt Atkison	1
Leonard Bend	2
Robert Boulton	1
Tho Hall	1
Tho Yarker	1
Geo Baxter	1
Talbert Talior	2
Christ Ludge	1
Barbara Hutton	2
Will Thompson	1
Ambrose Shutt	1

Greg Appleby	1	Christ Darnton	2
Greg Yearker	1	Robt Walterman	1
Jno Warkup	1	Christ Hodgson	5
Ann Warkupp	1	Will Douthwaitt	2
Mr Bowes	12	Will Temple	3
Margrett Rippon	1	Oswald Dobson	5
Cuth Cupas	2	Will Burdy	1
Ralph Hodgson	2	Will Watson	1
Will Luge	1	Tho Todd	1
	66	Tho Simpson	4
		Tho Talior	3
Staindroppe		Jno Craike	1
[Staindrop]		Will Spencer	1
Mich Waistall	1	Rich Robison	3
Ms Rodgers	2	Ms Dale	5
James Bell	1	Will Watson	1
Will Hall	2	Richard Brownlace	1
Mr Smart	6	Anth Bell	2
Richard Dickinson	1	Richard Crawdocke	1
Wm Walker	1	Tho Kemp	2
Ms Baimbricke	2	Talbott Bennett	2
Tho Boulton	2	Robt Greathead	1
Geo Nicolson	3	Margrett Thompson	1
William Nicolson	1	Henry Temple	1
Geo Chapman	2		**115**
James Bell	1		
m. 4, c. 2		**Shotton Teasdale Forrest**	
Jno Harrison	1	Issabell Emmerson	1
Mr Ewbankes	4	Ann Baimbricke	2
James Atkison	3	Leonard Allison	1
Robert Thompson	2	Jno Bell	1
Jno Walterman	1	Jno Allison	1
Mr Gilping	5	Jno Dixson	1
Talbot Dent	3	Jno Robson	1
Jno Marley	1	Will Watson	1
Christ Wild	3	Jno Palmerley	1
Jno Layfield	2	Jno Robison	1
Rich Pratt	3	Henry Robison	1
Cuth Liddell	1	Jno Allison	1
Geo Goundry	3	Arthur Lee	1
Jno Dinsdaill	1	Rebekka Parkin	1
Tho Hewettson	4	Jno Lazenby	1
Jno Marley	1	Henry Walton	1
Will Jnoson	1	Margrett Walton	1
Barbara Arrowsmith	1	Christ Turry	1

Antho Page	1	Jno Hornsby	2
Barbara Ture	1	Tho Waikliffe	2
Jno Linn	1	Will Rowntree	1
Mr Arthur Baimbricke	2	Tho Robinson	1
Simond Raine	1	Richard Dobson	1
Will Turry	1	Francis Carter	2
Will Walton	1	Tho Smith	2
Nichol Rosebecke	1	Geo Darnton	1
Jno Horne	1	Ralph Rowntree	1
Jno Rase	1	Tho Ovington	1
Peter Horne	1	Robt Appleby	2
	31	Issabell Dent	1
		Francis Gastell	2
Westwicke		Jno Heighley	1
[Westwick]		Eliza Waterman	1
Jno Holmes	2	Robt Jnoson	1
Christ Samples	3	Christ Jnoson	1
Jno Hullocke	1	Ms Ann Wytham	10
Tho Kipling	2		45
Edward Holmes	1		
Richard Swainstone	1	**Wakerfield**	
Henry Hodgson	2	**[Wackerfield]**	
Robert Rowlandson	2	Nichol Whitfield	1
Tho Wilson	1	Robert Bails	1
Henry Blenkisoppe	1	Robert Wade	1
		Christ Marley	1
m. 4, c. 3		Ann Bails	1
Lyonell Kipling	1	Bernard Simpson	1
Jno Smayles	1	Will Sutton	1
Christ Newby	1	Christ Hadwen	2
Christ Peell	2	Tho Jackson	2
Antho Appleby	1	John Talber	2
Jno Harrison	1	Robt Paverley	1
Henry Swainston	6	Will Wade	1
Stephen Airey Gent	4	Nichol Lumbley	1
	33		16
Whorleton		**Winstone**	
[Whorlton]		**[Winston]**	
Ambrose Jnoston	5	Cuth Marley	4
Will Shutt	1	Jno Thompson	2
Robt Dindsdale	1	Richard Garfoott	2
Henry Jnoson	2	Tho Smithson	3
Will Browne	1	Robert Slacke	1
Eliza Hodgson	1	Rich Darnton	2
Jno Soulby	1	Tho Longstaffe	1

Jno Newcomb junr	1	**Darlington Ward**	
Will Fawell	1	**North West Division**	
Tho Farrow	2		
Francis Clement	1	**Brough of Aukland**	
Dorothy Simpson	3	**[Borough of Auckland]**	
Jno Frankland senr	1	Tho Holmes	5
Jno Frankland junr	1	Will Conyers	2
Bernard Frankland	2	Will Thompson	1
Ellinor Brummell	1	Will Spenceley	4
Tho Foulthropp	1	Antho Allenson	4
Jno Clement	1	Jno Wright	1
Ambrose Clement	2	Will Gilford	3
Eliza Richardson	1	Rachell Crawdocke	4
Geo Swainston	1	Edw Lampton	2
Richard Wilson	1	Francis Wren Esqr	4
Robert Pearson	1	James Whitton	5
Ms Newcomb	2	Will Watson	5
Jno Wrangham	2	Jno Hadon	2
Mr Paiting	1	Mr Phillips	5
Will Sudderam	1	Jno Grindall	5
Edward Elwan	4	Eliza Simpson	2
Tho Suddell	2	Will Crawdocke	5
Jno Douthwaitte	4	Will Currey	1
Thomas Newton	2	Richard Larkey	1
Richard Ovinton	1	Jno Thompson	2
Francis Bunny	2	Joseph Worthy	3
Mary Viccar	1	Tho Roberts	1
Cuth Burrell	1	Will Jefferson	1
		Richard Ranforth	1
m. 4v, c. 1		Richard Apedale	1
Jno Seamer	2	Richard Pinkney	4
Edward Wright	2	Wid Apedaile	4
George Bunning	4	Cuth Apedaile	3
Jno Palmer	2	Hosea Bradforth	2
Bernard Douthwaitt	1	Richard Talior	1
Tho Warkup	3	Matt Browne	3
Margrett Wilson	3	Christ Nelson	2
Bartho Harwood	1	Jno Allison	3
Mary Jnoson	1	Edward Elgoe	5
Tho Gibson	1	Stephen Cuming	2
Gervus Gibson	3	Robert Heighington	1
	82	Jane Walker	1
		Ralph Crawdocke	4
		Jane Clater	3
		Theophilus Paise	4
		John Arrundaill	2

Sam Davison	18	Jno Lackey	1
Ralph Pace	4	Francis Richardson	2
Alice Webfoot	1	Ralph Colepitts Gent	4
Robert Gibson	2	Stephen Haigg Gent	5
Tho Lockey	1	Edw Middleton	3
Christ Dobson	6	Richard Longhorne	2
Ann Sparke	5	Tho Howett	3
Mary Gantley	3	Antho Bell	2
Margrett Walton	5	Antho Wheatley	1
Jno Ward	6	Marke Horner	2
Jno Lockey	2	Tho Watson	3
Eliza Spenceley	4	Stephen Wyly	1
Ann Law	3	Issabell Stobey	3
Ralph Worthy	3	Tho Brasse	6
Nichol Stobbart	2	Rich Portas	1
Jno Parnaby	2	Mr Fuiller	5
Jno Clerke	1	Jno Longstaffe	4
Tho Clerke	1	Ann Wilson	1
Geo Hodgson	5	Jno Longhorne	1
Cuth Whitfield	3	Josias Baimbricke	1
Geo Hodgson	5	Humphrey Chipchase	1
Antho Game	3	James Robson	1
Will Branksell	1	Jno Walton	1
Francis Dawson	2	James Croft	2
		Michaell Stobbart	2
m. 4v, c. 2		Phillip Watt	2
Robert Spenceley	4	Geo White	3
Ralph Douthwaitt	6	Tho Todd	2
Tho Medcalfe	2	Richard Wright	1
Francis Watson	1	Jno Bewicke	1
Will Lax	1	Will Shaw	2
Tho Slater	3	Jno Stobbart	4
Michaell Harrison	1	Richd Smelt Gent	6
Jno Lax	2	Jennett Wilson	2
Luke Nesom	2	Christ Curry	3
Francis Brackett	4	Will Dobson	3
Jno Lord Bishopp	35	Will Darnton	1
	263	Robt Ovington	2
			104

Bondgate in Bpp Aukland
[Bondgate in Bishop Auckland]

Newgate in Bpp Aukland
[Newgate in Bishop Auckland]

Jno Pinkney	4	Will Adamson	2
Bryan Walker	2	Will Hunt	1
Tho Smurfoott	3	James Bradforth	3
Nicholas Rowley	3	Ellinor Liddell	1
Jno Tunstal Gent	2		

Jno Roberts	1
Antho Clerke	1
Will Smurfoott	1
Geo Sickerham	4
Matt Tallentyre	1
Francis Swinbanke	2
Will Tallentyre	4
Mr Pleasance	3
Tho Rickaby	2
Cuth Whitfield	3
Christ Craw	2
Henry Casson	3
Mr Blackett	3
Ms Martha	3
Francis Wright	1
Will Leaver	5
Jno Ward	5
Tho Longstaffe senr	1
Eliza Whorleton	2

m. 4v, c. 3

Robert Jnoson	2
Richard B...	9
Will Barnes	1
Geo Harrison	5
Jno Dowson	1
Jno Dowson senr	4
Wid Grunden	2
Geo Gibson	3
Antho Robson	2
Jno Watson	1
Will Bulman	1
Jno Trotter	4
Matthew Robison	2
Will Whitfield	3
Robt Thompson	2
Jno Kirkham	1
Jno Adamson	2
Jno Whittfield	2
Geo Sukerhouse	3
Gerrard Trotter	3
Eliza Peckton	2
Gartrude Nuby	2
Tho Richardson	2
Jno Roberts	1
	114

St Andrw Aukland [Auckland St Andrew]

Francis Wren Gent	9
Robt Harrison	2
Cuth Dobson	4
Mich Talior	1
Will Plowman	1
Jno Wheatley	1
Joseph Lax	1
Antho White	1
Christ Lawson	3
Tho Maugham	1
Jno Greathead	2
Will Crow	1
Will Close	3
Wid Labron	2
	32

St Ellin Aukland [Auckland St Helen]

Cuthbert Carre Gent	13
Williamson Gent	2
Matt Smithson	4
Jno Garth	3
Will Ward	3
Jno Rickarby	2
Antho Gargrave	2
Ralph Dickinson	2
Jno Anderson	1
Will Downes	1
Jno Dickinson	1
Wid Reed	1
Tho Meaburne	1
Mr Windle	3
Will Stainbanke	1
	40

West Aukland [West Auckland]

Jno Eden Gent	8
Jno Tongue Gent	8
Tho Garth	4
Richard Coltman	2
Mrs Ellinor Eden	4
Cuth Allinson	2
Jno Wainman	1

Will Todd	2	Jno Jolley	3
Mich Richardson	4	Jno Dixson	2
Antho Airy	3	Richard Potter	1
Leonard Hunter	1	Jno Waters	1
Robert Mason	2	Will Bell	1
Christ Richardson	1	Jno Lister	1
Will Ward	1	Jno Mason	1
Will Longstaffe	1	Will Wall	1
Geo Garth	5	Jno Winter	1
Christ Stoddart	1	Robt Raine	1
Ralph Simpson	3		__1__
Wid Heighley	1		**111**
Robt Stoddart senr	3		

Branspeth cum Castle & Parke
[Brancepeth with Castle and Park]

Charles Anderson	1	Will Swinburne Gent	17
Geo Simpson	1	Doctor Brevent	8
Francis Farray	2	Walter Bell	1
Jno Blythman	2	Jno Rodham	2
Eliza Garry	1	Francis Mitchell	2
Jno Gargrave	1	Stephen Cocke	3
		Francis Curry	2
m. 5, c. 1		Francis Thompson	1
Will Wall	1	Jno Pearson	3
Will Richardson	2	Ralph Dowfoott	3
Mary Newby	1	Rich Emmrson	3
Tho Hodgson	1	Eliza Arrowsmith	1
Antho Garth	1	Geo Raxby	2
Will Tuggall	1	Margrett Wilson	2
Jno Lister senr	1	Peter Mason	2
Robt Stoddart junr	1	Will Jackson	1
Robt Ashsmith gent	2	Richard Byars	3
Will Thompson	2	Robt Eden Gent	4
Jno Teasdale	2	Stephen Arrowsmith	1
Tobias Child	1	Henry Atkison	4
Christ Thorrowberry	1	Antho Farrow	2
Jno Bulmer	1	Henry Fawden	3
Ralph Bulmer	1	Lady Hodgson	9
Geo Attas	1	Tho Coniers Gent	5
Robert Teasdaill	1	Tho Purdey	2
Christ Stoddart	1	James Feaster	1
Tho Hodgson	1	Jno Coleman	2
Jno Kay	3	Ann Dowfoott	3
Jno Fairbecke	1	Will Wright	1
Jno Hutchison	1	Issabell Hull	1
Geo Talior	2	Oliver Mills	1
Will Talior	1	Geo Browne	1
Jno Stoddart	2		

Will Mason	1	Robert Salkeild	1
Will Dowfoott	1	Robert Jackson	1
Charles Burnop	2	Matthew Holmes	3
Margt Middleton	2	Tho Blunt	1
Robert Byars	2	Jno Fawden	1
Robt Thompson	3	Jno Cooper	4
Tho Townes	2	Jno Robson	3
Ralph Coale Gent	11	Edward Harrison	2
Tho Hutchison	5	Will Hester	2
Tho Hutchison	3	Jno Feaster	2
Ralph Friend	2	Michaell Bryan	1
	130	Jno Lampton	1
		Ralph Holmes	3
m. 5, c. 2			61

Brandon

Tho Hind	5	**North Bedburne**	
Ralph Pickering	7	**[North Bedburn]**	
James Laing	2	Will Hodgson	3
Tho Pickering	3	Bartho Jackson	1
Richard Crookes	2	Ingram Todd	2
Robt Marry	2	Robert Fowell	3
Jno Vincent	2	Lanc Braidley	1
Charles Vincent	2	Tho Jackson	1
Jno Newton	1	Tho Marshall	2
Jno Rumfoot	1	Tho Hodgson	2
Tho Morrison	1	Tho Mousy	1
Geo Fawden	1	Henry Moosy	1
Christ Hutchison Gent	6	Wid Jackson	1
Jno Hull	2	Tho Carre	2
Jno Adamson	1	Tho Hutchison	1
George Mason	1	Robert Stobbart	3
Bartho Stevenson	1	Jno Marshall	2
	40	Jno Roberts	2
		Katharin Hodgson	2
		Jno Smurfoot senr	1
Bishottles		Jno Smurfoot junr	1
[Byshottles]		Antho Yeatts	1
Cuth Allison	2	Jno Carelesse	1
Rodger Talbott	5	Cuth Smurfoot	1
Will Wilkison	1	Mr Hutchinson	3
Jno Browne	2	Mr Talior	5
Collonell Stewart	12	Jno Hogge	2
Richard Wright	2	Jno Harrison	1
Phillip Michaell	6	James Robison	1
Antho Thompson	2	Mr Wytham	4
Jno Michaell	2	Will Snaith	1
Martin Rippon	2		

Francis Fowll	1	Jno Simpson	1
Cuth Coming	1	Jno Hodgson	2
Jno Chesmond	1	Jno Parkin	2
Robt Snaith	1	Robt Ramshaw	1
Eliza Grundwell	1	Jno Dowson	1
Simon Dickinson	1	Tho Craigs	3
Mary Dickinson	1	Geo Shaw	1
Tho Borlisonn	2		68
Richard Roper	1		
Christ Milner	1	**Bishoppley**	
	63	**[Bishopley]**	

m. 5, c. 3

		Jno Morgan	1
South Bedburne		Ralph Wall	1
[South Bedburn]		Jno Mowbray	3
Jno Crow	1	Henry Angles	1
Jno Walker	1	Jno Chapman	1
Robt Dowson	1	Henry Furnace	1
Antho Gartheron	1	Geo Dobson	2
Charity Preston	1		10
Leonard Maddison	1		
Ralph Bails	2		
Ann Dowson	1	**Counden**	
Geo Dowson	1	**[Coundon]**	
Ralph Walton	5	Jno Hartley	2
Christ Blackett Gent	7	Will Parkison	2
Will Maddison	1	Eliza Hartley	1
James Dobson	2	Lance Chapman	1
Ralph Hodgson	1	Will Parkins	1
Will Blackett	3	Geo Browne	2
Will Teasdale	1	Will Pearson	3
Jno Atkison	1	Tho Parkins	2
Geo Walton	1	Eliza Parkins	1
Will Jnoson	2	Jno Garry	2
Christ Blackett	2	Ralph Short	1
Will Teasdale	1	Jno Hopper	2
Jno Atkinson	1	Will Shearington	1
James Fellowes	4	Richard Hopper	1
Geo Carter	2	Humphrey Hopper	2
James Guttery	1	Will Parkins	1
Jno Jackson	1	Antho Pearson	1
Gilbt Midcalfe Gent	4	Ann Hopper	1
Bryan Palmerley	2	Tho Short	1
Moses Newby	2	Eliza Slacke	1
Hugh Gartheren	2	Will Short	1
Robert Gray	1	Richard Parkins	1
		Will Addy	1
			32

Crooke and Billiraw
[Crook and Billy Row]

Henry Fetherstone	5
Ann Greenwell	3
Jno Talior	1
Wid Hodgson	2
Tho Baker	1
Will Atkison	2
Cuth Hodgson	2
Antho Jackson	3
Bartho Marshall	2
Antho Wren	1
Jno Allerton	1
Henry Marshall	2
Cuth Ovinton	1
Will Dow	1
Tho Hodgson	1
Will Bell	1
Jno Salkeld	1
	30

m. 5v, c. 1

Escombe
[Escomb]

Wid Todd	3
Margrett Crow	2
Tho Todd	1
Will Marley	2
Geo Moore senr	3
Edward Newcombe	3
Will Cooks	2
Nichol Blades	1
Jno Browne	1
Tho Elwan	1
Jno Stobbs	1
Tho Thackwray	3
Jno Stephenson	3
Jno Spooner	1
Jno Phillips	1
Jno Curry	1
Jno Stobbart	1
Percivall Martindall	2
Bryan Pearson	3
Humphrey Smurfoot	1
Geo Moore junr	3
Tho Rickaby	1

Mary Todd	2
Henry Baimbricke	1
	43

Evenwood Towne
[Evenwood Town]

Jno Stephenson	3
Will Ray	2
Jno Hodgson	1
Charles Wren	1
Geo Cuming	1
Will Todd	1
Geo Todd	2
Tho Stephenson	2
Simon Robinson	1
Ann Stephenson	2
Antho Stephenson	1
Jno Marley	2
Christ Hopper	1
Geo Stephenson	1
Jane Lodge	1
Henry Atkinson	1
Lampton Downes	1
Ellin Chirkilt	1
	25

Evenwood Barrony
[Evenwood Barony]

Tho Robsonn	6
Will Bowes	4
Ms Grace Pearson	8
James Thompson	2
Jno Thompson	2
Jno Sidgewicke	2
Will Slacke	1
Tho Robinson	1
Ralph Foreman	1
Jno Gowland	1
Christ Sidgewicke	1
Tho Sanderson	1
Jno Gargrave	1
Antho Appleby	1
Ralph Coall	1
An Wild	1
Will Hodgson	1
Jno Heavieside	1
Ralph Sidgewicke	1
Jno Hodgson	1

Geo Viccars	2	Robert Pearson	1
Bryan Mounseir	1	Phillip Stoddart	1
Mary Allison	1	Christ Wood	1
Percevall Lamb	1	Tho Stobbs	1
Tho Todd	1	Jno Simpson	2
Ralph Tailor	1	Robert Natresse	1
Geo Bowes	2	Jno Natresse	1
Jno Gainsforth	1	Will Allenson	2
Dorothy Wild	1	Tho Dickinson	2
Tho Walton	1	Geo Wilsonne	1
Jane Dobbison	1	Geo Noble	1
Robert Addison	2	Christ Sureties	2
Francis Parkison	1	Jane Garfoot	1
	54	Jno Cornforth	2
		Wid Cuming	2
		Antho Trotter	2
Frosterley			49
Bridgett Chapman vid	1		
Tho Morgan	1		
Cuth Todd	1	**Hedley and Cornsey**	
Tho Mowbray	1	**[Hedley and Cornsay]**	
James Clerke	1	Mr Sanderson	9
Arthur Jopling	3	Geo Hedley	2
Geo Wall	1	Tho Hedley	1
Christ Wall	3	Martin Briggs	1
		Margrett Greenwin	1
m. 5v, c. 2		Humphrey Richardson	1
Tho Todd	2	Tho Allison	1
Mich Chapman	1	Matt Smith	2
Tho Teasdale	1	Richard Hedley	1
Ellinor Chapman	2	Will Rippon	1
Jno Chapman	1	Peter Achnell	2
Tho Chapman	1	Anthony Mills	1
Cuth Morgan	1	Jno Lindsey	2
	21	Will Cartley	2
		Tho Sanderson	2
		Robert Greenwin	1
Hunwicke		Rich Foster	1
[Hunwick]		An Greenwell	1
Jno Collingwood Gent	9		33
Tho Trotter Gent	7	**[corrected total]** es[?]	32
Will Wright	1		
Jane Phillip vid	1		
Wid Gley	1	**Helmington Row**	
Tho Sickerman	1	Cuth Jackson	3
Jno Stephenson	2	Martin Jackson	2
Will Wright	1	Robt Cuming	2
Geo Wilsonne	3	Tho Maior	1

Will Walker	2	Jno Hodgson Gent	4
Robt Isley	2	Cuth Peverall	1
Will Smurfoott	2	Bryan Todd	1
Jno Jnoson	1	Ralph Hodgson	1
Ann Greenwell	1	Nichol Chapman	2
Tho Charleton	2	Tho Hall	1
Robt Cooley	1	Henry Richdson	3
Robt Walton	1	Barbara Hearon	1
Tho Jackson	1	Blench Dixson	1
Ambrose Wilsonn	1	Francis Walker	1
Geo Farrow	1	Christ Huntershell	1
Nichol Cuming	1	Eliza Crow	1
Jno Jobling	1	Robt Fullensby	2
Tho Lindsey	1	Tho Hearon	1
Tho Gibson	1	Tho White senr	1
	27	Simon Lambert	1
		Will Thompson	2
Thornley and Helmparke		Tho Givengs	1
[Thornley and Helm Park]		Tho Givens senr	1
Tho Baker	2	Jane Giveings	2
Richard Garfoott	1	Ralph Pattison	1
Jno Teasdale	1	Ralph Giveings	1
Will Duckett	1	Christ Chaittor	2
Will Story	1	Ann Smith	1
Robt Readshore	1	Will Cole	1
Ralph Hodgson	1	Will Rosse	2
Wm Raw	1	Cuth Stainbanke	1
Jno Martindale Gent	3	Hugh Hearon	1
Wid Blarton	1	Will Lindsay senr	2
Robt Douthwaitt	1	Eliza Talior	2
Jno Hartley	1	Eliza Giveings	2
		Tho White	1
m. 5v, c. 3		Tho Hodgson	1
Stephen Walton	1	Will Lindsey	1
Jno Raw	1	Christ Giveings	2
Wm Greenwell	1	Wm Givens	1
Jno Garfoott	1	Wm Steall	1
Jno Grindon	1	Bryan Todd	1
Richard Marshall	1		62
Will Greenwell	1		
	22	**Linsacke and Softley**	
		[Lynesack and Softley]	
Hamsterley		Bartho Burlison	2
Tho Talior Gent	4	Geo Steeley	1
Henry Young Gent	4	Gerrard Stockley	3
Jno Benson	1	Ann Maddison	1

Jane Dowson	1	Antho Atkison	1
Richard Coale	1	Tho Simpson Gent	5
Anthony Hodgson	2	Mr Fetherstone	6
Michaell Parkin	1	Ann Hodgson	2
Jno Greenwell	1	Tho Simpson junr	3
Tobias Hutton	1		**36**
Will Natres	1		
Henry Viccars	1	**Shildon**	
Christ Dobson	1	Jno Wharton Gent	2
Jno Braidley	1	Will Richardson	4
Cuth Sanderson	1	Jno Crow senr	1
Will Jnoson	1	Jno Taller	2
Robt Emmerson	1	Wid Blythman	2
Roger Harding	1	Jno Crow	4
Geo Lindsey	1	Jno Nicholson	1
Ralph Stephenson	1	Edmond Midcalfe	1
Tho Hutchinson	1	Tho Bussy	2
Mich Blackett	1		**19**
Jno Sanderson	1		
Will Dobbison	1	**Stockley**	
Tho Palmerley	1	Jno Brabbant Gent	6
Antho Hodgson	2	Ms Baxter	5
Henry Coall	2	Ralph Douthwaitt	1
Eliz Hodgson	1	Geo Morrison	1
Jno Heavieside	1	Jno Morrison	2
Jno Tinkler	1	Tho Hull Gent	2
Mary Benson	2	Henry Hull	1
	38	Tho Hull	1
		Issabell Fawden	3
Newton Capp		Tho Smith	2
[Newton Cap]		Nichol Smith	2
Henry Pattinson	1	Tho Harrison	1
Jno Allison	1	Nicho Hull	1
Jno Trotter	2	Jno Tindall	1
Bryan Stobbs	1	Robert White	1
Bryan Wall	4	Will Addison	1
Will Pattison	2	Jno Hall	1
Will Bow	1	Gawen Forrest	2
Richard Wall	1	Geo Fuister	1
		Ann Wilkison	2
m. 6, c. 1		Robert Duckett	1
Antho Allinson cot	[-]	Henry Bell	1
Jno Pringle	1	Jno Fawden	1
Will White	2	Gawin Bell	1
Rich Cornforth	2		
Rich Cornforth junr	1		

Robert Byars   1
                                               __
                                               41
[*corrected total*]   es[?]   42

**Stanhopp Newlandsideridge and
Stanhopp Baileywicke
[Stanhope Newlandside and
Stanhope Bailywick]**

Jno Coltsforth	1
Jno Crawhall	2
Geo Brewicke	1
Geo Baimbricke	1
Jno Gray	1
Eliza Wall	1
Jno Hadwen	1
Tho Emmerson	1
Jno Johnson	2
Will Maddison	2
Will Watson	1
Geo Short	1
Cuth Wall	2
Tho Mowbray	2
Richard Norman	1
Will Blackett Gent	5
Jno Mowbray	2
Robt Morgan Gent	4
Tho Harrison	1
Will Rippon	1
Will Sidgewicke	1
Christ Wall	3
Maddison Gray	2
Edward Branham	1
Geo Walton	1
Jno Maddison	1
Michaell Walton	1
Stephen Maddison	1
Jno Westgarth	1
Nichol Nicholson	1
Geo Harrison	2
Tho Westgarth	3
Sr George Vaine	14
Antho Waidson	2
Ann Westgarth	2

m. 6, c. 2

Mr Featherston	10
Will Watson	2
Arthur Lonesdale	2
Jno Elwood	1
Geo Pratt	1
Will Dixson	1
Tho Walton	1
Godfrey Disbrey	1
Nichol Richardson	2
Richard Greensword	3
Geo Greensword	1
Jno Watson	2
Jno Colling	1
Tho Robson	5
Doctor Bazier	9
Will Emmrson	6
Ms Mary Phillipson	6
Ms Blackett	2
Will Wright	2
Geo Colling	1
Jno Coulsworth	1
Jno Walton	2
Rowland Wooler	1
Jno Dixson	1
Tho Walton	2
Ralph Trotter	1
Jno Battinson	1
Geo Myres	2
Geo Collingwood	1
Ralph Emmrson	2
Geo Harrison	1
Christ Thompson	2
Jno Emmerson	1
Jno Walton	2
Bryan Trotter	1
Widd Henderson	1
Henry Jnoson	1
Cuth Teasdale	1
Ralph Jnoson	1
Will Berwicke	1
Jno Walton	1
Widd Stephenson	1
Will Hutchinson	1
Tho Thomlinson	1
Cuth Myars	1

Francis Dixson	1
Jno Blackett	1
Mr Fetherstone	1
Tho Thompson	2
Mr Anderson	4
Nichol Hymas	1
Tho Hackward	1
Jno Rowell	1
Chris Lawson	1
Tho Blackett	1
Henry Wallace	1
Tho Hutchison	1
Will Watson	2
Robt Golightly	2
Geo Golightly	1
Jane Maddison	2
Ralph Golightly	1
Will Steward	1
	186
	[184]

Stanhope Parke Quarter
[Stanhope Park Quarter]

Jno Baimbricke	3
Margery Emmerson	2
Will Emmerson	1
Geo Emmerson	1
Peter Baimbricke	2
Mary Emmerson	2
Geo Baimbricke	2
Elizabeth Emmerson	4
Will Watson	1
Jno Thompson	1
Richard Watson	1
Ann Robison	2
Nichol Emmerson	2
Jno Harrison	3
Jno Wall	1
Richard Baimbricke	2
Jno Pelkington	6
Christ Harrison	3
Cuth Hall	1
Geo Crissopp	1
Geo Wall	1
Jno Ward	1
Jno Westgarth	2

Jno Fetherstone	1
Geo Stobs	2
Jno Stobbs	1

m. 6, c. 3

Jno Stobbs junr	4
Will Stobbs	1
Jno Myars	1
Geo Stobbs	1
Geo Brumwell	2
Lanc Trotter	2
Tho Talior	4
	64

Stanhopp Forrest
[Stanhope Forest]

Geo Emmerson	1
Margrett Emmerson	2
Guy Baimbricke	1
Jno Westwood	1
Jno Gibsonn	1
Jno Gray	1
Jno Westwood	1
Eliza Gibson	1
James Viccars	1
Jno Sheell	2
Ralph Hall	1
Will Fetherston	1
Will Sheell	1
Cuth Watson	1
Jno Hall	1
Ralph Gibson	2
Jno Emmerson	1
Tho Emmerson	1
Tho Emmerson	1
Mary Emmerson	1
Jno Gibson	1
Ralph Fetherstone	1
Ralph Hall	1
Cuth Hall	1
Cuth Watson	1
Jno Watson	1
Tho Emmerson	1
Tho Watson	1
Geo Rowell	1
Geo Hornsby	1

Jno Natresse	1	Will Smith	1
Issabell Watson	1	Jno Baimbricke	1
Ralph Fetherstone	1	Ralph Baimbricke	1
Will Harrison	1	Tho Watson	1
Ralph Emmerson	1	Jane Emmerson	1
Francis Little	1	Rowland Natresse	1
Jno Fetherstone	1	Jno Natresse	1
Ralph Harrison	1	Jno Peart	1
Tho Alsopp	1		**90**
Cuth Peart	1		
Jno Lonesdale	1		
Jno Harrison	1	*m. 6v, c. 1*	
Jno Harrison	1	**Witton upon Weare**	
Robert Emmerson	1	**[Witton-le-Wear]**	
Will Gibson	1	James Darcy Esqr	16
Jno Fetherstone	1	Mr Collingwood	5
Will Fairlesse	1	Mr Young	3
Geo Harrison	1	Mr Francis Oard	2
Ralph Harrison	1	Mr Ward	2
Jno Emmerson	1	Will Richardson	2
Tho Emmerson	1	Rich Vazie	2
Jno Lonesdale	1	Tho Talior	1
Geo Watson	1	Nichol Talior	1
Cuth Emmerson	1	Wm Talior	2
Robert Bramwell	1	Will Hutchison	1
Jno Natresse	1	Tho Ramshaw	1
Geo Harrison	1	Tho Bavens	2
Arthur Emmerson	1	Francis Dobbinson	2
Tho Alsopp	1	Will Westoe	2
Ralph Fetherston	1	Jno Rippon	1
Jno & Robert Rutter	2	Ralph Hodgson	2
Cuth Hall	1	Jno Cumming	1
Will Baimbridge	1	Chris Hutchinson	2
Cuth Emmerson	1	Jno Hutchinson	1
Margrett Emmerson	1	Jno Talior	2
Rich Hall	1	Tho Atkinson	1
Jno Baimbridge	1	Robert Russell	1
Geo Harrison	1	Tho Drewhitt	1
Geo Whitfield	1	Tho Milburne	1
Geo Emmerson	1	Humphrey Green	2
Geo Bramwell	3	Henry Blackett	2
Geo Emmerson	1	Robt Rippon	1
Jno Ewens	1	Geo Dixson	1
Geo Phillipson	1	Ralph Jelling	2
Rowland Natresse	1	Jane Booth	1
Geo Emmerson	1	Jane Vaux	1
		Jno Bowmer	2

Widd Snaith	2
Tho Myers	1
Wid Myers	2
Matt Allenson	1
Tho Emmerson	1
Tho Walton	1
Henry Smith	2
Tho Lilburne	1
Ralph Thompson	1
Ann Moscroft	1
Francis Heavyside	1
Will How	1
Will Talior	1
Tho Simpson	2
James Cooper	1
Mirriell Myres	1
Geo Bucke	1
Margrett Bouth	1
Henry Milburne	1
Jno Harland	2
Will How senr	1
Jno Booth	1
	96

Wolsingham Town Quarr
[Wolsingham Town]

Jno Wall	2
Michaell Wild	2
Will Reonaldson	1
Will Hopper	1
Michaell Chapman	2
Will Fleaming	2
Will Richardson	1
Jno Todd	2
Will Wilson	2
Robert Horsley	2
Tobias Trotter	1
Joseph Martindale	2
Ralph Reonaldson	1
Eliza Dixson	1
Lanc Air	2
Will Deacon Gent	4
Margrett Hodgson	1
Tho Greenwell	1
Jno Thompson	1
Tho Hopper	1

Jane Robinson	1
Henry Jackson	1
Will Thompson	1
Robert Kirley	2
Jno Harrison	1
Nichol Toward	1
Antho Toward	1
Will Toward	1
Doctor Guy Carleton	9
Ralph Vasey	1
Will Oliver	1
Geo Oliver	1
Jno Toward	2
Geo Clerke	1
Adam Goston	1

m. 6v, c. 2

Will Siddell	1
Matthew Armstrong	2
Tho Tenman	4
Christ Linn	1
Charles Siddall	1
Will Air	2
Rodger Harrison	2
Jno Thompson	1
Gabriell Wilson	2
Ann Harrison	3
Robert Wall	3
Will Jefferson	2
Jno Hutchison	2
Christ Welfoott	2
Mary Wallace	2
	89
[*corrected total*] es[?]	87

Wolsingham East Quartr
[Wolsingham East]

Jno Vasay Gent	5
Antho Dixson	2
Adnell Marshall	1
Tho Vasey Gent	4
Geo Chapman	2
Jno Greenwell	1
Grace Allison	1
Ingram Thompson	1
Ralph Dixson	1

Geo Trotter	1
Jno Stobbs	1
Henry Robinson	1
Robert Wasnutt	1
Matt Bell	1
Tho Greenwell	2
Cuth Martindale	2
Tho Dobbinson	3
Lanc Martindale	1
Jno Jopling	1
Albony Foster	4
Imego Stobbs	2
Ralph Bowes Esqr	7
Lady Mary Bowes	1
Geo Marshall	1
Michaell Bryars	1
Geo Chapman	2
Jno Simpson	1
Jno Marshall	2
Tho Rutter	1
Will Toward	1
Will Crooke	2
Guy Watson	1
	58

Wolsingham So Side Quarr
[Wolsingham South]

Jno Hall	1
Jno Magdon	1
Widd Dixson	1
Tho Wall	1
Christ Dixson	2
Arthur Jopling	3
Jane Ashley	4
Will Jackson	2
Antho Craigs	4
Mich Chapman	1
Geo Lindsey	2
Tho Lindsey	1
Will Hopper	1
Jno Hopper	2
Tho Trotter gent	3
Ralph Emmerson	1
Christ Teasdale	1
Wid Hopper	2
Jno Bailey	2

Jno Air	1
Christ Dobson	1
	37

Wolsingham Pke Quatr
[Wolsingham Park]

Mich Burnop	2
Jno Sampson	1
Jno Kirkley	1
Alice Coulson	1
Jno Harrison	2
Tim Allison	1
Richard Burnoppe	1
An Coulson	1
Tho Heighington	1
Mich Dixson	1
Robert Trotter	2
Antho Dixson	1
Robert Coulson	2
Ingram Chapman	2
Doctor Guy Carleton	1
	20

Stockton Ward
South West Division

Aislaby

Jno Garnett	7
Tho Fuiller	6
Ralph Blaclocke	1
Tho Newton	1
Wm Jnoson	1
Nichol Hutton	1
Christ Richardson	1
Richard Moore	4
Tho Cooke	1
Robt Burne	1
Tho Appleby	1
Tho Moore	1
Jno Richardson	1
Ann Richardson	1
Jno Clifton	1
Robert Moore	1
Geo Bosman	3
Francis Clifton	1

Jno Talbush	1	Ralph Davieson	2
	35	Will Foster	2
		Tho Wilson	2
Bishoppton		Nichol Emmerson	1
[Bishopton]		Tho Davieson	2
Tho Pearson	1	Will Chipchase	2
Will Soullby	1	Marmaduke Foster	2
Christ Jurdison	1	Tho Bell	1
Francis Heighington	1	Richard Cuthbert	1
Edward Scurfield	3	Jno Richardson	1
Tho Mawer	1	Alexdr Fawell	1
Tho Jackson	3	Stephen Merrington	2
Tho Welford	7	Robt Thompson	2
Jennett Cuming	2	Jno Jefferson	2
Richard Raw	1	Marmaduke Davieson	2
Jno Stephenson	2	Robert Wilson	1
Ralph Golds Brough	2	Rober Snawden	2
Tho Lax	1	Matt Teasdale	1
Eliza Mawer	2	Eliza Raw	1
Jno Middleton	2	Robt Wood	1
Jno Dobbin	1	Nichol Emmerson	1
Cuth Bird	1	Margrett Fuiller	1
Mary Welford	3		**34**
James Earle	3		
Tho Farrow	1		
Tho Reaw	1	**Cotham Mundevall**	
Tho Welford	1	**[Coatham Mundeville]**	
Jno Davison	2	Will Jackson Gent	4
Eliza Allison	1	Christ Teasdale	2
Tho Rutter	3	Robert Brewer	2
Jno Robinson	1	Simond Cooley	1
Tho Air	1	Will Blithman	3
Elizabeth Aire	1	Will Buckle	3
Jno Bulman	1	Richard Heighington	3
Jno Browne	1	Robert Bracke	3
Tho Rowntree	1	Antho Arrowsmith	1
Phillip Jackson	2	Richd Heighington	1
Will Craw	1	Jno Steadman	1
Jane Chilton	2	Tho Douthwaitt	3
Margrett Deanham	2	Jno Coats	1
Jno Stephenson	1		**28**
	61		
		m. 7, c. 1	
		Dindsdaile	
Carleton		**[Dinsdale]**	
[Carlton]		Rowland Place Esqr	8
Antho Elstobb	1	Ms Lazenby	3

Jno Peacocke	1
Jno Jnoson	1
Marmaduke Wetherall	3
Will Tates	2
Will Williamson	1
Gaskon Wilson	2
Robert Wastall	1
Rich Cosse	1
Geo Peacocke	1
Richard Peacocke	1
Will Medcalfe	1
	26

Elton

Tobias Mc Kendall	1
Will Jefferson	1
Will Scurry	2
Reonald Anderson	1
Christ Hodgson	1
Jno Taliorson	1
Matthew Thompson	2
Francis Sparke	1
Ralph Anderson	2
	12

Eggscliffe
[Egglescliffe]

Doctor Basier	7
Ralph Emmerson Gent	4
Henry Doughty Gent	2
Antho Wood	3
Will Wilkison	1
Jno Ingledew	2
Richard Nicholson	2
Tho Wilkison	1
Jno Allenson	2
Henry Bird	2
James Johnson	1
Richard Parkinson	1
Cuth Hodgson	1
Will Foster	1
Jno Baimbricke	1
Robert Baimbricke	1
Jno Nicolson	1
Francis Seamer	1
Mich Ingledew	2

Antho Todd	2
Tho Robinson	1
Bartho Hodgson	1
Will Anderson	1
Tho Anderson	2
Tho Preistwick	3
Francis Reed	1
Richard Coats	1
Michaell Ridley	1
Reonald Hodgson	1
Rowland Wilkison	1
Robert Swainston	2
Will Thewbatts Gent	2
Jno Taliorson	1
Jno Smith senr	2
Henry Todd	1
Jno Smith junr	1
Jno Dent	1
	61

Hurworth

Leonard Waistall	4
Rich Stockton	3
Mr Lister	5
Will Ward	2
Richard Dobbin	3
Jno Lattimer	1
Tho Walker	1
Robert Simpson	1
Charles Willis	3
Eliza Longstaffe	1
Mich Harrison	2
Christ Thompson	1
Matth Gaill	1
Mr Thompson	4
Jno Robison	1
Tho Elwood	1
Antho Middleton	1
Tho Middleton	1
Jno Mytton	1
Mrs Frances Burnett	4
Tho Bulman	3
Ambrose Gryseworth	3
	47

Harburne
[Hartburn]

Robert Rawling	2
Jno Midcalfe	1
Antho Harpley	2
Leonard Hoggart	1
Tho Grange	1
Robert Thompson	1
Eliza Fuiller	1
Will Midcalfe	1

m. 7, c.2

Robert Pears	1
Bridgett Medcalfe error	…
Robert Fuiler	3
Antho Fuiller	1
	15

Middleton on Row
[Middleton One Row]

James Askey Gent	5
Ralph Wilson	2
Rodger Wilson	2
Margrett Frear	1
Robert Marley	2
Jno Daile	1
Tho Cuningham	3
Robert Martin	2
Jno Smart	1
	19

Middleton St George

Will Killinghall Gent	10
Leonard Browne	2
Marmaduke Wetherall	4
Marmaduke Horseley	1
Jno Allinson	1
Geo Emmerson	1
Henry Wilkison	1
Will Wilkison	1
Robert Gates	2
Matt Vear Gent	2
Francis Foster	1
Jno Thompson	1
Christ Skarlett	1

Will Wetherall	1
	29

Norton

Mr Davison	7
Jno Mannell	3
Ralph Sharp	2
Tho Huntington	2
Tho Pepper	1
Francis Baimbricke	2
Simon Townsend	3
Jno Hudson	1
Tho Musgrave	1
Robt Swainstone	1
Margrett Green	3
Jno Blaixton	1
Jno Chipchase	2
Will Harrison	1
James Corner	2
Richard Adamson	1
Tho Chipchase	3
Bernard Jackson	3
Alis Pattison	3
Tho Wilson	2
Robt Davison	2
James Gattis	2
Valentine Blaixton	1
Will Berwicke	1
Tho Chipchase senr	2
Tho Chipchase junr	2
Peter Berwicke	1
Rodger Sharp	1
Tho Cattericke	2
Tho Thompson	1
Will Herring	1
Jno Foster	1
Tho Shepherd	1
Ellinor Donkin	3
Nicho Latkenby	1
Robt Blacke	1
Geo Swainston	1
Eliza Swaintone	1
James Wallace	1
Eliza Hodgson	1
James Gowland	2
Stephen Corner	1

Jno Chapman	3	Robt Andrew	2
Robert Wright	2	Wid Gaire	1
Tho Robinson	1	Jno Walton	3
Robert Davison	4	Richard Stephenson	2
Will Kitching	5	Jno Booth	3
Will Wheateley	2	Tho Aislaby	1
Tho Stockley	1	Robert Allan	2
Tho Thompson	1	Will Hope	1
Robert Chipchase	2	Tho Pyburne	2
Jno Halliman	1	Antho Stephenson	1
Mich Watson	1	Geo Crawfoord	1
Tho Jefferson	1	Martin Andrewes	2
Tho Smalwood	1	Jno Ramsay Gent	4
Will Chapman	1	Antho Pinkney	1
Richard Harrison	1	Henry Marre	1
Will Robson	1	Tho Lumbley	1
Robt Watson	2	Ambrose Creswood	1
Francis Kitching	3	Tho Peacocke	1
Ralph Row	1	Will Richardson	2
Jno Glover	1	Tho Blenkisopp	1
		Tho Claxson	2
m. 7, c. 3			42
Sr Thomas Davisonn	17		
James Medcalfe	1	**Long Newton**	
Jno Trainman	1	Sr Geo Vaine	7
Tho Hogge	1	Jno Oliver Gent	5
Ralph Richardson	1	Ralph Colling	2
Tho Huntington	1	Robert Thorp	2
Eliza Hodgson	1	Jno Fewler	2
	132	Margrett Colling	1
		Eliza Colling	1
		Jno Medcalfe	1
Newbiggins		Tho Robinson	2
[East & West Newbiggin]		Tho Moore	1
Mr Jno Woodhouse	2	Ralph Wilson	1
Jno Middleton	2	Robert Newlam	1
Tho Barker	1	Will Grainger	1
Cuth Beckfield	1	Jno Armstrong	1
Ralph Jefferson	1	Jno Moore	1
Ralph Jnoson	1	Edward Robinson	1
	8	Christ Hall gent	6
		Cuth Gibson	1
Neasham		Geo Talior	1
James Pinkney	1	Dorothy Roper	1
Richard Stephenson	2	Eliza Bishopwicke	1
Will Betson	1	Marmad Middleton	1
Ralph Walton	1		
Jno Stephenson	2		

Jno Whittfield	1	Ralph Wilson	1
Robert Peart	2	Tho Stephenson	1
Tho Thompson	1	Will Stephenson	1
	45	Christ Crossby	1
		Ann Swainston	2
Preston upon Tease		Geo Swainston	1
[Preston on Tees]		Tho Potter	1
Richard Story	1	Widd Calvert	2
James Sair	2	Will Bartram	1
Ralph Leafin	1	Michaell Watson	1
Tho Wilkinson	1	Jno Swainston	3
Ann Bowmer	1	Richard Harperley	2
	6	Will Tindale	1
		James Cooke Gent	5
Redmarshall		Tho Watson	1
Jno Jackson Gent	4	Jno Medcalfe	2
Mary Emmerson	1	Richard Gowland	1
Robert Stelling	2	Tho Sherrington	1
Martin Stell	1	Henry Baimbricke	1
Jno Graison	1	Will Jeckell	1
Robert Wrench	1	Peter Markham	1
Jno Stelling	1	Ralph Heron	1
	11	Solomon Crosseby	1
		Tho Fleatham	1
Stillington		Will Cuthbert	1
Christ Todd	8	Tho Heron	1
Richard Morpeth	2	Richard Story	1
Jno Robison	7	Mark Way	2
Will Baxter	1	Will Middeton	1
Mark Robison	1	Ralph Hall	1
Margrett Maltby	1	Tho Harpels	2
Jno Stubb	1	Jno Middleton	1
	21	Jno Lambert	4
			65
m. 7v, c. 1		[*corrected total*] es[?]	63
Stockton Towne			
[Stockton Town]		**Stockton Burrow**	
James Burdon	4	**[Stockton Borough]**	
Christ Fleathan	1	Mrs Alis Jenkins	3
Will Fewler	2	Tho Jessop	2
Robt Gibson	3	Will Power	1
Jane Chilton	1	Antho Coats	1
Bryan Baimbricke	1	Edward Fuiller	1
Jno Bunting senr	1	Robert Cockerill	1
Tho Atkinson	1	Jno May	1
Jno Bunting	1	Tho Merchant	1

Will Thompson	1	Jno Oisburne	1
Jno Mannard	1	Jno Baimbricke	1
Francis Carter	1	Ralph Bunting	1
Eliza Burdon	4		98
Eliza Fleatham	1		
Mr Jno Burden	4	**Little Stainton**	
Antho Fleatham	3	Robert Tatum	4
Jno Coats	1	Tho Newton	2
Robt Nicolson	1	Simon Hopper	1
Leonard Fewler	1	Ralph Allison	1
Tho Swainston	1	Jno Newton	1
Alis Harperley	2	Will Newton	1
Francis Fewler	1	Tho Stelling	2
Nichol Fleatham	2	Will Stobbs	1
Jno Wells Gent	6	Henry Jnoson	1
Robert Jackson Gent	5		14
Peter Swainston	1		
Christ Coats	1	**Sadbergh**	
Clement Anderson	1	**[Sadberge]**	
Mr Jno Atkinson	3	Jno Bradforth	2
Jno Thompson junr	1	Robert Kirton	1
Antho Wilsonne	1	Richard Mawer	2
Tho Hart	1	Richard Peacocke	2
Margrett Bailise	5	*Margrett Peacocke error*	…
Widd Welfoott	1	Jno Harrison	2
Wid Dale	3	Richard Middleton	1
Will Dent	1	Will Garry	1
Wid Thompson	2	Peter Welbankes	1
Will Heron	1	Francis Harrison	2
Mr Tho Watson senr	7	Matt Middleton	2
Jno Jeckell	2	Will Coolman	1
Jno Heron senr	1	Ralph Harrison	2
Robert Teasdale	1	Matt Middleton	2
Tho Swainston	4	Will Coolman	1
Tho Ward	1	Ralph Harrison	2
Zachar Heron	1	Tho Garmasey	2
Jno Heron junr	1	Jno Allen	1
Edward Woodmasse	2	Rich Awd	2
Will Jnoson	1	Richd Garmasey	2
Bryan Watson	1	Jno Cusson	2
Josias Ripley	2	Jno Carter	1
Cuth Fewler	1	Will Harrison	2
Tho Deenham	1	Geo Middleton	1
		Richard Garry	1
m. 7v, c. 2		Jno Coleman	1
Tho Steall	1	Francis Bucke Gent	5

Jno Addey	1	**Billingham**	
Jno Simpson	1	Jno Eden Gent	4
Robt Stainsby	1	Sam Bolton Gent	4
Henry Garth Gent	1	Simon Merriman	1
Michaell Walton	2	Will Kitching	2
Jno Kenney	1	*Jno Jeckell error*	...
Will Hardin	1	Tho Shepherd	1
Will Yarrow	1	Issabell Davison	1
	53		

Sockburne
[Sockburn]

m.7v, c.3

Will Collingwood Gent	8	Mary Davison	1
Tho Wyly	1	Eliza Jeckell	1
Matt Coopper	2	Margery Chapman	1
Geo Ovinton	1	*Geo Steare error*	...
Tho Martin	1	Will Mattison	2
	13	Jno Wairmouth	1
		Francis Deanham	1

Stockton Ward No East Division
[Stockton Ward North East
Division]

		Robert Shepherd	1
		Will Huntington	1
		Thom Chapman	1
Bradbury		Tho Ward	2
Jno Robinson	1	Michaell Burne	1
Mr Jno Farrer	2	Will Stobbart	1
Tho Stokeld	2	Ralph Wilkison	1
Robt Fawdwen	1	Rich Christopher	1
Robert Davison	1	Will Egglestone	1
Tho Sidgewicke	1	Jno Dunn	1
Tho Browne	1	Tho Gaills	1
Nichol Hilyard	1	Richard Rutledge	1
Robert Smith	1	Richard Chapman	2
Jno Hodgson	2	Robt Law	2
Mary Chapman	1	Will Thompson	1
	14	Jacob Mandwell	1
		Jno Dickinson	2
		Jno Page	1
		Gaskin Eden	1
Butterwicke		Jno Moore	1
[Butterwick]		Robert Pattinson	1
Will Butler Gent	8	Tho Ovinton	1
Ralph Butler Gent	3	Reenald Huntington	1
Jno Wilkison	1		**47**
Jno Wilkison	1		
Jno Rowlin	1	**Brearton**	
Humphrey Wilkison	2	**[Brierton]**	
	16	Tho Armstrong	1
		Antho Dunn	1
		Lawrence Thompson	1

Geo Crowl	1	Robert Walker	2
Robt Chilton senr	1	Robert Lawrence	2
Robt Chilton junr	1	Antho Burne	3
Ralph Chilton	1	Jno Pickering	1
	7	Michaell gent	1
		Will Huntington	1
Bishopp Middleham		Tho Yoole	2
[Bishop Middleham]		Jno Burne	1
Ralph Ward Gent	3	Matthew Garry	2
Will Parkins	1	Will Bushby	1
Peter Hutchison	2	Antho Law	2
Jno Stockton	2	Issabell Stephenson	1
Tho Kirkby	1	Jno Fletcher	1
Will Botchby	1	Christ Harrison	1
Jno Hutchison junr	3	Jno Walker	1
Francis Wood	1	Jno Hutchison	1
Jno Hutchison senr	1	Tho Liddell	1
Thomas Hymers	1	Tho Lamb	1
Will Moody	1	Jno Mason	1
Tho Bails	1	Tho Ward	1
Jno Brabbant Gent	2		35
Will Selby	1		
Jno Carre	1	*m. 8, c.1*	
Jno Hutchison	2	**Cornforth**	
Bartho Hutchison	1	Ann Hutchison	1
Cuth Hutchison	1	Richard Waugh	2
Jno Hutchison	1	Ralph Booth Gent	3
Henry Hutchison	1	Tho Hutchison	1
Robt Legg	1	Will Wood	2
Rich Wooddyfield	1	Henry Richardson	2
Ms Bedford	2	Tho Woodhouse	2
Mary Ward	1	Robert Colledge	2
Robert Lawes	2	Will Woodhouse	1
Will Lambert Gent	4	Susanna Woodhouse	2
Geo Weames	3	Wilfred Sewell	1
Mr Brabband	4	Jane Heron	1
Tobias Uswell	1	Jno Morland	1
	47	Robert Kearston	2
		Jno Woodhouse	1
Coopen Bewly		Jno Laing	1
[Cowpen Bewley]		Will Conyers	1
Jacob Dunn	1	Will Haswell	2
Jno Bowmer	1	Will Lasburne	3
Antho Haddocke	1	Will Smith	1
Richard Stoddart	2		32
Will Marshall	3		

Dalton Peircy
[Dalton Piercy]

Henry Barnes	5
Will & James Shearton	2
Jno Armstrong	1
Eliza Watson	1
Robert Watson	1
Tho Armstrong	1
Jno Boyes	1
Tho Boyes	1
Matt Corner	1
Robt Corner	1
James Jackson	4
Robt Chilton	1
	20

Embleton

Geo Oard	5
Jno Richardson	1
Robt Richardson	1
Tho Sander	1
Will Stobbart	3
Ralph Heard	1
An Walker	1
Jno Lister	1
Robert Robison	3
Ralph Dodgson	7
Jno Wardell	2
Jno Hickson	2
Jno Liddell	1
Tho Emmerson	1
Jno Hutchison	1
	31

Elwicke and Hall
[Elwick Hall]

Nichol Hall	3
Arch Deacon	5
Ms Alston	7
Will Thompson	1
Geo Lockey	1
Anthony Walton	1
Jno Jefferson	1
Jno Harrison	2
Will Darnton	1
Will Darnton	1

Robert Smith	1
Will Wardell	1
Tho Gibson	4
Will Ranson	1
Ninian Sherriton	1
Edward Parkin	1
Jno Jurdison	1
Wid Boyes	1
Wid Chilton	1
Jno Chilton	1
Geo Walton	1
Will Sherriton	1
	38

Foxton and Shotton

Mr Elstobb	5
Tho Story	1
Eliza Story	1
Geo Baxter	1
Robert Earle	1
Robert Buckle	1
Robert Smith	1
Will Lynn	1
Richard Lynn	2
Robert Lynn	1
	15

Fishburne
[Fishburn]

Francis Hunter	1
Nichol Farrow	4
John Gray	1
Edw Richardson	4
Will Barker	1

m. 8, c. 2

Christ Wardell	2
Jno Pannell	2
Will Mason senr	1
Robt Young	1
Will Widdyfield	2
Robt Wood	1
Will Mason junr	1
Tho Mothersell	1
Geo Atkison	1
Tho Reed	3

Geo Walton	1	Jno Watson	1
Tho Oard	1	Richard Oliver	1
Will Reed	2	Antho Armstrong	2
Francis Mason	3	Antho Dunn	1
Jno Horner	2	Bernard Dunn	2
Jno Shacklocke	1	Jno Gastell	1
Jno Schoolhouse	1	Tho Oliver	1
Antho Corner	2	James Craigs	2
	39	Edward Smurfield Gent	2
		Ann Reed	3
Greetham		Tho Armstrong	1
[Greatham]		Ralph Reed	1
Greatham Hospitall	13		**28**
Robert Jnoson	6		
Richard Errington	1	**Hartlepoole**	
Jno Elstobb	3	**[Hartlepool]**	
Widd Jurdison	1	Mr Hodgson	7
Richard Dunn	2	Mr Dobson	4
James Hall	1	Rich Wilsonn	4
Geo Johnson	1	Jame Martindale	1
Tho Hall	1	Jno Harrison	3
Francis Lowther	2	Richard Bell	3
Will Luckenby	1	Grace Parrett	7
Will Elstobb	1	Mr Marshall	3
Edward Sparke	1	Joseph Speding	2
Jno Smith	1	Jno Smith	3
Robt Elstobb	2	Tho Thompson	6
Will Wren	2	Ms Nicholson	3
Richard Clerke	3	Mr Shadforth	5
Alice Clerke	5	Robt Merriman	1
Patrick Drummond	2	Robert Routledge	3
Ralph Jnoson	2	Mr Lindsay	5
Robt Wilson	2	Wid Talior	1
Will Gibson	1	Will Allinson	1
Jno Dunn	1	Eliza Humble	2
	55	Nehemiah Martindaill	1
		Jno Humble	3
Hart Towne		Jno Davison	1
[Hart Town]		Richard Slater	2
Robert Brumley	1	Bernard Dunn	2
Jno Harrison	1	Jno Wells Gent	3
Robert Armstrong	1	Jno Claxton senr	2
Bartho Barker	1	Jno Millner	2
Will Jurdison	2	Bartho Pickton	2
Will Stratforth	2	Lowrence Hodgson	2
Will Mallam	2	Jno Sewell	4

Robert Humble	1

m. 8, c. 3

Rich Moore	2
Matt Davison	1
Widd Haisting	3
Rich Watt	1
Tho Robinson	2
Jno Merriman	1
Antho Reed	2
Jno Claxton	2
	103

Mordon

Rich Reed	3
Tho Conyers	1
Richard Watson	2
Tho Mawer	1
Will Watson	1
Mary Elstobb	1
Augustine Hickson	2
Richard Hilyard	1
Robert Ellison	1
Geo Smith	2
Tho Shootwell	2
Tho Steall	2
	19

Mansforth [Mainsforth]

Mr Hutton	5
Will Wreay	4
Cuth Harrington	1
Ralph Midcalfe	1
Geo Barnett	1
Jno Darnton	1
Antho Clerke	1
	14

Newton Bewly [Newton Bewley]

Michaell Jurdison	2
Issabell Merrington	1
Tho Harlend	1
Simond Chambers	2
Eliza Corker	1

James Carter	2
Robert Carter	3
Tobias Readhead	2
Jno Slater	1
Buly Grange	2
Nichol Hall	2
Marke Young	2
Will Emmerson	1
Tho Merrington	1
Jno Hewettson	1
Cuth Rawling	1
Jno Kell	2
Eliza Hubbecke	2
	29

Sedgefield

Joseph Nailor Gent	9
Robt Mason	3
Will Rickaby	1
Dorothy Barker	2
Tho Clement	1
Issabell Thompson	1
Jno Harrison	2
Tho Smith	3
Jno Ward	1
Will Walker	1
Marmaduke Chapman	1
Robert Browne	1
Richard Ray	1
Tho Sparke	1
Jno Gowre	3
Jno Reed	1
Jno Smith	3
Tho Wilkison	1
Will Thompson	1
Jane Rea	1
Ralph Smith	2
Lanc Richardson	2
Robt Chipchase	1
Jno Ward	2
Ann Routledge	3
Tho Sparke	1
Will Shotton	1
Henry Jnoson	1
Christ Readshaw	2
Jno Robison	1

Jno Lamb	1	Tho Bridge	1
Margrett Smith	1	Jno Thompson	1
Richard Wright	3	Robt Thompson	1
Ralph Thompson	1	Richard Cooling	1
Rich Hutchison	2	Will Cooling	1
Bartho Browne	1	Henry Cooling	1
Ralph Buckle	1	Nicho Frewell gent	14
Geo Smith	2	Sam Southgate	2
Jane Hodgson	1	Abraham Wright	1
Jno Hodgson	3	Alice Wilkison	1
Ralph Nicolson	2	Will Story	1
Geo Christon	1		**160**
Antho Allinson	2	[*corrected total*] es[?]	162
Hugh Parkinson	1		
Will Parkinson	1	**Great Stainton**	
Richard Gregson	1	Will Tunstall Gent	3
		Antho Dobbin	2
m. 8v, c. 1		Will Dobbin	1
Christ Dods	1	Will Newton	2
Will Browne	1	Jno Rickarby	4
Cuth Laburne	1	Will Norton	2
Will Browne	1	Tho Pearson gent	3
Will Green	1	Jno Wilkisonn	3
Jno Parkinson	1	Jno Marre	1
Tho Coltman	1	Will Scurfield Gent	7
Tho Middleton	2	Rich Jackson	3
Mr Farrow	6	Jno Jackson	2
Martin Hickson	1	Edward Wilson	1
Robert Jnoson Gent	5		**34**
Robert Moore	3		
Tho Oard	2	**Strainton**	
Ralph Oard	2	**[Stranton]**	
Tho Austin	2	Clem Fultherup Esqr	10
Robert Browne	3	Antho Dodsworth Gent	7
Robert Jnoson	1	Jno Smith Gent	2
Geo Straton	1	Richard Cooke	1
Ralph Smith	1	Antho Gibson	2
Robert Browne	1	Jno Richardson	1
Tho Warmouth	2	Antho Baills	1
Geo Gregson	3	Tho Thompson	1
Geo Davieson	1	Antho Merriman	1
Lyonell Ord	1	Will Gibson	5
Will Widdyfield	2	Nichol Close	1
Ralph Davison Gent	11	Will Merriman	1
Eliza Ward	1	Jno Errington	1
Jno Bridge	1	Jno Jackson	1

Ambrose Harrison	1
Antho Smith	1
Antho Widdison	1
Henry Thompson	1
Will Dodgson	2
Ann Harrison	1
Antho Wren	2
Robert Wood	1
Jno Busbey	1
Will Corker	1
Jno Jackson	1
	48

Seaton Carre
[Seaton Carew]

Will Bellasis Gent	7
Jno Dodgeworth	1
Christ Kearton	1
Will Wren	1
Jno Harrison	1
Francis Thompson	1
Richard Jnoson	2
Eliza Harrison	2
Tho Baills senr	1
Jno Baills	1
Tho Dodgworth	1
Robert Hutchinson	2
Geo Williamson	1

m. 8v, c. 2

Will Gowland	1
Robert Jnoson	1
Tho Baills junr	1
Nichol Bean	1
Jno Hall	1
Jno Dunn	1
Robt Jnoson	3
Will Jnoson	1
Will Jnoson	2
Antho Harrison	1
Geo Baills	1
Robt Jnoson	2
	38

Thorp Thewlis
[Thorpe Thewles]

Alexander Davison Gent	7
Antho Kendale Gent	2
Edw Urwing	2
Robt Haswell	1
Matt Nicholson	1
Jno Nicholson	1
Wid Wilson	1
Jno Lamb	1
Jno Ewbanke	1
Will Coughtman	1
Richard Greaveson	1
Michaell Ewbankes	1
Robt Conyers	1
Will Lamb	2
Marmaduke Davison	1
Francis Davison	2
Will Swainston	1
Richard Melsonby	1
Jno Chipchase	1
Matt Lockee	1
Wid Lamb	1
Geo Dixson	1
Jno Sidgewicke	1
Will Lamb	1
Rich Thompson	1
Will Golding	1
Robt Deanham	1
Mr Wallace	2
Bryan Todd	1
Nichol Wilson	1
Richard Cornforth	1
	42

Throston

Thomas Armstrong	1
Thomas Nicolson	1
Will Hett	1
Nichol Armstrong	1
Will Adamson	1
Jno Hett	1
Will Jurdison	1
Robert Smith	2
Robert Swallwell	1
Antho Watson	1

James Shearaton	2
Wid Armstrong	1
Will Merriman	1
Bartho Barker	1
Tho Hett	1
	17

Thrislington

Robt Shaw Gent	4
Eliza Shaw	2
	6

Whitton

Chris Kennett	3
Robt Chipchase	2
Mr Watson	3
Will Halliman	2
Jno Lynn	2
Mary Buckle	1
Ralph Cleeton	2
Ralph Maltby	1
	16

Woolvestone
[Wolviston]

Ralph Grange	2
Robt Richardson	2
Robt Moorey	1
James Smith	1
Will Jnoson	3
Gaskin Finch	2
Will Thompson	1
Widd Rawling	1
Tho Chilton	1
Geo Warmouth	1
Geo Trotter	1
Jno Mansforth	1
Jno Wild	1
James Rawling	1
Edw Davison	1
Wid Markham	1
Will Smith	3

m. 8v, c. 3

Will Halliman	3
Edw Chilton	2

Nichol Richardson	2
Geo Steare	1
Robt Lawson	2
Will Chipchase senr	1
Will Chipchase junr	1
Geo Davieson	1
Jno Thompson	1
Will Chipchase	1
Jno May	1
Geo Hickson	1
Will Huntington	1
Jno Boyes	1
Jno Witherof	1
John Shepherd	3
Hugh Finch	2
Jno Williamson	1
Gerrard Sidgewicke	2
Simon Thorp	3
	55

Easington Ward
South Division

Croxdale and Butterbye
[Croxdale and Butterby]

Jno Conyers Gent	10
Ralph Steall	1
Richard Mansforth	3
Rich Foster	1
Tho Todd Gent	2
Tho Dixson	4
Robt Bell	2
Jno Ingleby	2
Jno Hopper	2
Jno Wheetley	2
Geo Wilkisonn	2
Jno Cooke	1
Rich Bell	2
Will Gainsforth	1
Robt Dunn	4
Clement Farrow	11
Antho Salvin Gent	15
Edward Buttiman	1
Robert Suddicke	1

Lyonell Oard	2
	69

Cassop

Tho Howard	11
Mr Bullocke	10
Will Busby	3
Wid Busby	4
Ditto	3
Jno Davison	2
Antho Wilkison	2
Geo Reed	2
	37

Castle Eden

Will Todd Gent	4
Will Sigsworth	1
Geo Huntington	1
James Huntington	1
Jno Sparke	1
Rich Soulby senr	1
Tho Soulby	1
Will Arrowsmith	1
Jno Coats	1
Antho Watson	1
Tho Reedhead	1
	14

Easington

Sr Christopher Conyers	14
Robt Smith	1
Robt Paxton	1
Abraham Paxton	3
Will Jurdison	1
Jno Jurdison	1
Antho Wild	1
Christ Paxton	1
Rich Rawling	2
Mr Arch Deacon	6
Jno Iley	1
Dorothy Pattison	1
James Paxton	1
Wid Beere	1
Will Harrison	1
Cuth Henry	1
Tho Dawson	1

Geo Paxton	2
Geo Robison	2
Geo Wardall	1
Tho Robison	2
Ellinor Watson	2
Ralph Smith	1
Jno Cocke	1
Rich Rennison	1
Will Calvert	1
Robt Paxton	1
Henry Smith	2

m. 9, c. 1

Jno Harrison	1
Tho Paxton	1
Tho Nicholson	1
Geo Burdon	2
Geo Trewhatt	1
Wid Watson	1
Geo Jackson	2
Geo Hatherington	1
Mr Drover	1
Will Paxton	2
Tho Lowes	1
Mich Watson	1
Richard Jurdison	2
Christ Moody	1
Robert Paxton	1
Thomas Paxton	2
Tho Watson	1
Robert Appleby	1
	77

Haswell

Will Midford Gent	7
Jno Warmouth	1
Jno Hubbithorne	1
Jno Farbridge	1
Will Appleby	1
Mary Atkin	1
Jno Wolfe	1
Jno Heighley	1
Ralph Baxter	1
Jno Watson senr	1
Jno Watson junr	1
Edward Newby	1

Matt Cragsey	1	Jno Byars	1
Geo Talior	1	Geo Sparke	2
Will Talior	1	Nichol Byars	1
	21	Robt Emmerson	1
		Jno Sparke	2
Hawthorne		Jno Mair Gent	2
[Hawthorn]		Geo Craigs	1
Will Wright	1	Will Harrison	1
Robert Wright	2	Tho Byars	1
Tho Thompson	2	Jno Ovinton	1
Robert Sharpe	5	Tho Spaine	1
Rich Unthanke	1	Lance Potter	1
Antho Robinson	2	Tho Maior junr	1
Jno Jurdison	1		29
Will Ranison	1		
Geo Foster	1	**Kelloe**	
Michaell Robison	2	Jno Kennett Gent	14
Cuth Jurdison	1	Tho Lamb	2
Geo Robison	1	Will Arrowsmith	1
Tho Foster	1	Robt Ridley	2
Abraham Robison	1	Mr Pearson	6
Tho Liddell	1	Mr Foster	4
Will Hopper	1	Richard Arrowsmith	1
Jno Starne	1		
Geo Woofe	2	*m. 9, c. 2*	
Tho Robison senr	1	Will Sadler	1
Tho Robison junr	1	Rich Allan	1
Jno Dobson	1	Mr Atkinson	1
Robert Foster	1	Robt Atkinson	1
Rich Robinson	1	Christ Winter	1
Widd Foster	1	Jno Armstrong	1
Wid Robinson	1	Tho Ridley	1
Geo Wilson	1	Francis Tinmouth	1
	35	Jno Trollup Gent	7
		Jno Lawes	1
Hutton Henry		James Watson	1
Geo Moore	1	Edw Arrowsmith	1
Robt Potter	1	Robt Arrowsmith	1
Christ Smith	1	Robert Pearson	1
Tho Marley	2		50
Nichol Tweddell	1		
Tho Soulby	1	**Pittington**	
Nichol Easterby	1	Will Blaixton Gent	8
Jno Green	3	Christ Thompson Gent	4
Robt Moore	1	Christ Midfoord Gent	2
Christ Newby	1	Jno Foster	2

Jno Millner	1
Will Thompson	1
Robert Russell	2
Jno Hull	3
Tho Hotherley	7
Clem Watson	1
Tho Watson	1
Jno Watson	1
Ms Collingwood	6
Robt Haswell	1
Tho Caverley	1
Jno Younger	1
Matt Gargrave	1
Ralph Gargrave	1
	44

Sunderland Bridge

Lance Bowes Gent	6
Geo Biggings	2
Will Beaske	2
Eliza Browne	1
Will Farrow	1
Robert Roison	2
Nichol Crookes	2
	16

Shadforth

An Swallwell	1
Eliza Laikenby	3
Will Errington	2
Ralph Taton	4
Tho Whitfield	2
Bryan Younger	1
Antho Huntley	1
Will Huntley	1
Robert Jefferson	1
Will Errington	1
Wid Baley	1
Rich Errington	2
Robt Errington	1
Bartho Ingram	1
Ellinor Swalwell	2
Jno Swalwell	2
James Lister	1
Geo Swalwell	1

Jno Clerke	1
	29

**Shearburn and House
[Sherburn House]**

Jno Whitfield	1
Jno Whitfield junr	1
Jno Atkinson	3
Robt Cocke	1
Jno Gainford	1
Henry Cooke	2
Jane Pearson	1
Robt Rutter	2
Will Whitfield	2
Jane Lackenby	2
Will Hall	2
Will Davieson	1
Henry Westmorland	1
Jno Rowlin	2
Tho Rea	1
Jno White	1
Mich Pattison	1
Nichol Wyly	1
Barnes	3
Milne	1
Hospitall	8
James Hessop	1
	39

Shotton

Antho Byars	1
Edw Usher	1
Wid Thompson	2
James Reed	2
Lanc Horseley	1
Will Watson	1
Nichol Reed	2

m. 9, c. 3

Will Swallwell	1
Tho Hewson	1
Geo Jurdison	6
Jno Richardson	2
Robert Leighton	2
Will Appleby	2
Will Young	2

Phillip Richardson	1	Tho Paxton	1
Jno Errington	1	Bryan Starford	1
Ms Heath	3		19
Jno Humble	1		
Geo Blackett	1	**Thorp bulmer**	
Mr Dalivell	2	**[Thorpe Bulmer]**	
Richard Crooke	1	Will Howard Gent.	8
Geo Richardson	1	Christ Rawling	1
Geo Hatherington	1	George Atchison	…
Michaell Bryam	1	[*above entry crossed through*]	9
	39		
		Trimdon	
Hesledon		Margrett Lister	1
[Hesleden]		Tho Lodge	1
Jno Mair Gent	7	Bryan Weems	1
Jno Hodgson Gent	2	Robt Richardson	1
Tho Brownley	3	Margt Jackson	1
Jno Wilkison	2	Geo Hutchison	2
James Hall	2	Tho Weems	1
Tho Smith	1	Will Lister	1
Ralph Laine	1	Tho Harrison	1
Nichol Hall	2	Will Hutchison	1
Henry Atkinson	1	Ann Pearson	1
Richard Handman	1	Robert Brasse	1
Antho Tweddell	1	Robt Roper	5
Nichol Walker	2	Robt Pearson	1
Jno Watson	1	Jno Bacon	1
	26	Jno Shadforth	1
		Christ Stephenson	1
		Geo Wardell	2
Shearaton		Henry Airey	1
[Sheraton]		Jno Anderson	1
Geo Scurfield	1	Geo Woodroofe	1
Ralph Scurfield	2	Mr Warriner	2
Nichol Scurfield	1	Bryan Burleton	3
James Moore	1	Jno Brasse	1
Bryan Storford	1	Jno Stobbart	1
Mary Harford	1	Margrett Weemes	1
Robt Watson	1	Will Hardy	1
Richard Jobey	1	Will Hutchison	2
Guy Atkison	1	Will Jackson	1
Tho Wilson	1	Christ Coatham	1
Christ Smith	1	Nicho Roper	1
Will Lonesdale	1	Cuth Close	1
Francis Clerke	2	Bryan Keeper	1
Henry Green	1		43
Jno Pattison	1		

Wharrington
[Quarrington]

Henry Knaggs	1
Tho Lamb	2
Rich Darnton	1
Rich Darnton senr	1
Jno Knaggs	1
Ralph Wilkison	1
Jno Darnton	1
Bryan Ellinor	1
	9

m. 9v, c. 1

Windgate
[Wingate]

John Salvin Gent	5
Rich Hickson	1
Will Witherop	1
Jno Craiges	1
Jno Hickson	2
Geo Ovinton	1
Robt Sadler	1
Will Hall	1
Tho Bird	1
Peter Robison	1
Tho Harrison	1
Nichol Dodgson	1
Arthur Mowbran	1
Will Garfoot	1
Christ Smith	1
James Hall	1
Jno Elcott	1
Tho Waske	1
Tho Clerke	1
Phillip Mowbron	1
Jno Story	1
Amb Smith	1
Francis Smith	1
Geo Simpson	1
Ralph Bunting	1
Ralph Clerke	1
Will Wood	1
	32

Nesbett
[Nesbitt]

Robt Brumley	4
Will Wood	1
	5

Easington Ward
North Division

Burdon East and West
[East and West Burdon]

And Huntley	2
Tho Burdon	2
Robert Harison	1
Tho Blaixton	1
Mich Potts	1
Jno Wilkinson	1
Tho Huntley	2
Tho Johnson	2
Jno Blaixton	1
	13

Daelton
[Dalton]

Tho Sharp Gent		3
Geo Dale		4
Edward Dale		3
Tho Todd		2
Robert Fell		2
Edw Robison		2
		15
[*corrected total*]	es[?]	16

Dawden
[Dawdon]

Mr Collison	17
Jno Jnoson	1
Geo Jnoson	2
Jno Hornsby	1
Nichol Story	1
Robert Liddell senr	1
Robert Liddell junr	1
Geo Liddell	1
	25

Eppleton

Tho Shadforth Gent	13
Ditto more	3
Ralph Hall	2
Geo Ray	1
Marke Foster	1
Rich Reed	1
	21

Houghton in ye Spring
[Houghton-le-Spring]

Robt Chilton	3
Antho Watson Gent	1
Geo Wilson	1
Tho Walton	1
Tho Cooper	1
Nichol Ticer	1
Robt Dobson	2
Tho Chilton	1
Tho Browne	1
Ann Lampton	2
Percivall Backhouse	2
Will Backhouse	1
Tho Jnoson	1
Robt Rutter	3
Jno Wild	1
Francis Mason	2
Will Riddell	1
Geo Cant Gent	3
Jno Hope	2
Robert Wild	3
Ann Cooke	1
Robt Hutton Gent	15
Geo Palmer	2
Robt Ranson	2
Tho Burton	1
Margrett Watson	1
Jno Lampton	[-]

m. 9v, c. 2

Jno Lampton	3
Bartho Smith	1
Edward Lamb	1
Jno Byars	1
Margery Dobson	1
Jno Stokeld	1

Anthony Young	1
Will Ironside	2
Parsonage	15
Ralph Hall	1
Henry Williamson	2
	84

Hetton
[Hetton-le-Hole]

Tho Robison	1
Tho Hope	1
Mich Jnoson	2
Jno Tunstall	2
Mich Foster	1
Hetton Hall	10
Jno Foster	1
Rich Appleby	1
Antho Watson	1
Jno Welsh	2
Will Welsh	2
Tho Watson	1
Will Faulthorp	1
Mich Leavers	1
Jno Grinwell	4
Will Judgson	2
Jno Gargrave	1
Geo Stewart	2
Rich Fetherstone	1
Will Crow	2
Will Parkin	1
Widd Fetherley	1
Will Hope	1
Geo Wright	1
Will Foster	1
	44

Cold Hesledon

Tho Sharp	4
Jno Foster	1
Geo Wilson	1
Jno Foster	1
Geo Robison	1
Rodger Stedman	1
Geo Talior	1
Robt Shadforth	1
Jno Parkin	1

Jno Marshall	1
Tho Foster	4
	17

Herrington East and Middle
[East and Middle Herrington]

Ralph Robison	3
Henry Paidge	1
Rich Burrett	2
Will Punshen	1
Robert Talior	2
Robert Gibson	1
Jno Fetherstone	1
Francis Coupland	1
Rich Bucke	2
Jno Twentyman	2
Tho Nicholson	2
Will Watson	2
Robert Wilkison	2
Cuth Guy	2
Francis Morgan	1
Tho Kay	1
Tho Smith	2
Henry Fetherstone	2
Jno Swinburne	1
Stephen Haddocke	1
	32

West Herrington

Jno Shadforth Gent	5
Jno Smith Gent	5
Robt Alton Gent	7
Jno Richardson Gent	6
Tho Cooke	1
Jno Smith	1
Henry Lister	1
Tho Paxton	1
Geo Smith	1
Tho Cocke	2
Will Browne	1
Tho Colledge	3
Jno Cragge	1
Robt Leath	1
Jno Holliday	1
Will Lilburne	1
Joseph Willeby	1

Tho Robson	1
	40

Lumbley and Lampton
[Lumley and Lambton]

Will Wilson Gent	4
Jno Jackson	3
Tho Foster	2
Ann Todd	2
Geo Maddison	2
Tho Alison	3

m. 9v, c. 3

Jno Houtt	2
Mr Henry Lampton	8
Tho Rutter	3
Will Hodgson	2
Will Mattison	3
Robt Hall	2
Ralph Wilson Gent	32
Robt Thompson	2
Ralph Gray	3
Jno Brignell Gent	7
Will Potter	3
Jno Easterby	1
Rich Todd	1
Jno Welsh	1
Tho Howgall	1
Jno Liddell	2
Jno Stephenson	2
Tho Atkison	2
Christ Wolfe	1
Tho Liddell	2
Tho Hudson	1
Geo Nicholson	2
Will Hutchison	1
Will Wilson Gent	4
Jno Slackley	1
Ralph Gibson	1
Will Gibson	1
Rich Thompson	2
Will Clerke	3
Robert Clerke	2
Robt Sander	1
Will Stephenson	2
Mr Bristow	8

Tho Hall	4
Geo Hall	4
Robt Hall	2
Mr Lumbley senr	6
Mr Lumbley junr	5
Richard Clerke	1
Ralph Lowson	3
Peter Clerke	1
Tho Skoror	2
Wid Hugall	4
Wid Baimbricke	1
Robert Hodgson	1
Bryan Welsh	1
Jno Robison	2
Rob Clerke	6
Mr John Attan	11
Tho Coxsell	2
Ralph Carre	2
Ruster Pelidath	1
Robt Coxson	1
Rich Welsh	1
Jno Gowland	2
Jno Robison	1
Edmond Talior	1
Jno Renyson	1
Ussaly Wranghand	1
Jno Pilkington	1
Richard Crofton	1
Jno Sander	2
Will Thompson	4
Tho Fetherley	1
	201

Moorsley

Jno Mitchison	2
Will Mitchison	2
Rich Robison	2
Jno Newby	2
Jno Talior	1
Margrett Humble	1
Gilbert Clifton	1
Jno Moffatt	1
Jno Fruid	1
Mary Hind	1
	14

Murton East
[East Murton]

Jno Gregson	1
Edward Shepherdson	3
Tho Gregson	2
Will Shacklocke	1
Matt Robinson	3
Robert Johnson	1
Tho Young	2
Geo Robison	1
Bryan Younger	1
Jno Newby	1
	16

Newbottle

Robt Stephenson	3
Will Chilton	1
Mich Watson	2
Will Ranson	2
Wid Smith	1
James Watson	1
Edw Collier	2
Geo Watson	4
Will Wilson	2
Wid Matthew	1
Robt Chilton	2
Geo Chilton	2
Will Waster	1
Antho Ranison	1

m. 10, c. 1

Geo Wilsonn	2
Issabell Shaw	1
Widd Byars	1
Robt Chilton	1
Will Surrett	1
Will Thompson	1
Will Ray	1
Wid Blaclocke	1
Edw Charter	1
Tho Foster	1
Robert Ushar	1
Jno Turner	1
Geo Glendale	1
Widd Hall	1
Widd Dent	1

Robt Mason	1	Will Walton	2
Widd Ellett	1	Will Browne	2
	43	Mr Ingleby	5
		Jno Hewson	4
Pensher			**57**
[Penshaw]			
Robt Lampton Gent	15		
Mr Hamcoats	4	**East Rainton**	
Will Bowes Gent	6	Ralph Smith	1
Edward Myles	4	Will Chilton	1
Jno Hutson	1	Ellinor Brough	1
Geo Walker	2	Will Adamson	2
James Green	1	Christ Pearson	1
Will Washer	1	Margrett Brough	2
Henry Washer	1	Jno Botchaby	1
Will Ranson	1	Margrett Wheatley	1
Jno Hall	1	Robt Chilton	1
Tho Collyer	3	Tho Wilkison	1
John Smith	1	Avery Robison	2
Jno Richardson	2	Jno Cooper	2
Robt Guy	1	Phillip Brough	3
Matt Bird	1	Ralph Wilkison	1
Tho Day	1	Grace Foster	1
James Lester	1	Jno Brough	2
	47		**23**

West Rainton		**Ryhope**	
Mollison	6	Geo Raxby	2
Ralph Smith	2	Geo Fell	1
Will Adamson	2	Ralph Thompson	1
Jno Lampton	2	Rich Thompson	1
Jno Welsh junr	1	Jno Robinson	1
Ralph Younger	1	Robt Thompson	1
Robt Cooke	2	Jno Fell	2
Geo Harrison	1	Nichol Thompson	1
Matt Harrison	1	Tho Todd junr	2
Will Ogle	3	Tho Todd senr	1
Tho Bailey	2	Geo Thompson	1
Will Widdowes	2	Wid Thompson	1
Christ Orton	2		
Jno Paige	2	*m. 10, c. 2*	
Jno Welsh senr	3	Geo Holmes	1
Ralph Pendworth	2	Rich Coats	1
Antho Burden	1	Rich Thompson junr	2
Robt Coltman	1	Geo Fell junr	2
Geo Mann	1	Richard Leighton	3
Ralph Carre Gent	7		

Ralph Goodchild	1
	25

Seaham

Henry Dobbins	4
Robt Collingwood	4
Tho Martin	2
Jno Morgan	1
Widd Marshall	1
Geo Fell	1
Tho Harrison	1
Tho Todd	1
Will Smith	1
John Hatherington	2
Geo Robison	1
Geo Foster	1
Will Browne	1
	21

Seaton

Tho Middleton	1
Jno Wilson	2
Robt Fell	1
Richard Martin	1
Jno Atkinson	3
Jno Smith	1
An Murton	2
Ann Goodchild	1
Will Robison	3
Jno Sharp	1
Robt Ranison	1
Tho Wilsonne	1
John [*blank*]	[-]
	18

Sunderland p[er] Sea
[Sunderland]

Will Jennison	1
Jno Farrow	2
Geo Paxton	2
Wid Browne	2
Jno Hodgson	4
Jno Hickson	2
Rich Ireland	4
Isaac Dobson	1
Geo Lilburne Gent	9

Sam Marshall	2
Rich Cash	1
Ann Wilson	2
Stephen Carter	2
Rich Palmer	2
Richard Spencer	3
Will Potts	3
Wid Wardell	3
Wid Nicolson	3
Jno Sanderson	2
Rich Browne	1
Antho Fetherstone	1
Tho Baxter	2
Will Stewart	2
Jno Ridley	4
Matt Humble	4
Wid Cracknell	5
Geo Snawden	3
Widd Green	1
Tho Bond	2
Rich Anderson	5
Humphrey Howell	3
Jno Marley	2
Jno Donnell	1
Gawen Reed	2
Nichol Rigdon	2
Alexr Atkinson	1
Francis Hall	4
Robt Hickson	5
Edward Dossey	3
Geo Burton	1
Edw Beares	1
Edward Hinkes	2
Stephen Harlend	4
Barbell Burrie	2
Will Fawcett Gent	8
Robt Shearburne	3
Jno Lettony senr	2
Robt Bartram	2
Wid Watt	1
Rich Norton	2
Will Heppell	3
Charles Thompson	3
Will Crookes Gent	6
Tho Laissey	4
Will Coulson	4

Richard Hodgson	2
Tho Grundy	2
Nichol Tinmouth	2
Walter Ettricke Gent	8
Will Wilson	4

m. 10, c. 3

Alexr Humble	4
Nichol Thompson	2
Wid Robison	3
Robt Young	3
Robt Young junr	2
Geo Talior	5
Wid Myers	1
Robt Halliday	2
Jno Dreeton	2
Will Moore	3
Jno Little	2
Nichol Lax	3
Robt Chipchase	2
Wid Atkinson	3
Henry Hull	3
Jno Wilkison	3
Wid Potts	1
James Hodgson	4
Stephen Houlder	1
Jno Littleforth	3
Rich Curtis	3
Sam Nicholson	6
Geo Liddell	1
Robt Hall	1
Henry Bavington	2
Tho Coall	2
Edw Lee	3
Wid Thompson	3
Will Aggar	3
Robt Nicholson	4
Tho Newby	2
William Wharton	2
Henry Douthwaitt	5
Richard Wilson	4
Richard Robinson	1
Isaack Cockerill	3
Will Dickinson	2
Jno Cockerill	3
Robt Goodchild	1

Jno Lettony junr	3
Simond Bracke	1
Robt Pease	1
Jno Glover	1
Widd Clerke	1
Wid Martindaill	2
Wid Story	2
Ralph Elstobb	1
Will Cadwell Gent	4
Richard Barton	2
Lyell Hall	2
Matt Delavall	4
Wid Reed	2
Sam Hodgkins	2
Kendall Sidgewicke	4
Jno Groves	4
	308

Silksworth

Mr Middleton	5
Tho Nicolson	1
Cuth Maltby	1
Will Watson	2
Robt Robson	1
Ralph Marley	4
Will Lazenby	1
Geo Scott	1
Mr Pepper	5
Robt Gent	2
Christ Lazenby	2
	25

Tunstall

Ms Mary Shadforth	7
Antho Smith	3
Antho Air	2
Tho Air	2
	14

Bishoppwearmouth [Bishopwearmouth]

Mr Haddocke	5
Antho Reed	2
Will Miller	3
Jno Gervice	1
Jno Reed	2

Tho Bulmer	1	Will Wanles	1
Mr Holliman	8	Will Ellinor	2
Edw Henderson	1	Jno Talior	1
Jno Coopland	1	James Talior	1
Jno Goodchild	2	Will Browne	2
Tho Story	2	Jno Counden	1
Arthur Amery	1	James Coupland	1
Gerrard Potts	2	Geo Snawden	1
Jno Mills	2	Jno Ratcliffe	1
Rich Wood	1	Edw Snowden	1
Ms Grinwell	2	Robt Gray	1
Tho Atkinson	1	Rich Browne	1
Jno Oard	2	Tho Smith	1
Jno Shepherdson	4	Wid Robison	1
James Bilton	2	Geo Crozier	5
Will Thompson	1	Doctor Gray	9
Wid Chapman	1	Henry Foster	1
		Ralph Watson	2
m. 10v, c. 1		Jno Watson	3
Wid Gilroy	1	Wid Walkin	2
Mich Robison	2	Ralph Wilkison	1
Tho Story	1	Rich Arnold	1
Geo Hall	1	Tho Jnoson	1
Robert Read	1	Robert Oliver	2
Robt Fenwicke	1	James Foster	1
Andrew Gibson	1	Rich Gibson	1
Robt Thompson	1	Nichol Middleton	1
Jno Moiser	1	Widd Hilton	1
Tho Air	3	Christ Pattinson	1
David White	1	George Browne	1
Jno Allinby	1	Adam Blaixton	1
Edw Allinby	1	Robt Pattison	2
Tho Mason	1	Edw Robison	1
Will Snowden	2	Tho Chambers	1
Jno Ellinor	1	Jno Little	1
Jno Jnoson	3	Nichol Bryan	3
Rich Jnoson	1	Mr Lilburne	2
Jno Arnold	1	Robert Chilton	1
Will Chambers	1	Tho Minnikin	1
Ralph Hodgson	1	Cuth Talior	1
Wid Talior	1	Eliza Watson	2
James Atkinson	1	Jno Rose	1
Dorothy Teasdale	1	Rich Watson	1
Will Wilson	2	Ambrose Musgrave	1
Cuth Potts	1	Will Watkins	1
Cuth Atkew	1	Tho Mattison	1

Jane Browne	1	Geo Dobson	1
Rich Rose	1	Matthew Harecke	1
Will Watson	1	Stephen Harecke	1
Tho Anderson	1	Thomas Thompson	1
Widd Lawson	1	Tho Oliver	1
Robt Kirton	1	Tho Henderson	1
Marmaduke Smith	1	Tho Bonner	1
Will Talior	1	Jno Hutchinson	1
Henry Dixson	1	Oliver Bird	1
Will Smith	1	Geo Robson	1
Tho Hutchison	1	Geo Waithman	1
Tho Martin	2	Will Chilton	1
Richard Criswell	1	Tho Snawden	2
Ann Goodchild	1	Robert Browne	1
	166	Geo Raison	1
		Jno Moskins	1
Bishoppwearmouth Panns		Jno Cooke	1
[Bishopwearmouth Panns]		Tho Anderson	1
Geo Liddell	1	Tho Crozer	1
Robt Thompson	4	Tho Stewart	1
Robt Nicholson	2	Robert Stamp	1
Tho Laicy	4	Jno Cooke	1
		Cuth Turner	2
m. 10v, c. 2		Bryan Virtus	1
Will Aggarson	2	Richard Thompson	1
Tho Thompson	1		**38**
Jame Bentley	2		
Will Scurfield	5		
Theod Talior	1	**Chester Ward**	
Jno Menom	1	**West Division**	
Ralph Clerke	6		
Mrs Parker	6	**Butsfield**	
Will Thompson	2	Josias Dockray Gent	3
Edw Burdon	1	Will Darnell	2
Tho Harrison	2	Tho Greenwell	2
Geo Harison	9	Will Talior	2
Will Henderson	1	Will Lamesley	1
Alexr Rosse	1	Tho Rippon	2
Francis Hodgson	1	Jno Hopper	2
Jno Robinson	1	Jno Lindsay	1
	53	Will Greenwell	2
		Rowland Wilkison	2
Ufferton		Wid Greenwell	3
[Offerton]		Jno Bemond	1
Geo Lilburne Gent	6	Jno Hall	1
Francis Middleton Gent	5	Jno Hall	1

Jno Hickson	1
Will Darnell	2
Will Rippon	2
Tho Winter	2
Jno Tiplady	1
Henry Sewell	2
Robt Ramshaw	1
Jno Greenwell	1
Alice Greenwell	3
	40

Burnopp and Hamsteels
[Burnhope and Hamsteels]

Robert Stringer	2
Jno Reonaldson	1
Will Hind	1
Tho Bracke	4
Tho Reonaldson	1
Tho Pickering	1
Will Robson	3
Michaell Thompson	3
Jno Gallely	2
Widd Rippon	1
Tho Atkison senr	1

m. 10v, c. 3

Jno Talior	1
Tho Atkison junr	1
Nichol Pickering	1
Jno Pickering	1
Robt Greenwell	1
Cuth Burnop	3
Widd Midcalfe	3
Henry Cattricke	1
	32

Benfieldside

Widd Smith	4
Will Major	1
Wid Smith	2
Robert Jnoson	2
Jno Hunter	2
Clem Waugh	2
Nichol Cuming	1
Jno Beckworth	3
Cuth Beckworth	3
Cuth Hopper	2

Jno Blenkishopp	1
Rowland Pallister	1
Francis Lumbley	1
Francis Barkas	1
Robert Nicolson	1
	27

Crawcrooke
[Crawcrook]

Sr Francis Anderson	7
Robert Sanders	1
Roger Coupland	1
Geo Wetherop	1
Robert Fenwicke	1
Robert Hutton	1
Will Anby	1
Jno Greenway	1
Nichol Greenway	1
Wid Pickering	1
Wid Esterham	1
Will Welsh	4
Will Lainson	3
Tho Rackstraw	4
Nichol Robinson	2
Richard Hay	2
Christ Thompson	1
Christ Lamericke	1
	34

Choppwell Lordshippe
[Chopwell]

Robt Clavering Gent	11
Will Durrance	1
Tho Hopper	1
Robt Procter	3
Edw Barker	1
Jno Stephenson	2
Tho Layburne	1
Robt Foster	1
Jno Stephenson	1
Issabell Sureties	1
Antho Stephenson	1
Jno March	2
Robt Blaixton	1
Robt Suretyes	1
Margrett Jopling	1

Will Emmerson	3
Jno Harrison	1
Geo Hedley	2
Jno Sureties	1
Peter Lumbley	1
Tho Stephenson	1
Tho Atty	1
	39

Conside
[Consett]

Jno Blenkishipp	1
Geo Raw	2
Robt Blenkishipp	1
Jno Talior	1
Jno Rippon	2
Ms Jane Burnopp	3
Will Hubbecke	1
Andrew Jopling	1
Robert Wheatley	1
Charles Rippon	2
Jno Readshaw	2
Stephen Raw	1
Thomas Hopper	1
	19

m. 11, c. 1

Cornsaw
[Cornsay]

Margrett Rippon	3
Eliza Hilyard	1
Tho Talior	3
Jno Talior	1
Geo Rippon	1
Jane Greenwell	1
Jno Denning	2
Tho Kirkley	1
Geo Byerley	2
Richard Greenwell	1
Matthew Byerley	1
Ralph Walton	1
Tho Rippon	2
Jno Talior	1
Tho Darwell	2
Will Rippon	2
Jno Arrowsmith	2

Jno Stovehouse	4
	31

Esh

Sr Edward Smith	22
Robt Jopling	1
Francis Ifley	1
Jno Smith senr	2
Jno Smith junr	2
Robert Coming	2
Jno Gaire	1
Lawrence Young	2
Ann Brasse	3
Tho Jackson	5
Ellinor Palmer	1
Will Bryan	1
Lyonell Aire	2
Tho Johnson	1
Jno Woodmasse	2
Andrew Baxter	1
Joseph Collinson	1
Jno Aire	2
Nichol Talior	1
Tho Pinkney	1
Jno Foster	1
Ann Barttmanson	1
Jno Robson	1
	57

Ebchester

Matt Wrightson	2
Antho Jopling	3
Antho Fewster	2
Jno Jnoson	2
Matt Proctor	1
Antho Fewster	2
Cuth Atkison	1
Ralph Fewster	2
Antho Sureties	1
Jno Harrison	1
Jonathan Jewell	1
Christ Readshaw	2
Tho Readshaw	1
Wid Readshaw	1
Nichol Garthwaitt	2
	24

Edmondbyers

Jno Dury	1
Geo Readshaw	1
Robt Dridon	1
Alexr Read	1
Jno Greenwell	1
Jno Whitfield	1
Jno Lumbley	2
Clemt Parker	1
Jno Oliver	1
Humphrey Hopper	1
Ralph Hay	1
Cuth Snawball	1
Tho Lumbley	1
	14

Greencroft

Will Hall Gent	5
Jno Plumpton	4
Mary Greenwell	3
Ralph Milburne	2
Jno Jordan	2
Will Atkinson	4
Jno Kirkley	1
Tho Darnell	1
Geo Carre	3

m. 11, c. 2

Jno Raw	2
Jno & Will Grenwell	2
	29

Hunstonworth
[Hunstanworth]

Richard Thorp	3
Robert Eggleson	1
Mich Eggleston	1
Lance Egglestone	1
Will Marley	1
Margrett Dixson	1
Alexr Egglestone	1
Tho Wilkison	1
Issabell Jenning	1
Issabell Dixson	1
Nichol Wilkison	1
Geo Oard	1

Robert Hopper	1
Matt Eggleston	1
Robert Whitfield	1
Jno Snowball	1
Jno Whitfield	1
Jno Snowball	1
Jno Dixson	1
Rich Snowball	1
Robert Dixson	1
Tho Ward	1
Mr Forrest	1
Jane Proud	1
	26

Ivestone
[Iveston]

Geo Barker Esqr	6
Jane Hutchison	2
Geo Hopper	1
Rich Cradge	1
Eliz Mason	1
Will Hopper	1
Tho Burnopp	2
Ralph Foster	1
Antho Tailor	1
Tho Mason	1
Nich Burlison	1
Robt Wheatley	1
Tho Brantingham	1
Jno Hopper	1
Tho Mason junr	1
	22

Kimlesworth
[Kimblesworth]

Tho Harrison	3
Edw Harrison	1
Ralph Harrison	1
	5

Kyo

Tho Morley	5
Matt Grange	4
Lawrence Wilkison	4
Will Lawes	2
Jane Walker	1

Alexr Lampton	2
Jno Wheatley	1
Lyonell Carre	2
Robt Laing	1
Will Flother	1
Tho Darnell	2
Jno Smith	1
Widd Lawes	2
Wid Smith	1
Tho Sumrbell	1
Tho Maughan	1
Wid Ferry	1
Will Story	1
Jno Hutchison	1
	34

Langley Lordshipp
[Langley]

Edward Jackson	2
Lanc Jackson	2
Will Jopling	1
Jno Jopling	1
Jane Shawes	1
Will Jopling	1
Cuth Johnson	1
Jno Baxter	1
Mich Sheraton	1
James Cleaton	1
Issabell Talior	1
David Dunce	1
Will Midcalfe	1
Jno Galliley	2
	17

m. 11, c. 3

Lanchester

Tho Kirkby	3
Jno Foster	1
Cuth Dewfoot	4
Robt Grindon	1
Tho Smurfoot	2
Robt Kirkley	2
Jane Smurfoot	1
Richard Jopling	1
Jno Hilly	1
Will Ironside	1

Jno Wilkison junr	1
Jno Wilkison senr	1
Will Atkison	2
Ralph Browne	1
Will Jordan	1
Tho Atkison	1
Tho Whitfield	1
Geo Ditchburne	1
Geo Talior	2
Jno Hall	1
Jno Sanderson	2
Robert Lindsey	2
Jno Hornsby	3
Thomas Stokes	1
Henry Hornsby	1
Geo Hornsby	3
Edward Blackett	2
Ruth Ward	1
Geo Smith	1
Robert Carruthers	1
Geo Wheatley	3
James Foster	1
Whitehouse	2
Deanry	3
Lanchester Mill	5
Copighill	5
	65

Mugglesworth
[Muggleswick]

Nicho Layburne	1
Nichol Bowrley	2
Jno Readshaw	2
Cuth Richardson	1
Christ Atkison	2
James Layburne	1
Wid Redshaw	2
Tho Newton	1
Jno Harrison	1
Jno Jobling	2
Rowland Harrison	1
Jno Raw	1
Jno Atkison	2
Robert Merriman	1
Nichol Atkinson	1
Jno Hall	1

Edward Hopper	1
Jno Hopper	1
Rowland Harrison	2
Alice Ward	2
Wid March	1
Geo Oliver	1
Jno Dridon	1
Tho March	1
Jno Ward	1
Jno Bowrley	1
Nichol Harrison	1
Tho Hopper	2
Mr Dury	2
Jno March	2
Tho Lonesdale	1
Edward Ward	2
Margt Jopling	1
Will Wilkison	1
	46

Meddomsley
[Medomsley]

Tho Hunter	5
Will Hunter	1
Cuth Hunter	1
Tho Hunter	1
Richard Ramshaw	1
Eliza Hunter	1
Jane Bowmer	1
Jno Hopper	1
Cuth Hunter	2
Martin Ramshaw	2
Robert Hunter	1
Jno Hunter	2
Henry Walton	2
Sr John Swinburne	3
Will Hudson	1
Michael Cuming	1
Edw Layburne	2
Abrose Stephenson	4

m. 11v, c. 1

Geo Sureties	2
Richard Gally	1
Will Stephenson	1
Antho Armstrong	1

Mich Wilkison	1
	38

Roughley & Roughside
[Rowley & Roughside]

Robert Whitfield	1
Christ Oard	2
Wid Ward	2
Jno Sumerson	1
Geo Heads	1
Jno Maddison	2
Nichol Kirkley	1
Tho Emmerson	1
Thomas Row	2
Charles Rippon	2
Robt Readshaw	2
Robt Blenkisop	1
Cuth Palliser	2
Rowland Kirkley	2
Tho Readshaw	2
Jno Pallister	1
Wid Hedley	1
	26

Rytton
[Ryton]

Ralph Blaixton Gent	8
Mark Sanders	2
Jno Humble	1
Will Jolly	2
Hugh Calker	1
Robt Sureties	3
Jane Walker	1
Will Hutton	1
Jane Newton	2
Jno Stokoe junr	1
Robt Sander	1
Jno Hauxby	2
Mich Best	2
Nich Newton	2
Robert Stocton	1
Will Best	1
Will French	2
Jno Stokoe senr	3
Alice Coulson	1
Allice Jolly	2

Cuth Walker	1
Tho Jolley	3
	43

Ryton Woodside

Sr Thomas Tempest	22
Robt Addy	3
Susanna Rain	1
Tho Hodgson	2
Mr Francis Hedworth	4
Mr Will Hedworth	2
Henry Foster	1
Will Pattison	1
Tho Fieldhouse	1
Will Colling	2
Will Horsley	2
Robt Autumne	3
Richard Lumbley	1
Cuth Gray	2
Alice Waugh	3
Wid Anderson	1
Will Bood	1
Robt Carter	2
Jno Wilson	2
Henry Liddell	1
Robt Fenwicke Gent	1
Tho Humble	1
Will French	1
Geo Onley	1
Jno Pratt	2
Jno Walker	2
Edw Cuthbertson	2
Nicho Foster	1
Rich Robinson	1
Jno Newby	3
Jno Pearson	2
	74

m. 11v, c. 2

Swallwell
[Swalwell]

William Lonesdaill	2
Thomas Simpson	2
Geo Hebbron	1
Will Lawson	1
Christ Walton	2

Geo Lamesley	1
Tho Lonesdale	2
Robert Parkin	2
Will Mallaburne	1
Geo Pescod	3
Wid Jobling	1
Ralph Simpson	2
Jno Armstrong	1
Tho Robinson	1
Jno Dobson	1
Jno Gaill	2
Will Lonesdale	2
Geo Grainge	1
Jno Blackett	1
Tho Richardson	2
Peter Armstrong	1
Sr James Clavering	4
Jno Bawniley	2
Geo Lumbley	1
	39

Witton Gilbert

Will Sheele	1
Mich Talior	1
Robt Myres	2
Tho Fairbarnes	3
Jno Pallister	2
Will French	1
Mr Hobson	7
Rodger Thornton	1
Tho Wheatley	1
Will Dorman	1
William Hance	1
Geo Nicholson	4
Geo Owley	3
Nichol Birlaw	3
Will Talior	2
Jno Browne	1
Henry Mallam	1
Mr Dunkop	5
Tho Hodgson	2
Stephen Talior	1
Jno Day	1
Wid Talior	2
Geo Walton	2
Jno Mason	1

Mr Hutton	2
Robt Watson	1
James Mickleton	2
Nichol Talior	1
Jno Sneith	3
Jno Rainton	2
Gerrard Clerke	1
Wid Clerke	1
Edm Stoddart	1
Cuth Pallister	1
Henry Moore	1
Will Wrangham	1
Will Talior	1
Lance Harrison	2
Henry Moore	1
Edward Walton	1
Geo Pickering	1
Christ Jackson	1
Wid Jackson	1
Jno Jackson	2
Nichol Hornsby	1
Wid Hornsby	1
Tho Foster	1
Tho Jackson	1
Nichol Jopling	2
Henry Clerke	1
Witton Hall	7
Jno Mailland	[-]
Mich Hornsby	1
Robt Hopper	1
	92

Whickham

Tho Wood Gent	5
Jno Craigs	2
Robert Parkins	4
Jane Matthewes	3

m. 11v, c. 3

Tho Emmerson	2
Antho Wharton	5
Tho Grobe	6
Will Jackson senr	4
Robt Harrison	4
Alice Lishwood	2
Will Jackson junr	7

Rich Lish	3
Wid Jopling	5
Robert Elfinton	4
Tho Crawforth	9
Christ Gillery	3
Wid Lawes	3
Will Barnes	2
Jno Harrison	1
Wid Ogle	1
Marke Watson	2
Thomas Pescod	4
Tho Brignall	4
Henry Lewens	6
Tristram Fenwicke	5
Rich Harrison	2
Tho Harrison	2
Geo Walton	4
Robert Thirlewall	2
Tho Jackson	3
	109

Whichamfelside
[Whickham Fellside]

Sr Thomas Liddell	11
Jno Pallister	2
Jno Turner	4
Robert Sanders	2
Sr James Clavering	10
Robt Harding Gent	7
Lord Baltemoore	10
Tho Moore	2
Wid Maddison	2
Ann Robson	2
Tho Brignall	4
Guy Hudson	3
Jno Appleby	3
Jno Maddison	2
Jno Kennady	2
Wid Blackburne	1
Richard Pallister	1
Jno Healocke	1
Tho Layburne	2
Jno Sanders	1
Rowland Hodgson	3
Jane Robson	3
Tho Errington	2

Christ Emmerson	1	Tho Grange	2
Tho Bucke	1	Jno Swinburne	1
	82	Rowland Richardson	1
		Will Briggs	1
		Jno Dood	1
Whickham Lowhand		Will Little	2
Henry Liddell Gent	9	Will Jackson	2
Ms Liddell senr	8	Simon Trotter	1
Geo Hodgson Gent	2	Tho Pickering	1
Richard Ifly	1	Will Rowell	1
Will Pallister	1	Tho Garry	1
Issabell Ryce	1	Jno Carter	1
Jno Wilkison	1	Stephen Reonaldson	2
Ralph Liddell	3	Antho Wright	1
Will Anderson	1	Edward Wilkison	1
Will Ellison	1	Wid Jackson	2
Widd Hindmors	2	Robert Chambers	2
Tho Johnson	2		**89**
Will Hindmors	2		
Charles Jordan	1		
Robert Potts	2	**Winlaton West Lordshippe**	
Mary Hindmers	2	**[Winlaton West Lordship]**	
Thomas Parker	1	Robert Tempest Gent	6
Thomas Rewcastle	1	Jno Lawson	1
Eliza Harrison	2	Geo Ednam	1
Alice Bellancy	3	Henry Spencer	1
	46	Nathan Jewett	1
		Tho Smith senr	2
		Widd Smith	1
Winlaton East Lordshippe		Jno Richardson	2
[Winlaton East Lordship]		Jno Jopling	1
Sr Francis Anderson	6	Jane Heswell	2
Jno Clavering	14	Tho Foster	2
Charles Selby Gent	13	Francis Barkhouse	2
Lanc Hodgson Gent	12	Robert Procter	3
Tho Selby	2	Jno Beason	1
Geo Farrey	3	Jno Wild	1
Jno Gillery	3	Matt Barkhouse	1
Antho Dobson	2	Robert Hall	1
Richard Laverocke	1	Mr Timothy Shaftoe	2
		Tho Smith junr	2
m. 12, c. 1			**33**
Geo Robison	1		
Tho Chambers	1		
Tho Fawden	2		
Cuth Harper	2		
Mich Frost	3		
Widd Wilkison	1		

Chester Ward
East Division

Barmpstone
[Barmston]

Edward Smith	2
Richard Bowre	2
Jno Wilkison	1
Robert Wilson	1
Will Browne	1
Mich Parker	1
Mr Ritchison	2
Jno Wilson	1
Jno Laing	2
Eliza Pavy	1
Mr Pawle Liste	2
Henry Halliday	1
Will Wilson	1
Tho Matthew	1
	19

Boulden East
[East Boldon]

Will Fenwicke Gent	6
Will Smith	2
Richard Plawton	4
Richard Chambers	1
Will Atkison	3
Ralph Newland	1
Will Todd	1
Tho Atkison	2
Will Hodgson	2
Tho Welsh	1
Tho Newlands	1
Richard Hodge error	*1*
Eliza Stott error	*1*
Rich Welsh error	*1*
Jno Todd error	*1*
	24

Boulden West
[West Boldon]

Mr Richard Wrench	6
Richard Wrench	2
Gawen Maddison	2
Thomas Cornforth	1

Jno Sharp	1
Will Atkison	2
Will Teswhite	2
Will Browne	1

m. 12, c. 2

Geo Briggs	1
Will Readhead	1
Henry Maddison	1
Stroder house	2
Geo Trewhitt	1
Henry Smith	1
Jno Rawling	1
Eliza Clay	1
Robert Clerke	1
Ann Howorth	1
Richard Brouth	1
	29

Cleadon

Tho Gowre	9
Tho Wood	1
Rich White	1
Will Coulson	3
Tho Readhead	1
Jno Wake	3
Michaell Matthew	3
Jno Matthew	1
Tho Pattison	3
James Pattison	3
	28

Fullwell
[Fulwell]

Jno Young	3
Henry Matthew	2
Geo Brough	1
Tho Brough	1
Will Miller	1
Antho Talior	1
Tho Lumbley	3
Will Fawcett	2
	14

Hillton
[**Hylton**]

Tho Hunter	3
Ralph Bonner	2
Tho Atkison	2
Will Hilton	1
Barronett Hilton	10
Robert Granger	2
Geo Hilton	3
Jno Pemmerton Gent	3
Tho Sparrow	1
Jno Smith	1
Jno Gibson	1
Robert Peall	2
Geo Bell	2
Geo Scroggs	2
Robert Rockert	2
Robert Atkison	3
Thomas Paige	2
Jno Walton	1
Jno Wood	1
	44

Upp Heworth
[**Upper Heworth**]

Jno Watson	6
Christ Browne	2
Will Robson	3
Ann Davison	1
Jno Wilson Gent	2
Will Wood	1
Thomas Talior	4
Will Thompson	1
Geo Catchiside	1
Mr Jno Fell	1
Will Catchiside	1
Mr Wood	2
Tho Coulson	1
Rodger Dawden	1
Mr Ralph Fell	1
Will Greener	2
Tho Cuningham	1
David Jnoson	1
Roger Greener	1
Mary Graham	1
Widd Chilton	2
Will Davison	1

Will Hutchinson	1
Wid Browne	1
Wid Armstrong	1
Will Talior	1
Wid Thompson	1
	42

Hedworth

Robert Burton	3
Ralph Pattinson	3
Jno Swinburne	2
Robt Scott	1
Ann Burton	1

m. 12, c. 3

James Pattison	2
Jno Easterby	3
Matt Henderson	1
	16

Harton

Jno Smart	4
Richard Newton	2
Will Pearson	2
Tho Pearson	3
Will Harle	3
Tho Smart	3
James Laidler	2
Tho Atkinson	5
	24

Nether Heworth

Robt Ellison Gent	5
Will Softley	2
Jno Catchiside	1
Richard Huntley	1
Edward Nixson Gent	2
Margrett Wallis	2
Ms Branling	9
Jno Potter	2
Ralph Ellison	1
Tho Moody	2
Wid Deemster	2
Phillis Guddricke	2
Jno Sutton	1
Edward Branling	1

Jno Richardson	1
Luke Maxwell	2
Will Cesforth	1
Geo Story	1
Henry Archer	2
James Stoes	1
Tho Snawden	1
Jno Wallis	2
Robert Easterly	1
Tho Gibbons	2
Geo Thompson	1
Robert Story	1
Rich Grahame	1
Arthur Strother	1
Rowland Brewtish	1
Robert Hardy	2
Jno Hodge	1
Wid Catchiside	1
Jno Lowther	4
Antho Charleton	3
Tho Brunton	1
Jno Benwicke	2
Ralph Oxnett	1
Geo Fawell	3
Oswald Talior	2
Geo Ushar	2
Will Harrison	2
Wid Hall	1
Tho Oxnett	1
Geo Mitchell	1
Jno Willeby	1
Will Pearson	1
Will Askew	1
Ms Allice Reaves	4
Jno Hadwen	2
Gawen Moody	1
Jno Hodge	1
Geo Willis	1
Henry Jnoson	4
	95

Munckton
[**Monkton**]

Jno Walker Gent	3
Richard Fawell	3
Robert Aud	2

Richard Batty	4
Jno Fenwicke	2
Cuth Raw	1
Cuth Ellison Gent	22
Jno Easterby	3
Tho Softley	1
Jno Jnoson	2
Robert Thompson	2
Tho Kirsop	1
Tho Talior	1
Will Barker	4
Rich Reigh Gent	4
Tho Rockwood	1
Jno Talior	1
Ralph Talior	1
Wid Wilkison	2
Tho Kelsay	2
Will Foster	2
	64

m. 12v, c. 1

Munkwearmouth
[**Monkwearmouth**]

Stephen Talior	2
Tho Collier	3
Will Shepherdson	4
Ralph Shepherdson	3
Matt Whitehead	2
James Watson	2
Eliza Ogle	3
Will Thompson	5
Robt Scurfield	2
Rich Chapman	1
Francis Hall	4
Stephen Boyes	2
Will Colley	2
Christ Dinlay	2
Jno Harrison	3
Christ Gowland	3
Will Hudman	4
Jno Rumford	3
Cuth Bell	1
Rich Browne	3
Geo Hodgson	4
Jno Browne	1
Jno Smurfoott	3

Arthur Criske	1
Issabell Criske	1
Tho King	2
	66

Suddicke
[Southwick]

Tho Waike	2
Geo Gray	7
Eliza Read	1
Tho Atkison	1
Geo Waike	2
Robert Byart	3
Ralph Atkison	2
Geo Rickerby	1
Ralph Atkison	2
	21

South Sheels East Ward
[South Shields East Ward]

Jno Potter	3
Charles Chambers	3
Jno Clarke	2
Wid Hutchison	4
Robert Matthew	1
Tho Matthew	2
Will Talior	1
Edw Bodwell	3
Christ Rodgers	4
Tho Wolfe	3
Henry Carlisle	6
Tho Selby	2
George Readhead	2
Eliza Dagleish	4
Edward Clerke	6
Robert Thompson	2
Mary Clerke	4
Jno Chilton	6
Richard Parke	2
Jno Cutter	4
Jno Chipchase	1
Wid Hall	1
Will Davy	4
Geo Plunkett	1
Eliza Foster	2
Jno Trimble	2

Jno Hatton	2
Jno Larter	2
	79

So Sheels West Panns
[South Shields West Panns]

Will Harle	4
Robert Linton	5
Mary Linton	7
Cuth Coxson	2
Edw Killerby	1
Jane Coxson	6
George Carre	4
Lowrence Craft	6
Margrett Robison	4
Wid Newton	1
Jno Treddall	2
Will Ledgeman	2
Tho Rippon	1
Robert Collier	3
Will Harrison	2
Margrett Nicols	2

m. 12v, c. 2

Ellinor King	5
Jane Wheatley	4
Will Lawson	5
Charles Coatsworth	4
Ellinor Blythman	2
George Harle	2
Lowrence Blythman	4
Sam Harrison	3
Richard Row	10
Mich Coatsworth	5
Ralph Milburne	2
Tho Lodgert	2
James Smith	3
Ann Carre	2
Will Harrison	1
Charles Southerin	2
Christ Busby	1
Mary Cooke	3
Tobias Smith	2
Jno Atkinson	3
Tho Pattinson	5
Lance Greenway	2

Antho Andrew	3	Jno Halliwell	2
Ellinor Wright	4	Robert Archbald	1
Jno Wallace	4	Sam Greenway	2
Will Lodgeman	2	Jno Sutton	2
	137		106

**South Sheills First Constblry
[South Shields First Constabulary]**

**South Sheills 2d Constablry
[South Shields Second Constabulary]**

Tho Haswell	1	Geo Milburne	10
Jno Wright	6	Jno Thompson	5
Geo Selby	4	Mr Robt Loggan	6
Will Hall	6	Mr Ralph Anderson	8
Geo Selby	2	Tho Coupland	1
Henry Hall or Story	4	Robert Bell	5
Alice Pattison	2	Antho Minthorp	1
Adam Green	2	Robert Chilton	5
Henry Blackett	2	Jno Grundey	3
Will Bell	2	James Robson	1
Tho Carry	2	Robert Swaddell	1
Alice Watson	2	Geo Wallis	2
Ann Cooke	3		
Andrew Farnton	1		
Robert Archbald	2	*m. 12v, c. 3*	
Robert Archbald	1	Robert Maxwell	1
Cuth Readhead	2	Tho Cooke	2
Isaac Newton	4	Joseph Cooper	4
Jane Pattison	4	Will Thompson	1
Edward Readhead	2	Jno Foster	4
Margrett Hobart	3	Ann Nixson	1
Tho Bowdon	2	Will Watson	6
Will Sedgewelth	2	Robert Anderson	1
Jno Wilkison	3	Will Linton	5
Robert Wellings	2	Richard Ord	1
Margrett Dolles	2	Will Charleton	4
Lanc Story	2	Robert Murrow	2
Edward Mattison	3	Geo Winterburne	3
Will Bell	3	Edward Wallace	5
Ann Chapman	2	Will Feark	1
Jno Browne	5	Mr Anderson	1
Sam Greenway	6	Mr Geo Middleton	5
Robert Woolands	2	Robert Loggan	4
Tho Pearson	2	Will Bell	6
Peter Walker	2	Edward Vastis	1
Mary Posse	1	Wid Bulman	3
Margrett Davy	1	Jno Rutlish	2
Jno Tranwell	2		111

Usworth Greatt
[Great Usworth]

Will Lawson Esqr	10
Jno Cuthbert	1
Ralph Hilton	2
Richard Story	2
Rodger Harper	2
Rodger Sharper	1
Peter Graine	2
James Robison	1
Rodger Wallis	1
Jno Sherne	1
Jno Tod	1
Robert Robinson	1
Will Robinson	1
Tho Robinson	2
Jno Catchside	3
Richard Banke	1
Robert Carre	3
	34
[*corrected total*] es[?]	35

Washington

Henry Jnoson	5
Tho Sparrow	1
Geo Sparrow	2
Jno Sharp	1
Ann Steall	1
Will Pearson	3
Tho Foggett	1
Jno Scurfield	1
Will Welsh	2
Robert Green	2
Jno Braike	1
Marmaduke Walner	1
Jno Dening	2
Jno Fletcher	1
Jno Steall	2
Robert Readhead	1
Robert Waike	2
Tho Sharpe	1
Martin Waike	1
Matthew Foggett	1
Tho Newlands	1
Margrett Hutchison	1
Margrett Foster	1

Abigaill Hodgson	1
Barbara Lax	1
Mr James	10
	47

Westoe

James Harle	4
Tho Maxwell	3
Oswald Chambers	3
Thomas Harle	4
Will Biltham	4
Jno Jefferson	2
Ann Southerin	1
Jno Wilkison	4
Cuth Carr	3
Wid Haswell	2
Wid Richardson	2
Tho Carpenter	4
Tho Wolfe	2
	38

m. 13, c. 1

Whitburne
[Whitburn]

Matt Foster	2
Tho Gare	2
Will Browne	2
Cuth Maxwell	2
Richard Hicks Gent	8
Jno Bell	2
Will Burne	1
Richard Wright	2
Issabell Talior	2
Tho Roxby	2
Cuth Chambers	2
Tho Wright	3
Will Roxby	2
Robert Johnson	3
Edward Maxwell	2
Jno Stephenson	2
Jame Chapman Gent	6
Jno Wright	2
Will Bainbricke	3
Rodger Chambers	3
Richard Jefferson	2

Jno Embery	1
	56

Chester Ward Middle Division

Broome
[Broom]

Matthew Elwood	1
Jno Shockridge	2
Will Lees	1
Francis Blaixton	2
Ann Wright	2
Agnes Braidley	1
Martin Rutherford	1
Mr Jno Kirkby	2
Mr Nichol Bridge	3
Jno Lash	1
Tho Hall	1
Jno Barker	4
Antho Widdowson	1
Jno Cragge	3
Will Witherington	2
	27

Birkley
[Birtley]

Tho Catchside	1
Robert Catchside	4
Geo Billington	1
Lyonell Maddison	1
Alexr Turner	1
Jno Robison	2
Lyonell Maddison	2
Jno Glazenby	1
Alice Hall	4
Wid Thompson	1
Wid Maddison	2
Wid Fairbridge	1
Robert Glassenby	2
Ralph Maddison	1
Wid Jnoson	2
	26

Chester in Street
[Chester-le-Street]

Will Masterman	1
Peter Simpson	1
Wid Simpson	1
Katharin Gibson	1
Will Stobbart	4
Cuth Rytten	1
Tim Allison	2
Will Cleugh	2
Leonard Watson	1
Will Watson	1
Geo Watson	6
Robert Allison	1
Rodger Gibson	2
Ann Simpson	1
Cuth Watson	2
Robert Kirtley	1
Rodger Watson	2
Tho Gibson	2
Jno Matthew	2
Tho Wheldon	1
Mabell Fletcher	1
Ms Py	1
Jno Hedley	2
Martin Cleugh	3
Jno Gibson	3
Ralph Clerke	1
Robert Fletcher	3

m. 13, c. 2

Wid Nicolson	3
Cuth Rutter	2
Jno Procter junr	3
Ralph Clerke	1
Arthur Browne	2
Ralph Hedworth Gent	5
Mr Watson	4
Ralph Haswell	4
Rich Robison	2
Jno Cowen	2
Phill Gowland	1
Will Ranison	3
Edward Reed	2
Ms Sarah Webster	2
Katharin Coall	1

Will Hall	1
Geo Winship	2
Jno Pearson	2
Lowrence Fletcher	3
Wid Haswell	3
Antho Robson	3
Will Stuart	6
Wid Hodgson	4
Francis Henderson	1
Wid Haswell	6
Thomas Marley	4
Mr Richard Clerke	4
Humphrey Errington	2
Mr Ralph Millett	7
Richard Robison	1
Jno Aid	5
Ralph Sampson	3
Wid Bird	3
Tho Reed	2
Will Wortley	1
Tho Robison	1
Robert Robison	1
Tho Turner	2
Rich Haswell	4
Rich Oswald junr	3
Mr Ebdon	5
Wid Flether	1
Robt Askell	3
Jno Humble	1
Matt Chilton	1
Barbara Chilton	1
Ann Haswell	2
James King	3
Robert Rutter	1
George Rutter	1
Ms Maddison	6
Margrett Sneath	3
Ms Katharin Clerke	4
Mr Geo Clerke	4
Rodger Haswell	4
Rich Robisonn	2
	102
[*corrected total*] es[?]	202

Edmondsley

Mr Mich Jnoson	6

Mr Will Lampton	4
Geo Pearson	2
Martin Hartley	2
Robt Bushby	1
Tho Pearson	2
Eliza Bellarby	1
Nichol Ifly	1
Mich Hull	1
Mary Heighington	1
Robt Lax	2
Robert Wardell	3
Christ Wardell	2
Will Grunwell	2
	30

Harraton

Sr Jno Jackson	9
Mich Harrison	2
Cuth Punshon	4
Edward Wylam	1
Will Wylam	1
Jesper Wylam	1
Tho Younger	1
Antho Sampson	3
Rich Maddison	2
Robert Marley	4
Alexr Marley	1
Rich Reed	2
Ralph Marley	2
	33

m. 13, c. 3

Hedley

Will Marley	3
Ann Grundy	2
Robert Marley	1
Ralph Palmerley	1
Matthew Waikfield	1
Robert Leighton	1
Will Story	2
	11

Kiblsworth [Kibblesworth]

Will Jnoson Gent	9
Geo Talior	3

Will Cuthbert	1	**Lintsgreen**	
Geo Stott	1	**[Lintz Green]**	
Ralph Allen	1	Mr Tho Tempest	9
Geo Waster	1	Mr Blaixton	4
Tho Scurfield	2	Alba Hodgson	7
Wid Cuthbert	1	Mr Harrison	3
Wid Mitchison	1	Stephen Handcocke	2
Will Greenwell	1	Henry Handcocke	2
Tho Robson	5	Antho Bucke	2
Will Curry	2	Jno Heworth	1
Geo Farrer	1	Will Raw	4
Mr Bewicke	2	Henry West	1
Tho Simpson	2	Matt Rutherfoord	2
Wid Talior	2	Jno Stobbs	1
Ms Mary Greenwell	2	Rodger Stobbs	1
Antho Marley	2	Cuth Southerin	1
Will Seamer	1	Geo Harrison	1
Will Hunter	2	Will Stephenson	3
Cuth Lowes	2	An Robson	1
Will Curry	2	Jno Longstaffe	1
	46	Will Lonesdale	1
		Lance Jopling	1
		Geo Howers	1
Lamesley & Felside		Katharin Polestone	1
[Lamesley and Fellside]			50
Sr Thomas Liddell	28		
Mr Wilson	3		
Jane Clerke	3	**Peelton**	
Tho Robson	2	**[Pelton]**	
Robert Turner	4	Will Hall	3
Jno Heath	2	Geo Hall	4
Lowrence Airy	2	Alexr Hall	4
Tho Wilkison	4	Ralph Marley	3
Jno Haddocke	2	Wid Marley	2
Rob Cuthbert	1	Martin Davy	2
Jane Chipchase	2	Tho Sparke	2
Robert Wright	1		
Jno Emmerson	3	*m. 13v, c. 1*	
Tho Dickinson	3		
Henry Waike	2	Eliza Cook	4
Francis Bucke	1	Jno Grunwell	1
Rodger West	1	Stephen Wheldon	2
Henry Southerin	1	Wid Hall	2
Jane Tully	1	Tho Rutter	2
Will Talior	1	Wid Raxby	1
Ann Dickinson	1	Jno Jackson	1
	68		

Henry Johnson	1
	34

Plausworth
[Plawsworth]

Sr Christ Conyers	11
Ralph Hedword Gent	6
Rich Raw Gent	7
Ralph Short	2
Robert Darling	2
Nichol Watson	1
Jno Reed	1
Ralph Harbottle	1
Geo Harbottle	1
Tho Rippon	2
Jno Mowbray	2
Jno Woodmasse	2
Will Blackett	2
Jno Dixon	1
Henry Wheatley	1
Rich Atkinson	1
Jno Daring	1
	44

Ravensworth

Mr Ralph Surties	3
Robert Story	1
Christ Cuthbert	1
Edward Liddell	2
Will Fletcher	1
Will Wheatley	1
Robert Liddell	2
Tho Wheatley	2
George Forrest	1
Jno Weld Gent	3
Will Aukland	1
Wid Aukland	1
Jno West	1
Jno Reed	1
Wid Scurfield	1
Thomas Lee	1
	23

Urpeth

Cuth Baimbricke	2
Robt Errington	2

Jno Lawes	2
Wid Davison	2
Tho Reed	2
Nichol Farrer	2
Robert Hutchison	4
Will Mason	2
Jno Jopling	1
Ralph Marley	2
Tho Jopling	2
	23

Waldridge

Mr Ayton	2
Mr Newburne	3
Jno Watson	2
Will Coats	2
Robert Punchen	2
Will Allison	2
Rich Anderson	3
Stephen Whelton	1
	17

Goatshead
[Gateshead]
Pipewell Ward

Jno Bulman	5
Henry Bird	5
Clement Green	2
Mary Potts	2
Jno Gosten	3
Arthur Darling	4
Mr Gibson	2
Jno Watt	2
Robt Holmes	1
Humphrey Atkison	2
Geo Robison	3
Tho Teasdale	2
Mr London	1
Ralph Gibson	2
Lance Dawson	1
Eliza Middleton	1
Nehemiah Church	3
Will Crawkill	1
Tho Laverocke	1
Robt Clerke	2

m. 13v, c. 2	
Robt Rutter	3
Ralph Walker	2
Geo Wilkison	2
James Chambers	1
Jno Young	1
Jno Butcher senr	2
Jno Butcher junr	1
Robt Tweddell	1
Issabell Richardson	2
Cuth Hunter	4
Tho Hull	3
Jno Stobbs	1
Richard Shevill	1
Bartho Pigge	1
Mich Watson	1
Will Patterson	1
Will Calvert	1
Jno Richardson	2
Will Alder	2
Jno Browne	1
Cuth Sharp	1
Francis Hardy	4
Tho Waike	1
Tho Fisher	1
Geo Lawson	1
Lance Air	2
Ann Wallace	4
Christ Rawling	4
Jno Fenwicke	3
Robt Jobling	2
Jno Mabell	1
Robt Trollup	6
Sr Francis Liddell	11
Rich Bradford	1
Jno Moody	1
Will Stephenson	2
Tho Dalton	1
Ann Cookson	2
Rowland Oliver	1
Tho Gibbings	2
Ralph Hedley	1
Jno Chambers	1
Will Moore	3
Henry Crafton	2
Tho Fenwicke	3

Tho Mosse	2
Edward Grundy	2
Will Harrison	2
Will Stephenson	2
Edward Rolyeth	2
Mr Ord	7
Jno Rutter	3
Tho Hauxley	2
Eliza Hopper	2
Gilbert Thompson	1
Jno Readshaw	2
Geo Lubton	4
Alexr Talior & Thomas Appleby }	5
Barbara Henderson	3
Geo Airey	2
Jno Fulburne	1
Walter Alcocke	2
Ralph Bowrey	1
Tho Turner	2
Mary Gibson	1
Geo Carre	1
Lowrence Foster	1
Alexr Wilkison	1
Robt Lovitt	2
Jno Atkison	3
Robt Gall	4
Robt Andrson	4
Jno Bedford	4
Ms London	6
Jno Burrell	2
Mr Sober	10
Will Richardson	2
Matt Thompson	3
Thomas Potts	2
James Gastell	8
Tho Young	7
Robt Martindale	4
Jno Dedford	5
Will Rutter	1
Margrett Thackray	1
Will Barker	2
Tho Anderson	1
Joseph Jophcoatt	2

m. 13v, c. 3	
Tho Thompson	4
Jno Willis	2
Will Gibson	1
Geo Cooper	1
Tho Moore	6
James Holmes	1
Christ Cooke	2
Mr Alder	1
Jno Harrison	1
Richard Stoker	1
Tho Harbitt	2
Tho Henderson	4
Alexr Watson	2
	291

Pantward
[Pant Ward]

Jno Ladler Gent	6
Jno Thursby	2
Barbara Teasdale	1
Ralph Parkin	3
Francis Gaskin	5
Will Willis	1
Tho Cooper	2
Anthony Heworth	1
Thomas Chambers	1
Lyonell Matthewson	2
James Stoker	1
Oswold Browne	1
Richard Cash	1
Robt Eldstone	1
Geo Marshall	3
Jno Nicholson	1
Dorothy Clebburne	1
Simond Butterby	1
Edw Smith	3
Robt Jackson	5
Jno Glover	1
James Brasse	1
Rich Robison	1
Tho Walker	1
Geo Bell	2
Robert Layburne	3
Jno Yeatt	8
Nichol Newby	9

And Clow	3
Francis Collingson	5
Ralph Thompson	5
Jno Atkison	1
Jno Forbridge	1
Tho Goyle	1
Tho Foster	3
Jno Reonaldson	4
Robt Seamor	1
Jno Tutchell	1
Lucy Swellwell	1
Issabell Swan	2
Francis Bulman	4
Robert White	2
Rowland Wilson	1
Peter Bell	2
Arthur Mould	1
Henry Earle	1
Ralph Selby	3
Tho Rawling	4
Tho Milburne	1
Christ Haddocke	1
Will Todd	1
James Haddocke	1
Phillip Spencer	1
Francis Winde	1
Alexr Wright	1
Tho Stobbart	2
Nichol Craigs	1
And Moorhead	1
Edw Wetherley	2
Henry Jnoson	2
Tho Atkison	1
Francis Green	1
Mary Ellinor	1
Cuth Woodman	1
Mary Gibson	2
Cuth Barkworth	2
Rich Wallace	3
Cuth Hunter	2
Ditto Hunter	1
Christ Stoker	1
Thomas Blunt	3
m. 14, c. 1	
Robt Robison	6

Geo Bryan	5	Geo Randall	1
Jno Briggs	7	Mich Thompson	1
Emmanuell Gaskin	2	Will Coats	1
James Walker	1	Eliza Moore	1
Oswald Watson	2	Mich Young	1
Cuth Edward	1	Nichol Readhead	4
Christ Hardyside	2	Robt Stotts	1
Edwald Bulman	1	Ralph Wallace	1
Wid Dale	1	Mr Hunter	2
Will Golder	1	Ann Slelsip	1
Jno Clayton	6	Will Harrowgate	1
Will Pearson	1	Robt Fenwicke	1
Geo Smith	1	Issabell Bogge	1
Tho Fish	1	Tho Willoby	1
Ms Cole	6	Tho Errington	1
Jno Bleston	1	Stephen Hodgson	2
Margrett Emmerson	1	Geo Talior	3
Andrew Carre	1	Lance Newton	2
Wid Jackson	1	David Story	1
Stephen Thompson	1	Rich Burrell	1
Grace Garrett	1	Robert Todd	1
Will Garrett	1	Tho Moorhead	1
Jno Browne	1	Will White	1
Will Scott	2	Jno Wright	2
Hugh Rutter	3	Percivall Wharton	2
Richard Ewbanke	4		311
Robert Hastings	1		[310]
Tho Fergusson	1		
Wid Marley	4	**Bankward**	
Matt Mattsin Gent	7	**[Bank Ward]**	
Rich Pearson	1	Ralph Galliley	2
Eliza Foggane	1	Jno Patridge	6
Mr Will Jackson	5	Will Burton	2
Rowland Atkison	1	Matt Baitts	4
Jno Shevill	1	Jno Arey	4
Ms Ann Cole	12	Jno Japhrap	4
Cuth Blaikey	2	Robt Bulman	4
Cuth Readshaw	3	Marke Cooke	5
Mr Carre	6	Nichol Bracke	2
Peter Marley	2	Henry Ailup	5
Matt Burden	1	Jno Rudstone	5
Phillip Foster	4	Tho Henderson	5
Jno Fryer	2	Mary Wolfe	3
Jno Lumbley	2	Lance Fawcas	1
Wid Bell	5		
Robert Mould	6	*m. 14, c. 2*	
		Widd Swann	5

Tho Holmes	1	Francis Pryor	1
Nichol Saills	1	Robt Appleby	1
Marke Pattison	3	Will Mabin	1
Christ Newton	2	Mr Jno Willoby	9
Jno Pattison	2	Mr Jno London	8
Robert Heworth	1	Tho Tweddell	4
Ann Evens	1	Tho Thompson	2
Barbara Hunter	2	Tho Potts	6
Tho Simpson	4	Rich Newton	3
Geo Saills	2	Tho Heworth	2
James Air	2	Mich Atkison	6
Daniell Simpson	1	Peter Humble	8
Tho French	2	Luke Garnett	2
Margrett Ruddicke	2	Grace Appleby	7
Jane Nicholson	4	Jno Clerke	3
Robert Jnoson	4	Cuth Hering	5
Edw Robison	2	Tho Cumpton	7
Jno Jnoson	1	Nathaniell Wind	2
Will Rand	1	Tho Grahame	6
Katharin Clerke	2	Jno Partridge	5
Will Sanderson	4	Tho Partridge	5
Jno Hawkins	1	Bartho Turner	2
Mary Farrow	1	Jno Martin	4
Alice Bullocke	1	Arthur Gunn	2
Arthur Gun	8	Francis Rodgers	2
Jno Bownman	6	Jno Shadforth	6
Jno Pattinson	2	Jno Gastell	3
Will Pertis	2	Rodger Stephenson	2
Robert Lowrence	3	Wid Errington	1
Jno Harrison	2	Christ Newton	1
Margrett Addison	1	Wid Urrand	1
Robt Sutton	3	Jno Wilkison	1
Will Webster	3	Alice Pattison	1
Tim Tyssicke	4	Geo Wilkison	2
Jno Bowman	2	Ann Cooke	3
Richard Stockton	2	Joshuah Rudstone	2
Will Suddicke	4	Will Steall	1
Matt Arkley	3	Stephen Hodgson	2
Edward Bulman	2	Tho Shipley	3
Tho Glover	3	Jeffrey Leeke	2
Jno Mathers	2	Will London	5
Robt Bulman	8	Jno Appleby	4
Henry White	3		**321**
Nicholas Browne	5		
Edward Allen	2		
James Mathers	4		

m. 14, c.3

High Ward

Robert Browne	3
Jno Trumble	1
Jane Browne	3
Wid Anderson	1
Mary Blakey	6
Abraham Porter	3
Jno Bradforth	1
Jno Day	1
Henry Day	1
Ann Smith	1
Jno Trumble	1
Tho Porter	1
Alexr Hunter	1
Jno Thompson	1
Jno Bushby	2
Geo Smith	2
Mark Stephenson	2
Jno Brandling	1
Jno Hewison	1
Lanc James	1
Edward Smith	1
Nich Watson	1
Jno Lister	3
Ambrose Cheesbrough	3
Geo Chambers	2
Geo Dunnell	1
Tho Gray	1
Nichol Read	1
Lance Fletcher	1
Christ Wolfe	1
Will Crinkley	1
Will Hodgson	1
Peter Jackson	4
Will Riddell Esqr	17
Ann Hall	2
Jno Wetherburne	1
Peter Mills	1
Jno Johnson	1
Hugh Craister	5
Rich Walton	1
Jno Slater	1
Will Farrow	1
Tho Wilson	1
Rich Jones	2

Christian Garth	1
Jno Crawford	1
Rich Pattison	1
Jane Hogge	2
Tho Scott	1
Antho Hunter	1
Will Snaray Gent	3
Jno Hart	3
Margrett Addison	1
Jno Mirrucke	5
Henry Raw	2
Will Turner	1
Mr Geo Jnoson	9
Robert Pinker	1
Rich Bell	7
Rich Rutledge	2
Robt Carter	1
Tho Atkison	3
James Liddell Gent	6
Robert Preston	2
Tho Scurfield	1
William Scurfield	2
Mr Lyonell Maddison	10
Mr Ralph Carre	7
Will Rutter	2
Jno Catchiside	2
Robert Moody	2
Jno Blissons	1
Jno Fulburne	1
Henry Eden	1
Rich Rutledge	1
Ralph Eden	1
Geo Gledstone	1
Francis Collinson	3
Alexr Weetwood	1
Thomazin Wilson	2
Jno Masterman	2
Ann Wilson	9
Edward Hogge	1
Rodger Walker	1
Jno Willowby	2
Jno Porter	1
Tho Teasdale	1
Jno Parker	1
Will Grahame	1
Ann Browne	1

Mary Story	1

m. 14v, c. 1

High Ward

Nichol Gray	6
Jno Wolfe	1
Will Wallis	1
Will Talior	1
Edward Smith	1
Cuth Watson	1
Tho Spight	3
Jane Barras	2
Will Kell	1
Ralph Ogle	1
Lowrence Sigsworth	1
Tho Simpson	1
Mr Will Everston	6
Will Gibson	1
Robert Thompson	1
Luke Fletcher	7
Will Downison	1
Cuth Hudlestone	1
Tho Frizzell	1
Jno Wardhough	1
Tho Nelson	1
Peter Gray	1
Lowrence Parkin	4
Ms Coall	2
Geo Stewart	1
Wid Linger	1
Jno Ratcliffe	1
Tho Jackson	1
Jno Emmerson	4
Cuth Wightman	5
Wid Gibson	1
Robt Clerke	1
Ms Cole	4
James Snawden	1
Rich Harrison	1
Rich Craiston	1
Jno Landerer	1
Wid Pattison	3
Wid Hastings	2
Will Sewell	2
Richard Wilson	4
	281

Durham Citty
[Durham City]
St Nicholas

Will Hunter	6
Gabriell Wright	1
Jno Ellerington	3
Christ Whitfield	4
Mr Francis Crossby	10
Jno Hopper	4
Geo Walker	1
Wid Stephenson	2
Magd Gallely	1
Abraham Paxton	5
Mr Jno Sanderson	5
Will Wilkison	2
Mr Pemberton	4
Gabriell Glover	3
Geo Heighington	1
Hugh Hutchinson	5
Jno Southerin	2
Robert Maddingham	2
Robert Bankes	2
Rich Chipchase	1
Jno Stoddart	2
Jno Nicholson	2
Wid Swinhoe	2
Christ Nicholson	2
Will Dent	1
Tho Coulson	3
Tho French	2
Christ Mann	1
Alderman Wanlesse	5
Will Bird	2
Tho Ladler	3
Stephen Teasdale	4
Jno Scallocke	3
Will Catterall	1
Robt Clifton Gent	4
Clem Parker	2
Tho Richardson	4
James Olivant	1
Wid Richardson	1

m. 14v, c. 2

Mary Jurdon	1
Ralph Nicholson	5

Cuth Adamson	1	Richard Mawer	1
Cuth Hutchison	2	Geo Farrow	1
Jno Gray	6	Robert Errington	2
James Fairlasse	2	Mr Richard Padman	8
Tho Browne senr	5	Henry Wood	3
Robert Pearson	1	Robert Jnoson	2
Ms Bellerby	5	Tho Wilkison	3
Mr Ovinton	2	Mr Louther	3
George Welsh	2	Edward Foster	3
Ralph Lumley Gent	6	Luke Shepherdson	2
Humphrey Smith	2	Mr Jno Maior	2
Tho Snawden	2	Stephen Elrington	1
Alice Kemp	1	An Duxberry	1
Ann Foster	1	Edward Turner	1
Ralph Corbiske	1	Gilber Wilkison	2
Jno Lee	2	Thomas Jackson	3
Will Lee	1	Edward King	1
Jno Allison	3	Thomas Hawd	2
Robert Cornforth	4	Ann Browne	4
Edw Guy	1	George Page	5
Jno Simpson	2	James Peacocke	3
Margrett Davison	2	Ralph Baimbricke Gent	5
Robert Wall	2	Simond Hutchison	1
Ms Hall	9	Jno Bucke	5
Anthony Daile Gent	3	Edward Stelling	1
Nicholas Paxton	5	Matth Baills Gent	2
Jno Jefferson Gent	7	Edward Smith	3
Mr Richard Lee	12	Mr Hall senr	5
Geo Sparke	3	Mr Hall junr	4
Cuth Hutchison Gent	2	Alderman Shives	5
Mr Jno Stockdale	3	Mr Will Armstrong	6
Mrs Price	2	Alderman Airson	9
Mr Francis Colleand	9	Mr Pextell Foster	3
Mr Henry Rowell	8	Thomas Browne	1
Michaell Oliver	4	Mr Edward Threlkeld	7
Matthew Mawer	6		
Mr Francis Airson	1	*m. 14v, c. 3*	
Tho Richardson	2	Mr Robert Selby	2
Margrett Middleton	4	Jno Bullocke	1
Geo Rowell	7	Robt Hedley	1
Jno Summers	1	Robert Cowing	1
John Wharton	1	Hugh Jnoson	1
Tho Sutton	1	Hugh Hopper	2
Robert Bell	2	Nichol Greave	1
Jno Arrundale	2	Tho Stephenson	1
Richard Brice	4	Matt Craigs	2

Mr Richard Heighington	7
Nichol Ladler	4
Peter Rowell	3
Jno Haswell	1
Will Lee	1
Jno Spenceley	2
Mr Thomas Massum	6
Mr Clerke	2
Mr Hubbocke	12
Richard Hukson	5
Wid Burrow	2
Mr Jno Lamb	2
Tho Talior	7
Tho Richardson	2
Rich Archer	2
Will Heslop	3
Mr Coming	5
Mr Geo Cooper	8
Jno Walton	2
Edward Talior	5
Tho Ray	2
Mr Geo Hodgson	4
Robertt Fawell	1
Jno Goodhaire	1
Cuth Bainbricke	5
Richard Ward	2
Jno Catchside	5
Alexr Shaw	2
Hugh Rodham	2
James Fairlesse	2
Will Rackett	2
Will Drake	1
Christ Greenwell	1
Christ Shaw	1
Issabell Ward	1
Mary Peacocke	2
Bernard Focer	3
Tho Focer	3
Ms Manky	4
Geo Anderson	2
Wid Charleton	3
Jno Kirby	1
Jno Gray	9
Jno Hary	2
Ralph Waster	2
Robert Simpson	1

Issabell Hudson	1
Tho Walker	4
Mr Robt Blaixton	4
Jno Kent	2
Rowland Stoutt	1
Wid Ditchburne	2
Rich Kirton	2
Tho Broom junr	2
Nichol Lee	1
Widd Pearson	1
Mr Wilkison	1
Tho Dainby	2
Will Rodham	1
Geo Burdon	2
Henry Mailand	1
Mr Tho Cooper	1
Mr Jefferson	3
Anthony Pawsey	3
	588
[*corrected total*] es[?]	570

St Gyles
[**St Giles**]

James Rodham	2
Jno Davison	2
Sr Nicholas Coall	25
Mr Thomas Tempest	13
West Grange	8
Nichol Hull	4
Will Coulson	1
Robt Eppleton	1
Robt Huntley	4
Mich Walton	3
Andrew Hermison	2
Wid Chiton	3
Will Bee	2
Wid Hall	4

m. 15, c. 1

Henry Wilkison	2
Tho Miller	1
Robert Dobson	4
Mich Ladler	3
Will Hubbocke	3
Jno Barker	1
Will Harrinson	1

Oswald Bell	1	**Burrow of Elvett**	
Geo Crookes	1	[Borough of Elvet]	
Geo Robison	3	Christ Balland	2
Richard Hopper	2	Rich Kinlyside	4
Will Simpson	3	Mr Eden	5
Margrett Heath	1	Mr Brockett	6
Nicholas Bootley	2	Mr Jackson	3
Rowland Simpson	1	Mr Evers	7
Mr Tho Maior	8	Mr Gray	10
Jno Chilton	2	Mr Phillipson	4
Robt Richardson	1	Mr Blaixton	5
Phinehal Marshall	2	Mr Daikers	4
Tho Readhead	1	Mr Crosby	4
Ann Bushby	1	Mr Salvin	3
Ann Sheels	1	Wid Smart	1
Christ Hooley	1	Henry Braidley	2
Geo Robson	1	Ms Bradford	3
Will Jurdison	1	Ms Conyers	4
Tho Emmerson	3	Ms Wytham	5
Jno Allison	5	Abraham Smith	2
Jno Hair	1	Isabell Servant	1
Robt Tweten	1	Cuth Clerke	1
Antho Dobson	2	Doctor Wilson	7
Edward Kemmerstone	1	Mr Jno Conyers	7
Wid Dobson	3	Jno Mailland	3
Robt Jackson	2	Mr Jno Peacocke	5
Christ Bee	1	Jno Murras	2
Abraham Allison	1	Tho Winnis	3
Tho Snawden	3	Geo Ridley	4
Charles Robison	2	Wid Smith	2
Jno Miller	1	Tho Smith	2
Jno Maior	1	Geo Hunter	1
Henry Jnoson	2	Mr Sigsworth	9
Robt Heighington	5	Mr Bradsha	7
Robt Fairfax	1	Christ Shacklocke	3
Will Wilson	2	Mr Orton	5
James Coulson	2	Alice Loftis	4
Richard Coulson	2	Tho Phillippson	2
Mr Witham	2	Robert Beckles	3
Jno Harrinson	2		
Humphrey Chapman	1	*m. 15, c. 2*	
Rich Hutchinson	1	Wid Kitching	1
Wid Eden	2	Mr Morlland	9
Rich Martin	2	Jno Martin	11
Christ Wilkison	2	Lady Bellasis	12
	175	Lanc Talior	4

Mr Hedley	6	Jno Leath	1
Wid Gastell	1	Tho Kinlyside	3
Robt Neale	2	Henry Brice	2
Jno Kinlyside	4	Christ Bankes	2
	195	Jno Gibson	2
		Tho Maugham	1
Barony of Elvet		Jno Richardson	1
[**Barony of Elvet**]		Jno Holden	1
Jno Brice	5	Mr Cooper	2
Henry Sheels	2	Wid Hurst	1
Robt Scurfield	3	Mr Howard	1
Robt Hall	1	Will Marre	1
Mich Belly	2	Phillip Atkinson	1
Jno Drysdaill	3	Ms Cooke	5
Mr Backworth	5	Mr Gilbt Marshall	10
Robert Fisher	11	Gyles Raine	2
David Sharp	1	Will Raine	1
Thomas Humble	1	Mr Midford	2
Mr Densey	2	Mr Peacocke	9
Will Hinkes	3	Jno Dickinson	2
Will Atkison	1	Tho Gaire	1
Rich Anderson	2	Robt Kirkley	1
Christ Watson	1	James Pleasington	4
Jno Braidley	2	Rich Croft	2
Will Stobbart	1	Wid Mann	2
Ms Greenwell	4	Wid Sikes	1
Tho Bankes	1	Wid Liddell	3
Robert Mosse	1	Nicho Bradley	3
Wid White	1	Wid Coward	2
Geo Burne	1		153
Mr Hillyard	3		
Will Nukson	1	**Framwellgate**	
Geo Rowell	1	Jno Burnhop	3
Christ Bradley	2	Ms Hall	8
Mr Sallim	7	Mr Heath	5
Richard Suddicke	3	Rich Harrison	2
James Sowaby	1	Will Hutchison	5
Tho Parkin	1	Robert Mason	3
Jno Rowell	1	Mr Rich Hutchison	7
Tobias Softley	1	Tho Hutchison	2
Nichol Jnoson	2	Mr Mascall	6
Nichol Rumford	1	Will Kelsay	1
Geo Thompson	1	Will Jnoson	1
Wid Readhead	1	Tho Willices	2
Mr Brasse	1	Jno Brand	1
Mr Read	3	Ann Dixson	2

Mr Lampton	1	Nichol Hutchison	4
		Christ Liddell	4
m.15, c. 3		Jno Richardson	3
Robert Stelling	1	Tho Pearson	3
Rich Nicolson	1	Jno Heslop	4
Robert Frizzell	3	Cuth Bee	1
Nichol Hutchison	1	Eliza Cornforth	1
Ann Buttery	1	Will Jnoson	2
Jno Dodd	2	Jno Stott	1
Gilbt Watson	1	Rich Wiseman	4
Jno Thompson	2	Henry Kirkhouse	3
Antho Hutchison	2	Jno Wilkison	2
Christ Kintley	1	Luke Parkin	2
Jno Younger	1	Tho Stott	1
Issabell Harrison	1	Mr Edward Parkinson	9
Will Hutchison	2	Geo Sanders	1
Will Story	1	Jno Thornton	1
Will Heads	1	Mr Geo Forrer	10
Jno Barnwell	1	Jno Kennady	1
Will Wilson	1	Will Thompson	2
Tho Holmes	2	Jno Roxby	10
Matt Corner	2	Will Moorley	1
Tho Buttery	1	Geo Pattison	3
Jno Jnoson	1	Charles Wrenn	1
Percivall Hadley	2	Tho Smith	2
Robt Newby	8	Tho Snawden	3
Mr John Hall	6	Christ Clerke	1
Robert Read	4	Phillip Browne	2
Jno Kirkhouse	2	Tho Jnoson	1
Will Read	4	Mr Jno Hutchison	5
Robt Charleton	2		233
Mary Brabbard	1		
Jno Gowland	3	**Crosssegate**	
Rich Hutchison	3	**[Crossgate]**	
Jno Rumford	3	Will Hewson	2
Mr Robt Dixson	7	Jno Wood	2
Oswald Richardson	2	Edw Milburne	1
Robt Gowland	2	James Smith	2
Will Shepherd	2	Wid Talior	6
Jno Douthwaitt	2	Nichol Sheiffield	4
Richard Huntley	3	Will Feaster	6
Tim Stott	4	Will Mitchell	2
Edward Stott	3	Nichol Dixson	1
Hugh Stott	1	Rowland Stott	3
Issabell Hall	1	Jno Dearham	1
Rich Hutchison	2	Cuth Stoutt	1

Christ Skarrow	2	Will Browne	2
Will Rosse	2	Mr Jno Talior	7
Mr Heighington	12	Jno Smith	3
Tho Hutchinson	2	Geo Kirkley	1
Jno White	2	Robt Knaggs	1
Tho Hopper	1	Widd Snowball	2
Nichol Pearson	3	Jno Clerke	2
		Christ Richardson	1

m. 15v, c .1

Framwellgate: Crossegate
[Framwellgate: Crossgate]

		Jno Almonds	1
		Christ Vazy	1
		Matt Todd	2
Richard Mason	1	Jno Eggleson	1
Geo Wilson	2	Simond Smith	2
Ralph Wilson	5	Wid Hind	2
Mr Shepherdson	4	Mr Daikins	2
Jno Harrison	1	Wid Younger	1
Jno White	2	Christ Ranison	1
Jno Selby	2	Jno Rowell	2
James Storfoott	1	Tho Todd	1
Tho Frizzell	1	Mr Will Trollup	4
Matt Carelow	1	Francis Hunter	1
Rowland Harrison	1	Rich Pearson	3
Jno Walker	1	Matt Teasdale	1
James Harrison	2	Antho Vazy	1
Edward Hodgson	1	Nichol Smirke	2
Nichol Coultman	1	Will Kirkley	1
Wid Swalwell	1	Mr Power	7
Christ Coulson	1	Abraham Porter	1
Tho Dixson	1	Robt Burne	1
Richard Pinkes	1	Tho Preston	1
Tho Harrison	2	Will Manstin	1
Wid Teasdale	1	Mr Thompson	8
Tho Wade	1	Clemt Wilkinson	3
Wid Wilson	2	Wid Wilkison	3
Robt Hutchison	1	Tho Allison	3
Geo Moore	5	Jno Smith	2
Tho Marshall	1	Ralph Ratles	1
Widd Farrow	2	Jno Dobbins	3
Jno Lowther	2	Christ Dent	4
Geo Featherstone	1	Richard Bentley	3
Wid Richardson	1	Wid Teasdale	3
Jno Baley	1	Jno Jackson	3
Tho Cuming	1	Mr Blackett	5
Michaell Dearham	1	Ralph Shearwood	2
Martin Holmes	1	Wid Gibbons	1
Will Martin	1	Ralph Hopper	1

Jacob Gibb	1	Mr Moorcroft	2
Robert Fisher	2	David Neals	1
		Wid Racks	1
m. 15v, c. 2		Mr Kirkby	9
Mr Reads house	5	Geo Bullocke	1
Mr Henry Frizzell	6	Ms Myres	8
Matt Thompson	2	Mr Parkisons house	2
Stephen Harrison	2	Geo Talior	5
Nichol Richardson	1	Mr Hilton	4
Will Rowell	2	Mr Barkers	9
Jno Gairfield	2	Mr Newhouse	5
	236	Ms Walking	4
		Mr Conyers	8
South Baley		Ms Watson	7
[South Bailey]		Mr Broome	10
Humphrey Stephenson	6	Mr Matthews and }	8
Ms Church	5	Mrs Spearman }	
Ms Carnaby	6	Mr Lodge	5
Ms Blaixton	7	Mr Cholmley	11
Sr Thomas Tempest	10	Sr Francis Bowes house	11
Lady Mallerby	7	Humphrey Holden	3
Mr Will Newhouse	5	Mr James Mikleton	7
Mr Stappleton	8	Jno Darbyshier	6
Eliza Lee	3	Mr Martin	3
Wid Car	3	Mr Butterby	3
Ms Carre	3	Mr Phillips	3
Mr Eden	5	Wid Lamb	3
Mr Whittingham	7	Mr Newton	8
Mr Cooper	2	Richard Jopling	8
Doctor Carleton	10	Mr Row	8
Doctor Gray	9	Mr Christ Mickleton	8
Doctor Bazier	10	Wilfred Clerke	4
Doctor Wood	6	Cuth Colson	2
Doctor Nailor	11	Geo Baitman	6
	123	Ms Harrison	7
		Ms Hawden	6
North Baley		Mr Sissons	5
[North Bailey]		Jno Lord Bishopp	22
Robert Midford	4	Mr Dean	20
Matt Stout	2	Doctor Neill	8
Mr Baddiley	5	Doctr Wrench	9
Jno Miller	1	Doctor Smith	9
Mr Greens house	4	Doctor Brevent	7
Mark Dod	2	Mr Grinwell	9
Jno Smith	3	Doctor Dalton	10
Mr Gibson	5		

Ms Rodgers	3
	323
	[324]

m. 15v, c. 3

Island Norham and Bedlington Sheirs
[Holy Island, Norham and Bedlington Shires]

Ancroft

Mr Antho Cotten	1
Jno Sibbett	1
Adam Sibbett	1
Matt Miller	1
Jno Miller	1
Matt Steall	1
Jno Hope	1
Matt Sibbett	1
Will Ath	1
Adam Maine	1
Will Turbett	1
Will Gray	1
Peter Gray	1
Jno Grahame	1
Jno Ewart	1
Adam Brankstone	1
Tho Simpson	1
Eliza Lampton	1
Mich Grahame	1
Jno Robison	1
Jno Scott	1
Wid Greenhead	1
	22

Spittle
[Spittal]

Will Duncon	2
David Allen	2
Will Pallart	1
Will Milne	1
Tho Waters	2
Jno Strangewayes	1
James Lawson	1
Geo Edgar	1
Bartram Potts	1

Rynian Steall	3
Will Hambleton	1
Will Mavice	2
Peter Steward	1
Edward Colbraith	1
And Cocke	2
Will Trumble	2
Hector Hewson	1
Matt Balmbrough	4
Adam Gray	1
Michaell Hall	1
Thomas Burrell	2
James Crawforth	2
Will Dun	3
George Hamilton	2
Will Davison	7
Jno Unthanke	5
James Wild	1
	53

Tweedmouth

David Pearson	1
James Humes	4
Will Camell	1
James Edenton	1
Will Selby	2
Vincent Rutherford	1
Edward Reaveley	3
Tho Reaveley	2
Geo Wilson	1
Jane Boalam	1
Bartram Richardson	1
Mr Jno Bane	8
Mr Cuthb Charleton	7
Jno Foreman	2
Alexr Green	2
Wid Davison	1
Lowrence Coulson	5
Margery Cooke	6
Mabell Mitton	5
Will Strother	1
Jane Nickolson	1
James Swinhoe	2
Tho Calvin	1
Will Craston	2
Henry Gradon	2

Wid Smith	2	Geo Richardson	2
Lowrence Coleson	1	Wid Grahame	1
Geo Gradon	1	Tho Enderson	4
Tho Lamb	1	Mich Glendining	4
Robert Martin	2	Gawen Davieson	3
Will Sanderson	1	Mr Smith	1
Tho Dixson	1	Jno Carston	2
Ellinor Farrow	2		**153**
Edw Nelson	2		
Francis Armourer	3	**Scremerston**	
Rich Fenwicke	2	Adam Smith	1
Jno Nelson	5	Anthony Hall	3
Will Rule	3	Edward Moore	1
		James Avery	1
m. 16, c. 1		Tho Vert	1
Jno Sadler	1	Ralph Scott	2
Jno Hoggart	1	Oswald Dods	1
David Lisle	1	Andrew White	1
Tho Cowbron	2	Jno Farrow	1
James Cowbron	1	Lance Stephenson	2
James Gilchrist	1	James Neisbitt	1
Rich Steell	1	Robt Branxton	1
Robt Armourer	1	Jno Dawson	1
Will Cooke	5	Jno Short	1
Patrick Ramton	1	Geo Smith	1
Edward Moorhead	1	Thomas Farrow	1
Edward Hewett	1	Charles Ellett	1
Cuth Hewett	1	Will Avery	1
Robt Riddell	1	Tho Southerin	1
Edward Cockerin	1	Jno Cooke	1
Jno Hoggart	2	Ralph Arnett	1
Robert Lambert	1	Richard Cooke	1
Jno Davidson	2	Ralph Skade	1
Geo Jorsy	1	Tho Wood	1
Gabriell Gotterton	3	Rich Surry	1
Lanc Wilkison	1	Jno Harley	1
Luke Richardson	2	And Thompson	1
Thomas Oard	2	James Heckles	1
Will Finley	1	Jno Thompson	1
Tho Hamleton	1	Katherin Smith	1
Wid Rutherford	2	Ralph Anderson	1
Margrett Selby	3	Jane Carre	1
Jno Selby	2	Ralph Binny	1
Jno Richardson	2	Mich Grahame	1
Wid Cammell	1	John Smith	1
Will Richardson	1	Geo Dennis	1

Ralph Smith	1
James Tate	1
Jno Bell	1
Geo Dods	1
Adam Jackson	1
Will Dennis	1
Geo Dennis	1
Richard Scott	1
Nichol Smith	1
	49

Holy Island

Tho Jackson	1
Matt Talior	2
Matt Steell	1
Thomas Allison	3
Geo Mason	2
Geo Steell	1
Ralph Gray	1

m. 16, c. 2

Wid Winlow	1
Thomas Grahame	1
Will Watts	4
Samuell Steell	1
Robert Wallis	1
Jno Steall	1
Wid Hebburne	1
James Wallis	1
Will Moore	3
Henry Short	2
Lady Collingwood	4
Andrew Wilson	1
Will Stamp	1
Mary Moore	2
Edward Wilkison	1
Ellinor Wright	1
Geo Watson	1
Cuth Swinhoe	1
Will Hope	2
Tho Bewdle	1
Richard Readhead	3
Jno Patterson	1
Ralph Brady	2
Will Patterson	2
Wid Lilburne	1

Cornelius Hebburne	1
Jno Bulmer	2
Mary Grahame	1
Richard Grahame	1
Rich Day	3
Tho Jackson	1
Anthony Wallis	2
James Stobbs	1
Geo Smith	1
Tho Watson	1
Jane Eshley	1
Tho Bewdle junr	2
Lance Moore	6
Katharin Jackson	1
Ann Steall	1
Simond Lewen	1
Mr Bartram Ord	2
Will Gray	1
Mr Muscamp	2
Wid Wallis	1
Robert Lilburne	1
Henry Gray	2
Jno Bowden	1
Mr Jno Ord	3
Henry Gray	1
	91

Low Linn
[Low Linn]

Henry Ord	2
David Hewson	1
Mich Browne	1
Tho Browne	1
And Bell	1
James Spencer	1
Will Mow	1
	8

Shoreswood
[Shoreswood]

Bartram Clavering	1
Robert Gammelling	1
Robert Scott	1
Jno Bourne	1
Geo Avery	1
Will Carre	1

Jno Edgar	1
Will Hudspeth	1
Patrick Sproatt	1
Tho Watt	1
Henry Turner	1
Jno Carnes	1
Henry Scott	1
Edward Gleghorn	1
Rich Anderson	1
Jno Mann	1
Jno Atkin	1
Rodger White	2
Edward Wood	2
Alice Browne	2
Oliver Selby	1
Tho Sanderson	1
Robt Woodcocke	1
Will Carnes	1
Matthew Nesbett	1
Jno Trotter	1
Charles Wilkison	[?]
	29

Haggerstone [Haggerston]

Collonell Haggerstone	15
Francis Cotham	1
Geo Dixson	1
Geo Kellett	1
Robt Gray	1
James Dixson	1
Jno Lammerton	2
Will Haggarstone	1

m. 16, c. 3

Geo Crosby	1
Richard Watson	1
Stephen Pudsey	2
Henry Muscrop	1
Ralph Maine	1
Cuth Talior	1
Alexr Short	1
Robt Kellett	2
Jno Matthewson	1
Geo Purdey	2
Will Smith	2

	38

Felkington

Mr Will Ord	2
Lance Strother	1
Jno Summerbell	1
James Arnett	1
Wilfred Arnett	1
Tho Pattin	1
Wilfred Arnett	1
Jno Grean	1
Geo Grean	1
Edward Arnett	1
James Arnett	1
	12

Morten [Murton]

Mr Jno Gray	4
Will Mailland	1
Will Carre	1
Pat Minnikin	1
Jno Archbald	1
James Lough	1
	9

Twizell and House

Mr Claybburne	11
Jno Talior	1
Jno Harby senr	1
Jno Harby	1
Edward Young	1
Will Thompson	1
Rich Enderson	1
Patricke Tindale	1
Robert Atkin	1
Thomas Tate	1
Gervus Sanderson	1
Nichol Crawford	1
Rich Nesbitt	1
Will Patrickson	1
Oswald Steward	1
James Crawford	1
Jno Carre	1
Wid Mabell	1
Matthew Forge	1
Robert Preston	1
Tho Patricke	1

Jno Summer	1
Robert Robison	1
Alexr Carmichaell	1
Jno Clerke	1
Ann Thompson	1
Robert Bell	1
Tho Steward	1
Thomas Fettesse	1
Will Read	1
David Mardicke	1
James Crawford	1
Jno Catterson	1
Robert Mordon	1
James Smith	1
Tho Pattinson	1
Tho Oliver	1
Lance Brownhill	1
	48

Fenham

Will Bell	1
Tho Jnoson	1
Robert Atkison	2
Adam Snawden	1
Robert Dods	1
Jno Wilson	1
Will Watson	1
Tho Steward	1
Tho Moody	1
Ralph Thompson	1
Thomas Bell	1
Jno Steward	1
Ralph Watson	1
Ralph Tindale	1
James Watson	1
Will Hall	1
Nichol Steward	1
Margrett Bell	1
Robert Malcomb	1
Richard Braddey	1
Jno Scott	1
Geo Atkison	1
Tho Batehouse	1

m. 16v, c. 1

Will Henderson	1

Jno Steall	1
Tho Winlow	1
Eliza Atkison	1
	28

Fenwicke
[Fenwick]

Tho Selby	2
Geo Thompson	2
Jno Davieson	2
Tho Bell	1
Geo Davisson	1
Henry Heslop	1
Will Dods	1
Tho Duncon	1
Ralph Browne	1
Henry Watson	1
Richard Duncon	2
Geo Wood	1
Cuth Stewart	1
Wid Atkison	1
Wid Thompson	1
Jane Browne	1
James Wright	1
Jno White	1
Robert Wilson	1
Thomas Wade	1
Wid White	1
Wid Wright	1
Will Robison	1
Will Jnoson	1
Tho Acton	1
Tho Wright	1
Elias Boyde	1
Tho Bower	1
Jno Fergusson	1
Wid Shepherd	1
Wid Pringle	1
Thomas Browne	1
Tho Alexander	1
Ralph Fendar	1
Wid Thompson	1
Matt Steall	1
Tho Dixson	1
Wid Jacking	1
Wid Wilson	1

Jno Shepherd	1
Lowrence Lernwicke	1
Wid Beadland	1
Ralph Thompson	1
Alexr Wright	1
Andrew Fleming	1
Will Lisle	1
Vincent Thompson	1
Will Clough	1
Jno Beadnell	1
Wid Rutter	1
Simond Davison	1
	55

Bucktonn
[Buckton]

Jno Watson	1
Stephen Smith	3
Jno Younghusband	1
Robert Hope	1
Thomas Farley	1
Jno Craigs	1
Robert Atkinson	1
Cuth Read	2
Jno Thompson	1
Richard Wake	1
Geo Atkison	1
Oswald Wright	1
Will Trumble	1
Rich Purdy	1
Eliza Scott	1
Barbara Thompson	1
Geo Atkison	1
Will Spence	1
Will Purvis	1
Edward Jackson	1
Henry Bell	1
Ralph Nelson	1
Tho Fendar	1
Henry Wilsonne	1
Daniell Bullocke	1
Henry Loggan	1
Robert Ellis	1
Jno Elliott	1
Ralph Purvis	1
	32

m. 16v, c. 2

Heatton [Heaton]

Mr Robert Moore	3
Luke Ward	1
Ralph Cranston	1
Tho Kinstone	1
Will Crossby	1
	7

Grindon and Grindon Ridge
[Grindon and Grindonrigg]

Will Ord Esqr	4
Geo Holliday	1
Jno Bourthack	1
Geo Weddell	1
Alexr Atkison	1
Will Bone	1
Jno Weddell	1
Wid Ward	1
Jno Weddell	1
Tho Haugue	1
Jno Burne	2
David Trotter	1
James Bourne	1
Wid Carre	1
Tho Carre	1
Rich Foster	1
Will Hague	1
Collonell Strother	7
	29
	[28]

Kylo cum Membris
[Kyloe with parts]

Mr Francis Moore	2
Ms Read	2
Will Reaveley	2
Henry Parsell	1
Jno Thompson	1
Will Coward	1
Will Thompson	1
Jno Anderson	1
Jno Armstrong	1
James Carmichaell	1
Jno Middleton	1
Geo Thompson	1
Tho Gibson	1

Geo Davison	1
Antho Peacocke	1
Tho Smith	1
Rich Wake	1
	20

Berrington

Gilbt Swinhoe Esqr	5
Jno Shankes	1
James Gilroy	1
Wid Jackson	1
Tho Readpath	1
Robt Lisle	1
Richard Dennis	1
Bartram Atkinson	1
Adam Hemetson	1
Wid Nicholson	1
Will Cockson	1
Oswald Paxton	1
Tho Dunwell	1
Geo Mason	1
Michaell Sanderson	1
Jno Dixson	1
Robert Moody	1
Jno Miller	1
Will Cowbron	1
Richard Gibson	1
Jno Farrow	1
Jno Smith	1
Jno Paxton senr	1
Geo Maine	1
Robert Jackson	1
James Air	1
Vincent Fendar	1
Will Hood	1
Andrew Smith	1
Will Thrubron	1
James Fordy	1
Wid Carre	1
Geo Anderson	1
James Thrubron	1
Ralph Dennis	1
	39

Tilmouth
[Tillmouth]

Mr Robert Clayburne	2
Tho Knox	1
Adam Swan	1
Pet Robinson	1
Jno Matthewson	1
	6

m. 16v, c. 3

Cornhill

Mr John Foster	7
Major Armourer	3
Tho Archbald	1
Bartho Machell	1
Jno Archbald	1
Robert Chandler	1
	14

Ord

Jno Strangewayes	1
Wid Trumble	2
Geo Tweaddy	2
Wid Short	1
Adam Short	1
Will Bald	1
Tho Henderson	1
Tho Makin	1
Jno Edmondson	1
Wid Fitts	1
Will Lough	1
Tho Dawson	1
Wid Bourne	1
Robert Talior	1
James Cooper	1
Cornelius Armstrong	1
Will Carre	1
Ferdinando Rule	1
Wid Cleghorne	1
Tho Talior	1
Ralph Talior	1
Clement Wilson	1
Wid Carre	1
Tho Tate	1
Ralph Robison	2
Rodger Heslop	2
Robert Collingwood	1
Ralph Bell	1

Wid Richardson	1
Wid Allen	1
Will Thompson	1
Henry Greenhead	1
Rynion Mabell	1
Alexr Glesse	1
Christ Rule	2
Tho Short	2
Geo Short	1
Wid Mosseman	1
Patricke Temple	1
Adam Trumble	1
Archbald Renton	1
Alexr Short	1
Robert Ellott	1
James Richardson	1
Richard Fendar	1
Henry Hasty	1
Will Wilson	1
Matt Foster	1
Henry Hudspeth	1
Henry Ord Esqr	6
Tho Dennis	1
Gilbert Wood	1
Christ Lamb	1
Tho Halliday	1
Randall Roten	1
Luke Thompson	1
Geo Cockson	2
Jno Close	1
Wid Douglasse	1
Wid Fewler	1
Ralph Ramsay	1
Robert Ord	2
Wid Ord	2
Robt Lambert	1
Jno Dunce	1
Christ Coxson	1
Wid Thompson	1
	81

Hockliffe vel Hartley
[Horncliffe or Hartley]

Robt Ord	1
Alexr Crake	1
Gilbt Gastin	1

Jno Ord	1
James Croussy	1
Gawen Richardson	1
Jno Robson	1
Alexr Ord	1
Jno Ord	1
James Throwbron	1
Richard Yeoman	1
Robert Thompson	1
Widd Ord	1
Alexr Farrow	1
Jno Rowles	1
Will Comley	1
Gawen Rodger	1

m. 17, c. 1

Tho Rodgers	1
Wid Nicholson	1
Ellinor Nicholson	1
Gawen Foggart	1
Jno Thompson	1
Ralph Rickaby	1
Margery Thompson	1
Rowland Smith	1
Jno Strother	1
Will Hudspeth	1
Gawen Yeoman	1
Robert Given	1
Henry Ord	1
Will Givens	2
James Swinhoe	1
Jno Nesbitt	1
Tho Wedlesse	1
	35

Lone end
[Loan End]

Thomas Richardson	1
Robert Matthewson	1
Jno Rickaby	1
Wid Davison	1
Henry Yeoman	1
Will Simms	1
Robt Bartlemaine	1
Geo Simpson	1
Robt Nicholson	1

Will Clerke	1
Leonard Coxson	1
Robt Nicholson	1
Henry Ord	1
Jno Nicholson	2
Henry Richardson	1
	16

Beell on ye Hill
[Beal]

Will Selby Gent	2
James Attison	1
Jno Selby	1
Tho Watson	1
Bartram Gettes	1
James Tannah	1
Ralph Browne	1
Jennett Wilson	1
Fortune Carr	1
Will Hall	1
Jno Grahame	1
Richard Anderson	1
Will Selby	1
James Balmbrough	1
Robert Talior	1
Fortune Tannah	1
James Palmer	1
Andrew Cowbron	1
Ralph Richardson	1
Richard Boomer	1
Tho Grahame	1
Francis Steall	1
Jno Richardson	1
Tho Addison	1
Jno Selby	2
Tho Ellott	1
Richard Stamp	1
Will Smith	1
	31
[*corrected total*] es[?]	30

Cheswicke [Cheswick]

Edward Coall	2
Ralph Smith	2
Geo Jamison	1
Cuth Paper	2

Mr Edward Strangewayes	5
Geo Davison	2
Edward Lamb	1
Andrew Mitchelson	1
Tho Thompson	1
Jno Miller	1
Geo Smith	1
Wid Cooke	1
James Glasse	1
Bartram Peacocke	1
Will Moffitt	1
Peter Steall	1
Jno Hunkerstone	1
Robt Simpson	1
Jno Foster	1
James Hamleton	1
Rich Davison	1
Will Baxter	1
Geo Boomer	1
Geo Smith	1
Robt Rutter	1
Wid Carmichaell	1
Jno Weddell	1
	35

Thistlerigge and Norham
Castlegate
[Thistlerigg and Norham
Castlegate]

Andrew Pearson	2
Adam Coxson	1
Will Duncon	1
Tho Davison	1
Edward Davison	1
Jno Ward	1
Jno Smith	1
Nichol Hutchison	1
Ralph Thompson	1
Wid Purvis	1
Rich Coxson	1
Will Marshall	1
Tho Coxson	1
Tho Marshall	1
Andrew Wallis	1
Wid Rosse	1

Tho Purvis	1	Jno Baitts	2
	18	Mr Davison	4
		Tho Baitts	1
Thornton		Tho Moffitt	1
Daniell Selby	3	Geo Arnett	1
Will Gattes	1	Wid Glayne	1
Robert Bell	1	Francis Tate	1
Rich Selby	1	Margrett Scott widd	2
Jno Thew	1	Rodger Rowell	1
Andrew Thompson	1	Tho Sanderson	1
Tho Armstrong	1	Wid Armstrong	1
Geo Maben	1	Wid Learman	1
Will Crome	1	Andrew Armstrong	1
Jno Bowmaker	1	Leonard Ogle	1
Alexr Allen	1	Will Weddell	1
	13	Will Richardson	1
		Geo Trotter	1
		Robt Richardson	1
Norham		Will Bunting	1
Geo Haigg	1	Wid Fargy	1
Jno Amisley	1	Adam Pearson	1
Will Crawford	1	Geo Menam	1
Tho Lownon	1	Tho Henderson	1
Will Turnbull	1	Leonard Talior	1
Will Armstrong	1	Henry Sanderson	1
Gawen Richardson	1	Jno Trotter	3
James Knox	1	Will Mitcheson	1
Will Hettell	1	Robt Davison	2
Will Forside	1	Robt Newlands	1
Geo Talior	1	Tho Swinhoe	1
Jno Hague	1	Jno Lough	1
Geo Birnett	1	Geo Home	1
Will Talior	1	Wid Lewning	1
Leonard Foulerton	1	Geo Carson	1
Wid Scott	2		**71**
Geo Palling	1		
Geo Browne	1		
Geo Ogle	1	*m. 17, c.3*	
Robt Sanderson	1	**Duddoe**	
Will Neasbitt	1	[**Duddo**]	
Geo Richardson	1	Lady Clavering	8
Jane Dixson	1		
Gawen Hague	1	**Bedlington**	
Jno White	1	Jno Smith	2
Will Abernethy	1	Thomas Mitcheson	1
Edward Trotter	1	Jno Mitcheson	1
Tho Simpson	1	Jane Walker	1

Jno Todd	1
Richard Marshall	1
Robt Lawson	1
Will Wilson	1
Ann Marshall	2
Will Hunter	1
Geo Skipsey	4
Wid Errington	2
Robt Lishman	1
Tho Atchison	1
Arthur Archer	1
Robt Robison	1
Geo Almery	1
Wid Truckett	1
Robt Wilson	1
Tho Hall	1
Henry Craigs	1
Geo Smart	1
Jno Richardson	1
Jno Katharin	1
Ralph Midford	1
Dorothy Watson	1
Antho Blacke	1
Dionis Albane	1
Will Robson	1
Dorothy Lawson	1
Wid Potts	1
Jno Talior	1
Jno Henderson	1
Jno Potts	1
Jno Talior	1
Jno Henderson	1
Jno Potts	1
Jno Smart	1
Cuth Watson	1
Geo Watson	1
James Watson	1
Tho Watson	1
Mr Will Methwen	2
Tho Potts	2
Robert Warwicke	1
Mr Henry Delavall	6
Will Potts	1
Robert Milles	3
Richard Browne	2
Tho Watson	1

Jno Spaine	1
Jno Garrett	1
Thomas Smart	1
Matthew Curren	4
Cuth Midford	1
Christ Reay	1
Will Moody	1
	76

Camboise
[Cambois]

Cuth Young	2
Jno Errington	1
Edward Oliver	1
Jno Proder	1
Henry Dawson	1
Ralph Hunter	1
Ralph Mittforth	1
Tho Dawson	1
Thomas Blackett	1
	10

East Slickburne
[East Sleekburn]

Jno Davy	1
Dorothy Pearson	1
Robert Bell	2
Jno Davy senr	1
Gawen Pearson	1
	6

West Slickburne
[West Sleekburn]

Jno Jnoson	1
Rowland Jnoson	1
Henry Jnoson	1
James Watson	1
Robt Watson	1
Jno Bowden	1
Matt Midford	1
Henry Ewbankes	2
Henry Nicholson	1
Jno Lowrence	1
Geo Watson	1
Gawen Watson	1

Tho Gibson   1
                                       ——
                                       14

Allerton and Unthanke
[Allerdean and Unthank]
Ralph Trimble   3

Elwickhalfe
[Elwick half]
Rob Wallace   1
Will Bowre   1
Jno Browne   1
                                       ——
                                        3

Rosse
[Ross]
Jno Crozier   1
Rich Wake   1
                                       ——
                                        2

m. 17v, c.1

Netherton
Robert Dixson   1
Rich Wilson   2
Cuth Nicholson   1
Tho Potts   1
Rodger Wilsonn   1
Jno Barker   1
Geo Nicholson   1
Will Lesley   1
Geo Nicholson junr   1
Jno Browne   1
Robert Ward   1
                                       ——
                                       12

Goswicke
[Goswick]
Mr Tho Watson   7

m. 18, c. 1

An Accot of Non Solvants within the Countie Palatyne & Bishoppricke of Duresme

South East Division of Darlington

Great Aikliffe		**Great Aycliffe**

Great Aikliffe			
[Great Aycliffe]			
Richard Brasse	1	Geo Slator sen	2
Alice Grainger	1	Richd Stockald	1
Cuthbt Carr	1	Widd Grainger	1
Adam Sadler	1	Robt Laykin	1
Thomas Coltman	1	Robt Grysdale	1
Bryan Robinson	1	Symon White	1
Jane Clarkson	1	John Pallaster	2
Mary Sisson	1	Willm Nicholson	1
Geo Megson	1		47
Eliz Dowfoot	1		
Math Prowd	1	**Schoole Aikliffe**	
Mary Blaicke	1	**[School Aycliffe]**	
Mary Megson	1	George Peacocke	1
John Haswell	1	Michaell Wheatley	1
Geo Grisby	1	John Harryson	2
John Bell	1	Ann Adamson	1
Ann Carr	1	William Gramshaw	1
Mathew Burrell	1		6
Margtt Fairebecke	1		
Richd Stockeld	1	*m. 18, c. 2*	
Willm Richdson	1	**Blackwell**	
Richd Dobson	1	Thomas Gibson	1
Thomas Bownesse	1	Thomasin Chambers	2
Wm Alexander	1	Wm King	1
Dorothy Brasse	1	John Relfe	1
John Catheriche	1	Jane Willmson	1
Margtt Pyburne	1	Margtt Gouldsbrough	1
Willm Burne	1	Francis Grainger	2
Robt Davyson	1	Tho Robinson	2
Richd Corsey	1	Peter Gouldsbrough	2
Thomas Coward	1	Tho Blaymire	1
Jane Wattin	1	Tho Bergote	1
Richd Peirson	1	Ann Aukelan	1
James Bryarman	1	Leonard Robinson	1
Chr Hall	1	Ursley Rauson	1
Raphe Whitfield	1	Ann Low	1
Robt Brasse	1	Cuthbt Cornforth	1
		Robt Scott	1
		Nicholas North	2

John Middleton	1
Francis Langstaffe	2
Edward Mone	1
Thomas Dent	1
Henry Kirton	1
Margtt Longstaffe	1
Thomas Hunter	1
Richd Archlay	2
Willm Robinson	2
Geo Harryson	2
John Garthron	2
Chro Gray	1
John Goldbrouth	1
Ann Goldbrouth	1
Eliz Dobson	1
Francis Jollywill	1
	44
[*corrected total crossed out*]	45

Barmpton

Geo Harryson	1
Tho Labron	1
Stephen Cooper	1
Richd Shoe	1
Wm Thompson	1
Ann Richardson	1
Wm Thompson	1
Ann Richdson	1
Wm Summers	1
John Smith	1
John Cooper	1
Tho Fawcett	1
	12

Great Burdon

James Rainsdale	1
Wm Bullocke	2
Marmaduke Waugh	1
Anthony Robson	1
Robt Umphery	1
Tho Waugh	1
Isabell Raydon	1
	8

m. 18, c. 3

Brafferton

John Richdson	1
Robt Walker	1
Edward Simpson	1
Francis Hall	1
Denny Jones	1
Robt Gray	1
Dorothy Thompson	1
John Humble	1
Geo Peirson	1
Eliz Wilson	1
Tho Addy	1
Willm Norton	1
Richd Rickaby	1
Margtt Richardson	1
Thomas Close	1
	15

Byars Greene
[Byers Green]

Willm Emerson	1
George Emerson	1
Margtt Wright	1
Stephen Wright	1
Gracy Wright	1
Margtt Eltringham	1
Eliz White	1
Ann Todd	1
Widd Cairsley	1
Robt Cornforth	1
	10

Cockerton

Robt Bowes	1
Fran Richardson	1
Tho Emerson	1
Chr Gaskine	1
Raphe Smith	1
Tho Gibson	1
Margarett Sherewood	1
Fran Wastell	1
Tho Robson	1
Widd Hunter	1
Richd Atkinson	1
Fran Squire	1

Annas Dawson	1	William Hill	1
Widd Lee	2		23
John Lumby	1		
Robt Willd	1	**Conscliffe Low**	
Richd Wild	1	**[Low Coniscliffe]**	
Roger Totter	1	Rowld Oswald	1
Math Simpson	1	Willm Houldson	1
John Westall	1	Chro Brackenbury	1
Tho Gibson	1	Robt Armestrong	1
Wm Maine	1	Margtt North	2
Raphe Armestrong	1	John North	1
Tho Browne	1	Geo Wittly	1
Annas Lister	1	Eliz Hory	1
Raphe Robinson	1	Tho Hill	1
Margtt Mason	1	Tho Cowper	1
Willm Whitfield	1	Margtt Swinbanck	1
Margtt Richdson	1	Robt Stones	1
Michaell Jackson	1	Cuthbt Robson	1
Thomas Waistell	1	John Harryson	1
	32		15

m. 18v, c. 1		**Chilton Great**	
Conscliffe High		Michaell Munday	1
[High Coniscliffe]		Wm Hearing	1
Edward Thompson	1	John Steward	1
Margtt Allinson	1	Eliz Maltby	1
Wid Rennison	1	Jane Hunter	1
Thomas Armestrong	1	Willm Haddby	1
Toby Wray	1	Robt Hunter	1
Nicholas Wabrington	1	Jane Fishburne	1
John Hill	1	Tho Musgrave	1
John Vasye	1	Math Hawell	1
Wid Greathead	1	Ann Morner	1
Thomas Allinson	1	John Summer	1
Richd Robinson	1	Robt Kely	1
Thomas Dawing	1	Gilbert Ware	1
Cicillie Robinson	1	John Sober	1
Nicholas Todd	1	Raphe Whitfield	1
Christopher Wood	1	John Willinson	2
John Waicke	1	Robt Joblins	2
Hen Carter	1	Richd Harryson	1
Nicho Todd	1	Jane Richdson	1
Laurence Hewton	2		22
Phillip Downinge	1		
John Sockburne	1		

m. 18v, c. 2

Darlington Broughgate
[Darlington Borough]

Eliz Ward	1
John Kay	1
Eliz Heskatt	1
John Heskatt	1
Isabell Spence	1
Hen Shaw	1
Wm Robinson	1
Tho Clarvis	1
Adenall Houldon	1
Leonard Harryson	1
Anthony Scott	2
Eliz Simpson	1
Geo Taylor	1
Barnaby Wallas	1
Mary Mideruph	1
	16

Darlington Pribin
[Darlington Prebend]

Jane Dixson	1
Jane Wilkinson	1
Tho Lackanby	1
Isabell Hall	1
Willm Hodgson	1
Franc Gregory	1
	6

Darlington Bondgate

Tho Bell	2
John Watson	2
Ann Earthy	1
James Leadman	1
Tho Bushby	1
Hen Shaw	1
Wm Tindale	1
Mich Browne	1
Willm Wastell	1
Franc Thorp	1
Eliz Watson	1
Sam Leadman	1
Sarah Rudd	1
Chr Dannuell	1
Raphe Becke	1

Geo Langstaffe	1
Isabell Lamly	1
John Hannawell	1
Margtt Nicholson	1
John Richdson	1
Edward Todd	1
Raphe Elstob	1
John Preston	1
Mr Barnes	2
Edw Pearson	1
Hen Wright	1
Robt Browne	1
Tho Langstaffe	1
Hen Dunne	2
John Welley	1
Raphe Bellerby	2
James Winty	1
Tho Johnson	1
Lan Barenes	1

m. 18v, c. 3

Jenett Dun	1
Cicilly Clarson	1
Willm Bowrow	1
Willm Bowrow	1
Anthony Blades	1
James Bargiss	1
James Moorely	1
John Williaut	1
John Stansby	1
Ellin Shaw	1
Chr Sadwicke	1
Tho Morfitt	1
John Shaw	1
Willm Simpson	1
Raphe Chipse	1
James Wright	1
Robert Drummer	1
Ann Watson	2
Willm Bell	1
Mathew Tindall	1
Geo Langstaffe	2
Robt Timpron	1
Willm Hellcoat	1
Willm Marr	1
Fran Bayes	1

John Atkinson	1	Robt Cowper	1
Schoole house	1	Wm Soulby	1
Fran Jolly Mill	1	John Hackworth	1
Christopher Smith	2	Fran Mitchell	1
John Barnes	1	Wm Thompson	1
Edward Fisher	1	Chr Bowman	1
Jane Thompson	1	Wm Harryson	1
Robt French	1	Robt Knaggs	1
Henry Dun	1	Isabell Richardson	1
Tho Hodgson	1	Robt Rickerby	1
Geo Hugill	1	Fillis Simpson	1
Geo Richdson	1	Raphe Foster	1
Martin Ridley	1	John Warkin	1
Martin Almon	2	Geo Davidson	1
Chr Rayne	1	Wm Londsdale	1
	83	Margtt Blenkinshopp	1
			21

Denton

John Carlisle	1	**Ferryhill**	
Edw Otley	1	Robt Lodge	1
Rowld Atkinson	1	Robt Key	1
Geo Wright	1	Tho Blocke	1
Wm Biglin	1	Widd Doothfull	1
Tho Wright	1	John Richdson	1
Robt Allinson	1	John Carr	1
Tho Todd	1	John Harow	1
Wm Sidgwicke	1	Richd Richdson	1
Chr Todd	1	John Newton	1
Margery Hutton	1	Ann Gelson	1
Raphe Sidgewicke	1	Wm Laybourow	1
John Todd	1	Ann Watson	1
Ann Kitchin	1	Wm Gobling	1
Mary Simpson	1	John Stodert	1
Eliz Sidgewicke	1	John Luck	1
Dorothy Carlile	1	Raphe Sweetin	1
Duke Smart	1		16
Chr Kay	1		
	19		

m. 19, c. 1

Eldon

		Houghton in the Side	
		[Houghton le Side]	
Eliz Adamson	1	Robt Burdon	1
Robt Parkin	1	Wm Darneton	1
Tho Watson	1	Robt Davyson	1
Tho Burrell	1	Ann Darneton	1
Fran Hornsby	1	Hen Reins	1
		Richd Anderson	2
		Tho Hall	1

John Taylor	1
Marke Dennam	1
Geo Simpson	1
Phillis Burdon	1
Richd Burdon	2
John Dennam	1
	15

Haughton
[Haughton-le-Skerne]

John Bouffield	1
Leonard Hunter	1
Edw Brayon	2
John Bouston	1

m. 19, c. 2

Tho Beetson	1
Wm Clifton	1
Martin Reay	1
Geo Thompson	1
Widd Justis	1
Widd Hodgson	1
Robt Coulson	1
Tho Nanson	1
Widd Browne	1
Robt Sadler	1
Wm Sisson	1
John Collingwood	3
Robt Sisson	1
Tho Mansor	1
Margtt Young	1
Tho Turner	1
Margt Iveson	1
	24

Heighington and Old Parke
[Heighinton & Old Park]

John Hodgson	1
Hen Erington	1
Widd Horner	1
Anto Erryholme	1
Widd Skafe	1
John Harryson	1
Fran Fowell	2
John Purdson	1
Cuth Burrall	1

Tho Wilde	2
David Wilson	1
John Kendall	1
Geo Aurburne	1
Tho Hodgson	1
John Simpson	1
Dorothy Carton	1
Tho Auburne	1
Widd Heighinton	1
John Kitchinge	2
Margtt Mesom	1
Isabell Miller	1
Wm Miller	1
Geo Mesom	1
Widd Nicholson	2
Chr Emerson	2
Robt Wheatley	1
Percivall Hobson	2
Chr Smerson	1
Geo Newton	1
Willm Wilde	1
Widd Dawson	1
Isabell Harryson	1
Richd North	2
Eliz Franklyn	1
Willm Skafe	1
Wm Robinson	1
Hen Preastman	1
John Harryson	1
Chr Johnson	1
Widd Burrall	1
Widd Staintny	1
Widd Barres	1
Peter Hugh	1
John Newton	1
John Gray	1
Geo Bywell	1
Robt Robinson	1

m. 19, c. 3

Widd Lawson	1
Raphe Mebourne	1
Widd Crawfoote	1
Tho Welfoote	1
Widd Lambe	1
Antho Eriholme	2

Willm Redchester	1
	62

Hett

Jane Greene	1
Jane Hogge	1
John Moburne	1
Wm Lister	1
James Fery	1
Tho Jurpin	1
Fran Ferry	1
Edw Unthanke	1
Widd Lister	1
Willm Bell	1
Richd Allen	1
Cuth Layton	1
Willm Walker	1
Edw Charleton	1
Raphe Chesterwicke	1
John Turpin	1
Cuth Hopper	1
James Corner	1
John Ellison	1
John Sharpe	1
Dorothy Ferry	1
Martin Best	1
Cuth Kay	1
John Weapon	2
	25

Killerby

Fran Simpson	1
Chr Little	1
Geo Robinson	1
Tho Natter	1
Stephen Clarke	1
John Rutter	1
Geo Raper	1
	7

Middleston
[Middlestone]

Chr Downes	1
Willm Hickson	1
John Stelling	1
	3

Merrington Church
[Kirk Merrington]

Robt Hickson	1
Tho Fleatham	1
Hugh Dods	1
Mary Masterman	1
Antho Richdson	1
John Richdson	1
Chr Smith	1
Robt Richdson	1
Hen Simpson	1
John Bankes	1
Humphrey Clerke	1
Antho Heighinton	1
Margt Martin	1
Fran Heavysides	1
Jane Richdson	1
Wm Masum	1
Wm Hasly	1
	17

m. 19v, c. 1

Midridge
[Middridge]

Wm Wallis	1
Edw Chilton	1
Tho White	1
Willm Hunter	1
Widd Hunter	1
Willm Allen	1
Widd White	1
Tho Bell	1
Willm Palleser	1
Robt Walker	1
Willm Jaines	1
Geo Byarley	1
John Jeckell	1
Willm Bell	1
Willm Thompson	1
Tho Simpson	1
James Haueside	1
Geo Clayton	1
John Craggs	1
Geo Watson	1
Richd Palleser	1

Robt Craggs   1
                                      ——
                                      22

Oxnetfield
[Oxneyfield]
In ye new house   3

Preston upon Skerne
[Preston-le-Skerne]
John Coatworth   1
Denny Hutchinson   1
Mary Atkin   1
John Granston   1
John Sweetings   1
Hen Hasswell   1
Ann Wilkinson   1
Hen Eadon   1
Hen Younge   1
Martin Garth   1
Mirrell Tunbridg   1
Mirrell Wood   1
John Barker   1
Edw Anson   1
Ann Smith   1
                                      ——
                                      15

Redworth
Eliz Renwicke   1
Geo Pattinson   1
Antho Bell   1
Tho Martin   1
Robt Dobson   1
Wm Welfoot   1
Geo Simpson   1
Rich Renwicke   1
Cuth Simpson   1
James Richdson   1
Tho Atkinson   1
Richd Renwicke   1
Wm Aulwood   1
Hugh Watson   1
Chr Todd   1
Wm Pattinson   1
Wm Hewson   1
Margtt Dodd   1

m. 19v, c. 2
Wm Watson   1
Margtt Welfoot   1
Wm Gibson   1
John Younge   1
Edw Thursbye   1
Peter Applebye   1
John Simpson   1
John Parker   1
James Harde   1
Mary Robinson   1
                                      ——
                                      28

Tudoe
[Tudhoe]
Dorothy Cord   1
Ann Walker   1
Richd Browne   1
Alice Peele   1
Hen Ellery   1
Mr Coop   1
Chr Rickison   1
Roger Turping   1
Hen Richardson   1
Mary Allen   1
John Briggs   1
Hen Coser   1
John Coser   1
Jane Redhead   1
Ambrose Bell   1
Robt Sparke   1
Jane Wilson   1
Margtt Horner   1
Geo Kirkely   1
Tho Thirkly   1
James Elinger   1
John Sidgsworth   1
Martin Harper   1
Richd Smith   1
Mich Ellery   1
Tho Browne   1
John Fecher   1
John Gill   1
Wm Row   1
Hen Wheatly   1
Mich Wheatley   1

Willm Wheatley	1
	32

Wallworth
[Walworth]

Wm Arowsmith	1
Geo Jackson	1
Isabell Smart	1
Geo Parkinson	1
Allan Filder	1
Hugh Thompson	1
John Richdson	1
	7

Woodholme
[Woodham]

Antho Wilson	1
Richd Aikrigg	1
John Jackson	1
John Morgan	1
	4

m. 19v, c. 3

Willington

Tho Watson	1
Tho Hollymann	1
Antho Jackson	1
John Parkin	1
Wm Friend	2
Robt Cooke	1
John Clayton	1
Eliz Pearson	1
John Atkinson	1
Geo Stockdale	1
Denny Wall	1
Wm Gowland	2
John Fawell	1
Widd Smart	1
Widd Moss	1
Isabell Browne	1
Richd Wall	1
Wm Mayd	1
John Thornton	2
Mr James Claxton	1
Char Pickergin	1
Cuth Pattinson	1

Eliz Hadsman	1
Nicholas Cuninge	1
Charles Pickering	1
Phillip Carter	1
	29

Whitworth

Richd Hopper	1
Jane Adamson	1
Elianor Hemsley	1
Jane Nicholson	1
James Hewson	1
John Farrow	1
Mary Adamson	2
Robt Wilson	1
	9

m. 20, c. 1

Summerhouse

Widd Sodgson	1
Ann Burrell	1
Wm Norton	1
Mary Langstaffe	1
Katharine Headman	1
Tho Harryson	1
	6

Streetlam
[Streatlam]

Tho Latches	1
Rich Johnson	1
John Shaw	1
Margtt Hay	1
Robt Jackson	1
John Jackson	1
Willm Robinson	1
Isabell Show	1
Geo Nicholson	1
Tho Taylor	1
Eliz Robinson	2
Margtt Lazenby	1
Geo Beggett	2
Robt Nicholson	1
Cuth Dent	1
John Milton	1
John Brayfett	2

Tho Steadman	1	*m. 20,c. 2*	
Robt Sowerby	1	Anne Peirson	1
Denny Atkinson	1	Eliz Sidgwicke	1
Cuth Pattinson	1	Willm Cockfield	1
Marke Rakestraw	1	Jane Watson	1
Hen Robinson	1	Chr Wright	1
John Dent	1	John Frizwell	1
	27	Stephen Wood	2
Stainderopp		Toby Aynesley	1
[Staindrop]		Geo Robinson	1
John Farrow	2	Jane Robinson	1
Tho Colpetts	2	Mary Longstaffe	2
Robt Wilking	1	Chr Hodgson	2
John Vickers jun	2	Lewis Cradocke	1
John Vicker senr	1	John Simpson	3
John Atkinson	1	Wm Highwood	1
Geo Robinson	1	Mary Aynesly	1
Eliz Richdson	1	Edw Armestrong	1
Peter Applegarth	1	Anne Hopper	1
Margtt Stumble	1	Hen Farrow	2
John Alder	1	Barbary Arrowsmith	2
Margtt Alder	1	Margtt Bell	1
Eliz West	1	Eliz Skare	1
Mich Cockfield	1	John Allen	1
Jane Baxter	1	Geo Atkinson	1
John Waugh	1	Widd Todd	1
Geo Kirkin	1	Tho Dennyson	1
Anne Richardson	1	Cicillie Cradocke	1
Eliz Birly	1	Margtt Ridley	1
Geo Corker	1	Bridgett Hartley	1
Tho Stout	1		76
Tho Richardson	1		
Symon Sayfield	1		
Willm Docker	2	**Shotton**	
Katharine Viccars	1	James Borne	1
Jane Wood	2	Kath Mutres	1
James Richardson	1	Mary Heldon	1
Antho Richardson	1	John Houlden	1
Toby Brasse	2	Geo Bell	1
Grace Aynesley	1	Widd Langstaffe	1
Eliz Rowlandson	1	Cuth Hill	2
Robt Wilkin	1	Willm Edell	1
Chr Docker	1		9
Eliz Hudson	1		
		Teasdell Forrest	
		[Teesdale Forest]	
		Willm Walton	1

John Walton	1	Isabell Hutchinson	1
Widd Parkin	1	Hen Lambes	1
Cuthbt Watson	1	Anne Bowes	1
Antho Walton	1	Percivall Simpson	2
John Broumewell	1	Dorothy Show	1
John Robson	1	John Sidgsworth	1
Rebecca Houston	1	Widd Bland	1
Arthure Gastale	1	Geo Sutton	1
Willm Newby	1		14
John Walton	1		
	11		

Whinston
[Winston]

Westwicke
[Westwick]

Willm Dewfoot	1	Sam Bynion	1
Tho Dewfoot	1	John Dixon	1
Charles Bland	1	Annas Robinson	1
Elianor Wilson	1	John Newcombe senr	2
Schoole house	1	Kathar Dowthwayt	1
	5	Anne Hugh	1
		Geo Hewarth	1

Whorleton
[Whorlton]

		Robt Langaran	1
		Eliz Tilburne	1
Isabell Soulby	1	Eliz Jackson	2
Henry Ovington	1	John Brownlasse	1
Bartram Marley	1	Mary Hinde	1
Dorothy Hudson	1	Cicillie Harker	1
Eliz Dindsdale	1	Antho Robinson	1
Johanna Armitage	2	John Hudson	1
Geo Appleby	1	John Powell	1
		Richd Wilson	1
		Richd Bainbridge	1
m. 20, c. 3		Bernard Browne	2
Margtt Shutt	1	Jane Wilson	1
Oswold Soulbye	1		23
Antho Dinsdale	1		
Willm Cowerd	1		
Anne Bainrbigge	1	**Boadlam**	
	13	**[Bolam]**	

Wackerfeild
[Wackerfield]

		Widd Trotter	1
		Kathar Wetherell	1
		Anne Taylor	1
Elianor Chambers	1	Robt Dent	1
Eliz Taylor	1	Geo Robson	1
Nicho Maddison	1	Adam Colvin	1
Mary How	1	Geo Hay	2
Margtt Barker	1	Anne Thompson	1
		Eliz Taylor	1
		Mary Jackson	1

Geo Linsley	1	Leonard Hodgson	1
	12	Kathar Stanford	1
			24

Cleatham
[Cleatlam]

		Eggleston	
Geo Unite	1	Richd Loansdale	1
Jane Barnes	1	Antho Robson	1
Kathar Kiplin	1	Jacob Walker	1
Margtt Wraugham	2	Richd Murton	1
Chr Coward	1	Eliz Lawson	1
Ann Taylor	1	Mary Bland	1
Tho Prowds	1	Jacob Pinkney	1
Ann Shawe	1	Raphe Dixon	1
Chr Crawford	1	Mich Newby	1
Dan Brice	1	John Harker	1
Jane Smith	1	James Pinkney	1
Nich Ray	1	Antho Wilson	1
Mary Dowthwayt	1	Tho Dixon	1
Wm Hall	1	Robt Milner	1
Wm Hall	1	Chr Pinkney sen	1
Jo Renyson	1	Wm Addyson	1
	17	Hen Lightley	1
		Chr Harryson	1

m. 20v, c. 1

Cockfeild
[Cockfield]

		Kath Raine	1
		John Wrightson	1
		John Lawson	1
Rich Mackreth	1	Isabell Robinson	1
Willm Lodge	1	Wm Clarke	2
Robt Lodge	2	Cuth Browne	1
Wm Rand	2	Wm Murton	1
John Claper	1	Chr Harker	1
Raphe Stanford	1	Mr Sanderson	1
Robt Jefferson	1	Robt Peake	1
Nich Jefferson	1	Kathar Headlam	1
Eliz Garbett	1	Mabell Peacocke	1
Eliz Summer	1	Chr Adamson	1
Ann Doughthwayt	1	Wm Dent	1
Ann Smith	1	Raphe Dawson	2
Raphe Shaw sen	1	Chr Dixon	2
Raphe Shaw junr	1		37
George Pattinson	1		
Tho Watt	1	**Gaineford**	
Hen Bramley	1	**[Gainford]**	
Wm Burden	1	Widd Watson	1
Raphe Lodge sen	1	Ann Smith	1
Peter Fairbancke	1	John Ward	2

Antho Blaxton	2
Patricke Halston	1
John Brounteth	1
Robt Kay junr	1
Wm Percevell	1
Alice Boswell	1
Francis Dent	1
Wm Tinckler	1
Mathew Lampton	1
John Elwen	2
Robt Lanton	1
Jane Crawford	2
Jane Simpson	1
Margtt Joyner	1
Willm Percivell	1
John Hood	1

m. 20v, c. 2

John Cowling	2
Tho Milburne	1
John Rumforth	1
Wm Sheraton	1
Robt Steed	1
Anne Peirson	1
Antho Wayde	1
Jane Milburne	1
Sr Jos Crad	-
Isabell Abbott	2
Robt Dent	1
Robt Stodart	2
Hen Jermine	2
	39

Headlam

Margtt Atkinson	1
John Hellinrew	2
John Smith	1
Chr Dent	1
John Robson	1
Alice Lambert	1
Chr Burton	1
Percivell Ellin	1
Tho Smith	1
	10

Hylton [Hilton]

John Watson	1
Tho Marley	1
Edw Tinckler	1
Hen Marley sen	1
Hen Scott	1
Edw Tinckler	1
John Sutton	1
Wm Halls	1
	8

Ingleton

John White	1
Florence Wayde	1
Anne Bough	1
Mary Marley	1
Willm Fenwicke	1
Chr Dowell	1
Wm White	2
John Farrow	1
Isabell Cowperthwayt	1
John James	1
Isabell Gibson	2
Tho Rand	1
John Wayd	1
Peter Johnston	1
The Schoolehouse	1
	17

Langton

Widd Spencer	1
Wm Clarke	2
Chr White	1
Fran Eskill	1
John Browne	1
Robt Bryan	2
John Stappleton	2
Robt Bryon sen	1
Rich Francke	1
Wm Lockson	1
Hen Spencer	2
Wm Moscroft	1
Widd Finley	1
Nich Charleton	1
John Carleton	1
John Eskill	1

Peter Askill	1
	21

Langley Forrest
[Langleydale]

Widd Clayburne	1
John Taylor	1
Widd Botcherby	1
Chr Coates	1
John Hodgson	1
Willm Walton	1
John Heblethwayt	1
Geo Coates	1
Thomas Shaw	1
John Mayers	1
	10

m. 20v, c. 3

Middleton Bounds

Wm Bainbrigge	2
Chr Rayne	1
John Peacocke	1
Anne Bainbrigg	1
Cuth Beadlale	1
Chr Lowes	1
Eliz Kelly	2
James Bainbrigg	1
Joane Bridge	1
Jacob Rutter	1
Cuthbt Gibson	2
Hen Bainbrigge	1
Roger Gibson	1
John Ritson sen	1
John Wilson	1
	18

Murton Tinmouth
[Morton Tinmouth]

John Sutton	1
Garkin Dunn	1
Marke Goundry	1
	3

Newbiggin in Teasdell
[Newbiggin on Tees]

Ursula Loansdale	1

Arthure Emmerson	1
John Allinson	1
Margtt Allison	1
Anne Jackson	1
Cuth Nattris	1
Fran Hodgson	1
Anne Newby	1
	8

Peirce Bridge
[Piercebridge]

Rowld Lancaster	1
Tho Bomer	2
John Waugh	1
Raphe Newland	1
Anne Hillderth	1
Geo Parling	1
John Cowling	1
John Bell	1
Rich Smith	1
Tho Smith	1
Mich Reap	1
Edw Penshow	1
John Carter	1
Ellin Sisson	1
Mary Richdson	2
Fran Shaw	2
Robt White	2
John Smith	1
Hen Potter	1
Mich Roper	1
John Bramly	1
Richd Jober	1
Fran Hodgson	1
Wm Esliaby	1
Tho Harryson	1
Richd Colling	1
Ellin Bradshaw	1
Tho Newlands	1
Raphe Hodgson	1
Wm Browne	1
Robt Murton	1
Raphe Parking	1
Fran Jober	1
Edw Hodgson	1
Eliz Hodgson	1

Mich Gray	1	**Bondgate in Bis:pp Auwkland**	
School house	1	**[Bondgate in Bishop Auckland]**	
John Darntonhopp	1	John Maddison	1
	42	Robt Corner	1
		Rich Thompson	1
Raby and Kaverston		John White	1
[Raby with Keverstone]		Hugh Roberts	1
John Todd	2	John Summer	1
Chr Peirson	1	John Wilkinson	1
James Thompson	1	Mary Summer	1
Richard Elgy	1	Nich Judson	1
	5	Mich Spencer	1
		Tho Harryson	1
m. 21, c. 1		John Lazenby	1
Brough of Awkland		Marmaduke Crawford	1
[Borough of Auckland]		Wm Milburne	1
Tho Wright	1	Geo Cockerfield	1
Marmaduke Davyson	1	Wm Rawell	1
Jane Leever	1	John Wasy	1
Tho Hart	1	Barbary White	1
Willm Hayton	1	Margery Fleminge	1
Margtt Dounes	1	Nicho Milburne	1
Eliz Lampson	1	Raphe Chapman	1
Dorothy Nanbell	1	Tho Man	1
Wm Wilson	1	Hen Downes	1
James Mott	1	John Wilson	1
Geo Curry	1	Geo Brickeld	1
Bryan Lachle	1	Chr Walker	1
Willm Middleton	1	Hugh Roberts	1
Eliz Shawwood	1	John Wheatley	1
Mabell Gowland	1	Ann Middleton	1
John Clerke	1	Richd Ward	1
Cuth Thompson	1	Ann Dent	1
Richd Wilson	1	Wm Flemmin	1
Jane Baley	1	Tho Chapman	1
Stephen Wright	1	James Worsupp	1
John Dawson	1	Eliz Robinson	1
Jane Colling	1	Ann Stobbs	1
Bryan Barker	1	James Worst	1
Tho Bawswitt	1	Henry Nelson	1
Eliz Bainbrigg	1	John Robinson	1
Francis Means	1	Thomas Winter	1
Ann Wall	1	Widd Fothergill	1
Eliz Cooke	1	Grace Foster	1
	28		

m. 21, c. 2

Alexandr Thompson	1
John Hall	1
Margtt Cuttle	1
Barbary White	1
Francis Salkeld	1
Mary Gyles	1
John Browne	1
Wm Cradocke	1
John Jordan	1
Raphe Sparke	1
Samuell Bankes	1
Richd Thompson	1
Tho Temple	1
Tho Summers	1
Wm Darnton	1
Tho Foster	1
John Bewicke	1
John Liddell	1
	60

Newgate in Bis:pp Auwkland
[Newgate in Bishop Auckland]

John Roberts	1
Jane Graham	2
John Adamson	1
Geo Moore	1
Jane Nealson	1
Humph Wharton	1
Geo Wilson	2
Antho Roberts	1
Tho Scott	2
Robt Key	1
Willm Failler	1
John Tallentyre	1
Richd Gibson	1
John Langstaffe	1
Ottinell Rider	1
Antho Browne	1
Tho Thompson	1
Widd Wetherell	1
Mary Nealson	1
James Simpson	1
Widd Sober	1
Widd Wiggan	1
Nicho Wilson	1

Geo Eggleton	1
Alice Willaby	1
Margtt Smith	1
Ann Burlison	1
Hen Thompson	1
John Hedley	1
Hen Hedley	1
Margtt Curry	1
Margtt Spenceley	1
Willm Carleton	1
John Lambe	2
Hen Bails	1
Raphe Duglasse	1
Bryan Longstaffe	1
Raphe Parkin	1
Tho Walton	1
John Mason	1
Tho Rainsforth	1
Richd Steadman	1
John Adamson	1
Wm Gills	1
Richd Hunt	1
Gaskin Downes	1
Tho Hunter	1
John Ward	1
Peter Nelson	1
Wm Stobbs	1
John Hunter	1
John Johnson	1
Otnell Rider	1
Wm Wilson	1
Widd Hadwen	1
Fran Robinson	1
John Kirkham	1
	61

m. 21, c. 3

St Andrew Awkland
[Auckland St Andrew]

Wm Crow	1
Tho Maughan	1
Barnaby Bell	1
Widd Byerley	1
Robt Robinson	1
Jane Lawson	1

Widd Dickinson	1	Ann Stephenson	1
	7	Widd Baxter	1
		Jane Best	1
St Ellin: Awkland		Tho Baxter	1
[Auckland St Helen]		Robt Middleton	1
Widd Reed	1	Jane Simpson	1
Willm Stanbanke	1	Alice Wilde	1
Tho Meburne	1	Wm Hope	1
John Burne	1	Fran Henderson	1
John Rowling	1	Isabell Stevenson	1
Tho Newby	1	Robt Shield	2
Mich Teasdale	1	Widd Dunn	1
Cuth Straitforth	1	Tho Deputy	1
James Colling	1	Geo Newby	1
Jane Stainbancke	1	Symon Raine	1
Raphe Gargrave	1	Eliz Garforth	1
Chr Lambert	1	Isabell Mason	1
Tho Vaux	1	Wm Gainforth	1
Tho Pauly	1	Margtt Newby	1
Ann Dawson	1	Arthure Stockdale	1
Chr Hodgson	1	Ann Smith	1
Musgrave Errington	1	Ann Sidgworth	1
Jennett Waistell	1	Eliz Bryan	1
Humphry Bell	1	Tho Bellas	1
Tho How	1	Robt Darnton	1
Antho Garminsway	1	Margtt Sandrson	1
John Daniell	1	Mary Mounsey	1
Stephen Windell	1	Margtt Wren	1
Isabell Rennyson	1		
John Parkinson	2	*m. 21v, c. 1*	
Jane Stainebanke	1	Ann Bucke	1
Willm Stainebanke	1	Eliz Bayles	1
	28	Richd Dent	1
		Willm Plummer	1
West Awkland		Widd Preston	1
[West Auckland]		Widd Grainger	1
John Gibson	1	Robt Eden	1
Bryan Dent	1	Marke Parkinson	1
Duke Dale	1	John Hinde	1
Wm Finley	1	Raphe Simpson	2
Wm Mounsey	1	Widd Clifton	1
Wm Wall	1	Tho Parkinson	1
Raphe Coltman	1	Tho Chester	1
Raphe Summer	1	Bryan Dent	1
Widd Maughan	1	Widd Allinson	1
Wm Parkinson	1	John Hodgson	1

Arthure Stockdell	1	Chr Lumley	1
John Hodgson	1	Geo Kiplinge	1
John Anderson	1	Bartho Mallam	1
	60	Willm Acwith	1
	[59]	John Hull	1
		Eliz Betterby	1
Branspeth		Mich Mason	2
[Brancepeth]		Raphe Wright	1
John Harkley	1	Tho Fitch	1
Isabell Emerson	1	Eliz Mason	1
Wm Blenkinshopp	2	Robt Barker	1
Geo Blenkinshopp	1	Widd Marley	1
Rich Noble	1	Roger Hull	1
Ann Acquith	1		**61**
Nicho Acquith	1		
John Button	1	*m. 21v, c. 2*	
Eliz Horseley	1	**Branspeth Castle**	
Charles Acquith	1	**[Brancepeth Castle]**	
Geo Younge	1	William Friend	1
Margtt Emmerson	1	Raphe Johnson	1
John Taylor	1	George Mitchell	1
George Martin	1		**3**
Eliz Fuester	1		
Widd Stout	1	**Brandon**	
Widd Browne	1	John Crookes	1
Geo Willowby	1	John Grinwell	1
Widd White	2	Widd Lampton	1
Robt Taylor	1	Rich Robson	1
Hen Emmerson	1	Widd Pinkney	1
Raphe Mason	2	Wm Arrowsmith	1
John Suddicke	1	John Swalwell	1
Robt Bainbrigge	2	Timothy Arkley	1
Margtt Thompson	1	Tho Bell	1
Edward Browne	1	Jane Arkley	1
John Mason	1	Ellinor Gaire	1
Richd Willowby	1	Margtt Pinkney	1
Margtt Wright	1		**12**
Tho Marley	1		
Hen Marley	1	**Byshottles**	
Hugh Mason	1	Thomas Bankes	1
John Doffett	2	Tho Moores	1
Robt Parkin	2	Fran Westley	2
Step Barker	2	Ann Salkeld	1
Tho Duckett	2		**5**
John Wright	2		
Ellinor Wodderupp	1		

North Bedburne
[North Bedburn]

Thomas Mosy	1
Chr Hodgson	1
Tho Story	1
Antho Coming	1
Thomas Lawe	1
Antho Jackson	1
Henry Pattinson	1
Willm Byreland	1
	8

South Bedburne
[South Bedburn]

Richd Herreside	1
Antho Hodgson	1
Richd Atkinson	1
Tho Atkinson	1
Margtt Wright	1
Mabell Nicholson	1
Bryan Todd	1
	7

Bishoppley
[Bishopley]

Tho Colepitt	1
Arthure Morgan	1
John Athy	1
Eliz Nower	1
Margtt Armestrong	1
Antho Golightly	1
Geo Bell	1
	7

Counden
[Coundon]

Richd Parkins	1
Wm Addy	1
Widd Hopper	1
Chr Dixon	1
Robt Parkins	1
Roger Stockell	1
Ellis Wilson	1
Wm Morgan	1
Luke Wilson	1
Richd Parkins	1

Jane Nicholson	1
Antho Parkins	1
Tho Plumpton	1
Robt Parkins	1
Thomas Pearson	1
	15

m. 21v, c. 3

Escombe
[Escomb]

John Todd	1
Hen Bandricke	1
Bryan Todd	1
Jane Hodgson	1
John Stobbs junr	2
Richd Hodgson	1
Tho Steele	1
Bridgett Stobbs	1
	9

Evenwood

James Chirkilt	1
Joseph Prestley	1
Chr Stevenson	1
Tho Bowes	1
John Brumley	1
Tho Taylor	1
Willm Smorfoot	1
John Boath	1
John Wright sen	1
John Wright jun	1
Richd Robbinson	2
Thomas Hoggart	1
Tho Sewell	1
Willm Brumbley	1
Raphe Wass	1
Antho West	1
Jane Medcalfe	1
Jane Made	1
John Hansome	1
Bulmer Boyes	15
Fran West	1
John Browne	1
Antho Bullocke	1
Kathar Bell	1
James Bullocke	1

Robt Wardell	1
Edward Slee	1
	28

Evenwood Barrony
[Evenwood Barony]

Ellinor Hodgson	1
Margtt Hodgson	1
Wm Gasterley	1
James Hoard	1
Wm Young	1
Hen Smith	1
Jane Craw	1
Leo Hodgson	1
Jane How	1
John Crow	1
Willm Gowland	1
Anthony Phillipps	1
William Shield jun	1
Jane Gowland	1
	14

Frosterley

Thomas Cornforth	1
Tho Mowbray	1
Antho Chapman	1
James Clerke	1
Clement Chapman	1
Arthure Jobling	1
Clement Chapman	1

m. 22, c. 1

John Gartheron	1
Cuth Morgan	1
John Walton	1
Hen Estobb	1
Mary Chatt	1
Eliz Walton	1
	13

Hanwicke
[Hunwick]

Tho Ward	1
John Lumley	1
Margtt Wright	1
John Berwicke	1

Kathar Silvertoppe	1
Geo Walker	1
Sanders Archer	1
	7

Hedley on the Hill [Hedley]

Ann Hogg	1
Ann Jobling	1
	2

Helmington Row

Tho Gibson	1
Robt Tirrell	1
Tho Jackson	2
Tho Charleton	2
Hen Jackson	1
John Sickerwham	1
Mary Walker	1
Geo Hall	1
Nicho Hall	1
Widd Maior	1
Nicho Raine	2
John Layton	2
Ann Linsley	1
Isabell Linsley	1
George Hall	1
Nicholas Elstobb	1
	20

Helmparke
[Helm Park]

John Pickering	1
Richd Garfoot	1
Tho Story	1
Simon Coleman	1
Willm Simpson	1
Mary Garfoot	1
Ann Heavyside	1
	7

Hamsterley

Willm Givens	1
Wm Steele	1
Tho White junr	1
Geo Wilson	1
Tho Rose	1

Widd Hardy	1	Raphe Braidley	1
Geo Hall	1	Robt Emmerson	1
Abraham Whitley	1	John Emmerson	1
Gilbt Mcnelly	1	Henry Bell	1
John Jackson	1	Richd Bell	1
Peter Hodgson	1	Tho Smith	1
John Yard	1	John Hutton	1
Eliz Little	1	Robt Newton	1
Grace Hodgson	1	Widd Sandrson	1
Tho Shepheard	1	Tho Hodgson	1
Edward Punton	1	Raphe Newby	1
Peter Natris	1	John Hutton	1
		Willm Johnson	1
m. 22, c. 2		Geo Braidley	1
Widd Fericke	1	Tho Hodgson	1
Wm Graham	1	Willm Emmerson	1
Tho Whitfrickle	1	John Ashburne	1
Wm Fericke	1	Ann Maddyson	1
Antho White	1	John Greenwell	1
Widd Givens	1	Eliz Hodgson	1
Jeffery Newby	1	John Heavyside	1
Hugh Little	1		40
John Nattris	1		
	26	**Newton Capp**	
		[Newton Cap]	
Linsacke & Softley		Wm Byerley	2
[Lynesack and Softley]		Robt Watson	1
Raphe Watson	1	John Gills	1
Willm Estobb	1	Willm Watson	1
John Parmerly	1		5
Mary Speedlin	1		
Wm Hodgson	1	**Seildon**	
Chr Hodgson	1	**[Shildon]**	
Wm Robinson	1	Raphe Worthy	1
John Jackson	1	Widd Fowler	1
Tho Appleby	1	Isabell Hudson	1
Richd Alder	1	Willm Watson	1
Tho Heblethwayt	1	Tho Buffy	1
Geo Alderson	1		5
Raphe Potter	1		
Margtt Dobison	1	*m. 22, c. 3*	
Geo Potter	1	**Stockley**	
Willm Archer	1	Widd Robson	1
Wm Hodgson	1	John Taylor	1
Geo Braidley	1	John Bell	1
Robt Braidley	1	Robt Pearson	1

Tho Pearson	1	Nicho Fetherston	1
Edw Westwood	1	Widd Emmerson	1
John Hixton	1	Eliz Little	1
Ann Fletcher	1	Tho Viccars	1
Wm Blackey	1	Lan Robinson	1
John Bontfloore	1	John Haward	1
Barbary Bruntingham	1	Raphe Watson	1
Nicho Ushaw	1	Fran Pigg	1
John Porter	1	Widd Fetherston	1
Widd Rodham	1	Tho Reedfarne	1
Jane Teasdale	1	Cuth Nattris	1
Ann Smith	1	John Hetherington	1
Mich Smith	1	Peter Viccars	1
Geo Clarke	1	Widd Bainbrigge	1
Tho Coleson	1	Fran Renwicke	1
James Shevell	1	Hen Bromer	1
Widd Blacke	1	Raphe Emerson	1
Widd Harryson	1	Tho Viccars	1
John Colson	1	Geo Norton	2
Robt Duckett	1	Isabell Lee	1
Geo Jackson	1	John Witton	1
	25	Eliz Bainbrigge	1

Stanhopp
[Stanhope]

		Raphe Watson	1
		John Nattris	1
Tho Raine	1	John Fetherston	1
Widd Horsman	1		28
Geo Bainbrigge	1		
Ellinor Ward	1		
John Westgarth	1	*m. 22v, c. 1*	
Eliz Ward	1	**Stanhopp Quarter**	
Margery Emmerson	1	**[Stanhope Quarter]**	
	7	Raphe Sidgsworth	1
		Raphe Harryson	1
		John Bell	1

Stanhopp Park
[Stanhope Park]

		Wm Stobbs	1
		Wm Teasdale	1
Isabell Chapman	1	Wm Morley	1
Chr Viccars	1	Wm Watson	1
Math Walton	1	Nicho Vepond	1
Rich Gosling	1	Nicho Lee	1
Cuth Whitfield	1	Henry Suddocke	1
	5	Willm Walton	1
		Robt Hale	1

Stanhop Forrest
[Stanhope Forest]

		Raphe Walton	1
		Hugh Teasdale	1
John Coulterd	1	Lancelott Walton	1
Geo Westwood	1	Widd Walton	1

John Bell	1	Dorothy Hall	2
John Reedley	1	Richd Bucke	1
John Walton	1	Willm Hodgson	1
Henry Ellam	1	Grace Moore	1
Willm Robinson	1	Grace Fadwen	1
Tho Maddyson	1	Fran Dobbyson	1
Katharine Peart	1	Robert Myers	1
John Gastin	1		
Nicho Westgarth	1	*m. 22v, c. 2*	
Arthure Dewson	1	Tobias Fanden	1
George Jobling	1	Margtt Ellinor	1
Chr Teasdale	1	Andrew Collingwood	1
Widd Phillippson	1	Raphe Emerson	1
Robt Golightly	1	Tobias Benson	2
Tho Greenside	1	Geo Simpson	1
Mary Halliday	1	Michael Fanden	1
Widd Henderson	1	Peter How	1
George Harryson	1	Tho Allinson	1
Chr Harryson	1	Eliz Jackson	1
Widd Collingwood	1	Tho Thompson	1
Lowry Maddison	1	Tho Addison	1
Chr Stoker	1	Ann Seames	1
Robt Crome	1	Willm Taylor	1
	39		**27**

Thornley

John Wilson	1
Widd Wilson	2
Wm Stott	1
Tho Stott	1
Widd Garfoot	1
Cuthbt Oard.	1
Willm Greenwell	1
John Garfoot	1
Widd Dawson	1
Geo Layton	1
Math Greenwell	1
Richd Marshall	1
	13

Witton upon Weare
[Witton-le-Wear]

Wm How sen	1
John Booth	1
Dan Wright	1
Mary Hall	1

Willington Qrtr
[Wolsingham town]

Henry Emerson	1
Simon Buston	1
Robt Lynn	1
Fran Lynn	1
Margtt Bassell	1
Tho Coulson junr	1
John Maughan	1
Phillip Maughan	1
Geo Curry	1
Wm Browneridge	1
John Aray	1
Roger Dun sen	1
Roger Dun junr	1
Richd Mawbray	1
Eliz Dawson	1
Richd Joplin	1
John Andrew	1
Hugh Ramsey	1
Tho Collinson	1

Isabell Allerton	1	John Wilson	1
Robt Marshall	1	John Bell	1
Raphe Wall	1	Willm Geston	1
Laurence Taylor	1	Hen Batson	1
Bridgett Oliver	1	Tho Jackson	1
John Lawson	1	Richd Jefferson	1
Wm Robinson	1	Widd Strafford	1
Isabell Dowson	1	Geo Usher	1
Ann Grinwell	1	Dorothy Cleaton	1
Tho Stevenson	1	Matt Heighington	1
John Thompson	1	Margtt Harryson	1
Joseph Walker	1	Wm Reanoldson	1
John Unthanke	1	Wm Toward	1
Wm Crooke	1		**25**
Chr Wall	1		

Woolsingham St Side Quarter
[Wolsingham South]

Rich Kelly	1	Willm Parkin	1
John Nelson	1	John Foulerby	1
Jane Brearley	1	Cuthbt Nivey	1
Robt Linskill	1	Alexandr Bell	1
Robt Wass	1	Cuthbt Lowish	1
Mich Harryson	1	Chr Golightly	1
Geo Stephenson	1	John Jackson	1
Robt Chapman	1		**7**
Robt Hopper	1		
Cuth Kirkley	1		

Woolsingham Park Quartr
[Wolsingham Park]

Raphe Dixson	1	Geo Toward	1
John Fielding	1	Widd Viccars	1
Mich Cooper	1	Widd Joplin	1
James White	1	Michaell Burnopp	1
	48		**4**

m. 22v, c. 3

Woolsingham Et Quarter
[Wolsingham East]

m. 23, c. 1

Stockton Ward

Geo Marshall	1		
Mich Bryers	1	**Ayslaby**	
Albony Foster	1	**[Aislaby]**	
Jane Wren	1	John Cooke	1
Matt Greenwell	1	Chr Colinson	1
Rich Marley	1	Margtt Ducke	1
Jane Hudspeth	1	Geo Dent	1
Margtt Fogg	1	Tho Newton	1
Alice Falken	1	Susanna Newton	1
John Aire	1		
Tho Raw	1		
Godfrey Stephenson	1		

Tho Chapman	1
Margtt Wilson	1
Richd Turner	1
Tho Appleby	1
Eliz Middleton	1
Hen Chapman	1
Esther Bowman	1
Tho Hinell	1
Cuthbt Nicholson	1
Tho Reed	1
John Tailbush	1
	17

Bishoppton
[Bishopton]

John Stevenson	1
Wm Clarke	1
Willm Fewler	1
Margtt Wilson	1
John Bewserlaw	1
John Hart	1
Mich Newton	1
Willm Challens	1
John Earle	1
John Rew	1
Willm Smith	1
Margtt Reaw	1
John Towers	1
Hen Layburne	1
Phillis Williamson	1
Duke Farow	1
Willm Clarke	1
Richd Layburne	1
John Johnson	1
Raphe Hart	1
Robt Todd	1
John Garnett	1
Mary Cowper	1
Thomas Newton	1
Richd Dinsall	1
Jane Chilton	1
John Stoddart	1
Wm Reay	1
Willm Foster	1
	29

Carleton
[Carlton]

Peter Farrie	1
Dorothy Glandall	1
Hen Heaton	1
Chr Peart	1
Edw Bushbie	1
Raphe Anderson	1
John Ranson	1
John Robson	1
Antho Mills	1
Richd Robson	1
James Norton	1
Margtt Fewler	1
Alex Fawell	1
	13

m. 23, c. 2

Cotham Mundivell
[Coatham Mundeville]

John Arrowsmith	1
Tho Overman	1
Ann Davyson	1
John Dent	1
Tho Johnes	1
Antho Clarke	1
Chr Haxwell	1
	7

Elton

Willm Rawling	1
Jane Watson	1
Eliz Brass	1
Ann Reed	1
Ann Clarke	1
Tho Akie	1
	6

Egglescliffe

Barbary Ayre	1
Tho Robinson	1
Yovans Cathericke	1
Robt Reed	1
Tho Aire	1
Wm Bainbrigg	1

Willm Wilson	1	Duke Ward	1
	7	Willm Neasham	1
		Geo Denam	1
Harworth		Eliz Bullman	1
[Hurworth]		Ann Lodge	1
Rich Lanby	2	Tho Deanam	1
John Allinson	1	Fran Anderson	1
Marmaduke Ivinson	1	Robt Godling	1
Humph Steedman	1	Sam Ovington	1
Mary Walker	1	Tho Coats	1
Chr Mawen	2	Ninian Gresham	1
Sam Phennicke	1	Geo Farmer	1
John Snawden	1	Phillip Coulson	1
Wm Brass	1	John Smith	1
Raphe Algood	1	Peter Wilkinson	1
John Cousson	2	Tho Bailes	1
Tho Cully	1	Eliz Franking	1
Chr Grayne	1	Hen Craggs	1
Wm Hardy	1	Willm Arrowsmith	1
Richd Smith	1		63
Chr Denam	1		
Tho Neasham	1	**Harburne**	
John Dunings	1	**[Hartburn]**	
John Bulman	1	Tho Thompson	1
Wm Willmson	1	Willm Ramford	1
Wm Harryman	1	Martin Carter	1
Wm Walker	1	Wm Parkin	1
Chr Dinsdall	1	Rosina Peers	1
John Bromley	1	John Emmerson	1
Ann Bellamy	1	Margtt Ray	1
Wm Tunstall	1	John Rainford	1
Geo Bulman	2	Jane Graham	1
Charles Willy	1	John Gent	1
Wm Pyburne	1	Margtt Banks	1
John Potter	1	Tho Ambgell	1
Joane Stockton	2	Antho Harpley	1
John Atkinson	1		13
Edw Mawen	1		
Eliz Spence	1	**Middleton on Row**	
Richd Gresham	1	**[Middleton One Row]**	
Wm Bulman	1	Widd Stockdall	1
Dorothy Fenwicke	1	Chr Browman	1
		Tho Wilson	1
m. 23, c. 3		Wm Wilkinson	1
Jane Stevenson	1	Tho Bedson	1
John Johnson	1	Constance Andrew	1

Wm Andrew	1	Math Weare	1
Robt Seaman	1	Robt Young	1
Andrew Gilmore	1	Raphe Colling	1
Ann Allinson	1		24
Eliz Culley	1		
James Hodgson	1	**Rede Marchall**	
Wm Savill	1	**[Redmarshall]**	
Chr Gibson	1	Edw Teasdall	2
John Hudson	1	Tho Browne	1
Tho Hutchinson	1	Leo Simpson	1
Edw Pinkard	1	Eliz Forrest	1
Antho Dale	1	John Thompson	1
Jane Horsley	1		6
Mary Savill	1		
Thomas Savill	1	**Stillington**	
John Harryson	1	Wm Baxter	1
	22	Margtt Maltby	1
		John Stubb	1
m. 23v, c.1		Margtt Reedman	1
Middleton St Geo[rge]		Richd [*blank*]	1
John Harperley	1	Francis Hartburne	1
Robt Gates	1	Francis Cully	1
	2	Volentine Martin	1
		Richd Wadley	1
Long Newton		Margtt Jackson	1
John Pearkson	1	John Johnson	1
Wm Thompson	1	John Hardy	1
Jane Corner	1	Geo Bridgewell	1
Margtt Newham	1	Alison Markeham	1
Ellinor Walker	1		14
Ann Wilson	1		
Thomas Pearson	1	**Stockton Town**	
Geo Hodgson	1	Wm Fuler	1
Mary Burne	1	Wm Wilson	1
Eliz Stobbs	1	Chr Crosby	1
Richd Richdson	1	Tho Hutson	1
John Clarke	1	Widd Reditt	1
Richd Hodgson	1	Wm Crosby	1
Jane Raine	1	Jane Stephenson	1
Robt Browne	1	Widd Thompson	1
Ann Warmouth	1	Margtt Burne	1
Isabell Boyes	1	Wid Thompson	1
Ann Greenbury	1	Ann Jhison	1
John Newham	1	John Ushaw	1
Eliz Newham	1		12
Fran Pinder	1		

m. 23v, c. 2

Stockton Burrow
[Stockton Borough]

Geo Denham	1
Raphe Crossland	1
Jonathan White	1
Wm Story	1
Widd Fowler	1
Tho Southgate	1
Widd Allinson	1
Widd Heron	1
Widd Wood	1
Widd Robinson	1
John Johnson senr	1
Wm Stocke	1
Wm Claxton	1
Widd Robinson	1
Widd Allinson	1
Widd Saderton	1
Raphe Oaks	1
Widd Wheardon	1
Widd Sheryton	1
Widd Browne	1
Widd Jones	1
Roger Bainbrigg	1
John Wilson	1
John Browne	1
John Bainbrigg	1
Robt Banks	2
Widd Fewler	1
Alice Eden	1
Widd Denham	1
Widd Denham	1
Robt Banks	1
Widd Bainbrigg	1
	33

Stainton Little
[Little Stainton]

John Hugiston	1
Ann Dawson	1
Mary Ushaw	1
John Johnson	1
Wm Newton	1
Jane Wilkinson	1
Tho Newton	1

Jane Atkinson	1
	8

Sadbury
[Sadberge]

Wm Lee	1
Wm Cullis	1
Widd Bartell	2
Widd Wilkinson	1
John Harperley	1
Tho Barnes	1
Martin Barnes	1
John Tallon	1
Widd Audd	1
Widd Hutchinson	1
Robt Balmbrough	1
Widd Robson	1
Martin Angle	1
John Armstrong	1
Widd Bell	1
Fran Mawer	1
Rich Cockerall	1
Tho Marley	1
	19

m. 23v, c. 3

Bradbury Const[abulary]
[Bradbury]

Wm Davyson	1
Peter Lukopp	1
John Robinson	1
Wm Greave	1
John Cristall	1
Richd Browne	1
	6

Butterwick

Edw Richardson	1
Eliz Wilkinson	1
Richd Cooke	1
Hen Portes	1
	4

Bellingham [Billingham]

Gawen Reed	1
Wm Thompson	1

John Christopher	1
Robt Christopher	1
Hen Stobart	1
Isabell Stayes	1
Jos Mandivell	1
Wm David	1
John Christopher	1
Wm Jeckell	1
Wm Hull	1
Tho Warmouth	1
Chr Warmouth	1
Tho Stevenson	1
Ellinor Browne	1
Fran Skarth	1
Margtt Harburne	1
John Best	1
Eliz Layne	1

[*above entry crossed through*]

Tho Chapman sen	1
Tho Hodgson	1
John Huettson	1
Jane Booke	1
Tho Stevenson	1
Marma Robinson	1
Robt Clerke	1
Tho Huettson	1
Margery Stevenson	1
	27

Bishopp Middleham
[Bishop Middleham]

Barth Reay	1
Wm Robson	1
Jo Doney	1
John Barton	1
Tho Robinson	1
Wm Rutter	1
John Emmerson	1
Raphe Nicholson	1
Willm Thompson	1
Fran Maunder	1
Rich Botchby	1
Wm Wood	1
Tho Stockton	1
John Bothby	1
John Raw	1

Tho Wright	1
John Robinson	1
Robt Cocker	1
Eliz Reed	1
Ann Wilkinson	1
Raphe Widdowes	1
Mary Robinson	1
Chr Parker	1
Geo Dodd	1
Hen Grinwell	1
Mary Middleton	1
Robt Fissicke	1
Margtt Mawyer	1
Antho Midford	1
Dorothy Blyth	1
Mary Middleton	1
Thomas Stockton	1
	32

m. 24, c. 1

Coopen Bewly
[Cowpen Bewley]

Will Bowmer	1
Wm Emerson	1
Robt Sitteron	1
John Flecke	1
Wm Law	1
Ann Maughan	1
Eliz Huntington	1
Wm. Clifton	1
Mich Bushby	1
Raphe Tindale	1
Rich Clarke	1
Richd Robinson	1
John Swallwell	1
Wm Stephenson	1
Wm Robinson	1
Tho Clerke	1
Tho Stephenson	1
Chr Boomer	1
	18

Cornforth

Wm Smith	1
Wm Hunter	1
Fran Gerrard	1

Tho Brunstill	1
Robt Smith	1
John Hutchinson	1
Tho Lambe	1
Margtt Allis	1
Duke Allis	1
Ann Chipchase	1
Mary Colledge	1
Wm Layburne	1
James Hudspeth	1
Jane Davyson	1
Geo Richardson	1
Chr Fawett	1
Phillip Hudspeth	1
Mary Haswell	1
Mary Marley	1
Dorothy Turpine	1
Tho Haswell	1
Robt Widdyfield	1
Robt Hutchinson	1
Robt Kyrton	1
	24

Dalton Pearcy
[Dalton Piercy]

Eliz Robson	1
John Hobkirke	1
	2

Embleton

Florence Thompson	1
Robt Fawcett	1
Eliz Robson	1
	3

Elwicke
[Elwick]

Robt Swallwell	1
Richd Craggs	1
John Ambleton	1
Laurence Laverocke	1
Geo Littleforth	1
Isabell Watson	1
Wm Crow	1
Tho Hodgson	1
John Wood	1

Widd Harryson	1
Geo Pattinson	1
Nicho Harryson	1
Tho Reed	1
James Gallowlie	1
	14

m. 24, c. 2

Elwicke Hall
[Elwick Hall]

John Best	1
Chr Denton	1
Widd Emmerson	1
Wm Martin	1
Ann Pattinson	1
Fran Richdson	1
Myles Jefferson	1
Geo Michell	1
John Jorden	2
Jane Richardson	1
	11

Foxton

Margtt Watson	1
James Ranson	1
Tho Maltby	1
Lan Brewster	1
John Smith	1
Eliz Smith	1
Eliz Maltby	1
	7

Fishburne
[Fishburn]

John Shacklocke	1
Margtt Cattericke	1
James Sever	1
Wm Stodart	1
Robt Corner	1
Geo Robinson	1
Wm Craggs	2
Jane Johnson	1
Wm Werren	2
Wm Martindale	1
Ellinor Smith	2
Robt Wilkinson	1
Hen Middleton	1

Jane Carter	2	Volentine Sparke	1
Ann Hassen	1	Simon Smith	1
Raphe Woodhouse	1	John Swanwicke	1
Geo Adamson	2	Raphe Hart	1
Jane Mason	1	Robt Martin	1
John Clerke	1	Widd Sparke	1
Wm Robson	1	Geo Miller	1
Jane Farrow	1	Widd Dennyson	1
Nich Nevelson	1	Tho Thompson	1
John Buss	2	Widd Foster	1
	29	Rich Martin	1
		John Fletcher	1
Greatham		John Cully	1
Robt Sparke	1	Widd Wilson	1
Widd Tinmouth	1	Tho Huettson	1
Widd Eddinngton	1	Widd Warmouth	1
Widd Shepherd	1	Widd Nicholson	1
Geo Habacke	1	Edw Sparke	1
John Robinson	1	Andrew Dawson	1
Edw Prance	1	Widd Thompson	1
Marke Mallance	1	Widd Rewton	1
John Yeell	1	Widd Errington	1
Wm Newby	1	Hen Watson	1
Geo Coats	1	Widd Largeman	1
John Hutchinson	1	Widd Archer	1
Richd Elstobb	1	John Marley	1
Widd Lister	1	Widd Johnson	1
Widd Dun	1	Geo Hubacke	1
Widd Andrew	1	Widd Heaslery	1
John Yeell	1	Willm Fletcher	1
John Pearne	1	John Robson	1
Widd Atkinson	1	Tho Wardell	1
Robt Court	1	James Rainton	1
Edw Atkinson	1	Widd Emerson	1
Tho Atkinson	1	Mich Harryson	1
		Hen Hall	1
m. 24, c. 3		John Sparke	1
Tho Rippon	1	Tho Smith	1
Robt Dun	1		70
Gaskyn Dun	1	[*corrected total*] es[?]	69
Edw Oliver	1		
John Sheraton	1	**Hart**	
Willm Speddin	1	Raphe Reed	1
Marke Atkinson	1	Eliz Nicholson	1
Peter Marlin	1	Robt Passmoore	1
John Sparke	1	Mich Johnson	1

Wm Nicholson	1
Tho Burdon	1
Widd Wilson	1
Eliz Wright	1
John Nicholson	1
Geo Atkinson	2
Wm Smith	1
Hen Wilson	1
Widd Maugham	1
Robt Hutchinson	1
Wm Wright	1
Robt Toby	1
Math Thomlinson	1
John Twedell	1

m. 24v, c. 1

Wm Johnson	1
Widd Mansforth	1
Letty Cooke	1
Wm Wilkinson	1
John Snowden	1
Wm Mackley	1
Tho Rew Croft	1
Wm Turbatt	1
Robt Craggs	1
Jane Craggs	1
Antho Dun	1
John Hallyman	1
John Martin	1
Jennett Lee	1
Robt Stothart	1
Alex Ferrybie	1
Margtt Dun	1
Mich Todd	1
John Mansforth	1
Alice Meburne	1
Jane Mansforth	1
John Curry	1
Margtt Coulson	1
Eliz Mace	1
Robt Chilton	1
Robt Cooles	1
Robt Gibson	1
James Mansforth	2
Chr Moody	1
John Lee	1

Robt Turbett	1
Rich Johnson	1
John Wright	1
Marke Bates	1
Peter Graveson	1
Geo Wilson	1
Tho Rennyson	1
Tho Hallyman	1
	58

Hartlepoole
[Hartlepool]

Clement Browne	1
Wm Bull	2
Widd Taylor	1
The Towne Hall	1
Mr Smurfield	2
Antho Easton	2
Jo Harryson	2
Wm Harryson	2
Raphe Whitehead	2
Dorothy Cuminge	1
Margtt Revell	1
Margtt Moore	2
Nicho Bacon	1
Tho Lagnell	1
John Stevenson	1
Eliz Ware	1
Margtt Sherewood	1
Tho Humble	1
Tho Robinson	2
John Davyson	2
Wm Parrott	1
Eliz Gibson	1
Antho Middleton	1
Margtt Finley	1
Ellin Twedell	1
Tho Haswell	2

m. 24v, c. 2

Eliz Buttree	1
Bryan Martindale	2
Margtt Sharpe	2
John Thompson	1
John Middleton	1
Chr Bacon	1

Margtt Revell	1
Wm Robinson	1
Robt Patterson	1
Wm Uffington	1
Wm Ogle	1
James Whitehead	1
Widd Hayson	1
Widd Laverocke	1
Eliz Hart	1
Geo Ward	1
	54

Mordon

Tho Hardman	1
Ellinr Ramshaw	1
Hen Key	1
Richd Thaxton	1
Marke Watson	1
Phill Islababy	1
Isab Elstobb	1
Margtt Clement	1
Tho Story	1
Eliz Clarke	1
Antho Heavyside	1
Robt Lambert	1
Tho Earr	1
Barbary Smith	1
John Bowman	1
Tho Skarlott	1
John Shottwell	1
Humphrey Shottwell	1
Symon Theakston	1
Chr Appleby	1
Tho Wind	1
Susan Chapman	1
Geo Conyers	2
Ellinr Shecklocke	1
Tho Marr	1
	26

Mansford
[Mainsforth]

Raphe Midcalfe	1
Geo Barnett	1
	2

Newton Bewly
[Newton Bewley]

Isabell Merrington	1
John Sleater	1
Jane Ranson	1
Wm Hunter	1
John Smith	1
John Slaiter	1
Alice Habacke	1
John Huettson	1
John Leaton	1
Cuthbt Harling	1
Alice Eggleston	1
Willm Emmerson	1
	12

Sedgefield

Willm Gore	1
John Richdson	1
Margtt Hodgson	1
John Hodgson	1
Willm Lambe	1

m. 24v, c. 3

John Fletcher	1
Robt Harryson	1
Bernard Robinson	1
Barbary Morris	1
Wm Harryson	1
Tho Gent	1
Marmaduke Richdson	1
Mary Blackley	1
Richd Browne	1
Mich Old	1
John Southgate	1
John Carr	1
Antho Lax	1
Robt Cradocke	1
John Cradocke	1
Florence Ivyson	1
John Hodgson	1
James Heslopp	1
Ellin Browne	1
Geo Richdson	1
Eliz Wheatley	1
Lan Lambe	1

Leo Gibson	1	Raphe Story	1
Robt Richdson	1	Bryan Stobert	1
Willm Lee	1	Raphe Richardson	1
Tho Joblin	1	Robt Hodgson	1
Mich Dodd	1	John Ellinor	1
Margtt Richdson	1		78
Widd Young	1		
Ann Rayson	1	*m. 25, c. 1*	
James Coward	1	**Great Stainton**	
Geo Sparke	1	Tho Varey	1
Ann Fletcher	1	Robt Colling	1
Widd Humble	1	John Binks	1
John Austin	1	Geo Empton	1
Jane Robinson	1	Tho Clayton	1
John Emmerson	1	Tho Allinson	1
John Croft	1	Robt Sumpter	1
Tho Robinson	1	Rich Greavson	1
Tho Dent	1	Wm Taylor	1
Jane Walker	1	Isabell Robson	1
Robt Hodgson	1	Wm Greaveson	1
John Gibson	1	Willm Richdson	1
Gerrard Ferrar	1	Wm Rickarby	2
Ann Gill	1	Tho Wadly	1
John Smith	1	Raphe Garth	1
Mary Chipchase	1	John Marre	1
Edw Layton	1	Geo Jackson	1
Tho Robinson	1	John Marr sen	1
Antho Dixson	1	Jane Greaveson	1
Willm Coltman	1		20
Ann Bottshaby	1		
Mary Stevenson	1	**Strainton**	
Willm Gore	1	[**Stranton**]	
Jane Estobbs	1	James Habacke	1
John Chipchase	1	Tho Moody	1
Tho Chipchase	1	Tho Foster	1
Willm Sparke	1	Tho Atkinson	1
John Heighinton	1	Widd Greaveson	1
Tho Heavyside	1	Willm Emmerrson	1
Wm Dixon	1	Hen Moore	1
John Bailes	1	Nich Merrance	1
Wm Hate	1	James Bowmer	1
Ellinr Surratt	1	John Merryman	1
John Emmerson	1	Ann Browne	1
Mary Burden	1	Mary Browne	1
Geo Bentley	1	Willm Bowmer	1
John Sadler	1	Widd Thompson	1

Edw Kenton	1
John Browne	1
Isabell Harryson	1
John Atkin	1
Wm Atkin	1
Wm Lane	1
Wm Burdon	1
James Wilson	1
Cuth Walker	1
John Bushby	1
Nicho Sweetin	1
Mary Story	1
Tho Burden	1
Tho Wittingham	1
Geo Ward	1
Marke Ward	1
Widd Emerrson	1
Jane Atkin	1
Willm Hall	1
Tho Bowmer	1
Widd Sewell	1
Geo Emerrson	1
John Robinson	1
Susan Oliver	1
Robt Allen	1
Antho Smith	1
Chr Foster	1
John Atkinson	1
Tho Leatton	1
John Ellerton	1
	44

Seaton Carce
[Seaton Carew]

Widd White	1
Robt Dun	1
Bartho Goatt	1

m. 25, c. 2

Widd Foster	1
Antho Harryson	1
Rich Deninge	1
Wm Wood	1
James Ranson	1
Widd Dun	1
Tho Willinson	1

Tho Littlefaire	1
Antho Littlefare	1
John Smith	1
Widd Wood	1
John Walker	1
John Jackson	1
Robt Dun	1
Widd Smith	1
Hen Browne	1
Widd Bouncer	1
Tho Johnson	1
Ellin Jackson	1
Willm Ward	1
Geo Browne	1
Geo Yoale	1
John Lackenby	1
Widd Middleton	1
Geo Kerton	1
Antho Johnson	1
Geo Ratcliffe	1
	30

Thorp Tewly
[Thorpe Thewles]

Widd Rickarby	1
John Wilkinson	1
Widd Lister	1
Richd Pranse	1
Tho Forrest	1
Wm Danfoot	1
Robt Maltby	1
Willm Clayton	1
Tho Hall	1
Robt Seadlocke	1
Tho White	1
Willm Waike	1
Wm Lister	1
Raphe Bambrough	1
John Hartburne	1
Wid Wilkinson	1
Eliz Rainshaw	1
Tho Ewbancke	1
John Walker	1
Wm Eggleston	1
Ann Sidgswicke	1
Tho Blakey	1

Bryan Todd	1
	23

Throston

Wm Swalwell	1
John Brodbent	1
Robt Adamson	1
	3

Whitton

Tho Smith	1
Raphe Maltby	1
Tho Walker	1
Willm Morgan	1
Robt Bainbridge	1
Nicholas Thompson	1
Richd Hallyman	1
Margtt Bambrigg	1
John Walker	1
	9

m. 25, c. 3

Woolveston
[Wolviston]

Robt Smith	1
Tho Smith	1
Wm Lanericke	1
Jane Sanders	1
Wm Foster	1
Thomas Trotter	1
Hen Rawling	1
Robt Rousbie	1
Robt Smith	1
John Thorpe	1
Widd Davyson	1
Widd Johnson	1
Willm Roper	1
Widd Middleton	1
James Watson	1
Widd Thorpe	1
Tho Pranke	1
Tho Foster	1
Robt Coules	1
Willm Watson	1
Widd Toggill	1
James Gowlin	1

John Clerke	1
Alice Davyson	1
Mary Wood	1
Tho Rawlinge	1
Mich Watson	1
Widd Robson	1
Leonard Lawson	1
John Roper	1
Hen Wood	1
Tho Thorpe	1
Geo Buckle	1
Wm Thorpe	1
John Thorpe	1
Wm Laverocke	1
Raphe Ellinor	1
	37

Cassopp
[Cassop]

Robt Shaftoe	1
Tho Haith	1
Wm Collingwood	1
Geo Ewbancke	1
Alice Carr	1
Alice Barrow	1
Eliz Burdon	1
	7

Castle Eden

Wm Hardy	1
Richd Humble	1
Willm Dave	1
John Wilkinson	1
Geo Coats	1
Widd Taylor	1
Geo Cocke	1
	7

Easington

Eliz Walker	1
Geo Paxton	1
Simon Fletcher	1
Tho Goat	1
Chr Smith	1
Robt Walker	1
Luke Taylor	1

Robt Richdson	1
Richd Bee	1

m. 25v, c. 1

Edm Paxton	1
Widd Graham	1
Richd Wolfe	1
Mich Hickson	1
John Lambert	1
John Walker	1
John Hickson	1
Mich Hickson	1
Chr Dotchson	1
Widd Foster	1
Rich Wildon	1
Willm Stodart	1
Widd Gains	1
Mary Wheatlam	1
Robt Smith	1
Chr Kendall	1
Wm Bee	1
Robt Bacon	1
Willm Bee	1
Widd Ellison	1
Widd Paxton	1
Widd Clarke	1
Widd Harryson	1
Widd Wilden	1
John Lawes	1
Widd Burdon	1
Wm Snawden	1
Tho Eggleston	1
Geo Paxton	1
Antho Story	1
John Paxton	1
John Wilkinson	1
Phillip Blench	1
Antho Thompson	1
Mary Gibson	1
Robt Foster	1
Peter Wildon	1
Geo Martin	1
Gilbert Paxton	1
Richd Wilkinson	2
Robt Pescod	1
Geo Foster	1

Antho Middleton	1
Tho Foster	1
Chr Chapman	1
Widd Harryson	1
	56

Haswell

John Gambee	1
Willm Crofton	1
Gerrard Gebson	1
Gawen Hall	1
James Gelson	1
John Packton	1
John Michall	1
Fran Sharpe	1
Tho Shepheard	1
John Dobson	1
Robt Dobson	1
Willm Robson	1
Thomas Atkinson	1
Ellinor Middleton	1
Ann Haswell	1
Eliz Winter	1
	16

m. 25v, c. 2

Hawthorne
[Hawthorn]

Widd Liddell	1
Chr Kinge	1
Robt Davyson	1
Richd Sharpe	1
Widd Hart	1
Tho Davyson	1
Dorothy Kinge	1
Widd Foster	1
Widd Westland	1
John Davyson	1
John Anderson	1
Maudlin Todd	1
Widd Garstrange	1
Widd Wilton	1
Widd Hunter	1
Richd Davyson	1
Richd Foster	1
	17

Hutton Henry

Wm Hodgsmanhay	1
Raphe Newby	1
Wm Smith	1
Tho Corner	1
James Byers	1
Widd Ellinor	1
Edw Lawe	1
John Potter	1
Robt Goodson	1
Abraham Liddell	1
John Whitworth	1
Richd Liddell	1
John Simpson	1
Robt Colman	1
Wm Wilson	1
Mirrell Ovinton	1
Hen Harryson	1
Fran Newton	1
	18

Nesbett
[Nesbitt]

Isabell Pattison	1
Wm Arrowsmith	1
Rich Robinson	1
Isabell Doue	1
Eliz Tiplady	1
Chr Davy	1
Robt Wordey	1
Ann Cooke	1
Robt Doue	1
Hen Smith	1
Edw Cumin	1
John Thropell	1
Ellin Wilson	1
	13

Sunderland Bridge

Mich Bislyby [?]	1
Robt Awde	1
Mary Head	1
Robt Adamson	1
	4

Shadforth

John Bullocke	1
Fran Huntley	1
Barbary Dobson	1

m. 25v, c. 3

Robt Wilson	1
Phillip Haddocke	1
Jane Smith	1
Wm Hudson	1
Widd Gambesby	1
Margtt Burd	1
Hugh Bowman	1
Tho Huntley	1
Wm Man	1
John Murrow	1
	13

Shearburne
[Sherburn House]

James Heslop	1
Wm Davyson	1
Peter Middleton	1
Richd Bullocke	1
Simon Pearson	1
Fran Steele	1
Margtt Middleton	1
Tho Bussoe	1
Richd Pattinson	1
Robt Wood	1
Tho Ruderford	1
Marma Bee	1
Widd White	1
	13

Shotton

Char Usher	1
Marma Wildon	1
John Readhead	1
John Humble	1
Wm Corner	1
Volentine Smith	1
Tho Wheldon	1
Alice Shadforth	1
Geo Thompson	1
Wm Stodart	1
Wm Pattison	1

John Crooke	1
Eliz Errington	1
Margtt Gent	1
Nich Usher	1
Chr Armestrong	1
John Pattinson	1
John Lambert	1
Tho Addyson	1
Richd Jackson	1
Antho Wilson	1
Wm Byers	1
Widd Young	1
Phillip Humble	1
Margtt Smith	1
Phill Blensh	1
Eliz Etherington	1
Willm Blackett	1
	28

Hesledon
[**Hesleden**]

James Wilkinson	1
Antho Wilkinson	1
Geo Smith	1
Marke Wilkinson	1
John Lampton	1
Ann Reed	1
James Sanderson	1
Tho Hodgson	1

m. 26, c. 1

John Oliver	1
Wm Shetforth	1
Wm Usher	1
John Goatte	1
Lawrence Dobbyson	1
Mathew Gray	1
Chr Twedall	1
Willm Stobart	1
Widd Lambe	1
Widd Goatt	1
James Downe	1
James Usher	1
	20

Shearton
[**Sheraton**]

Tho Paxton	1
Robt Browne	1
Willm Robinson	1
Tho Robinson	1
Widd Markham	1
John Markham	1
Wm Markham	1
Widd Chatter	1
Robt Megger	1
Tho Craggs	1
Wm Cheatter	1
Wm Ladell	1
Bryan Starforth	1
	13

Trimdon

John Wouldhave	1
Robt Calvert	1
Robt Cooper	1
Tho Calvert	1
Ann Soullbie	1
Wm Coats	1
Tho Stobbert	1
Vell Gent	1
John Hutchinson	1
Robt Jackson	1
Kathar Robinson	1
Tho Atkinson	1
Robt Corbett	1
Margtt Stodart	2
Wm Ropper	1
Nich Ailes	1
Alice Horsly	1
Alice Swalwell	1
Geo Hutchinson	1
Robt Gray	2
Richd Foster	1
Nicho Ropper	1
Samson Stobert	1
Cuthbt Hutchinson	1
Margtt Willoe	1
John Adamson	1
Cuth Close	1
	29

Wharrington
[Quarrington]

Raphe Wilkinson	1
John Darnton	1
Wm Moore	1
Raphe Laverocke	1
John Hall	1
Henry Humble	1
Geo Coats	1
Math Stott	1
Tho Vaige	1
Hen Humble	1
John Hall	1
Raphe Laverocke	1
William Moore	1
Bryan Ellinor	1
	14

m. 26, c. 2

Wingate

Wm Harryson	1
Rich Crakes	1
Geo Cocke	1
Eliz Smith	1
John Erdon	1
Antho Smith	1
Tho Smith	1
Robt Story	1
Margtt Atkinson	1
John Thompson	1
Wm Newton	1
Robt Hall	1
Leo Burne	1
Richd Smith	1
	14

West and East Burdon

Richd Todd	1
Thomas Foster	1
John Burdon	1
John Stockell	1
Tho Lister	1
Widd Atkinson	1
Kathar Atkinson	1
	7

Daelton
[Dalton]

Wm Readhead	1
Nicho Denton	1
John Wray	1
Tho Steedman	1
Richd Reed	1
Marke Horsman	1
James Dove	1
Mich Shadforth	1
John Ellison	1
	9

Eppleton

Geo Clarke	1
Jane Young	1
Widd Chilton	1
	3

Haughton in the Spring
[Houghton-le-Spring]

Wm Smith	1
Margtt Dobson	1
Raphe Hall	1
Eliz Smith	2
Margtt Phenwick	1
Isab Sickerwham	1
Edw Nicholson	1
Tho Harryson	1
Lan Smith	1
Ann Nicholson	1
Wm Walton	1
John Watson	1
John Hall	1
Ann Stockell	1
Richd Dobson	1
John Parker	1
Dorothy Hopper	1
Eliz Tyres	1
Hen Pickering	1
Raphe Pigg	1
Marmaduke Farrow	1
Wm Clifton	1
Hen Lairman	1
Raphe Day	1

m. 26, c. 3	
Oliver Watson	1
Robt Chapman	1
Ellinor Dobson	1
John Arnot	1
Margtt Willy	1
Isab Brimton	1
Barbary Mason	1
Margtt Curry	1
	33

Hetton
[Hetton-le-Hole]

Francis Hobson	1
Geo Foster	1
Lan Appleby	1
David Clegholme	1
Geo Hutton	1
Widd Rand	1
Widd Wright	1
Widd Hall	1
John Leavers	1
Tho Meburne	1
Cuth Browne	1
Widd Leavers	1
Widd Cofferan	1
John Smith	1
Richd Shepherdson	1
Wm Herring	1
John Shepheard	1
Richd Marley	1
John Robinson	1
Wm Parkin	1
Wm Carr	1
	21

Middle Herrington

Robt Davyson	1
Richd Sminke	1
Tho Foster	1
Widd Ward	1
Widd Hall	1
Robt Laurence	1
Tho Horne	1
John Hutchinson	1
John Greene	2

Richd Appulby	1
Richd Truett	1
John Allen	1
Geo Robinson	1
John Dixson	1
Luke Hutchinson	1
Widd Bayles	1
Wm Dixson	1
Alex Simpson	1
Dan Sharpe	1
	20

West Herrington

Tho Robson	1
Richd Hedley	1
Robt Taylor	1
Richd Mires	1
Tho Snowdon	1
Wm Merryman	1
Wm Thompson	1
Wm Peterburne	1
Cuthbt Craggs	1
Isabell Wilkinson	1
Tho Wilson	1
Wm Cryton	1
Isab Purdon	1
Wm Douglasse	1
Tho Brough	1
Wm Foster	1
Geo Clarke	1
Tho Steele	1
John Lightly	1
Widd Cocke	1
Dan Skipper	1
Hen Holliday	1
Robt Lawrence	1
	23

m. 26v, c. 1	
East Murton	
Willm Robinson	1
Richd Murray	1
Robt Frudd	1
Widd Shacklocke	1
Richd Gibson	1
Hugh Heslopp	1

John Harryson	1
	7

Newbottle

Willm Thompson	1
Wm Ray	1
Widd Blacklocke	1
Edw Charter	1
Tho Foster	1
Robt Usher	1
John Turner	1
Geo Glendale	1
Widd Hall	1
Widd Dent	1
Robt Mason	1
Widd Ellott	1
Wm Hutchinson	1
Robt Surrett	1
Robt Hilton	1
John Fotherlay	1
Edw Robinson	1
Widd Thompson	1
Geo Lister	1
Widd Sharp	1
Mich Chicken	1
Robt Ladler	1
John Smith	1
Cuth Robinson	1
Wm Rutter	1
Tho Thompson	1
John Chilton	1
Richd Parker	1
Edward Whitfield	1
Widd Mason	1
Widd Howard	1
Widd Hodgson	1
Raphe Thompson	1
Tho Thompson	1
Mich Nathaniell	1
John Johnson	1
Widd Ellott	1
	37

Pensher
[Penshaw]

Sibbell Gleay	1

Widd Baylay	1
Anne Lidworth	1
Ellinor Waughby	1
Margtt Robinson	1
Eliz Chilton	1
Fran Place	1
Widd Thompson	1
Widd Hird	1
Widd Marshall	1
John Waster	1
Wm Waineman	1
Willm Bell	1
John Day	1
Robt Baker	1
Tho Wilson	1
Tho Smith	1
Wm Halliday	1
Tho Harryson	1
Andrew Glendinan	1
	20

West Rainton

Wm Browne	1
Wm Atkinson	1
Eliz Cooke	1
John Meaburne	1

m. 26v, c. 2

Robt Ridley	1
Richd Atkinson	1
Edw Robinson	1
James Charleton	1
Ellinor Gray	1
John Gray	1
Raphe Widdowes	1
Geo Cooke	1
Tho Ridley	1
Nicho Slater	1
Wm Shaw	1
Tho Harryson	1
Robt Fulthorpe	1
Mich Askell	1
Tho Atkinson	1
Robt Smeals	1
Tho Gallie	1
John Waugh	1
Tho Bell	1

Richd Crake	1	John Browne	1
John Dobbyson	1		10
John Coall	1		
Simon Ogle	2	**Ryhop**	
Raphe Place	1	**[Ryhope]**	
Robt Harbett	1	Robt Hymass	1
Tho Bell	1	Geo Thompson	1
Hen Carr	1		
Widd Langstaffe	2	*m. 26v, c. 3*	
Widd Davyson	1	Rich Jackson	1
Widd Wilkinson	1	Tho Thompson	1
Widd Clarke	1	John Wilson	1
Widd Toppin	1	Tho Wilkinson	1
Widd Dryden	1	Widd Watson	1
Mary Browne	1	Robt Wilkinson	1
Widd Verance	1	John Allanson	1
Widd Slater	1	Edw Gowland	1
John Young	1	Tho Swallwell	1
Widd Coulson	1	Richd Smith	1
Jane Coulson	1	Stephen Smith	1
James Feathamly	1	Willm Fenwicke	1
John Hugill	1	Sam Todd	1
Henry Hugill	1	Willm Scott	1
Wm Rowntree	1	John Winspeere	1
Laurence Hutchinson	1	Alice Foster	1
Chr Horne	1	Widd Gibson	1
Tho Short	1	Edw Thompson	1
Tho Taylor	1	Tho Pickering	1
Richard Robinson	1	Robt Mitchinson	1
Richd Young	1		22
Widd Stephenson	1		
Richd Young	1	**Seeham**	
Tho Taylor	1	**[Seaham]**	
	58	Wm Collingwood	1
		John Swallow	1
East Rainton		Joseph Liverseed	1
Dan Sharp	1	Sam Lister	1
John Thompson	1	Ann Easterby	2
Jane Bouncher	1	Tho Bee	1
John Alder	1	Raphe Rokabie	1
John Lister	1	Edw Whittingham	1
Margtt Smith	1	Geo Eales	1
John Welsh	1	Eliz Thompson	1
Tho Turner	1	Rich Elwood	1
Willm Chilton	1	Geo Cresswell	1
		Richd Wayton	1

Charles Laverocke	1	Ann Burdon	1
Wm Smith	1	Math Smith	1
John Heslopp	1	John Coats	1
Alice Denton	1	Ingram Browne	1
Edw Liddell	1	Wm Hutchinson	1
	19		**14**

Seaton

Bishopp Warmouth
[Bishopwearmouth]

Widd Hutton	1	Tho Robinson	1
Wm Ellott	1	Tho Huttinson	1
Luke Rutherford	1	John Milburne	1
James Bee	1	Willm Snawden	1
Tho Davyson	1	Robt Snawden	1
Margtt Smith	1	Widd Craw	1
	6	Raphe Jackson	1
		Cuth Shepherdson	1

Silksworth

Ann Martin	1	Parcivall Snowdon	1
Tho Brough	1	Wm Dun	1
Hen Atkinson	1	David Mathew	1
Robt White	1	Dan Dun	1
Antho Myres	1	Lan Marshall	1
Ellinor Sidgswicke	1	Wm Lee	1
James Collingworth	1	Robt Curtis	1
John Aynsley	1	Tho Suddicke	1
Barbary Rutter	1	Edw Hearinge	1
Ann Lazenby	1	Widd Moore	1
Edw Chapman	1	Widd Widdas	1
Mabell Bee	1	Tho Walker	1
Isabell Denton	1	Raphe Burne	1
Gilbert ye Miller	1	Hen Taylor	1
	14	Nich Wood	1
		Wm Bilton	1

Tunsdale
[Tunstall]

Mich Ridley	1	Wm Smith	1
Robt Chilton	1	Willm Burton	1
James Collingwood	1	John Ellott	1
Margtt Gowland	1	Rich Thompson	1
Char Ushaw	1	Widd Davyson	1
Marke Morgan	1	Antho Middleton	1
Raphe Cowper	1	Widd Foster	1
		Widd Shepherdson	1
m. 27, c. 1		Widd Dazy	1
		John Cooper	1
Alice Myers	1	James Messenger	1
Antho Batchelor	1	John Rennyson	1
		John Thompson	1

Willm Watson	1	Geo Hendrson	1
Tho Layinge	1	Antho Taylor	1
John Suddicke	1	Robt Coulden	1
Widd Thompson	1	Hen Browne	1
Math Hunter	1	Raphe Ellinor	1
Widd Bilton	1	Hen Foster senr	1
Tho Richardson	2	Tho Johnson junr	1
Wm Athew	1	Widd Slingesby	1
Widd Davyson	1	Martin Weeling	1
Tho Chalor	1	Widd Todd	1
Widd Sanderson	1	John Creeson	1
Antho Teasdale	1	Reinold Ridley	1
Edw Smith	1	Robt Knagg	1
Widd Johnson	1	Widd Watkin	1
Widd Sanderson	1	Widd Skurfield	1
Martin Willings	1	Tho Scott	1
Widd Harbottle	1	Robt Shepherdson	1
Rich White	1	Widd Curtis	2
Chr Horne	1	John Hutton	1
John Stevenson	1	Margtt Burton	1
Rich Rose	1	Robt Taylor	1
Robt Chambers	1	John Coopland	1
Widd Dixon	1	Widd Robinson	1
… Wilson	1	Wm Smith	1
…es Whitherburne	1	Alex Reed	1
Stephen Hutton	1	Geo Ray	1
		Tho Johnson	1
m. 27, c. 2		John Dixson	1
Widd Bee	1	Robt Arnold	1
Geo Lairman	1	Geo Johnson	1
Widd Arnold	1	Wm Appleby	1
Robt Curver	1	Tho Skinlay	1
Widd Hindmas	1	Parcivall Headley	1
Tho White	1	Marke Watson	1
John Wood	1	Gerard Chapman	1
Tho Hall	1	Tho Robinson	1
Edw Robinson	1	Tho Martin	1
Rich Reed	1	Clement [*blank*]	1
Edw Jackson	1	Tho Anderson	1
Geo Bell	1	Geo Bellee	1
John Waters	1	Mary Johnson	1
Tho Robinson	1	Widd Watson	2
James Creery	1	Tho Cheater	1
Hugh Bilton	1	John Wilson	1
John Fenwicke	1	Wm Watson	1
James Dykes	1		

Geo Browne	1
	130

Bishopp Warmouth Panns
[Bishopwearmouth Panns]

Math French	1
Tho Richardson	1

m. 27, c. 3

Widd Fairlesse	1
Geo Foster	1
Richd Taylor sen	1
John Hunter	1
Empty house	1
Rich Cadling	1
John Jackson	1
Raphe Browne	1
Edw Beednell	1
Widd Fairlesse	1
Tho Thompson	1
Tho Kirkewood	1
Tho Smith	1
Symon Ward	1
Richd Clarke	1
Chr Bell	1
Geo Shotton	1
Rich Gillery	1
Wm Foster	1
Widd Lacy	1
Nich Dixson	1
Edw Cole	2
Ephraim Potts	1
John Davie	1
Tho Addyson	1
Rich Atkin	1
Ann Hilton	1
Rich Taylor	1
Tho Willowby	1
Hugh Shepheard	1
Robt Cockfield	1
John Richdson	2
Tho Beard	1
Tho Bearay	1
Martin Wilkinson	1
Fran Hodgson	1
John Wood	1

John Thompson	1
Widd Page	1
James Francklyn	1
Tho Oliver	1
John Hills	1
Wm Trumble	1
Wm Tellfoot	1
John Coward	1
John Atkinson	1
Rich Leadbetter	1
Raphe Thompson	1
Rich Addison	1
Chr Hodgson	1
Jane Bell	1
Tho Simpson	1
Rich Addison junr	1
Wm Henderson	1
Tho Bell	1
Edward Taylor	1
Wm Beale	1
Widd Page	1
Tho Richdson	1
John Beale	1
Nich Thompson	1
Tho Stones	1
Widd Fairlesse	1
	67

Ufferton
[Offerton]

Robt Harbottle	1
Usse Nicholson	1
John Taylor	1
Wm Haricke	1

m. 27v, c. 1

… Dobson	1
… Clifton	1
… Walker	1
… Steele	1
…n Parker	1
… Andrson sen	1
Mich Helliday	1
Phillip Pharoah	1
Geo Oliver	1
Raphe Steward	1

Tho Studdert	1
Edw Holliday	1
	16

Burnopp
[Burnhope]

Hen Manger	1
Math Natty	1
Cuthbt Gray	1
Geo Snawden	1
Willm Robson	2
Widd Midcalfe	1
Edw Thompson	1
	8

Craw Crooke
Crawcrook]

Widd Newton	1
Hen Milburne	1
Leonard Charlie	1
Ann Coocke	1
John Greene	1
John Smith	1
Thomas Starrie	1
Mary Dunn	1
Robt Scott	1
Nicho Thompson	1
David Gray	1
John Lawson	1
Thomas Hedley	1
Rogr Cesterson	1
Chr Coopland	1
Geo Haggerston	1
Ann Thompson	1
Tho Staport	1
Hen Milburne	1
Tho Watson	1
Widd Dunn	1
Cuthbt Andrson	1
Tho Wilson	1
John Cocke	1
Robt Singleton	1
Walter Weddell	1
Chr Hudspeth	1
Roger Maughan	1
Reinold Forster	1

Willm Lawson	1
Robt Fenwicke	1
Robt Jackson	1
Chr Wetherbie	1
Widd Newton	1
John Greener	1
Robt Chesman	1
George Cooke	1
Widd Ward	1
Edward Ousonate	1
Thomas Kirkehouse	1
Willm Greenay	1

m. 27v, c. 2

Clement Greenay	1
Geo Watson	1
Humphrey Bell	1
Isab Greenay	1
	45

Chopwell

Tho Hopper	1
Willm Rodgers	1
Edw Barker	1
Robt Forster	1
John Stephenson	1
Isabell Suretie	1
Robt Hunter	1
Robt Francke	1
Robert Fenwicke	1
Daniel Hogg	1
John Murdagh	1
Robt Rossby	1
Widd Wilkinson	1
Symon Browne	1
Robt Ilye	1
Nicho White	1
Henry Stockoe	1
Peter Lumley	1
	18

Conside
[Consett]

Raphe Reed	1
William Storye	1
Widd Neall	1
Robt Baites	1

John Curtlay	1
Robt Batty	1
	6

**Cornesaw
[Cornsay]**

Math Iveston	1
Robt Punshon	2
Wm Dixon	1
Willm Wright	2
Lan Dearam	1
Raphe Carrothers	1
Edward Kirkley	1
Ann Hill	1
Tristram Blenkinshop	1
Tho Thomson	1
Widd Pickering	1
	13

Esh

John Robson	1
Widd Cleaton	1
Leo Corby	1
John Gaire sen	1
Widd Wray	1
Ellinor Palmer	1
Tho Nagds	1
Widd Forster	1
John Rackett	1
John Atkinson	1
Tho Etherington	1
Widd Athy	1
John Griffin	1
Widd Cominge	1
Jane Johnson	1
Widd. Baxter	1
	16

m. 27v, c. 3

Ebchester

Tho Suretyes	1
Tho Jopling	1
John Harryson	1
Tho Elliott	1
Widd Wilson	1
Hen Atkinson	1

Joseph Hopper	1
Willm White	1
Eliz Atkinson	1
	9

**Green Croft
[Greencroft]**

Rich Wilkinson	1
Math Humble	1
Wm Forster	1
Jane Hall	1
Robt Hall	1
Geo Curtle	1
Rowld Gallile	1
Geo Wray	1
Widd Hall	1
	9

Iveston

Tho Mason junr	1
Raphe Forster	1
Tho Mason	1
Hugh Fletcher	1
John Wheatley	1
John Rutherford	1
Widd Dickenson	1
Kathar Pickering	1
James Jone	1
John Hopper	1
Margtt Kirkeley	1
Wm Jobson	1
Robt Harryson	1
Tho Pace	1
Antho Taylor	1
Ann Vince	1
Richd Hendrson	1
Wm Dobinson	1
Mary Marling	1
Ann Lawson	1
	20

Kyo

Tho Sumerbell	1
Tho Maughan	1
Widd Ferry	1
John Wheatley	1

Lyonell Carr	1
Widd Smith	1
James Walker	1
Alexdr Lampson	1
	8

Langley

Wm Midcalfe	1
John Joplin	1
Widd Robinson	1
Jane Shawes	1
Widd Joplin	1
Widd Gallile	1
John Stainsby	1
	7

m. 28, c.1

Lanchester

Tho Kirby	1
John Reed	1
Margtt Curry	1
Ann Ditch	1
Margtt Ditch	1
John Graham	1
Tho Wright	1
Hen Rippon	1
Margtt Simpson	1
Rich Pearson	1
Susan Ironside	1
John Hopper	1
Ann Ward	1
Tho Gray	1
Ann Chapman	1
Jane Allison	1
	16

Mugglesworth
[Muggleswick]

Tho Thompson	1
Mich Trotter	1
Chr Dixon	1
Rowld Stockoe	1
Eliz Layburne	1
Wm Ramshaw	1
Ann Newton	1

Widd Ward	1
	8

Meddomsley
[Medomsley]

Robt Lighton	1
John Somersett	1
Widd Carr	1
Cuth Richardson	1
John Hunter	1
Robt Greenwell	1
Chr Jefferson	1
Jane Howard	1
Robt Hunter	1
Antho Marley	1
Geo Newton	1
Ellinor Leighton	1
Edw Fairburne	1
Hen Barran	1
	14

Rowly & Roughside
[Rowley & Roughside]

Widd Hedley	1
John Wilson	1
Wm Hall	1
John Little	1
Denny Middleton	1
	5

Ritton
[Ryton]

Ambrose Todd	1
Robt Coulson	1
Wm Finlasse	1
Widd. Nickson	1
Wm Richardson	1
Tho Smith	1
Wm Denninge	1
John Graham	1
John French	1
Wm Coulson	1
Jos Barnes	1
Thomas Robinson	1
Widd Robson	1
… Robson	1

… French	1

m. 28, c. 2

Peter Dickson	1
Mary Low	1
Wm Bordon	1
Wm Armstrong	1
Tho Middleton	1
Tho Todd	1
Widd Allan	1
Tho Hopper	1
Gawen Snowden	1
Geo Bowden	1
Widd Nicholson	1
John Watson	1
	27

Ritton Woodside
[Ryton Woodside]

Widd Morton	1
John Cisterson	1
Geo Lonewye [?]	1
Widd Robson	1
John Rennicke	1
Wm Porter	1
Fran Taylor	1
Geo Walker	1
Math Searns	1
Tho Grosare	1
John Londsdale	1
John Kalle	1
Robt Johnson	1
Luke Browne	1
Tho Hornsbye	2
Widd Wright	1
Hen Thompson	2
Wm Wanare	1
Arch Elliott	1
John Fawcett	1
Raphe Ellison	1
Willm Dood	1
Tho Hedley	1
Geo Lawson	1
John Gilbertson	1
Tho Graddon	1
Tho Browne	1

Wm Matson	1
Widd Dood	1
Tho Stockoe	1
Widd Greenay	1
John Ansally	1
Tho Watson	1
Widd Birbecke	1
Rich Dickson	1
Widd Joysey	1
Widd Hodgson	1
Robt Hodgson	1
Lan Hodgson	1
John Walker	1
Tho Greeny	2
Wm Ramsey	1
Edw Smith	2
Mich Hunter	1
Geo Daglease	1
Rich Hedley	1
Antho Poore	1
Edw Hedwath	1
Robt Raine	1
Leonard Banbury	1
Rich Robson	1
Lan Simpson	1
Tho Young	1
John Lister	1

m. 28, c. 3

Widd Taylor	1
Willm Barnes	1
Wm Thompson	1
John Coming	1
Widd Siddbotham	1
Robert Willkinson	1
Widd Young	1
Raphe Douglas	1
Willm Pratt	1
Alexdr [*blank*]	1
John Hodgson	1
Tho Pearson	1
John Bootland	1
David Pomar	2
Wm Marshall	2
John Wilson	1
John Stockoe	1

Tho Lodge	1	Tho Watson	2
Frances Lodge	2	Tho Stockoe	1
Andrew Robson	1	Chr Curry	1
Tho Richardson	1	Robt Wheldon	1
John Yowton	1	Geo Farlam	1
John Browne	1	Widd Yarrow	1
Wm Pattison	1	Widd Bambridge	1
John James	1	Tho Woodmass	1
John Bigland	1		
Geo Lawson	1	*m.28v, c. 1*	
Tho Morthwayte	1	… Temple	1
Robt Coulson	1	…lip Bell	1
Rich Browne	2	John Stockoe	2
Thomas Hendrson	1	Thomas Frame	1
Edw Crissop	2	Bartram Daglishe	1
Widd Sheffield	1	Tho Scoot	2
Chr Lavericke	1	Hen Pattinson	1
Wm Laybourne	2		36
Geo Hunter	2		
Matt Taylor	1	**Witton Gilbert**	
Nich Johnson	1	Nich Harryson	1
Tho Stockoe	1	John Hopper	1
Willm Hedworth	1	Eliz Palister	1
Wm Story	1	Eliz Sander	1
Widd Dood	1	Dorothy Hopper	1
	107	John Johnson	1
		John Johnson	1
		Hen Wilson	1
Swalwell		Tho Snath	1
Geo Gainge	1	Matt Sheeld	1
John Blackett	1	Tho Sneet	1
Peter Armestrong	1	Margtt Yealder	1
Geo Bainbrigge	1	Isabell Taylor	1
Robt Cocker	1	Andrew Nicholson	1
Tho Woodnes	1	Tho Twiddell	1
Tho Temple	1	Mary Smith	1
Math Nicholson	1	Alexdr Atkinson	1
Robt Daglishe	1	John Barker	1
Widd. Curry	1	John Taylor	1
Widd Clugh	1		19
John Dobson	1		
Geo Bambridge	1		
Widd Davyson	1	**Whicham**	
Widd Thompson	1	**[Whickham]**	
Antho Bainbridge	1	Geo Robinson	1
John Chatt	1	Wm Peareth	1
John Jenning	1	Widd Peareth	1

Widd Carr	1	John Harryson	1
Raphe Ferry	1	Widd Mackpans	1
Tho Brabbon	1	Char Wallasse	1
Wm Harbottle	1	Geo Beanmond	1
Wm Lucky	1	John Thompson	1
Tho Carrus	1	Willm Fowe	1
Wm Kirkley	1	Widd Thompson	1
Rich Carr	1	Widd Dods	1
Widd Thompson	1	Rich Marley	1
Mich Thompson	1	Matt Foster	1
James Preacher	1	Arch Wighman	1
Wm Clenn	1	Rich Usher	1
Geo Carr	1	Hen Usher	1
Edw Maxwell	1	Raphe Thompson	1
Tho Purdy	1	Marke Nattarous	1
Wm Wreetson	1	John Blackett	1
Tho Daglishe	1	Tho Hodgson	1
Wm Joblin	1	Widd Edmondson	1
Widd Bedlinton	1	Wm Parker	1
Willm Willas	1	James Laithes	1
John Robson	1	Mich Stockoe	1
Widd Denson	1	Rich Wilson	1
Leo Hall	1	Widd Watson	1
Robt Man	1		70
James Rasbecke	1		
John Welton	1	**Whickham Fellside**	
Nich Honam	1	John Fletcher	2
John Taylor	1	Widd Bell	1
Geo Richdson	1	Andrew Mathew	1
Widd Willmson	1	Tho Rigg	1
Widd Wiggam	1	Tho Dawson	1
John St John	1	Robt Man	1
Lancelott Lambe	1	Edw Moore	1
John Rennoldson	1	Tho Ladler	1
Widd Browne	1	John Smith	1
Ralphe Andrwood	1	James Hopper	1
		Widd Forrest	1
m. 28v, c. 2		Andrew Henning	1
Widd Lethon	1	Tho Stafford	1
John Arkell	1	John Storye	1
Widd Alladwood	1	Hen Trumble	1
Widd Johnson	1	Tho Jobson	1
Walter Rose	1	Wm Bayliffe	1
Widd Blenkinshopp	1	Rich Chandler	1
John Wilkinson	1	Wm Stephenson	1
Wm Harbottle	1	James Hebleworth	1

John Watson	1	John Hoggon	1
Arch Gibson	1	Geo Cuthbert	1
Wm Randale	1	John Spencer	1
Widd Lawes	1	Widd Hackworth	1
Wm Daglishe	1	Tho Forrest	2
Widd Copper	1	Geo Parkinson	1
Widd Cuthbert	1	Geo Thompson	1
Widd Trumble	1	Abigall Smith	2
Widd Clarke	1	Robt Purdy	1
John Lawson	1	Widd Maddyson	2
Chr Lee	1	Rich Pallister	1
Widd Dickson	1	Ann Robson	2
James Howard	1	John Halelocke	1
Widd Whitfield	1	Tho Laybourne	2
Jane Shell	1	John Saunders	1
Widd Hudson	1	Chr Emmerson	1
Tho Lumbley	1	Tho Bucke	1
Wm Storye	1	Widd Blackburne	2
		John Maddyson	2
			94

m. 28v, c. 3

Hen Ramshaw	1		
Robt Carr	1	**Whickham Lowhand**	
Roger Harryson	1	Geo Bainbrigge	1
John Maddyson	1	John Corbye	1
Wm Marshall	1	Mich Auckland	1
Tho Watson	1	Raphe Gayre	1
Widd Laybourne	1	Lan Bridges	1
Tho Richardson	1	Rich Wright	1
Geo Scott	1	Edw Smith	1
Tho Errington	1	Widd Emmerson	1
Widd Hurr	1	Tho Johnson	1
John Lyle	2	Widd Stockoe	1
Math Sanders	1	Widd Haddericke	1
James Daglishe	1	Robt Friend	1
Robt Whitlocke	1	Geo Taylor	1
Tho Holyday	2	Widd Surrat	1
Robt Askew	2	Robt Yare	1
John Bonner	1	Jeffery Arthur	1
Mich Langas	1	Margtt Fraine	1
Mich Wheatley	1	John Denning	1
Wm Wheatley	1	Hector Carnaby	1
Alexdr Laine	1	Geo Wilson	1
Tho Nixson	1	John Atkinson	1
Robt Coming	1		
Tho Pattison	1	*m. 29, c. 1*	
Widd Hunter	1	Robt Murrays	1

Geo Wilson	1	Wm Archer	1
Wm Parker	1	Wm Caygill	1
John Mason sen	1	Widd Gayre	1
John Young	1	Chr Peacocke	1
Widd Taylor	1	Fran Errington	1
Stephen Parker	1	Wm Davyson	1
Wm Frame	1	John Doby	1
Alexdr Thompson	1	Raphe Harddericke	1
John Doods	1	James Marley	1
David Carmell	1	Robt Michaelmas	1
John Hall	1	James Watson	1
Wm Baines	1	Tho Smith	1
Margtt Liddell	1	Wm Rea	1
Wm Carnes	1	Widd Stobbs	1
John Hunter	1	Wm Smith	1
Peter Simpson	1	Roger Heaton	1
Wm Simpson	1	John Peacocke	1
James Minean	1	Geo Fraine	1
Bryan Davyson	1	Antho Lyddell	1
Geo Browne	1	Robt Byers	1
Andrew Hogg	1		
Wm Wrightson	1	*m. 29, c. 2*	
Wm Coole	1	John Holmes	1
Phillip Durham	1	Edward Hutchinson	1
Widd Skurfield	1	Edw Carr	1
Widd Wheatley	1	Mary Waters	1
Tho Bell	1	Rich Howson	1
Wm Robinson	1	John Stockoe	1
John Hutchinson	1	Widd Hogg	1
John Gilwyn	1	Geo Green	1
Tho Stephenson	1	Robt Blakecliffe	1
Math Marwood	1	Wm Laycocke	2
Margtt Lawson	1	Geo Doods	2
Tho Coole	1	Sam Rice	1
Geo Easterly	1	Antho Drighton	1
John Wilkinson	1	Geo Bland	1
Robt Wilkinson	1	Antho Parkinson	1
John Winde	1	Robt Lyddell	1
Antho Bayliffe	1	Widd Croser	1
Nicho Johnson	1		108
Stephen Atkinson	1		
Widd Bainbridge	1	**Winlaton Et Lord:pp**	
Widd Pattison	1	**[Winlaton East Lordship]**	
Cuth Carr	2	Tho Grundye	1
James Foster	1	John Nixon	1
John Watson	1	Robt Archer	1

John Rowell	1	Widd Wilson	1
Nicho Cleaton	1		
Wm Weaton	1	*m. 29, c. 3*	
John Forster	1	Robt Hudspith	1
Jane Harryson	1	Widd Turner	1
Math Newton	1	Jeffery Robson	1
Math Nixon	1	Raphe Harding	1
John Bootland	1	Willm Trotter	1
James Younge	1	Geo Swadell	1
Robt Trotter	1	James Aynesley	1
Widd Swan	1	John Browne	1
Math Nixon senr	1	Widd Hendrson	1
Widd Hall	1	Robt Cell	1
Widd Sarry	1	Reynold Robson	1
Alexdr Harryson	1	Widd Dod	1
Widd Burnet	1	John Little	1
Widd Dawson	1	Lan Robson	1
Cuth Robinson	1	Geo Wilson	1
Widd Hedlay	1	Robt Harper	1
Phillip Story	1	Cuth Nixon	1
Tho Storye	1	Rich Heppell	1
John Watson	1	John Forster	1
Widd Hood	1	Edw Nicholson	1
Marke Smith	1	Matt Grayson	1
John Ward	1	Widd Champley	1
Geo Younger	1	Wm Errington	1
Wid Lawson	1	John Jackson	1
George Ogle	1	John Thompson	1
James Simpson	1	Walter Reed	1
Bartram Biggins	1	John Carr	1
Roger Douglasse	1	Hen Cutter	1
David Carr	1	Matt Robson	1
John Nixon	1	Widd Chapman	1
Antho Vepon	1	Geo Nixon	1
John Marrer	1	Widd Pattison	1
Widd Carr	1	Tho Gray	1
Widd Oliver	1	Mich Bell	1
Robt Jobson	1	Widd Cutter	1
Widd Robinson	1	Reynold Scott	1
Tho Hopper	1	Nicho Sunderland	1
Robt Sprout	1	Widd Benson	1
Marma Swinburne	1	Widd Walker	1
Widd Day	1	Wid Youton	1
Widd Greenay	1	John Taylor	1
Wm Hart	1	John Hunter	1
Raphe Champley	1	Matt Gray junr	1

Robt Tempest	1
Widd Vepon	1
Isab Dickenson	1
John Hedlay	1
John Bromfield	1
Cuth Stapor	1
Humph Errington	1
Rich Pattinson	1
Peter Briggs	1
Robt Anderson	1
Geo Chicken	1
Wm Gallile	1
Adam Sprott	1
Geo Pratt	1
Wm Storye	1
John Watson	1
John Bulmer	1
Hen Forster	1
John Whinshipp	1
Geo Stockoe	1
Rich Richardson	1
Chr Taylor	1
Tho Urwin	1
Widd Wardroper	1
John Rumley	1

m. 29v, c. 1

James Cooke	1
John Poid junr	1
Willm Maughan	1
Geo Bell	1
Alexdr Poid	1
John Morpeth	1
	124

Barmiston
[Barmston]

Wm Wilson	1
Tho Mathen	1
John Clarke	1
Wm Dent	1
Tho Brough	1
George Sandrson	1
Rich Dixson	1
Ellin Sallan	1

John Davy	1
	9

Bowldon Et
[East Bolden]

Wm Wiseman	1
Robt Plonnton	1
Kathar Wayd	1
James Wellbanke	1
John Watson	1
Tho Twiddell	2
Wm Hutchinson	1
Geo Rippon	1
Alice Wood	1
John Hunt	1
John Hodge	1
Eliz Carnabie	1
Wm Gorling	1
Mary Atkinson	1
William Wood	1
Humphrey Robinson	1
Robert Steele	1
	18

Bowdon Wt
[West Bolden]

Wm Robson	1
John Arrow	2
Wm Hodgson	1
John Smales	1
Ann Johnson	1
Tho Hall	1
Wm Hall	1
Raphe Hodgson	1
Tho Wheldon	1
Wm Skoray	1
Willm Atkinson	1
Geo Hodgson	1
Mareatt Trewitt	1
John Wilson	1
Robt Hoburne	1
	16

Cledon
[Cleadon]

Matt Lettmoore	1

Steph Hodgson	1
Tho Page	1
Robt Wood	1
John Chetner	1
John Richdson	1
Antho Younger	1
Matt Doctor	1
Isabell Richdson	1
Gawen Toppin	1
Widd Richardson	1
	11

m. 29v, c. 2

Fulwell

Tho Codlin	1
John Young	1
John Cooke	1
Francis Appleby	1
Widd Watson	1
Smith shopp	1
John Taylor	1
	7

Hilton
[Hylton]

Willm Todd	1
John Todd	1
Mich Taylor	1
Robt Bell	1
Willm Semany	1
Michaell Bell	1
Tho Wallas	1
John Carnaby	1
Tho Taylor	1
Widdow Taylor	1
	10

Upper Heworth

Tho Comingham	1
David Johnson	1
Roger Greener	1
Mary Graham	1
Willm Davyson	1
Wm Hutchinson	1
Widd Browne	1
Widd Armestrong	1

Wm Taylor	1
Widd Thompson	1
	10

Hedworth

Tho Pattison	1
John Middleton	1
Willm Johnson	2
Tho Dun	1
Wm Catchfield	1
Rich Dalston	1
Bell Taylor	1
James Oard	1
Rich Davyson	1
Ruth Scott	1
John Thompson	1
	12

Harton

Tho Thompson	1
John Haswell	1
James Browne	1
Ellinor Young	1
Roger Rogwood	1
Duck Ree	1
Willm Bronkson	1
John Paxson	1
Elizabeth Atkinson	1
Willm Parkinson	1
Thomas Atkinson	1
	11

Nether Heworth

James Ingledew	1
Matt Reed	1
Widd Turner	1
George Emerrson	1
Matt Shotton	1
John Straughan	1
Hen Hewith	1
Wm Rawe	1
Willm Taylor	1
Jane Browne	1

m. 29v, c. 3

John Taylor	1

Tho Thompson	1	Wm Taylor	1
Widd Thompson	1	Robt Rosden	1
Rich Littell	1	Robt Potter	1
Widd Potts	1	John Eledert	1
Uzin Middford	1		**61**
John Lee	1		
Geo Richdson	1	**Munckton**	
John Hull	1	[**Monkton**]	
John Robinson	1	Luke Burneson	1
Michaell Howith	1	Tho Kellsay	2
John Davyson	1	Widdow Wilkinson	2
Robt Hodgson	1	James Barton	2
Sam Hall	1	Tho Kellsay	2
Tho Dickson	1	James Crissop	1
Widd Johnson	1	Wm Foster	2
John Turner	1	Widd Lemonn	1
Widd Reedhead	1		**13**
Widdow Walker	1		
Thomas Johnson	1	*m. 30, c. 1*	
Wm Johnson	1	**Munckwearmouth**	
Tho Dichburne	1	[**Monkwearmouth**]	
Tho Richdson	1	Arthure Criske	1
John Lowther	1	Isabell Criske	2
Andrew Smith	1	Tho King	2
Widd Southeren	1	Eliz Wright	1
Tho Dickson	1	John Johnson	1
Wm Spencer	1	John Clarke	2
Antho Oliver	1	Wm Shepherd	1
Wm Dichburne	1	Wm Bambrough	2
Edw Aukland	1	Wm Trotter	1
Widd Hutchinson	1	Tho Wetherhead	1
Willm Peace	1	Oswan Beaukiston	1
James Graham	1	Tho Whittingham	2
James Shepherdson	1	Willm Whittingham	1
John Willowbie	1	Willm Thompson	1
Widd Watson	1	Mary Taylor	1
Tho Gibbon	1	Rich Todd	1
Mich Hewith	1	Willm Bell	1
John Robinson	1	Ellinor Gowland	1
Geo Nicholl	1	Tho Dotchson	1
Widd Thompson	1	Geo Lilburne	1
Robt Rea	1	Willm Browne	1
Richd Walker	1	Antho Harryson	1
Antho Armestrong	1	Lan Wright	1
Geo Boodes	1	John Tinmouth	1
John Goffton	1	Fran Ray	1

Mary Addyson	1
John Rea	1
Robt Thompson	1
Tho Fitch	1
Robt Meburne	2
Ann Wear	1
Geo Creggs	1
Tho Watson	1
Arthure Duglass	1
Willm Bland	1
Peter Watters	1
Eliz Watters	1
Ann Potts	1
Ellinor Bell	1
Eliz Ellis	1
Ben Sadler	2
Eliz Foster	2
Hen Wilson	1
John Boyd	1
John Browne	1
Wm Snawden	1
John Addyson	1
John Wilkinson	1
Tho Wouldhaue	1
Geo Tinmouth	1
John Ousha	1
Wm Burne	2
Rich Chapman	2
Nicho Harygad	1
Cuth Cowert	1
Eliz Wear	1
	66

Suddicke
[Southwick]

Rich Bell	1
Rich Snale	1
Ann Turpin	1
Tho Morris	1
Chr Lowe	1
Mich Bainbridge	1
Eliz Almond	1
Willm Cocke	1

m. 30, c. 2

Hen Roxlie	1

Jane Lambard	1
Willm Rickbie	1
Hen Page	1
Alice Lincashore	1
Geo Urpeth	1
Patricke Crosar	1
Wm Page	1
	16

South Sheeles East Ward
[South Shields East Ward]

Robert Mathew	1
John Hunter	1
George Carter	1
John Madkreth	1
Matthew Swan	1
John Waller	1
John Tinmouth	1
Wm Watson	1
Marke Scott	1
Widd Blacke	1
Wm Humphrey	1
Char Braikerdar	1
Lan Humphrey	1
Robt Moneumry	1
Andrew Walker	1
Andrew Alexander	1
Geo Stephenson	1
James Johnson	1
James Venke	1
Robt Greene	1
John Hind	1
James Birkes	1
John Gibson	1
Gerard Whittingham	1
Cuth Anderson	1
John Blacke	1
Wm Bennett	1
Edward Rawson	1
Wm Flecke	1
John Johnston	1
Robt Younge	1
Tho Pearson	1
Luke Coocke	2
Geo Bell	1
John Willyson	1

Wm Vent	1
Dan Vent	1
Robt Rell	1
John Tennent	1
Wm Flecke	1
Geo Jackson	1
Rich Fleck	1
James Wood	1
Robt Mathew	1
Geo Rowley	1
John Wayd	1
Alexandr Bayle	1
Robt Young	1
Tho Shell	1
Oliver Cove	1
Widd Dearham	1
John Davyson	1
Gawen Davyson	2
Edw Morrow	1
John Thompson	1
John Tinmouth	1
John Thompson	1

m. 30, c. 3

Margtt Wallis	1
Widd Gray	1
Humph Scott	1
Widd Wagon	1
Rich Johnson	1
Wm Black	1
James Hareegate	1
Widd Glennett	1
Hen Empty	1
Arthure Harle	1
Widd Brady	1
Robt Rowell	1
Tho Robinson	1
Tho Buglesse	1
Widd Rennyson	1
Matt Buston	1
Widd Robinson	1
Dan Vent	1
Tho Padgate	1
Eliz Hilton	2
	80

South Sheeles Middle Ward
[South Shields Middle Ward]

Mary Pesse	1
Margtt Davy	1
Widd Daglishe	1
Edw Hottson	1
Sam Greenaway	1
John Jackson	1
Robt Archbold	1
John Grant	1
Widd Atkinson	1
Matt Dun	1
Wm Watson	1
Mary Dam	1
Mich Pawton	1
Thomas Lister	1
Margtt Dossie	1
Tho Pawton	1
John Wallas	2
Tho Dixson	1
Geo Dun	1
John Sutton	2
Widd Wealand	1
Ann Coper	1
	24

Sheeles West Panns
[South Shields West Panns]

Geo Dodd	1
Tho Hind	1
Bartho Greene	1
Lewis Cootes	1
Rich Cootes	1
Wm Cootes	1
Simon Greene	1
Robt Gray	1
John Johnson	1
John Dickenson	1
Tho Hunter	1
Geo Studert	1
Marke Fear	1
John Errington	1
Geo Shaftoe	1
Roger Scott	1
Mungoe Stanfort	1
Tho Dickson	1

Geo Harryson	1
Robt Portter	1
Wm Newton	1
John Lightes	1

m. 30v, c. 1

Mary Lambe	1
Geo Dunce	1
Tho Archer	1
Raphe Lee	1
Robt Heath	1
Geo Young	1
Ann Bamer	1
Rowld Cuminge	1
John Daglesse	1
Toby Wood	1
Chr Graham	1
Phillip Nesby	1
Geo Young	1
Mich Story	1
John Reinald	1
Walter Davyson	1
Luke Young	1
John Walker	1
Chro Wright	1
Chr Empty	1
Willm Lee	1
Marke Shaft	1
Cuth Thompson	1
Abraham Garthside	1
John Wallas	1
Tho Wetherburne	1
Matt Coots	1
Raphe Watson	1
Tho Rutter	1
Roger Graham	1
Robt Murros	1
Geo Wood	1
Widd Rough	1
Tho Spean	1
Rich Newton	1
John Dickson	1
	58

St Sheeles Et Panns
[South Shields East Panns]

Robt Peacke	1
Leo Nelson	1
James Dickson	1
John Pringle	1
Cuth Doxworth	1
John Eters	1
Tho Feach	1
John Longmire	1
Mary Carter	1
Geo Bell	1
John Bell	1
Robt Murros	1
Joseph Heweth	1
Isabell Anderson	1
John Pattison	1
Uswen Dennam	1
Robt Adamson	1
Margery Gaskin	1
Wm Duggills	1
Hen Smith	1
Edw White	1
Mary Noble	1
Lewis Anderson	1
Mich Heslop	1
Wm Charleton	1
James Foster	1
John Carter	1
Hen Duggis	2
John Gilcrist	1
James Gray	1

m. 30v, c. 2

Andrew [*blank*]	1
Edw Atkinson	1
Robt Rogison	1
James Robson	1
Edw Vastis	2
John Young	1
Tho Weare	1
John Rippon	1
Edw Thompson	1
Fortune Bomer	1
Robt Wright	1
Edw Wallis	1
Tho Wright	1
Geo Taite	1

John Hall	1	Robt Allan	1
Edw Littell	1	Tho Dickson	1
Robt Andrson	1	Raphe Huggell	1
Robt Maxwell	1	Chr Jefferson	1
John Cooke	1	James Hovy	1
Mr Linton	1	James Browne	1
James Sotter	1		**17**
Roger Cooke	1		
Mabell Browne	1	**Westoe**	
Mich Feach	1	Tho Readhead	1
Richd Oard	1	Leo Browne	1
Ann Nixon	1	John Cocke	1
Wm Thompson	1	Margtt Haward	1
Robt Maxwell	1	John Readhead	1
Robt Swadell	1		
	61	*m. 30v, c. 3*	
		Tho Pring	1
		Wm Lawson	1
Great Usworth		Step Gibson	1
Tho Rogers	1	Tho Browne	1
Marke Brough	1	Luke Humble	1
Margtt Storye	1	Edw Helston	1
David Drydan	1	Margtt Row	1
Wm Lawson	1	Jane Rutherford	1
Robt Nixon	1	Isab Sutheren	1
Eliz Cuthbert	1	Rich Reedhead	2
Andrew Bell	1	Tho Robinson	2
James Hall	1	Steph Gibson	2
James Stodart	1	Willm Hodgson	1
Edw Younge	1	Rich Carr	1
Willm Clarke	1		**22**
Tho Younge	1		
Tho Lodge	1	**Whitburne**	
	14	**[Whitburn]**	
		Tho Lettony	1
Washington		Wm Young	1
Wm Brough	1	Robt Farnton	1
Widd Maxway	1	Raphe Dixon	1
Wm Skurfield	1	James Browne	1
Tho Pomer	1	Wm Collicke	1
Rixon [*blank*]	1	Tho Moore	1
Antho Story	1	Tho Young	1
Chr Pearson	1	Cuth Hutchinson	1
Parcivall Cox	1	Tho Carr	1
Alice Newlands	1	Chr Hall	1
Rich Sparrow	1	Steph Jefferson	1
Antho Thompson	1		

Tho Lilburne	1
Peter Hudson	1
Wm Lee	1
John Cocke	1
Cuth: Huntley	1
Tho Watson	1
Tho Farrow	1
Robt Wetherall	1
Robt Milburne	1
Edw Maxwell	1
Tho Wright	1
Wm Gowland	1
John Thomlinson	1
Wm Lisle	1
Widd Thomlinson	1
Widd Hutchinson	1
Widd Bell	1
Ann Gowland	1
Ann Wetherall	1
John Hutchinson	1
Widd Croft	1
Geo Wright	1
Tho Hutchinson	1
Mary Younge	1
Wm Atkinson	1
Edw Kitchin	1
Jane Preston	1
Margtt Watson	1
Willm Maxwell	1
	41

Broome
[**Broom**]

Ann Wright	2
Agnes Braidley	1
Widd Carnaby	1
James Bell	1
Tho Harryson	1
Margery Emerrson	1
	7

Brickley
[**Birtley**]

Raphe Maddyson	1
Richd Farbridge	1
John Bracke	1

Widd Greene	1
Raphe Pearson	1
Widd Glesenby	1
Widd Atkinson	1
Widd Robinson	1
	8

m. 31, c. 1

Chester
[**Chester-le-Street**]

Geo Potts	1
John Pearson	1
Richd Punshon	1
Robt Cowper	1
Widd Durham	1
Geo Shaw	1
Jane Ellett	1
Widd Ladler	1
Ann Rutter	1
Jane Lawson	1
John Tunnall	1
James Harry	1
Widd Peatridge	1
Widd Cuthbert	1
Tho Andrew	1
Rich Thompson	1
Widd Fishe	1
Widd Johnson	1
Robt Robson	1
Peter Heath	1
Fran Hendrson	1
Tho Atkinson	1
Robt Punshon	1
Widd Carr	1
Tho Sharper	1
Jane Pearson	1
Widd Lewens	1
John Marley	1
John Donkin	1
Widd Gelson	1
Mich Lough	1
Ann Lupton	1
	32

Harraton

Raph Harbottle	1

John Dodgson	1	Nich Emerson	1
Wm Richdson	1	James Young	1
Humph Sparrow	1	Tho Wallas	1
Geo Dunn	1	Tho Hodgson	1
Wm Howlett	1	Edw Closper	1
Wm Robinson	1	Cuth Bell	1
Widd Hendrson	1	David Gladers	1
Widd Waters	1	Raph Wild	1
Willm Story	1	John Wild	1
Widd Dofton	1	John Todd	1
Widd Howett	1	Robt Browne	1
Wm Newby	1	Gerrard Markpeen	1
Tho Dason	1	Widd Wild	1
John Fishe	1	Raph Boogan	1
James Bromer	1	John Coats	1
Margt Eland	1	Hen Lambert	1
Mary Deanham	1	Emann Wheatley	1
James Browne	1		23
Tho Browne	1		
Hen Howett	1	**Lintsgreen**	
Wm Simpson	1	**[Lintz Green]**	
Ann Smith	1	Ann Robson	1
Rich Widdan	1	John Longstaffe	1
Widd Gibson	1	Wm Lonesdale	1
	25	Lan Joplin	1
		Geo Hewers	1
		Kath Poleston	1
m. 31, c. 2		John Dun	1
Hedley		Wm Browne	1
Fran Stevenson	1		8
Robt Denton	1		
Wm Spurry	1	**Pelton**	
	3	Tho Charleton	1
		Geo Wheldon	1
Kibblesworth		Char Studdert	1
John Stephenson	1	John Fennicke	1
Geo Browne	1	Antho Winsling	2
Ann Walker	1		6
	3		
		Plausworth	
Lamesley and Lamesley Fell Side		**[Plawsworth]**	
Widd Silly	1	Raph Birkall	1
Widd Hindson	1	Cuth Appleby	1
Tho Walker	1	Edw Lodge	1
Edw Trumble	1	John Hall	1
Raphe Jackson	1	Tho Robinson	1
Wm Robinson	1		

Widd Winter	1
Widd Watson	1
Peter Slater	1
James Murrow	1
Willm Harbittle	1

m. 31, c. 3

Tho Wellbyes	1
Geo Carlisle	1
Widd Carlile	1
Edmond Clerke	1
Robt Dixson	1
Widd Rickarby	1
John Benson	1
Alex Coats	1
John Lee	1
Rich Smith	1
Widd Hinde	1
	21

Ravensworth

Antho Bell	1
Walter Forrest	1
John Walliman	1
Tho Sanders	1
Geo Catchfield	1
John Bainbrigg	1
Raphe Barroes	1
Edw Rodgers	1
	8

Urpeth

Emann Robson	1
Marke Ceson	1
Raph Harryson	1
James Cutter	2
Tho Bland	1
Tho Milner	1
Edw Maddyson	1
Robt Longstaffe	1
Hen Watson	1
Tho Pearson	1
Mary Charleton	1
Tho Walke Milne	1
	13

Waldridge

Isabell Kirkley	1
Rich Brough	1
Wm Adamson	1
Tho Adamson	1
George Jopling	1
	5

[Island, Norham and Bedlington Shires]

Ancroft

Wm Athe	1
Tho Graham	1
Adam Maine	1
Wm Swinhoe sen	1
Wm Turbett	1
Wm Grey	1
Gilbt Grey	1
Raphe Lambe	1
Wm Swinhoe	1
Raphe Frizell	1
Peter Graham	1
Robt Halliday	1
John Graham	1
John Ewert	1
Adam Brankston	1
Wm Dickson	1
Tho Simpson	1
John Lambert	1
Eliz Simpson	1
John Short	1
Andrew Hogg	1
Mich Graham	1
John Robinson	1
Leonard Gaston	1

m. 31v, c. 1

John Scott	1
Adam Maine	1
Geo Duncombe	1
Tho Dunnes	1
Widd Girnhead	1
Widd Linsey	1
Widd Taylor	1

Widd Wrey[?]	1
Widd Lee	1
John Wallis	1
Widd Moore	1
Widd Tindall	1
Edw Gray	1
Roger Maine	1
Robt Finley	1
Elizabeth Steele	1
Widd Wilson	1
John Palin	1
Andrew Howe	1
James Steele	1
Andrew Neasbitt	1
	45

Beell
[Beal]

Rynion Graham	1
James Atteson	1
John Selby	1
Tho Watson	1
Barth Gettes	1
James Tannah	1
Raphe Browne	1
Fortune Carr	1
Wm Hall	1
Tho Ellott	1
John Graham	2
John Anderson	1
Wm Selby	1
James Bamborough	1
Fortune Tannah	1
James Palmer	1
Andrew Cowburne	1
Raphe Richdson	1
Rich Bonner	1
Francis Steele	1
Jane Davyson	1
	22

Berrington

Robt Lister	1
Geo Anderson	1
Bartram Atkinson	1
Adam Hewetson	1

Wm Cockson	1
Geo Hudspeth	1
Oswould Paxton	1
Tho Sandrson	1
Geo Robinson	1
Tho Dumbell	1
Geo Mason	1
Mich Sandrson	1
John Dixon	1
John Miller	1
Willm Cowburne	1
Rich Gibson	1
John Farrow	1
John Paxton sen	1
Robt Jackson	1
James Ayre	1
Vincent Fender	1
Tobias Hucke	00
John Avery	1
John Paxton	1
	22
[*corrected total*] es[?]	23

Buckton

John Watson	1
John Younghusband	1
Robt Hope	1

m. 31v, c. 2

Robt Atkinson	1
John Thompson	1
Richd Wake	1
Geo Atkinson	1
Oswould Wright	1
Wm Trumble	1
Richd Purdy	1
Barbary Thompson	1
Wm Spence	1
Wm Purvis	1
Edw Jackson	1
Hen Bell	1
Raphe Nelson	1
Tho Fender	1
Hen Wilson	1
	18

**Cheswicke
[Cheswick]**

Edw Binney	1
Rich Strangwayes	1
Chr Strangwayes	1
John Miller	1
Geo Smith	1
John Hungerston	1
Geo Simpson	1
Wm Wray	1
Eliz Heslopp	1
James Glasse	1
Tho Hogg	1
Wm Moffitt	1
Peter Steele	1
Widd Carmichaell	1
John Weddell	1
Geo Dunkin	1
Geo Gastin	1
James Hambleton	1
Rich Davyson	1
Wm Baxter	1
Robt Rutter	1
James Richdson	1
Wm Young	1
Widd Cooke	1
	24

Fenham

Wm Bell	1
Tho Johnson	1
Robt Dodds	1
John Wilson	1
Raphe Bellheard	1
Willm Watson	1
Tho Steward	1
Tho Moodey	1
Tho Bell	1
John Steward	1
Raphe Tindall	1
Wm Hall	1
Nicho Steward	1
Margt Bell	1
Robt Mabcombe	1
John Scott	1
Tho Balehouse	1

Wm Hendrson	1
Tho Atkinson	1
Tho Winlowe	1
Hen Steele	1
	21

Fenwicke [Fenwick]

Henry Heslopp	1
Wm Dodds	1
Tho Duncon	1
Raphe Browne	1

m. 31v, c. 3

Hen Watson	1
Richd Duncon	2
Geo Wood	1
Cuth Stower	1
Widd Nicholson	1
Widd Thompson	1
James Browne	1
James Wright	1
Jo White	1
Tho Wadd	1
Widd White	1
Widd Wright	1
Wm Robinson	1
Wm Jackson	1
Tho Ackton	1
Tho Wright	1
Elyas Boyd	1
Tho Bower	1
John Fargison	1
Widd Shepheard	1
Widd Pringle	1
Tho Browne	1
Tho Alexandr	1
Raphe Fender	1
Widd Thompson	1
Matt Steele	1
Tho Dickson	1
Widd Jackling	1
Widd Wilson	1
John Shipherd	1
Lawrence Learnwicke	1
Widd Beadlin	1
Alexdr Wright	1

Andrew Fleminge	1
Willm Liste	1
Wm Clough	1
Widd Rutter	1
Symon Davyson	1
	43

Felkington and Greenslead
[Felkington and Grievestead]

Steph Gastell	1
John Cockstin	1
Wm Edgar	1
Cuth Scott	1
Tho Moffit	1
Jo Summerbell	1
Geo Browne	1
James Arnett	1
Wilfride Arnett	1
Eliz Peterson	1
Tho Pattin	1
Robt Neasbitt	1
Arm Thompson	1
John Smith sen	1
John Smith	1
James Harvy	1
James Arnett	1
Elenor Habkirke	1
Robt Huetson	1
Gawin Carnes	1
Patricke Russell	1
Rowld Arnett	1
Jasper Wheallis	1
Jane Clarke	1
	24

m. 32, c. 1

Grindon and Grindon Ridge
[Grindon and Grindonrigg]

Geo Holyday	1
John Bowertharke	1
Geo Weddell	1
Willm Bone	1
John Weddell sen	1
Tho Hayne	1
Widd Smith	1
Tho Carne	1

Richd Forster	1
Wm Hague	1
Christian Burne	1
Widd Browne	1
Geo Tindall	1
James Greenlaw	1
Wm Dodds	1
Wm Arnett	1
	16

Horcliffe
[Horncliffe]

Robt Ord	1
Robt Gray	1
Gilbert Gastin	1
John Ord	1
James Trousbie	1
Hen Richdson	1
John Robson	1
Alex Ord	1
John Ord	1
Hen Bowmaker	1
Alexdr Dodds	1
Wm Clarke	1
Thomas Bourne	1
Richd Simpson	1
Geo Strother	1
John Clarke	1
Richd Yeoman	1
Robt Thompson	1
Widd Ord	1
Alexdr Farrow	1
Hen Richdson	1
John Rowles	1
Raphe Palline	1
Willm Comely	1
Hen Richdson	1
Wm Wade	1
Gawen Roger	1
Tho Roger	1
Widd Nicholson	1
Ellinor Nicholson	1
Gawen Foggert	1
John Thompson	1
Raphe Rickerby	1
Margery Thompson	1

Rowld Smith	1
Alexdr Marshall	1
Raphe Gomery	1
Wm Crake	1
Wm Faire	1
	39

Haggerston

Fran Eatham	1
Geo Dixon	1
Tho Kellett	1
Robt Grey	1
James Dixon	1

m. 32, c. 2

Widd Kellett	1
Wm Haggerston	1
Geo Crosby	1
Richd Watson	1
Hen Muscropp	1
Raphe Mayne	1
Cuth Taylor	1
Ann Atkinson	1
Alexdr Short	1
	14

Holy Island

Tho Jackson sen	1
Math Taylor	2
Math Steell	1
Geo Mason	2
Geo Steell	1
Raphe Gray	1
Widd Winter	1
Sam Steell	1
John Steell	1
Widd Hebbourne	1
James Wallis	1
Andrew Wilson	1
Wm Stampe	1
Edward Wilkinson	1
Cuth Swinhoe	1
Wm Hope	2
Cornelius Hebbourne	1
John Bulmer	2
Richd Graham	1

Antho Wallis	2
James Stobbs	1
Tho Bewdle junr	2
Wm Gray	1
Widd Muschampe	2
Widd Wallis	1
Robt Lilbourne	1
Abigall Gray	2
Hen Gray	1
Geo Allison	1
Jo Harryson	1
Edw White	1
	39

Heaton

Char Waugh	1
Widd Johnson	1
Reinald Rutterford	1
Wm Donellson	1
Tho Farrow	1
Wm Waugh	1
Widd Anderson	1
John Waugh	1
Tho Moffitt	1
James Farrow	1
Tho Gigson	1
Nich Swan	1
Lan Pallierd	1
Geo Hill	1
Luke Ward	1
Raphe Granston	1
Tho Kirston	1
Wm Crossby	1
Edw Crossby	1
Ellinor Ogle	1
John Swan	1
John Forrest	1
John Thompson sen	1
John Thompson	1
Geo Crossby	1
Robt Donellson	1
Geo Ferrey	1
John Gray	1
Patricke Wetherhead	1
	29

m. 32, c. 3

Kylay cum Membris
[Kyloe with Parts]

John Andrson	1
John Armstrong	1
James Carmichall	1
John Middleton	1
Geo Thompson	1
Geo Davyson	1
Antho Peacocke	1
Tho Smith	1
Rich Waike	1
	9

Lowlynn
[Low Linn]

David Hewson	1
Mich Browne	1
Tho Browne	1
James Spence	1
Wm Mowe	1
	5

Low End
[Loan End]

Robt Mathewson	1
John Mitchelson	1
Widd Davyson	1
Hen Yeoman	1
Wm Sunins	1
Robt Bartleman	1
George Linsay	1
Robt Nicholson	1
Leo Coxson	1
	9

Morton
[Murton]

Patricke Minikin	1
John Archbald	1
James Lough	1
Wm Mallin	1
Wm Carr	1
Tho Dennis	1
John Hogg	1
Hen Forrest	1

Gilbt Wood	1
	9

Norham

Adam Peircy	1
Roger Peircy	1
Wm Richdson	1
John Ainsley	1
Widd Ramsey	1
Widd Richdson	1
Gawen Richdson	1
Widd Steward	1
Widd Burne	1
James Knox	1
Geo Allison	1
Widd Mathewson	1
Step Anderson	1
Robt Tate	1
Patricke Trotter	1
John Marshall	1
Wm Neasbitt	1
Bryan Pearson	1
Geo Richdson	1
James Dixon	1
John White	1
John Thompson	1
John Fowlerston	1
Tho Moffitt	1
Widd Glayne	1
John Knox	1
And Neasbitt	1
Rogr Rowle	1
John Bowmaker	1
Widd Armestrong sen	1
Wm Simmington	1
Geo Beanston	1
Hen Smith	1
Widd Learman	1

m. 32v, c. 1

Leo Hogg	1
Widd Beanston	1
Willm Rowle	1
Andrew Armstrong	1
Wm Richdson	1
Roger Knox	1

Robt Richdson	1
Wm Bunting	1
Margtt Ord	1
David Leech	1
Ellinor Fargis	1
Wm Knox	1
Adam Peircy	1
Geo Memum	1
Leo Taylor	1
Widd Browne	1
Widd Fowlerton	1
John Coxston	1
Margtt Hallywell	1
Tho Swinhoe	1
Oswald Dodds	2
Wm Turnbull	1
Geo Birnitt	1
Geo Ogle	1
Wm Woodell	1
Hen Byers	1
Margtt Byers	1
Geo Baites	1
Margtt Bowmaker	1
Widd Ayre	1
Stephen Sandrson	1
	66

Newbiggen
[Newbiggin]

John Learmouth	1
Nicho Archbold	1
George Feltes	1
Tho Davyson	1
Geo Hume	1
Widd Lowning	1
	6

Ord

Geo Twiddey	2
Widd Short	1
Wm Bald	1
Tho Hendrson	1
Tho Makin	1
Mirill Fittis	1
Tho Dawson	1
Widd Bourne	1

Robt Taylor	1
James Cowper	1
Cornelius Armestrong	1
Wm Carr	1
Ferdinando Rule	1
Widd Cleggeren	1
Tho Taylor	1
Raphe Taylor	1
Clement Wilson	1
Widd Carr	1
Tho Tate	1
Robt Collingwood	1
Raphe Bell	1
Widd Richdson	1
Widd Allan	1
Wm Thompson junr	1
Hen Greenhead	1
Rynion Maber	1
Alexdr Duglas	1
Chr Rule	2
Geo Short	1

m. 32v, c. 2

Widd Mossman	1
Patricke Temple	1
John Dunce	1
Archbold Renton	1
Alexdr Short	2
Robt Ellett	1
James Richdson	1
Richd Fender	1
Hen Haisty	1
Wm Wilson	1
Math Forster	1
Hen Hudspeth	1
Tho Dennis	1
Gilbt Wood	1
Chr Lamb	1
Tho Halliday	1
Randall Roton	1
Luke Thompson	1
Geo Coxson	2
Widd Douglas	1
Widd Fewler	1
Chr Coxson	1
Widd Thompson	1

John Warriner	1	Nich Crawford	1
Wm Thompson sen	1	Rich Neasbitt	1
Widd Coxson	1	Wm Patrickson	1
	59	Oswald Steward	1
		John Carr	1
Thornton		Math Forge	1
Cuth Landereth	1	Robt Preston	1
Wm Gates	1	Tho Patrickson	1
Robt Bell	1	John Summer	1
John Thew	1	Robt Robertson	1
Tho Armestrong	1	Alexdr Kirkemichaell	1
Geo Maben	1	Geo Clarke	1
Widd Crome	1	Tho Steward	1
John Bowmaker	2	Tho Fettesse	1
	9	David Mordike	1
		Robt Mordon	1
		James Smith	1
Thistlerigg		Tho Pattison	1
Adam Coxon	1	Tho Oliver	1
Wm Duncomb	1	Lan Brownhill	1
Tho Davyson	1	John Patterson	1
Edm Davyson	1		**28**
Robt Wetherston	1		
David Donelson	1		
	6		

Norham Castlegate

John Wadd	1
John Smith	1
Nich Hutchison	1
Widd Purvis	1
Rich Coxon	1
Tho Coxon	1
Tho Marshall	1
Andrew Wallis	1
Widd Rosse	1
Tho Purvis	1
	10

Twizell

Edw Young	1
Wm Thompson	1
Richd Enderson	1
Patrick Tindall	1
Robt Atkin	1
Tho Tate	1
Jarvis Sanderson	1

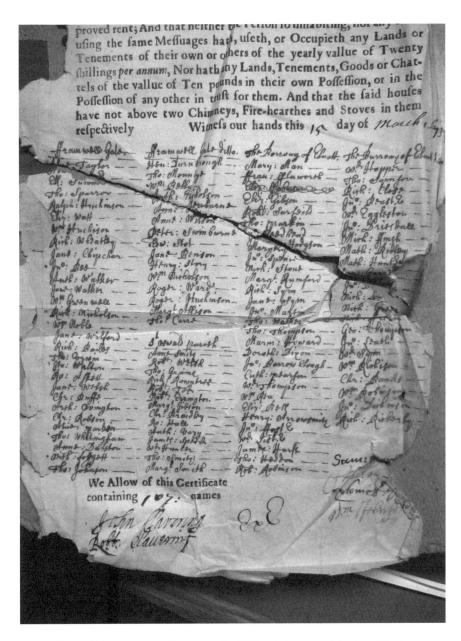

Figure 6. Exemption certificate, March 1674 (n.s.), for parts of the city of Durham:
Framwellgate, St Oswald, and the Barony of Elvet.TNA E179/327, part 2, no.1 (pieced
together from fragments). The names on this certificate are, suspiciously, identical
with those on certificates of Jan. 1671 (n.s.).The 1674 certificate has presumably been
copied either from the 1671 certificates, or from a yet earlier common source which no
longer survives. These certificates, despite their date, complement the Lady Day 1666
Asessment, which lacks information on the exempt for the City of Durham. See table p.
218–219.

APPENDIX I

Surviving Durham Hearth Tax Documents

Durham hearth tax documents held at the National Archives[1]

Assessments and Returns
NA E179/106/27 *1664 Lady Day collection*
Forty four parchment membranes comprising the fragmentary remains of the assessment for the 1664 Lady Day collection. The heading is illegible but the document was delivered to the Exchequer on 30 June 1664. The chargeable householders are listed by name with their hearth numbers expressed in Roman numerals. The not chargeable are omitted. The hearth total is noted at the end of each division with the corresponding money total in Arabic figures. The membranes are very damaged and large parts are missing.

NA E179/245/27 *1665 Michaelmas collection*
Fifty two membranes comprising the duplicate for the three collections Michaelmas 1664 to Michaelmas 1665. The heading is faded but the date 1665 can be deciphered. The signatures of the justices can be found on m. 52 with the delivery date to the Exchequer of 9 November 1666. The householders are listed in two parallel columns of chargeable and not chargeable though the not chargeable are sometimes omitted. On the final membrane is a summary of the amount of money returned by each division and the county total.

NA E179/106/28 *1666 Lady Day collection* (the document here published)
Thirty two parchment membranes on which the householders are divided into solvents listed from m. 1–17 and non-solvents from m.18–33. Although the list was drawn up after the collection was made it has been drafted as a survey or assessment. The membranes measure 7 inches (17.8 cms) wide by 19–20 inches (48.2–50.8 cms) long and each is double ruled at the head and lengthwise into three columns. The width of each set of columns are respectively from left to right are 1/5 inch (0.3 cms) 1 7/10 inch (4.3cms) and 1/2inch (1.3cms) with a final margin of 1/10inch (0.2cms). The hearth numbers are given in Arabic with totals at the end of each community. Any corrections to the totals are given slightly to the left of the original incorrect total.

The membranes were numbered in Arabic at the top right-hand corner by the compilers but this numeration was almost entirely obscured when the membranes

---

[1] Much of the work for this volume was done before the Public Record Office was re-named the National Archives. At this early stage it was expected that the citing of their references would be NA as used in this volume. It has since become TNA. The term membrane is used throughout for each piece of parchment whereas the term rotulet is used on the National Archives database.

were sewn together at their heads. Many of the membranes have suffered slight wear and tear on the left-hand side. There has also been some damage and loss at the head of the first four membranes. The position of the identifying inscription in a seventeenth-century hand at the end of the verso: County of Durham Fire hearths &c 1665.6 suggests that at one time the document was stored upside down.

NA E179/106/26 *1669 Michaelmas – 1670 Michaelmas collections*
Thirty six parchment membranes forming the badly fragmented remains of most of the enrolled duplicate for the county of Durham enrolled at the Quarter Sessions in January 1671 [written as old style January 1670] The householders are listed in two parallel columns of liable and not liable and the numbers are written in Roman numerals. This would appear to be an assessment for the three collections Michaelmas 1669 to Michaelmas 1670. Another fragment of this duplicate for part of the west division of Chester Ward is catalogued under E179/244/38.

NA E179/375/5 *1671 Lady Day & Michaelmas or 1672 Lady Day & Michaelmas and 1673 Lady Day collections*
Three membranes headed an 'account' of the increase and decrease in the number of taxable hearths since Michaelmas 1670. The document is undated but from the comments within it and the fact that no duplicate was compiled between Michaelmas 1670 and 1673 it must refer to the collections in 1671 or 1672 and those of Lady Day 1673. The list only records the increases and decrease in hearth numbers listed against the appropriate householder.

NA E179/106/25 *1673 Michaelmas – 1674 Lady Day collections*
Seventy six parchment membranes comprising the combined assessment and return for the two collections Michaelmas 1673 and Lady Day 1674. The heading is faded and no enrolment date can be discerned although the justices' signatures can be found on m.36. The named householders are listed according to ward as solvents and non-solvents. The final two membranes give a brief summary of the total hearth numbers in the Durham city parishes and the wards followed by the sum of money due. The names of the non-solvents can be matched to the exemption certificates in E179/327.

Exemption certificates
NA E179/327 *1671 Michaelmas and 1672–1674*
Included in part 3 of this piece are 90 paper exemption certificates for Durham most dated January 1671 (new style) listing the not chargeable by name. A similar number dated between 1673 and 1674 (new style) can be found in part 2, also listing the not liable by name. Some of these are printed in Appendix IV of this volume.

Durham hearth tax documents held at the Durham County Record Office
DRO D/Sa/E/882–890 *Hearth Tax Lists for Tudhoe Township, 1667–1675*
Among the extensive estate papers kept by the Salvin family (of Croxdale) are a
series of hearth tax lists for Tudhoe township, made by the constables. On the
reverse of D/Sa/E887, listing the hearth money collected in Lady Day 1673, is a
list of freeholders running from 1667 to 1675, including exemption certificates
issued by churchwardens. A transcript is printed as Appendix II of this volume.

Durham hearth tax documents held at Durham University Archive
Durham University Library, Halmote Court Miscellaneous Books No. 95.
Hearth Tax lists for West Auckland, 1671–1675
Among the Halmote Court records (primarily relating to the bishopric estates),
is the notebook kept by John Kay, grieve (a collector of various dues) of West
Auckland (see p. xxxii). Kay's notebook includes copies of the constables' hearth
tax lists for the township of West Auckland from 1671 to 1675, and exemption
certificates issued by the churchwardens of St. Helen Auckland. There is also a
list of West Auckland constables 1662–1700. These are printed as Appendix III
of this volume.

Arrears and Auditors' Papers at the National Archives
For those readers wishing to delve further into the hearth tax administration in
Durham there are other pieces held at the National Archives covering the arrears
and auditors' papers. These have been summarised below:
Arrears
 NA E179/106/20 1662 Michaelmas collection.
 NA E179/106/21 1663 Lady Day collection.
 NA E179/106/22 desperate arrears for 1662 Michaelmas – 1664 Lady Day
 collections.
 NA E179/106/23 arrears for the 1662 Michaelmas – 1664 Lady Day
 collections.
 NA E179/106/24 arrears for the 1666 Lady Day collection.
 NA E179/358 Schedule of non-distraint for the collections 1669 Lady Day –
 1670 Michaelmas.
 NA E179/359 Schedule of non-distraint for the collections 1671
 Michaelmas – 1673 Lady Day
Auditors papers
 NA E179/106/29 State of account for 1664 Michaelmas – 1665 Michaelmas
 and arrears from 1662 Michaelmas – 1664 Lady Day.
 NA E179/361 Unsorted bundle including summaries of accounts for 1664
 Michaelmas – 1665 Lady Day collections.
 NA E179/356 Unsorted bundle including auditors papers for the 1670
 Michaelmas – 1671 Michaelmas collections in which Durham is included with
 Northumberland, Newcastle upon Tyne and Berwick upon Tweed. E179/356

also contains a note of the receiver general's salary for Northumberland and bishopric of Durham, dated 18 February 1673 and a note of the appointment on 11 May 1670 of receiver general for Northumberland, Durham, Newcastle upon Tyne and Berwick upon Tweed, dated 19 February 1673; also an abstract state of account of the receiver-general for the year and a half ended Lady Day 1673; and a communal assessment, dated 11 January 1671, county Durham, including totals of hearths chargeable and not chargeable.

NA E179/158/117 Summaries of accounts for the 1671 Lady Day – 1671 Michaelmas collections in which Durham is included with Northumberland, Newcastle upon Tyne and Berwick upon Tweed.

NA E179/265/28 and 29 Two auditors' books listing the receipt of the assessment rolls at the office of the King's Remembrancer in which Durham is included.

NA E179/357 Unsorted auditors' papers which include a copy of the oath sworn by the Durham receiver and a note of tallies struck by him for Durham.

NA E179/358 Schedule of non-distraint for Durham, Northumberland, Newcastle upon Tyne and Berwick upon Tweed for the 1669 Michaelmas – 1670 Michaelmas collections.

Additional documents are constantly being identified in the National Archives. For the latest list of Hearth Tax documents for County Durham, see the web-site www.nationalarchives.gov.uk/E179/

Appendix II

Tudhoe Constables' Hearth Tax lists

The following have been transcribed from the hearth tax lists for Tudhoe township surviving in the Salvin papers in Durham County Records Office D/Sa/E882–890, along with the Exchequer Return for 1674 in NA E179/106/25. The 1673 exemption certificate for Tudhoe is printed in Appendix IV, p. 239, from E179/327 part 2.

[DRO D/Sa/E/ 882]

May 3 1667

A presentment of the Fire Hearths within the Constablewick of Tudhoe in the Parish of Brancepeth ye Michall: 1666 and Lady Day 1667.

A Note of ye Fyre Hearths in Tuddoe as they were collected by Tho: Pickering Constable for a whole year ended att Lady Day: 1667

		Hearths	
p.[aid] his owne	Henry Trewhitt	3	
p. Mr Featherstone	Richard Willson	2	
p. his owne and mothers	Henry Sidgewick	2	
p. his landlord Sa:[lvin]	Emery Richardson	1	
Idem	Anthony Harper	1	
p. Widd: Richardson	Thomas Dawson	1	1 layed down for Tho: Pickering
p. John Bracke	Thomas Rawe	1	
p. Widd: Browne	Thomas Taylor	1	
p. his owne	Thomas Harper	1	
	~~Christopher Rickeson~~	~~1~~	
the old House pull'd down ye last winter; and rebuilded this Spring; the Hearth layd againe April 29th 1667	William Dell	1	paid but p. one half year
	Roger Turpin	1	
p. his owne	John Richardson	2	
p. widd: Dunns	George Richardson	1	
p. her owne	Sarah Briggs Widow	1	
p. his owne	John Brack	1	
p. his owne	Francis Heighinton	1	
p. his owne	William Redhead	1	
p. Fratre	Ralph Dunn	2	
p. Mr. Sidgewicks	John Atkinson	2	
p. his own & sonnes	William Byerley	5	
p.Mr. Sidg: Cottage	Ellinor Jackson	2	

	Widdow	
p. his own	John Sparke	1
p. Widd: Shortriggs	James Ellinor	1
p. Mr Sidgewickes	Thomas Pickering	1
4 more never was layd & yett unfinished	Mr Ra: Salvin in his House	4
p. his owne	Nicholas Fishburne	1
p. Richard Willsons	George Ilye	1

3 of these Hearths lay'd since April the 10 1666

Pd. Afterwards to Tho. Pickering: & he gave itt to ye collectors Deputyes when they came to receivbe in this Towne in ye latter end of June, nr beginning of July 1667

p. Rich: Byers	Thomas Walker	1
p. his owne	Henry Jackson	1
p. his owne	John Wheatley	1

May 4th 1667 Tho: Pickering paid £4 5s in yet collected according to whose names are crossed out in this note (& a whole yeare)

Made October 5th 1667 a presentment according to this was dd: in to Jo: Applegate att Durham: by Tho: Pickering Constable & 45s paid by his according to this list by one half yeare ended at Mich: 1667 as he collected itt.

<u>Tuddhoe</u> A presentment of ye Fire Hearths given att Mich: 1668 by Richard Willson Constable and Collected by him.

Henry Trewhitt	4
Richard Willson	2
Hen: Sidgewick	2
Jo: Harper & Mr Salvin	1
Antho: Harper	1
Tho: Dawson	1
Tho: Rawe	1
Tho: Taylor	1
Tho: Harper	1
William Bell	1
Roger Turpin	1
Jo: Richardson	2
Ann: Dunn	1
Sarah Briggs	1
Jo: Brack	1
Fra: Heighington	2
William Readhead	2
George Richardson	1
John Attkinson	2
2. William Byerleys	5

Ralph Dunn	3
John Sparke	1
Jarr: Walker	1
Tho: Pickering	1
Mr. Salvin	5
Nicho: Fishburn	1
George Iley	1
Tho: Walker	1
John Wheatley	1
John Roundhead	1

& this ye first part of
his little new house att
Watergate

Made par Lady Day 1669: Henry Trewhitt & Henry Sidgewick Constables collected
after this same presentment

[DRO D/Sa/E/883]

Wee whose names are hereunto Subscribed doe affirme & hereby certifye that A Margaret Horner, Widow; Dennise Willson widdow; Thomas Bell; John Corser; Henry Corser; Jane Redhead widdow; Ambrose Bell; Robert Spark; George Kirkley; Thomas Browne; John Sidgewick; Matthew Harper; Richard Smith; Margaret Hillery; Margaret Browne Widdow; Allee Real Widdow; John Gill; Henry Wheatley; Dorothy Card; Henry Hillery; John Fletcher; William Rawe; Mary Allen Widdow; Anne Walker; Richard Brown; Thomas Thickald; Henry Richardson; & Temperance Cooper Widdow; all of them of the Townshipp of Tudoe in the parish of Branspeth are poor indigent People; & their Houses under the yearly vallew of fifteen shillings Rent & most of them doe frequently receive the Almes of Charity of the Parish & poor Cess: And therefore wee doe conceive are in noe sort lyable to pay Harth money. Given under our hands this first day of May. In the nineteenth yeare of his Majestyes Reign over England A.D. 1667.

Jul: Threckeld Curat de Branscepeth
He: Hull Churchwarden

Will: Wilson   his mark: *W*
Church Warden

~~Henry Trewhitt~~	4
Rich. Willson	2
Hen: Trewhit	4
Of which one not 1 d	
Hen: Sidgewick	1
Widdow Sidgwick	1
Wm. Wilson	1
Rich. Haward empty	1
Tho: Raw	1
Tho: Taylor	1
Tho: Harper one p Ellery	2 one p Ellery
Chr: Killeby	2 one p his mothers
James Ellinor	1
Rog. Turpin	1
John Richardson	1
Hen. Richardson	1
Mich. Wheatley	1
Will Wheatley	1
Ann Dunn	1
Will. Readhead	2
John Readhead	1
John Bracke	1
Fra. Heighington	2
John Briggs	1

Thomas Baston	1			
John Corser	1			
Amb. Bell	1			
Sara Briggs	1			

Non-solvents		[Charged]		
Jo: Harper	1	Geo: Richardson	1	
Tho: Harper	1	Emery Richardson	1	
Mich: Hillery	1	John Atkinsons	2	
Ann Browne	1	Will: Byerley	2	
Rich: Smith	1	Will: Byerley	3	
Matth: Harper	1	Ralph Dunn	3	
Jo: Sidgewick	1	Will Bell	--	
Widd: Johnson	1	John Sparkey	2	~~& of Mary Kisley~~
Widd: Sparke	1	Mar. Kirkley being in one of them		
Ann Woodifield	1	Jar. Walker	1	
Dennis Wilson		Tho. Pickering	1	
Margaret Horner		Mr Salvin	5	
Henry Carter		Mr Fishburn	1	
Tho: Bell		Geo. Iley	One p. with peale	
John Fletcher		Tho.Walker	1	
Willm: Bell		Hen. Jackson	1	
John Gill		John Wheatley	1	
Willm Rawe		Hen. Wheatley	1	
Ann Walker		Rob. Sparke	1	

[DRO D/Sa/E/884]

Tuddowe list of Hearths

William Wilson -	1
Henry Sidgewick -	1
Ann Sidgewick -	1
Anne Walker *	2
Henry Trewhit -	4
Rich Wilson -	2
Henry Lowasby -	1
Jo Weatley -	1
Henry Jackson -	1
William Raw -	1
Tho Walker -	1
Alice prele -	1
George Iley -	1
Nich: Fishburne -	1
Jo: Gilly -	1
Nich: Ellery -	1
Tho: Beccles -	1
Rich Smith -	1
Jo: Cawser -	1
Tho: Lawsen -	1
Tho: Dawson -	1
Jo: Briggs -	1
Margaret Horne *	1
Henry Wilson *	1
Anne Dunne -	1
Mary Allan *	2
Henry Richison -	1
Henry Elliray -	1
Anth. Harper -	1
Wid: Johnson *	1
Jo: Harper *	1
Jo: Brack -	1
Mart: Harper -	1
Jo: Sedgwicke -	1
Mr Ra. Salvin -	5 & 3 never used
Tho: Pickering -	1
Gerard Walker -	1
Jo: Spark -	1
Mary Kirkby -	1
Will Bull *	1
Margaret Flecke *	1

Ralph Dunne -	3
William Bierly -	2
William Bierly -	3
Jo: Alisham -	2
Emoray Richison -	1
Geo: Richison -	1
Tho: Bell *	1
Henry Cawser *	1
Sarah Briggs -	1
Anne Bell -	1
Will: Wheatley -	1
Nich: Wheatley -	1
Jo: Richison -	1
Ann Widdifield -	1
Roger Turpin -	1
James Elliner -	1
Dorothy Clarke -	1
Eliz: Rickerson -	2
Tho: Taylor -	1
Tho: Raio -	1
Rich: Howard -	1 empty
~~Mr Salvin -~~	~~1 empty~~
Tho: Harper -	1
Fr: Heighington -	2

Aug: 11th : 1670 This then surveyed [by] Tho: Hall

[DRO D/Sa/E/885 1670]
A Coppy of ye certificat for Harth Money for ye Townshipp of Tudhoe signed by ye Curat of Branspeth 4 Church wardens and 2 Justices
August 31th 1670

Wee the Minister of the Parish of Branspeth in the County of Durham and Churchwardens of the said parish for the Townshipp and Constabulary of Tudhoe being of the said parish, Doe hereby certefye unto his Majesties Justices of the peace for the said County of Durham, that wee doe believe that the respective houses wherein the persons heere under named doe inhabit are not of greater vallue than twenty shillings per annum upon the full improved Rent. And that neither the persons soe inhabiting nor any other using the same messuages, hath, useth, or occupieth any Lands or Tenements of theire owne, or others of the yearly vallew of twenty shillings per Annum, nor hath any Lands, Tenements, Goods or Chattels, of the yearly value of Ten Pounds in theire own possession, or in the possession of any other in trust for them. And that the said Houses have not above two Chimneys, Fire hearthes and stoves in them respectively. Witness our hands this 31st day of August A.D. 1670

Micheall Wheatley	Henry Hillary	John Carter
Ann Walker	Christopher Rickeson	Alice Peale
John Harper	William Wheatley	Temperance Cooper
Thomas Ha-rper	Ann Widdefielde solv-d	John Briggs
Michaell Hillery	Mary Allen	Mary Kirkley
Thomas Butcher	Widdow Willson	Robert Sparke
Richard Smith	Widdow Hornner	Henry Wheatley
Matthew Harper	Henry Corter	
John Sidgwick	Thomas Bell	
Widdow Johnson	John Fletcher	
Dorothy Carde	William Dell	
Thomas Dawson	William Rawe	
Ambrose Dell		

I doe believe (because I am soe informed) that the persons before mentioned are not lyable to pay Harth Money. Will: Threckeld Curat, ibid., John Bracke: B, Jo. Harland, Henry Chapman, John Cleckle Churchwardens.

Wee allow of this Certificate containing thirty three names
Nicho: Richardson Mayor
Jo: Morland

March: 24 1670 this certificate allowed of bodie of Mr. Francis Crosby, when james Ellinor Constable paid him eighteen months arrear for Harth Money due at Mich: last past 1670 / for Tudhoe Constablery

[DRO D/Sa/E/886 1670]

Harth money collected by Ja: Ellinore Constable of Tudhoe, & given in a note allowed off by Mr Francis Crosby Rec't March 23: 1670

Paid 3 halfe years arrears for Tudhoe Constablrey

Tudhoe Townshipp Fyrehearths payable par 3 half years Arreares att Mich: 1670 & to be collected by Warrant: by James Ellinor: Constab:

March: 23: 1670

1. Imp. Mr Hen: Trewhitt	4	per these 3 payments / and one pulled downe since Mich: 1670	
2. Ittm Rich: Willson	2		
3. Ittm: Hen: Sidgewick	2		
4. Ittm: Willm: Willson	1		
5. Ittm: Thomas Rawe	1		
6. Ittm: Thomas Taylor	1		
7. Ittm: Antho: Harper	1		
8. Ittm: James Ellinor	1	[constable]	
9. Ittm: Roger Turpin	1		
10. Ittm:John Richardson	2	[1 written over as 2]	
11. Ittm:Ann Dunn: Widow *	1	1 putt out (by Mr. Crosby) none of Mᶜ Christian's menthen present	
12. Ittm:Sarah Briggs: Widow	1		

for Butcher Race and Westgate

13. Ittm: John Brack	1		
14. Ittm: Francis Heighington	2	& answered for them himself	
15. Ittm: Willm: Redhead	2		
16. Ittm: John Readhead	*1	not demanded	
17. Ittm: George Richardson	1		
18. Ittm: Emry Richardson	1		
19. Ittm: John Atkinson	2		
20. Ittm: ye William Byerleys	5	one of these not paid for W: B: senior pretending it a Butcher Shopp	
21. Ittm: Ralph Dunne	3	one putt out by Mr Crosby	
22. Ittm: John Sparke	1		
23. Ittm: Jarrard Walker	1		
24. Ittm: Thomas Pickering	1		
25. Ittm: Mʳ. Salvin	5		
26. Ittm: Nicho: Fishburn	1		
27. Ittm: George Ilye	1		
28. Ittm: Thomas Walker	1		

29. Ittm: John Wheatley   1
30. Ittm: Hen: Jackson   1

Richard Haward and Infants and partner the house empty and not habitable./././ this marked according to ye non Solvents and was not paid for

[DRO D/Sa/E/887]

Harth money Collected by Roger Turpin Constable for Lady Day 1673

		b	
3.	Hen. Trewhitt	- 3	
2.	Rich: Willson	- 2	
2.	Hen: Sidgewick	- 2	
1.	Wm Willson	- 1	
1.	Hen: Hillery	- 1	
1.	Tho. Taylor	- 1	
1.	Anthony Harper	- 1	[added in]
1.	James Ellinor	- 1	
1.	Roger Turpin	- 1	
2.	Jo: Richardson	- 2	[1 rewritten as 2]
1.	Sarah Briggs	- 1	
1.	Geo: Richardson	- 1	
1.	Amery: Richard:	1	
2.	Jo: Attkinson	- 2	
3.	Wm. Byerley junr	3	
1.	Wm. Byerley senr	3	
1.	Tho. Byerley	1	
2.	Jo: Allen	- 2	
1.	Ra: Dunn	- 1	
1.	Jarr: Walker	- 1	
1.	Tho: Pickering	- 1	
5.	Ra: Salvin	- 5	
1.	Nicholas Fishburn:	- 1	
1.	Geo: Iley	1	
1.	Tho: Walker	1	
1.	Jo: Wheatley	1	
2.	Wm Redhead	2	
1.	Jo: Redhead	-1	
1.	Jo: Brack	-1	
2.	Fra: Heighingt.	2	
	£2 .5. 0.		

A perfect Schedule of all ye Freeholders names and Estates in the Constablery and townshipp of tudhoe April 22th 1673

£84		£ s. d.
	Imprimis Mr Jo: Sidgewick of Elvett in ye Citty of durham	84.0.0
6. 13. 4	Ittm. Mr Anthony Salvin of Croxdale	6.13.4
30. 0. 0	Ittm Mr Henry Fetherstonhagh of Stanley	30.0.0

6. 0. 0	Ittm Martin Nicholson of Willington	6.00.0
7. 6. 8.	Ittm Richard Byars Heires of Branspeth	7.06.8
3. 13. 4	Ittm Mr William Wilkonson of ye Citty of Durham Mercer	3.13.4
9. 0. 0	Ittm Widdow Shortrigg of Broome ye Land hers for her Life; and her sonn Peter Shortrigg; who lives at or about London, her next Heire	9.0.0
2.3.4.	Ittm Elizabeth Browne of Sunderland Briggs [Bridge] her land for her life; and her sonn George next heire	2.3.4
79.0.0	Ittm Mr Ra: Salvin of Tudhoe	79.0.0
19.0.0	Ittm Henry Sidgwick of ye same	19.0.0
2.6.8.	Ittm Henry Trewhitt of ye same	2.6.8
16.0.0	Ittm William Byerley of ye same senr & junr	16.0.0
14.0.0	Ittm John Richardson of ye same	14.0.0.
2.3.4	Ittm John Sparke of ye same	2.3.4
4.10.0	Ittm George Sidgewick of the same	14.10.0
2.3.4	Ittm John Sparke of Butcher race House	2.3.4
2.3.4	Ittm Francis Heighington of Butcher Race;	2.3.4
2.3.4	Ittm. Sarah Briggs of Tudhoe Widd: her Land for her Life; And her sonne J: Briggs her Heire	2.3.4
2.3.4	Ittm Ann Card of Durham; Widow; and relict of Francis Card deceased; and ye Heire yt appears is a child and under age; their Land -----	2.3.4
2.6.8	Ittm Richard Willson of Tudhoe	2.6.8
2.3.4	John Wheatley of ye same	2.3.4
		~~399.0.0~~
		Intoto £ 299: 0s: 0d

[DRO D/Sa/E/888 1673]

Tudhoe Ladyday 1673

A Note of ye halfe yearly paym't of Harth money in his Townshipp Collected and paid in by Roger Turpin Constable

 Paid May 3 1673 at his way goeing from this Towne

Tudhoe / Halfe yearly payment of Harth money payable to his Matye [majesty] for this Constabulary as it was collected by Roger Turpin Constable; at his way going May 3d 1673 /./././.

Harths

East Rawe

Anthony Harper for his wone house; to be added to ye East Rawe; which makes upp the number 45. in all

3. Imprimis Henry Trewhitt for his House	3
2. Ittem: Richard Willson tenant for Mr Fetherstones House	2
2. Ittem: Willm Willson for the House he now Farms of Mr. Salvin	1
1. Ittem: Thomas Taylor for Elizabeth Browns House	1
1. Ittem: Henry Hillery for his Brother Thomas' House	1
1. Ittem: James Ellinor for Mr. Salvins House he now Farms	1
1. Ittem: Roger Turpin at his way going from Mr. Salvins House he now Farms	1
2. Ittem: John Richardson for his owne House	2

West Rawe

1. Ittem Sarah Briggs for her house she now lives in	1
1. Ittem George Richardson Tennt for Mr Sidgewicks House	1
1. Ittem Amery Richardson Tennt for Mr Sidgewicks House	1
2. Ittem John Atkinson Tennt for Mr Sidgewicks House	2
3. Ittem Willm Byerely junior for his owne House	3
1. Ittem Willm Byerley senior for his owne House	1
1. Ittem Thomas Byerley for his shopp in ye same House	1
2. Ittem John Allen for Mr. Sidgewicks Cottage House Tennant	2
1. Ittem Ralph Dunn Tennt for John Sparcks House	1
1. Ittem Jerrard walker Tennt for Widow Shortriggs House	1
1. Ittem Thomas Pickering Tennt for Mr Sidgewicks House	1
5. Ittem Mr Ralph Salvin; for his owne House	5
1. Ittem Nicholas Fishburne; for his House	1
1. Ittem George Iley Tennt for Richard Willsons house	1
1. Ittem Thomas Walker Tennt for Richard Byars House	1
1. Ittem John Weatley for his own House	1

Henry Johnson Widdow her house in ye West Rawe

Jo Allen late Constable gott pulled out of Mr Crosby Booke in his tyme

Watergate
2. Ittem William Redhead for his House   2
1. Ittem John Redhead for ye House he lives ibid   1

Butcher Race Houses
1. Ittem John Brack: for his House, ibid   1
2. Ittem Francis Heighington for his House ibid   2
                          in all 45 Harths that pays   in toto   £.2.5.0

[DRO D/Sa/E/889.1 1674]

Wee the Minister Churchwarden and overseer of ye poore of ye parish of Branspeth doe hereby certefy yt we verily believe yt ye Inhabitants of ye Townshipp and Constabelry of Tudhow in ye said parish hereafter named pay noe contrebutions towards ye Church or poor by reason of their poverty; neither is any house wherein any them doth inhabit of ye improved yearly Rent of twenty shillings. Neither they nor any other using ye same doe occupy any Lands or Tenements of their owne or others to ye valew of twenty shillings a yeare, Nor have they any lands Tenements goods or Chattels, in their owne possession or others for their use to ye valew of Tenn pounds. Neither are any of ye houses wherein they inhabitt part of any Orchard or Garden belonging to any site [seat] or farme house formily. Neither is their more than two Chimneys in any of ye said houses witness our hands ye 5th February Anno Domini 1674. In all twenty fower
T.F., L. Widdow, G.K. single woman LFKC

P.R. Curt [curate]
Wm. Redhd Chwdn [churchwarden]
Th: Pickering Justice of ye pecce

Feb 5 1674 soe allowed by us
Rich: Blis
Frin: T/K

[DRO D/Sa/E/889.2 1674]

Wee the Minister Churchwarden and Overseer of the Poore of the Parish of Branspeth
doe hereby Certefye that wee verily beeleive that the Inhabitants of the Townshipp and
Constabulary of Tuddoe in the sayde Parish hereafter named pay noe Contribution
towards the Church or poore by reason of theire povertye neither is any House wherein
any them doth inhabitt of the improved yearly Rent of twenty shillings, neither they nor
any other useing the same doe occupye any Lands or Tenements of theire owne or others
to the valeiwe of twenty shillings a yeare, nor have they any Lands, Tenements, Goods
or Chattels, in theire owne possession or others for their use to the valeiwe of Tenn
pounds. Neither are any of the Houses wherein they inhabitt part of any Orchard or
Garden belonging to any State or Farme house formerly; neither is their more than two
Chimneyes in any of the sayde Houses. Wittness our hands the 25th day of February
Anno Domini 1674

Thomas Richardson
Ann Browne
Richards Smith
Matthew Harper
Richard Crookes
Thomas Harper
Ann. Johnson Widd.
Margaret Horner Widd.
Thomas Rawe
Michaell Wheatley
Mary Cooper
Thomas Bell
Margaret Bell
John Fletcher
John Gill
Ann Jackson
Henry Wheatley
Will: Rawe
Will: Wheatley
All these are non solvents

upon a diligent and deliberate scrutiny I
am informed, and doe verily believe that
the contents of this Certificate are true;
viz: That the persons named; non solvents;
are no way qualified to pay Harth Money

Testor. Ego.
Gull. Threckeld Curat
de Branspeth
his marke
Will: T keld

9 March : 1674
seene and allowed by us
Jo: Hall Major
Jo: Morland

[DRO D/Sa/E/890 1675]
A Coppye of ye Certificate for ye poore of Tuddoe: non-solvents for Harth Money
September 6th 1675

Wee the Minister Curate Churchwardens and Overseers of the Poore of the Parish of Branspeth doe heereby Certefie that wee verilye beleive that the Inhabitants of the Townshipp and Constablery of Tuddoe in the sayde Parish pay noe Contribution towards the Church or poore by reason of their great poverty neither is there any house wherein they now dwell or inhabitt of the improved yearly Rent of twenty shillings, neither they or any of them useing the same doe occupye any Lands or Tenements of theire owne or others to the value above mentioned nor have they any Lands, Tenements, goods or chattels, in theire owne possession to the value of Tenn pounds; neither are any of the houses wherein they now inhabitt parte of any Orchard or Garden belonging to any estate or farmehouse formerly neither is there more than 2 Chimneyes in any of the saide Houses.
Wittness our hands the 6th day of September Anno Domini 1675 /./././

Dan: Brevint
Wm. Thirkeld cur[at] of Branspeth
Wm. Redhead Churchwarden
                        his T marke
Henry Sidgewick : Overseer

non solvents
Chr: Rickstron
Tho: Richardson
John Fletcher
Michaell Wheatley
Wm Wheatley
Ann Browne
Richard Smith
Matthew Harper
Richard Crooks
Tho: Harper
Ann Johnson Widd:
Marg't Horner Widd:
Francis Legg
Tho: Bell
Marg't Bell Widd:
John Gill
Ann Jackson Widd:
Henry Wheatley
Wm Rawe
Mary Cooper

Marg't Johnson Widd:
Henry Richardson

Sept 6th 75
Wee allow this certificate according to the Authority given by Act of Parliament being
in number 22 [exempt]
Tho: Cradock
Ra: Davison

1670s Hearth Tax records for Tudhoe in the National Archives

The 1673 exemption certificate for Tudhoe is printed in Appendix IV, with
E179/327 part 2. Below, is the transcript from the Exchequer Return for Lady
Day 1674.

[NA E179/106/25]
Lady Day 1674 Tudhoe (Darlington Ward, South East)

PAYERS:

William […]	1
Henry […]	3
Rich: Hutton	1
[…] Wheatley	1
Tho: Walker	1
Mich: Eldridge	1
Mr. Ra: Salvin	5
Jerr: Walker	1
Ra: Dunn	2
Wm: Bierley	1
Wm: Bierley	2
Jo: Atkinson	1
Jo: Richardson	2
Anth: Harp	1
Francis Heighington	2
Wm: Redhead	3
Jo: Brack	1
Ro: Turpin	1
Ann Walker	1
Rich: Swan	1
Rich: Smith	1
Jo: Sidgwicke	1
Rich: Bull	1
	35

Non-Solvents	
Hen: Sidgewicke	1
Hen: Wheatley	1
Hen: Jackson	-
Wm: Raw	1
Alice Peele	1
Geo: Isley	1

Nich: Fishburne	1
Jo: Gills	1
Math: Harper	1
Tho: Pickering	1
Jo: Sparkes	1
Mary Kirkley	1
Margaret Fletcher	1
Eman: Richardson	1
Geo: Richardson	1
Sam Briggs	1
Amber Bell	1
Jo; Dawson	1
Margt Horner	1
Jennt Wilson	1
Ann Dunn	2
Mar: Allen	1
Wm: Wheatley	1
Roger Turpin	1
Jam: Ellinor	1
Wd: Johnson	1
Christ: Rutcliff	1
Hen: Hillary	1
Wd: Johnson	1
Jo: Harp	1
Tho: Tayler	1
Tho: Rawe	1
Jo: Bracke	1
	34

Appendix III

Extracts from John Kay's notebook, West Auckland Grieve

The following are hearth tax lists, and a list of constables, recorded for West Auckland in John Kay's notebook, Durham University Library, Halmote Court Miscellaneous Books No. 95. The source is described above in Appendix I. Kay's notebook was transcribed by the late Mr Forster in the 1980s, and has been checked against the original manuscript.

[West Auckland Constables' lyable list, September 1671]
[Note: '+' in this list has been added in a different ink]

September 4th 1671   Corn(d) Dunelm
A list of those Persons who are lyable to the duty of hearth money for one halfe yeare ending at Ladyday last by the Acts of Parliament Exhibited by us whose names are hereunto subscribed being Constables for the Township of West Auckland.

	number of chimneys
John Eden Esq	9 +
John Kay	3
William Langstaffe the elder	1
Christar Dobeson	1
William Thompson	2
William Todd	2
Frances Farrow widdow	2
Mrs Ellin Eden for Mr Robson house	4
Christopher Stothart senior	2
[...] Cargrave	2 +
Robart Stothart junior	3
Robert Raine for Garffoot house	1
Widdow Heighley	1
Georg Simpson	2
Charles Nubye	1
Robart Teasdall	1
Robart Askith	2
John Listar senor	1
Charles Andarson	2
Elizabeth Garry and Jo Teasdall junor	2
Robart Stothart senor	3
Thomas Todd	2
John Teasdall senor	2 +
Anthony Ayre	3

John Dickson Holme milne	1
Georg Taylor	2
Thomas Hodchson senor	1
John Jolly lough milne	1
Michall Richardson	4
John Tong gent	8 +
Richard Coltman and widdow Coltman	2
Anthony Garth's widdow	2
Thomas Garth and John Garth	4
Richard Coltman for Blithmans house	2
Robart Russell for wide open	1
Cuthbert Grundy for Will Thompson house at lough	2
Georg Moore for widdow Alleson house	2
Robart Maison for widde open houses	2
Richard Musgrave for Walker house	1
Widdow Tuggall	1
John Waineman for Thornberry house	1
Widdow Reed for William Ward house	1
William Vickars	2
Georg Garth	5
John Stothart	2
Marmaduke ouarman Staindrop field house	1
Richard Hodchson oth fine	1
Christar Stothart Green Feild	1
Widdow Boulmar oth fine	1
Georg Attis oth fine	1
William Taylor	1
Railph Boulman for Mrs Marley	1
Will Boulmar widdow oth ffell	2

lyable 107 hearths

Constable John Kay; Anthony (Ayre)

[St. Helen Auckland and West Auckland, Churchwardens Exemption Certificate, September 1671]

We the ministar of St. Ellen Auckland and Churchwardens of the same doe certifie unto his Majesties Justices of the Peace for the County of Durham that we doe beleave that the respective houses wherein the Persons heare undernamed do inhabit are not of greater value than 20s per annum upon the full improved rent and that neither the Persons soe inhabiting nor any other Possessing the same messuages hath useth or occupeth any lands or tenements of there own or others of the yearly value of 20s per annum or hath any lands tenements goods or chattels of the value of xs. in their own possession or in the possession of any other in trust for them and that the said houses have not above two chimneys fire hearths and stoves in them respectively. Witness our hand this 4th day Sept. A.D. 1671.

Town and township of St. Ellin Auckland.
John Parkinson
Jennet Waistall
Susan Garmondsway
Thomas Todd
Cuthbert Startfoord
Thomas Nuby
James Colin
John Danyell
Elizabeth Reignoldson
Thomas Vaux
Allice Rawlinge
Humffrey Bell
John Burne
Jaine Earmonsway
Christar Stainbanck
Thomas How
Thomas Langstaffe
Margaret Robinson
Christopher Hinde
Railphe Cargrave
Thomas Pooly
Widdow Garth
John Moabourn
Privat Bakehouses
Cuthbert Carr Esqr.
Mrs Anne Williamson
William Wardd
John Garth
Thomas Moabourne

John Rickabie

we allow of this certificate containing in number 30 names for St. Ellin Auckland
[signed]
Cuthb. Carre
Robt. Eden

[Sept. 1671 exemption certificate continued, for West Auckland]
Town and Township of West Auckland September 4th 1671

John Hutcheson
Thomas Chestar
Brian Dent
John Gibson
Katherine Cliffton
Will Rumbet
Marmaduke Baile
Allice Maugham
John Hinde
Mark Parkeson
Robart Eden
John Hodchson
Mary Priston
Margery Nubye
William Plumer
Robart Darlinton
Matthew Grainger
Margret Wron
Mary Hugall
Anne Burke
Thomas Bellasis
Anne Sidgwicke
Widdowe Coltman
Anne Steavenson
John How
William Wall
William Mounseer
Arthur Storkdall
William ffinleye
Richard Dent
William Robinson
William Gainforth
Widdow Carffoot

Mary Nuby
Simon Raine
Thomas Deputie
Richard Wattars
Railph Simpson
Robart Sheild
Widdow Dunne
ffrancis Henderson
John Litston Junor
William Hope
Mary Simpson
Alice Will
William Parkeson
Robart Middleton
Widdow Best
Thomas Baxter
John ffarberke
Allice Bullock
Widdow Barkston
Thomas Parkeson
Thomas How
Isabell Maison
Vallintine Bradbett
Anthony Dowson
ffrancis Willye
John Bell
John Maison

West Auckland
Private bakehouses
John Eden Esq.
Robart Askith
George Garth
Richard Coltman
Robart Stothart Senor
John Garth
Georg Ellis
William Taylor

Smithye harthes
Robart Maison
Christopher Dobeson
John Adamson

Thomas Plummar

[signed]
Henrye Robson Curate
John Garth and Christopher Dobeson Churchwardens

We allow of this certificate on having in number 75 names for West Auckland
[signed]
Cuthb. Carre
Robert Eden

[Assessment, March 1675. Appears in notebook between Sept 1671 and March 1672]

A list of the Surveys for West Auckland March 15th 1674/5

	Chimneys
Mr John Eden	10
Michall Richardson	+
+ Margret Coltman	1
+ Rochard Dent	1
+ Will Wall	1
+ William Mounser	1
+ Jan Bullock	1
+ John Farbeck	2
Thomas Anderson sen.	1
+ Mary Bailes	1
John Anderson milner	1
Robert Teasdall	2
+ Will Parkeson	1
+ Marmaduke Daile	1
+ Anne Steavenson	1
Anthony Ayre	3
Thomas Herryson	1
John Teasdall senior	2
+ Alles Mawhen	1
Thomas Todd	1
+ Margaret Herrison	2
George Taylor	3
Robart Stothart	4
Mary Simpson	1
John Teasdall jun.	1
+ John Maison	1
Charles Anderson	2
John Litstar sen.	1
John Litstar jun.	1
+ Frances Henderson	1
+ Arther Stockdall	1
+ William Meabourn	1
+ Leonard Hunter	1
+ Railph Simpson	1
+ Robart Shield	1
+ John Hodchson	1
+ William Langstaffe	1

+ Brian Wall	2
+ Marke Parkeson	1
Robert Asworth	3
+ Anthony Dawson	1
Richard Walker	2
Widdow Debetyer	1
Elliner Eden	emty
Widdow Heighley	1
Robart Stothart jun.	emty
+ Railph Gowland	1
Charles Nuby	1
+ Simone Raine	1
Christar Stothart	1
George Atis	1
William Bonner	1
William Taylor	1
Richard Hodchson	1
Railph Boulmer	1
William Thompson fine	1
John Dickeson milne	1

[signed]
Michall Richardson
For
George Marshall
    Collector.

[West Auckland, March, 1672]

A list for West Auckland 15th March 1671/2.   Chimneys

John Kay	3
+ widdow Nubye	1
+ Will Robeson	1
+ Will Rumbat	1
+ John Hutcheson	1
+ Will Langstaffe	1
+ John Hind	1
+ Robert Eden	1
+ James Nubye	1
+ Alice Bullock	1
+ Mary Joneston	1
+ Musgrave Avrington	1
+ William Plumer	1
+ Thomas Hodgson jun.	2
+ widdow Wild	1
Christar Dobeson	2
+ Will Bell	3
+ Margret Wren	1
+ Thomas Baxtor	1
+ William Raine	1
+ Thomas Plumer	2
+ John Bell	1
Robart Middleton	3
+ widdow Eden	2
+ widdow Buck	2
+ John Adamson House	1
William Thompson	2
Brian Mounseer	1
William Todd	2
widdow Farrow	3
Mr Robson	emty
Christar Stothart senior	2
John Gargrave	3
+ William Gainford	1
widdow Stothart	2
Robart Raine	1
John Brown	1
John Addamson shop	1
+ widdow Garfoot	1
Georg Simpson	1
widdow Reed	1

William Vickars	2
Christar Thornberry	1
Richard Musgrave	1
widdow Tuggall	1
John Swinbank	1
+ John Gibson	1
Robert Corby	2
William Thompson lough house	2
Lough Milne	1
John Garth	3
Mr John Tong	8
Richard Coltman	2
George Garth	5
John Stothart	2

John Kay survear for Henry Thorp Collector

List of West Auckland constables 1662–1700

Jo Kay Constable	John Litstar for West Auckland	1662
Robart Stothart Junor	Leonard Hunter for Rydding	1663
John Teasdall for the Garth	Jo Hutcheson Constables	1664
[?] Stothart	Francis Nuby for Garry land	

Georg Attis & Thomas Hodchson Constables   1665
Charles Andarson & Brian Mounseer for Tod House
Christ. Stothart Junor & Jo Farbeck Constables   1666
Christ. Richardson for Wreane House & Railph Boulmar   1667
Will. Plumer halfe yeare Jo Maison halfe yeare
Railph Boulmar for Hodceson land   Constable   1668
October 22 William Langstaffe for his Pt of Cottage
& Jo Burdon for Holm intake entered Constables   1669
October 21 John Kay served Constable for the ..... [towne?]
and Anthony Ayre for Staindrop Feeld House for outside   1670
Michall Richardson October 22 for the towne
John Stothart for the outsider   1671
- - - - - - - - - - - -

October 22nd Will Hodceson for Walls Houses for the towne
        and hired John Gargrave for the town
Ralph Boolmer for Mrs Marley land   1672
- - - - - - - - - - - -

October 14th
George Garth of Bolton Garths for outsider
William Mounseer for the town half a year   1673
May 5th John Farbeck for the other halfe year   1674
John Maison hired for Thomas Hodchson Constable for
a yeare & hired for Richard Coltman for the outsider   1675

        October 15 for a yeare
[....] halfe a year   1676
Aprill 25 Thomas Pulmer   Christ Dobson for Robt Teasdall   1676
[..]bar 13th Jo Bell & Robt Middleton halfe a year Constables
        for ...? houses   1676

April 20th Rbt Anderson & Robt Middleton for Will Thompson house
        ath fine   Constables for West Auckland   1677
October 14th Robt Middleton   Constable for the towne
        & O..bart Anderson hired for Richard Hodchson fine   1677

[....] 17th 1678 Anthony Ayre for the towne one whole yeare
[........] Anderson for Hodchson for the summer halfe year   1678

May 7th 1678   Jo Teasdall senor Constable halfe yeare
                               John Todd Constable halfe yeare for his house
                               Robt Andarson hired for Thornbok

----

[1679?] October 14 Railp Bumbrey Constable a whole yeare for outside
        Thos Todd house halfe a yeare & Tho Pattinson for the other halfe
        yeare for Hugall House   Robt Anderson for them all.

November 12 1680 Robt Henderson house a yeare. Robt Anderson hired
        Georg Taylor for his house a yeare stood himself

November 12 1681 Thomas Todd Constable for Robt Stothart house
        Jo Bonsor for outside for Richardson called Atis land

Novermber 12 1682 Jo Maison Constable   Garth House
        Will Andarson for his house
October 16th 1683 Jo Litstar for the towne
        & Swinbank for outside   Jo Maison hired.
October 28th 1684 Ather Stockdall for his house
        Francis Henderson for his   Rob't H'deson for both.
Aprill 9th 1685 Railph Simpson and Nickolas Sheild for the towne halfe year
November 23 1685 John Todd for the towne and William Boolmar for the outsider for
a yeare Constable
        Ralph Alixandar   Anthony Dowson hired Jo Maison Constable for halfe a
yeare
May 9th 1687 Robert Slack   John Gowland Constable for this summer halfe yeare for
West Auckland
November 23rd 1687 Anthony Garth Constable for the outsides for this yeare coming
and Railph
        Gowlland for halfe a yeare for the towne

        John Heighley for the towne Aprill 18th 1688 a year

        Thomas Smithson for the towne [16]89
        Edward Simpson

        John Gills and John Garth [...] for a year   [16]90

        Robart Middleton Robart Henderson Farrow House a yeare [16]91
                        Hired
        Christar Dobeson for widdow Todd

        William Bainbrig for tugall a year   [16]92

Anthony Dowson halfe a year|
William Thompson a yeare | 1693
Railph Gowland halfe a year |

John Jaimes a yeare for the towne   1694
Christopher Stothart for his house at Green Feild for outside

April 10th William Paterson and Thomas Anderson smith
        Constable for the towne this yeare   1695

Christar Dobeson Constable for the Towneship |
        mirril Vickars house | 1696
John Farrow for outside this yeare |

Thomas Hodchson Constable and Christar Plummar for the twone this yeare 1697

widdow Taylor for outside hired Robert Slack
Joshua Bell for the towne   1698

Mr John Peas for the township one yeare
John Thompson halfe a yeare   1699
& William Hodchson at Martinmass halfe a yeare 1699

John Kay a whole yeare
and Michall Richardson a whole year for   1700
and Robart Slack hired for them both.

216

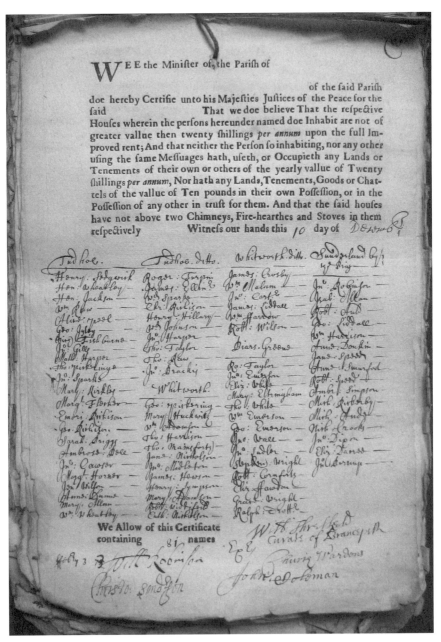

Figure 7. 1673 Exemption Certificate for Parish of Whitworth, including
Tudhoe. NA E179/327 part 2 no. 73. Transcribed on pp.239–40.

Appendix IV

Exemption Certificates 1671–1674

The surviving Certificates of Exemption from the Hearth Tax for County Durham are in the National Archives at Kew. Unfortunately there is, as yet, no complete listing of these certificates in the National Archives. There are two series of them. E179/327 part 3 contains 90 certificates dated 15 January 1670 (1671 n.s.). E179/327, part 2 contains 88 certificates, with various dates between 20 May 1673 and 18 September 1674. Part 1, in the same E179/327 box, contains certificates from Dorset and has nothing to do with Durham. However, there are probably stray Durham Certificates mixed in with those for other counties which have not yet been listed, just as there are stray certificates from other counties filed with these Durham Certificates. Both E179/327 part 3 and part 2 were specially listed in 2003 for this volume, by Duncan Harrington FSA, and selected certificates, from both bundles were then transcribed by him for this Appendix.

Nearly all these Exemption Certificates are on printed paper forms. Printed certificates survive generally from June 1670 until Lady Day (25 March) 1674, when the hearth tax was farmed out for the second time. The normal wording for these forms was as follows:

WEE the Minister of the Parish of

        of the said Parish doe hereby Certifie unto his Majesties Justices of the Peace for the said   That we doe believe That the respective houses wherein the persons hereunder named doe Inhabit are not of greater vallue then twenty shillings *per annum* upon the full Im-proved rent; And that neither the Person so inhabiting, nor any other using the same Messuages hath, useth, or Occupieth any Lands or Tenements of their own or others of the yearly vallue of Twenty shillings *per annum*, Nor hath any Lands, Tenements, Goods or Chat-tels of the vallue of Ten pounds in their own Possession, or in the Possession of any other in trust for them. And that the said houses have not above two Chimneys, Fire-hearthes and Stoves in them respectively   Witness our hands this   day of

One of these forms is reproduced on p.216

One of these forms is reproduced on p.216

Printed here are the surviving exemption certificates among the Exchequer records for 1672–4 (NA 179/327, part 2), for those places without lists of non-payers in Lady Day 1666. The following table lists the townships without non-payers in 1666, with the number of non-payers in the exemption certificates of

15 January 1671 (NA 179/327, part 3), c.1672-4, and in the 1674 Return. Only the 1672-4 certificates are printed here, as these were largely exact copies of the 1671 certificates and survive with slightly better coverage of the places with no data in Lady Day 1666.

Table 8: Townships without any data for the non-chargeable households in the 1666 return, together with data from exemption certificates and the 1674 return for the same places.

Township	PARISH	1666 assessment Paying	1666.0 assessment Non-paying	15 Jan 1671 n.s. certificates E179/327pt3	c. 1672-4 certificates E179/327pt2	1674 Paying	1674 Non paying
Archdeacon Newton	DARLINGTON	13	No data	3	3	10	3
Barnard Castle	BARNARD CASTLE	133	No data	117	120	150	131
Benfieldside	MEDOMSLEY	15	No data	12	12	No data	No data
Brierton	STRANTON	7	No data	No data	With Burntoft 10	With Burntoft 26	With Dalton?
Butsfield	SATLEY	23	No data	No data	7	27	With Weston 19
Cold Hesleden	DALTON-LE-DALE	11	No data	No data	No data	With Dalton 19	No data
Crook & Billy Row	BRANCEPETH	17	No data	1	1	20	1
Croxdale & Butterby	CROXDALE	20	No data	Butterby only 2	Butterby only 2	Butterby & Wharrington 16	No data
Dawdon	DALTON-LE-DALE	8	No data	No data	No data	No data	No data
Dinsdale	DINSDALE	13	No data	2	2	No data	No data
Durham, St Giles	DURHAM, ST GILES	66	No data	50	50	93	54
Durham, Crossgate	DURHAM, ST MARGARET	109	No data	40	41	107	47
Durham, Framwellgate	DURHAM, ST MARGARET	88	No data	42	43	103	43
Durham, South (Low) Bailey	DURHAM, ST MARY THE LESS	19	No data	No data	No data	41	0
Durham, North (Low) Bailey	DURHAM, ST MARY-LE-BOW	53	No data	6	6	60	47
Durham, St Nicholas	DURHAM, ST NICHOLAS	195	No data	48	48	Durham City 266	48
Edmondbyers	EDMONDBYERS	13	No data	3	3	12	No data
Edmondsley	CHESTER-LE STREET	14	No data	No data	2	14	14

Township	Parish	1666 assessment Paying	1666.0 assessment Non-paying	15 Jan 1671 n.s. certificates E179/327/pt3	c. 1672-4 certificates E179/327pt2	1674 Paying	1674 Non paying
Elvet, Barony	DURHAM, ST OSWALD	67	No data	50	50	80	50
Elvett, Borough	DURHAM, ST OSWALD	46	No data	14	14	47	15
Gateshead, Bankward	GATESHEAD	103	No data	28 omits?	29 omits?	115	151
Gateshead, High Ward	GATESHEAD	132	No data	145	145	140	No data
Gateshead, Pant Ward (West Ward 1674)	GATESHEAD	143	No data	46	46	99	46
Gateshead, Pipewell Ward	GATESHEAD	121	No data	27	27	149	29
Hunstanworth	HUNSTANWORTH	24	No data	No data	2	23	2
Kelloe	KELLOE	21	No data	18	18	19	20
Kimbleworth	WITTON GILBERT & KIMBLESWORTH	3	No data	4	4	?	4
Lumley & Lambton	CHESTER-LE STREET	70	No data	174	179	50	191
Marwood	GAINFORD	25	No data	1	1	31	1
Moorsley	HOUGHTON-LE-SPRING	10	No data	No data	No data	10	61
Neasham	HURWORTH	26	No data	26	26	28	No data
East & West Newbiggin	BISHOPTON	6	No data	No data	No data	No data	No data
Norton	NORTON	69	No data	72	72	62	72
Pittington	PITTINGTON	18	No data	20 see note	10	?	No data
Preston on Tees	STOCKTON ON TEES	5	No data	8 omits?	33	39	33
Sockburn	SOCKBURN	5	No data	3	3	?	No data
Thorpe Bulmer	HART	2	No data	No data	No data	?	No data
Thrislington	BISHOP MIDDLEHAM	2	No data	No data	No data	?	No data
South Shields	SOUTH SHIELDS	146	216	No data	No data	?	West Panns only 204
Sunderland	SUNDERLAND	115	No data	98	98	185	101
Westerton	AUCKLAND ST ANDREW	7	No data	2	2	with Windlestone 26	with Windlestone 4
Winlaton West Lordship	RYTON	19	No data	90	No data see note	17	No data

E179/327 part 3:
1671

These exemption certificates are in reasonable condition. They were written on printed paper forms, except no.92, a stray certificate from Derbyshire, which has found its way into this file. When Duncan Harrington listed this file, he re-numbered the certificates from 1 to 96, in pencil on the back of the sheets. The old numbers are very erratic and repetitive, suggesting that this was once a number of separate files, and that in making up this file the original order has been frequently reversed. This is indicated not only by the old numbering, but also by internal evidence (e.g. no.63 continues in no.62). They may have been re-ordered several times. At one time they were on a string, but this has been removed. The names of both parishes and townships are listed here as they are given in the certificates, and have not been modernised. The date, 15 January.1670 (1671 new style), has been changed throughout from 15 January 1672. These appear on the whole to be fair copies. The signatures of the justices appear to be verisimilitudinous. Often only the first townships named are within the parishes under which they are listed, and the remainder have been copied in from returns from a neighbouring parish. Sometimes parishes and townships were confused by the copyist; for example, Westhoe was not a parish, but a township within the parish of Jarrow. Nevertheless, in this list the name of the 'parish' has been put down as it is on the printed forms. The place names are as in the documents themselves and have not been modernised. The number of names 'allowed' are frequently not the same as the number of entries, but this does not always look like bad copying. Such discrepancies are noted in the following table of contents.

Only those asterisked have been transcribed for this Appendix. Such a very small number have been included from these certificates, because the material is mostly duplicated in the 1673–4 certificates. It appears that the names of the exempt in 1673–4 were often simply copied, sometimes with variant spellings, from the same source as these earlier certificates. Before the duplication was apparent, a much larger number were transcribed. They will be found in the database of the British Academy Hearth Tax Research Project at Roehampton University.

No.	Parish: townships (in brackets number of exempt in each township)	Date	No. of names	Comment, old numbering.
1	Barnardcastle	15 Jan 1670	81	
2	Barnardcastle	15 Jan 1670	36	joined to 1
3	Middleton in Teasdaile: Newbiggin (10), Middleton (14), Eggleston (8), Marwood (1), Forrest of Langleydayle (15)		48 Cert. says 51	
4	Winston: Winston (21), Whorleton 17), Stainton (23), Streatlum (1), Westwicke (3), Teasdayle Forrest (8)		73	
5	Staindropp: Staindropadh (36), Rabye (34), Cleatlum (12)		82	
6	Gainford: Pearcbridge [Piercebridge] (28), Gamford (27), Staintthropp (24)		79 Cert. says 78	
7	Cockfield: Cockfield (9), Wackerfield (11), Hilton (4), Tinmouth (1), Bolam (11), Sumerhouse (7), Headlum (7), ~~Pearcbridge~~		50	
8	Whitworth: Whitworth (18), Briars Greene (13), Sunderland by the brig (16), Darlington South West Division: Langton (16), Ingleton (13)		76 Cert. says 77	
9	Churchmerrington: Faryhill (19) Hett (24), Tudhoe (33)		66 Cert. says 76	Old no. 18
10	Churchmerrington: Windleston (26), Westerton (2), Midleston (2), Churchmerrington (16), Chilton Great and Little (21)		67 Cert. says 68	Old no. 17
11	Great Aycliffe: Preston Supra Skerne (15), Woodham (2), Midridge (32), Eldon (20)		69	Old no. 16
12	Great Aycliffe: Redworth, Midridge & Newbigin (19), Scholle Acliffe (4), Great Acliffe (37), Brafferton (8)		68	Old no. 15
13	Haughton: Oxnelfeild (1), Haughton (28), Great Bardon (3), Barmpton (8), Archdeacon Newton (3), Haughton one the side (6), Heighington (52)		101	Old no. 14
14	Highconscliffe: Wallworth 6), High Conscliffe (20), Low Conscliffe (12), Blackwell (28)		66	Old no. 13
15	Durnton: The Burrough in Darlington town (58), Bondgate in Darlington (22)		80	Joined to 16. Old no.11.
16	Durnton: Bondgate in Darlington (36), Prebend Raw in Darlington (4), Cockerton (20), Killerby (9), Denton (16)		85	Joined to 15. Old no.12.

No.	Parish: townships (in brackets number of exempt in each township)	Date	No. of names	Comment, old numbering.
17	Southchurch: South Church (9), Coundon (17), Newton Capps (5), Hunwicke (10), Escombe (12), Witton upon Weare (33)		86	Old no. 9
18	West Auckland: West Auckland (57), St Ellin Auckland (27), Shildon (5)		89	Old no. 8
19	Eavenwood: Linside [Lynesack] (30), Evenwood Barrony (52)		82. Cert. says 83	Old no. 7
20	Stanhopp: Frosterlah (11, and 11 entries scored through), Stannupp Towne (39), Stanupp Forrest (3)		53. Cert. says 52	Joined to 21. Old no.5
21	Stanupp: Stannupp Park Quarter (10), New Landside quarter (3), Bishopley (4), Southside quarter (7), Hamsterley (25), South Bedburne (4)		53	Joined to no 20. Section in the last column cut out. Old no.6
22	Wolsingham: Wolsingham		93	Old no. 10
23	Wolsingham: Crooke & Bill Raw (1), Hedley & Cornsey (14), Thornley & Helme Parke (12), Wolsingham Eastside Quarter (33), Wolsingham Parke (5)		65	Old no. 4
24	Branspeth: Bransputh & the parke (36), Stockley (22), Willington (13) Helming Raw (6)		77. Cert. says 79	Old no. 3
25	Bishopp Auckland: The Burrow of Auckland (43), Newgate in Auckland (31), Bondgate in Aucklande (12)		88	Joined to 26. Old no. 1
26	Bishopp Auckland: Bongate in Auckland (48), Bysholtells and Brandon (15)		63	Joined to 25. Old no. 2
27	Stockton: Stockton Towne		35	Old no. 14
28	Stockton: The Burrow of Stockton		32	Old no. 12
29	Hurworth: Neasham (26), Hurwouth (50)		76	Old no. 13
30	Bushopton: Bishopton (32), Dinsdael (2), Stockburne (3), Midleton & the Row (1)		68	Old no. 10
31	Redmarshall: Sadbury & Newbiggin (25), Little Stainton (5); Reed Marshall (4), Stillington (10), Carleton (13) , Cotton Munderidge [Coatham Mundeville] (9)		66	Old no. 11
32	Egscliffe: Eggscliffe (25), East Harborne (14), Elton (7), Long Newton (33)		79. Cert. says 81	Old no. 9
33	Norton: Norton (71), Preston upon Tease(8)		79. Cert. says 80	Old no. 8
34	Bishopp Midleham: Dalton (7), Priarton & Brontoft (10), Midlehame (36), Mainsforth (2), Cornforth (13)		68. Cert. says 69	Old no. 7
35	Hart: Hart Towne (45), Elwicks (17)		62 Cert. says 61	Old no. 6

No.	Parish: townships (in brackets number of exempt in each township)	Date	No. of names	Comment, old numbering.
36	Stranton: Stranton (31), Hartinpoole (50), Throston (2)		83. Cert. says 84	Old no. 5
37	Greatham: Gretham (59), Seaton (28)		87. Cert. says 63	Old no. 4
38	Billingham: Wolveston (30), Billingham (32), Coupan (22), Newton (15)		99	Old no. 3
39	Sedgfeild: Mordon (20), Bradburye (11), Great Strainton (22), Whitton (9), Thorpe (19)		81. Cert. says 83	Old no. 2
40	Sedgfeild: Sedgfield (49), Fishbourne (19), Butterwick (3), Emmelton (5), Foxton (7)		83	Old no. 1
41	Chester: Pensher (26), Lumley & Lampton (82)		108	Joined to 42. Old no. 16
42	Chester: Lumley & Lampton		93	Joinrd to 41. Old no. 17
43	Houghton in the Spring: East & Midle Harington (19), West Herington (16), Newbottle (36)		71	Old no. 15
44	Bishopp Wearmouth: Warmouth Pans (44), Offerton (31)		75	Joined to 45. Old no. 14
45	Bishopp Wearmouth: Sunderland by the Sea		98	Joined to 44. Old no. 13
46	Bishopp Wearmouth: Tunstall (9), Ryhop (20), Bishopp Wearmouth (23).		52	Joined to 47. Old no. 11
47	Bishopp Wearmouth: Bishopp Wearmouth,		99	Joined to 46. Old no.12
48	Easington: Easington		58	Joined to 49. Old no. 5
49	Easington: Hathorne (18), Haswell (17), Shadforth (18)		53	Joined to 48. Old no.6
50	Monck Hesleden: Hutton Henry (28), Sheraston (10), Monke Heslton (16)		54. Cert. says 55	Joined to 51. Old no.3
51	Monck Hesleden: Castle Eden (12), Sholton (27)		39	Joined to 50. Old no.4
52	Kelloe: Shinkliffe (22), Buterbye (2), Wharington (9), Cassop (10), Wingat & Wheatly (13, Cert. says 14 - hearths?)		56	Joined to 53. Old no.1
53	Kelloe: Trimdon (30, Cert. says 34 - hearths?), Kelloe (18, Cert. says 19 - hearths?)		48	Joined to 52. Old no 2. Last part of final column cut off.
54	Houghton in the Spring: Houghton (34), Hetton (9), Appleton (4), East Murton (7), Cold Heslinton (10)		64. Cert. says 66	Joined to 55. Old no. 9

No.	Parish: townships (in brackets number of exempt in each township)	Date	No. of names	Comment, old numbering.
55	Dalton: Dalton (8), Seaham (15), Slingley (5), Burdens (6), Silksworth (14)		48	Joined to Old no. 10 joined to 9
56*	Pittington: Sheerburne (17), Pittington (20)		37	Joined to Old no. 7
57	Houghton in the Spring: West Raniton (50), East Renton (10)		60	Joined to Old no. 8 joined to 7
58	Chester: Tanfield, Lintsgreen		60. Cert. says 59	Old no. 8
59	Chester: Plausworth (30), Kiblesworth (4), Ravensworth (65), Hedley (2)		101, Cert. says 102	Old no. 7
60	Chester: Warrage (4), Harraton (37), Orpeth (14), Pelton (5)		60. Cert. says 62	Old no. 6
61	Chester: Chester Middle Devition. Chester Towne (76), Birkley (1)		77. Cert. says 78	Old no. 5
62	Westhoe: Neather & Upper Heworth (19), Westoe (21), Harton (10)		50	Old no. 32
63	Neither Heworth: Neather & Uper Hewworths,		63	Old no. 31
64	Jarroe: Usworths Great & Litlle (25), Hedworth (5), Munckton (28)		58. Cert. says 57	Old no. 29
65	Washington: Bowdons Esat & West (25), Washintone (27), Barmeston (5)		57. Cert. says 58	Old no. 30
66	Bolden: Sudicke (4), Hilton (21), Bowdens East and West (34)		59. Cert. says 60	Old no. 28
67	Monckwearmouth: Munckwearmouth (41), Fullwill (12), Sudicke Towne (12)		65. Cert. says 64	Old no. 27
68	Whitborne: Cleadon (12), Whitburne (43)		55	Old no. 26
69	Southsheilds; Southsheilds		46	--
70	South Sheilds Southsheilds		73. Cert. says 72	Old no. 25
71	Southsheilds: Southsheil West Panns		77. Cert. says 76	Old no. 24
72	Southsheilds: Southsheeld Constab:		68	Old no. 23
73	Gateshead: Paul Ward		19	Old no. 22
74	Gateshead: Pipewell Ward (27), Pant Ward (27)		54. Cert. says 55	Old no. 21
75	Gateshead: Highward		45	Old no. 20
76	Gateshead: Goatshead Highward		63	Old no. 19
77	Gateshead: The east devition of Chester Ward. Goatshead Bank Ward (29),Goatshead Highward (37)		66. Cert. says 70	Old no. 18

No.	Parish: townships (in brackets number of exempt in each township)	Date	No. of names	Comment, old numbering.
78	Ash: Kyoe (6), Esh ((14), Langlee (6), Whitton Gilber (19), Burnup & Hamsterells (1)		46. Cert. says 45	Old no. 17
79	Lanchester: Lanchester (36), Green Croft (7), Iviston(12), Butsfield (7)		62. Cert. says 63	Old no. 16
80	Meddomsley: Meddoms Lee (18), Row Blackston (8), Benfield side (12), Conside (8), Rowside Rawley [Roughley and Roughside] (2), Mugloesworth (7), Edmonds Berry (3), Hunstandworth (2)		60. Cert. says 65	Old no. 15
81	Ryton: Ryton Towne (33), Craw Crooke (33), Chapwell Constab (14)		80	Old no. 14
82	Ryton: Riton woodside		64	Old no. 13
83*	Ryton: Idem [i.e. Winlington East Lordship continued] (84), Winlinton West Lordship (5)		89. Cert. says 90	Old no. 12
84	Whickham: Swallwell (26), Winlington East Lordship (41)		67	Old no. 11
85	Whickham: Whickham Felside		80	Old no. 10
86	Whickham: Chester West Devision		110	Old no. 9
87	[Durham] St Giles College par		50	Old no. 4
88	St Giles: City of Durham: St Nicholas parish (48), High Baylife (6)		54. Cert. says 55	Old no. 1
89	Framwelgate: Crosgate (41), Framwellgate (42)		83. Cert. says 84	Old no. 2
90	St Oswoldes: St Osweldes parish(14), Barronre of Elfett (50)		64. Cert. says 65	Old no. 3
91	Parish of Wickinton: [? Wighton, Norfolk] Herbert Astley wasa JP for NORFOLK	n.d.	13	Gives no. .of hearths
92	Lullington & Coton in the Elmes [DERBYSHIRE]	6 Jan. 1662		MS
93	Wanting in maior Christians account for 2 years ended LD 16 Chas II [1664]			
94	Declaration Major Christians accompt 3 ½ years ended Michaelmas 1670	4 June 1674		
95	Dividing slip for Chester Ward			
96	Dividing slip for Stockton Ward			

E179/327 part 3
1671

The transcriber, Duncan Harrington, FSA has identified the divisons within the parishes to make comprehension easier. Such identification is not present in the original documents, many of which run on, so that it is often difficult to see the divisions. See also the note at the beginning of the listing of the contents of this appendix.

No. 56 Printed Old no 7
Parish of Pittington
15 January 1670 (1671 n.s.)

Sheerburne [Sherburn]
Simond Person
James Haslop
Robart Wood
Petter Collers
James Stell
John Farrow
Robart Davison
Richard Pattison
Petter Midleton
Thomas Rotherforth
John Gamiforth
William Shaw
Marke Pattison
Rolph Bunting
John Smith
Ralph Burdy
Mylese Jefferson

Pittington
Hen Maugham
Elinor Robinson
John Burder
Hen Waister
Widow Heath
Ralph Eppleton
John Roper
John Stewby
Alc Sander
Thomas Dauson
Widow Hedly
Alyes Eubanke
Widow Hall
Johne Sudduick

Willi Blackburn
Widow Story
Widow Adamson
William Jackson
William Rickerby
William Dunney
Allowed 37 names
    JPs: Will Blakiston, Jo. Morland

Part of no. 83. Printed. Old no 12
Parish of Ryton
15 January 1670

**'Idem' i.e.Winlington East Lordship
[Winlaton East Lordship]**
Robt Hudspeth
Rich Dickison
Ralp Harding
Wm Trotter
Geo Swaddell
James Ainsley
Wid Brown
Hen Robson
Robt Kell
Wid Robson
John Litle
Lanc Robson
Geo Wilson
Robt Harper
Cuth Nickson
Hepl Roger
John Foster
Wid Nickson
Matt Gray
Wid Champley
Wid Erington
John Jackson
John Thomson

John Carr
Wid Cutter
Robt Ariler
Matt Rob[er]tson
Wid Chapman
Geo Nickson
Tho Wrey
Mich Bell
Wid Cutter
Rei Scott
Nich Sandeland
Wid Beason
Wid Walker
Wid Yowton
Geo Fisher
John Huntley
Matt Gray senr
Rob Temp[es]t
Lu?es Tempest
Wid Nepont
Issa Dickenson
John Bramfield
Hum Errington
Ruth Pattison
Petter Bridg
Robt Anderson
Geo Chicken
Wid Gally
Adam Sproate
Geo Peate
John Watson
John Bullmer
Henry Foster
John Winshop
Geo Stokoe
Rich Richardson
Cha Tayler
Tho Grundy
Tho Irwin
Wid Wardroper
John Rumly
Jam Cock
Jo Boyd junr
Wm Maughan
John Wall
Alex Poyd
Jon Duglas

Roger Prockter
Tho Maxwell
Wm Selver Tepper
John Poyd
Wid Stokoe
Wid Thomson
John Thomson
Ral Stoke
John Bullmer
Tho Bootland
Tho Hay
Wid Allyson
Geo Crisp
John Crisp

**Winlinton West Lordship
[Winlaton West Lordship]**
Tho Smith
Nick Smith
John Rutter
John Rotherford
Wm Crooke

Allowed 90 names
JPs: Will Blakiston, Jo Morland

E179/327 Part 2
1673–4

These exemption certificates are apparently all for the year ending Lady Day 1674. These, like those in part 3, appear to be fair copies. All are on printed paper forms, except where indicated as MS (Manuscript). They have various dates between 20 May 1673 and 18 September 1674, but many of the certificates were signed by JPs on 3 Feb 1673 (1674 new style), in anticipation of Lady Day 1674. This date has been altered throughout and appears to have been initially entered as 1675. When Duncan Harrington listed this file, he re-numbered the certificates, in descending order, from 89 to 1, in pencil on the back of the sheets. The old numbers are very erratic, suggesting that in making up this file the original order has been frequently reversed, as indicated by the old numbering. The present order is roughly by wards and these are indicated: Darlington, Chester, Stockton, Easington, Bedlingtonshire, Island and Norham Shires, Durham City. As in the 1671 certificates, it is often only the first townships named that are within the parishes under which they are listed, and the remainder have been copied in from returns from a neighbouring parish. Once again parishes and townships were sometimes confused by the copyist. In this list the name of the 'parish' has, nevertheless, been put down as it is on the printed forms. It appears that the names of the exempt in 1673–4 were often simply copied, sometimes with variant spellings, from the same source as the 1671 certificates. The place names in this list are as in the documents themselves, and have not been modernised. The number of names 'allowed' are frequently not the same as the number of entries, but this does not always look like bad copying. Such discrepancies are noted in the following table of contents.

Those asterisked have been transcribed for this Appendix

No	Parish: township (in brackets number exempt in each township)	Date	No. of names	Comment, old numbering
	DARLINGTON WARD			
89	Bishopp Auckland cols. divided under Bondgate (60), Byshottells & Brandon (15) and Bransputh & the Parke (40)	10 Oct 1673	115	signed by justices 3 Feb 1673. No. 46
88*	Bishopp Auckland cols divided under Stockley (22), Willington (13), Helmington Row (6), Crooke and Bille Row (1), Hedley & Cornsey (14), Thornley & Helme Parke (12), Wolsingham East side quarter (33)	ditto	101	no 47

No	Parish: township (in brackets number exempt in each township)	Date	No. of names	Comment, old numbering
87	Wolsingham Parke (5), Frosterlah (11), Stannupp Towne (37), Stannupp Forrest (3), Stannupp Parke quarter (10), Newlands side quarter (3), Bishopley (4), Southside quarter (7), Hamsterley (24).	ditto	104	no 48
86	St Ellin Auckland listed under South Bedburne (4), Linside (30), Evenwood & Barrony (55)	ditto	89	Signed by justices 3 Feb 1673 no 49
85	St Ellin Auckland listed under West Auckland (57), St Ellin Auckland (27), Shildon (5), South Church (9)	ditto	98	no. 50
84	Bishopp Auckland, Coundon (17), Newton Capp (5), Hunwicke (17), Escombe (12), Witton upon Weare (34)	ditto	85 List says 86	no 51
83	[Durham] St Giles	12 Mar 1673	50	Torn, no. 15
82	Bishopp Auckland; The Burrow of Auckland (42), Newgate in Auckland (31)	10 Oct 1673	73	no. 45
81	Wolsingham	20 Oct 1673	94	no. 52
80	Darlington; Darlington towne (59), The Burrough, Bondgate in Darlington (58)	12 Nov 1673	117	Signed by justices 3 Feb 1673 no. 53
79	Darlington: Prebend Row (4), Cockerton (20), Killerbye (9), Denton (19), Wallworth (6), High Conscliffe (21), Low Conscliffe (13)	ditto	92	Signed by justices 3 Feb 1673 no. 54
78*	Darlington: Blackwell (28), Oxnelfeild (1), Haughton (28), Great Burden (3), Barmpton (8), Archdeacon Newton (3), Haughton on the side (6)	ditto	77 List says 79	Signed by justices 3 Feb 1673 no. 55
77	Ayckliffe: Ayckliffe constb (37), Brafferton Constab (10), Preston Constab (8)	28 May 1674	55	no number
76	Heighington; Heightington (52), Redworth Mildridge and Nebiggin (19), [x'd out entries for Se..oole Acliffe (4), Great Ayckliffe (37)	13 Nov 1673	71 List says 70	Signed by justices 3 Feb 1673 no. 56
75	Parish of Bishop Auckland; Brafferton scored through(8); Preston supra Skerne scored through (15) ; Woodham (2); Midridge (32); Eldon (21); Windleston (26); Westerton (2); Midleston (2)	10 Oct 1673	85 List says 82	Signed by justices 3 Feb 1673 no. 57

No	Parish: township (in brackets number exempt in each township)	Date	No. of names	Comment, old numbering
74*	Parish of Churchmerrington; Churchmerrington (16); Chiltons Great & Little (21); Ferry Hill (19); Hett (24)	10 Dec 1673	80	Signed by justices 3 Feb 1673 no. 58
73*	no parish; Tudhoe (33), Whitworth (18); Biars Greene (14); Sunderland by the Brig (16)	ditto	81	Signed by justices 3 Feb 1673 No. 59
72*	Parish of Gainford: Langton (16); Ingleton (13); Cockfield (9); Wackerfeild (11); Hilton (4); Morton Tinmouth (1); Bolam (11); Summerhouse (7); Headlum (7); Peearchbridge (28)	12 Oct 1673	107	Signed by justices 3 Feb 1673 no. 60
71*	Parish of Gameford: Gainford (31); Stainthorppe (61); Rabye (34)	ditto	126 List says 131	Signed by justices 3 Feb 1673 no. 61
70*	Parish of Winston:	14 June 1673 changed from 1674	20	Two had 2 hearths. no old number.
69*	Parish of Gainford: Cleatlum (12); Winston (21); Whorleton (15); Stainton (23); Streatlum (1); Westwicke (3); Teasdayle Forrest (10); Newbiggin (10)	12 Oct 1673	95	Signed by justices 3 Feb 1673 no. 62
68*	Parish of Gainford: Middleton (14); Eggleston (8); Marwood (1); Forrest of Langley Dayle (15)	10 Oct 1673	38 Cert. says 37	Signed by justices 3 Feb 1673 no. 63
67*	Parish of Gainford: Barnardcastle (117)	12 Oct 1673	117	Signed by justices 3 Feb 1673 no. 64
66	Parish of Staindrop (4)	15 Oct 1674	4	none
65	Parish of Cockfield (1)	6 Oct 1674	1	none
64*	Barnardcastle (1)	9 Oct 1674	1	none
63*	Barnardcastle (1)	9 Oct 1674	1	none
62*	Barnard Castle	9 Oct 1674	1	
	CHESTER WARD			
61	Parish of Jarro:South Shields 2nd constab (49); South Shields 1st constab (18)	12 Jan 1673	67	no. 38

No	Parish: township (in brackets number exempt in each township)	Date	No. of names	Comment, old numbering
60	Parish of Southsheilds: South Sheilds West Pans 2nd constab (60); Cleadon (12); Whitburne (45)	12 Jan 1673	117	no. 40
59	Parish of Jarro: South Sheilds West Pans 1st Constab. (138)	12 Jan 1673	138	no 39
58	Parish of Whickeham: Wickham Fell side (79); Swallwell (26)	13 Jan 1673	105	no. 30
57	Parish of Whickeham: Lints Green x'dout (20), Whickham	12 Jan 1673	106	No. 23
56*	Parish of Goatshead: Pipewell (27), Pant Ward (46) x'd out South Shields 1st constab (18)	12 Jan 1673	73	No. 37
55*	Parish of Goatshead: Wilton/Witton Gilbert x'd out (19) Burnup & Hamsteeds x'd out (1), Goatshead Banke ward (29)	12 Jan 1673	29	No. 35
54*	Parish of Goatshead:: Gateshead highward	12 Jan 1673	145	No 36.
53	Parish of Medamsley: Crawcrooke (34), Chapwell Const. (14), Meddomsley (19), Ebchester (7), Benfeild side (12), Conside (8), Roughside & Row Lee (2), Mongleswicke (7), Edmond bire (2), Hunstanworth Const (2)	10 Feb	108	No. 33
52	Chapelry of Ash:	10 Feb	14	
51	Parish of Lenchester: Lenchester (36), Greencroft (7), Iveston (12); Butsfeild (7), Kyoe (6), Ash x'd out (14), Langley (6)	10 Feb 1673	74	No. 34
50	Parish of Witton Gilbert:	10 July 1674	24	
49*	Parish of Chester: Chester Towne (76), Birtley (1), Warridge (4) Harraton x'd out (13)	8 March 1673	81 Cert. says 82	No. 26
48*	Parish of Chester: Harraton (37), Orpeth (12), Edmonsley (2), Pelton (5), Plausworth (30), Ki[m]blesworth (4)	8 March 1673	90 Cert. says 89	No. 27
47	Parish of Ryton: Winlaton East Lordshipp (124)	8 Mar 1673	124	No. 31
46	Parish of Ryton: Winlaton East Lordship x'd out (5), Ryton Woodside (64), Ryton Towne (33)	2 Feb 1673	97	No. 32
45	Parish of Lainsley: Ravensworth (66), Hedley (2), Tanfield x'd out (41)	5 March 1673	68	No. 28

No	Parish: township (in brackets number exempt in each township)	Date	No. of names	Comment, old numbering
44	Parish of Tanfeild: Tanfield (41), Lints Greene (20)	2 March 1673	61	
43	Parish of Muncke Wearmouth: Munk Warmouth (42), Fullwell (12), Suddick (16), Hilton (21)	5 March 1673	91	No. 41
42	Parish of Washington: Bowden East & West (59), Washington (27), Barmeston (5), Usworth Great and Little (25), Hedworth (5)	6 March 1673	121 Cert. says 131	No 42
41	Parish of Munck Wearmouth: Munkton (28), Nether & Upper Heworths (82)	5 March 1673	110	No. 43
40	Parish of Munck Wearmouth: Westhoe (21), Harton (10)	5 March 1673	31	No. 44
	STOCKTON WARD certificates			
39*	Parish of Sedgefield (63)	18 Sep 1674	63	Reverse has list of hearths decayed
38	Parish of Grindon: In Thorpe Fewley constab. (21); In Whitton constab.(7)	20 Mar 1673	[28]	
37	Parish of Bishopp Midleham: in Cornforth (13); Mainsforth (3); Midleham (28)	7 July 1673 changed from 1674	44	
36	Parish of Eaglescliffe (34)	14 June 1673 changed from 1674	34	
35	Parish of Long Newton (30)	25 May 1673 changed from 1674	30	
34	Parish of Sadberdge (20)	25 May 1673 before 1674	20 Cert. says 21	
33	Parish of Byshopton: (19) Little Stainton (4)	2 June 1673 before 1674	23	

№	Parish: township (in brackets number exempt in each township)	Date	No. of names	Comment, old numbering
32	Parish of Billingham:Wolveston (30); Billingham (32), Coupan (22), Newrton (15)	20 June 1673	99	No. 18
31	Parish of Greatham: Gretham (63), Seton (28)	22 Jan 1673	91	No. 19
30	Parish of Hartinpoole: Stranton (33), Hartinpoole (51), Thorston (2)	10 Sept 1673	[86]	No. 20
29*	Parish of Harte: Harte Towne (46), Elwicke (17), Dalton (8), Brierton & Brentoft (10), Middleham x'd out (38)	10 Oct 1673	81 Cert. says 115	No. 21
28*	Parish of Norton: Cornsforth x'dout (13), Norton (72), Preston super Tease (33)	10 Dec 1673	118	No. 22
27*	Parish of Norton: East Harborne (14), Elton (7), Long Newton x'd out (34), Sadburye & Newbiggin x'dout (23), Read Marshall (4), Stillington (10), Carleton (13)	10 Dec 1673	48 Cert. says 49	No. 23
26*	Parish of Midelton: Cotam Mundwell (9), Bishopton x'dout (32), Dinsdayle (2), Sockburne (3), Midleton on the row (21), Ayslebye (9), Neasham (26)	20 May 1673	70 Cert. says 100	No. 24
25*	Parish of Norton: Hurworth (49), Stockton burrough (32), Stockton Towne (35)	16 Feb 1673/4	116 Cert. says 117	No. 25
	EASEINGTON WARD			
24	Parish of Trimdon: Shinkliffe (22), Butterbye (2), Wharington (9), Cassop (10), Wingate and Wheatley (13), Trimdom (30)	22 Jan 1673	86 Cert. says 186	No 1
23	Parish of Munkhasleton: Kelloe (18), Hutton Henrye (22), Sheraton (10), Monke Hesleton (16), Castle Eden (12)	6 Jan 16??	78	No. 2
22	Parish of Easington: Shotton (27), Easington (60)	2 Feb 1673	87	No. 3
21*	Parish of Pittington: Shadfoorth (11), Hallgarth (7), Pittington (10), Shearburn (17)	1 June 1673	45	
20	Parish of Easington: Query the whole of this sheet scored through. Heathorne (18), Haswell (19), Shadforth (18), Sheerburne (17), Pittington (21)	2 Feb 1673	93	No. 4
19	Parish of Houghton: West Rainton (51), East Renton (10), Houghton (33)	10 Fen 1673	94	No. 5

No	Parish: township (in brackets number exempt in each township)	Date	No. of names	Comment, old numbering
18	Parish of Bishopp Wearmouth: Hetton (9), Appleton (4), East Murton (7), Cold Heslington (10), Dalton (8), Seaham (15), Seaton & Slingley (5), Burdens (6), Silksworth (14)	10 Feb 1673	78	No. 6
17	Parish of Bishopp Wearmouth: Tunstall (9), Ryhop (20),	22 Feb 1673	29	No. 7
16	Parish of Bishopp Wearmouth: Bishopp Wearmouth (122)	20 Feb 1673	122	No. 8
15*	Parish of Bishopp Wearmouth: Sunderland by the sea (98)	12 Mar 1673	98 Cert. says 108	No. 9
14	Parish of Bishopp Wearmouth: Warmouth Pans (65), Offerton (10), East & Middle Herrington (19)	12 Mar 1673	94 Cert. says 104	No. 10
13	Parish of Houghton: West Herrington (16), Newbottle (36), Pensher (26)	10 Feb 1673	78	No 11
12*	Parish of Chester: Lumley & Lampton (179)	12 Mar 1673	179 Cert. says 189	No 12.
BEDLINGTONSHIRE				
11	Bedlington:	15 Apr. 1673[a]	36	MS
10	Bedlington: Chapington & Cleeswell hill (4), Camos & Blyth panns (3), Neatherton(3), Sleckburne East & West (8)	nd	18	
ISLAND & NOARHAM SHIRES				
9	Balinbrough [Northumberland]: Elwicke	6 July 1673[b]	6	MS
8	Kello: Kello Towne cum membris	1 Mar 1673	115 Cert. says 125	
7	Holy Island: Holy Island with Fenwicke	15 Mar 1673	74 Cert. says 75	
6	Cornehill	18 Mar 1673	56	
5	Norham: Noarham Towne	20 Mar 1673	64	

[a] Altered from 1672 or 74.

[b] Altered from 1674

No	Parish: township (in brackets number exempt in each township)	Date	No. of names	Comment, old numbering
4	Tweedmouth: Poor of Horkley Goswicke & Beale (63), Poor of Felkeington Grindon & Thornton (58), Poor of Twizell (25), Poor of Morton (10)	16 June 1674[c]	156 Cert. says 157 but one entry scored through	MS in bits
3	Tweedmouth: The Poor of Tweedmouth (55), Poor of Spittell (64), Poor of Ord (36), Poor of Morton (13)	18 Sep 1672 Ex 26 Sep 1673, changed from 1672	168 Cert. says 167, but entry added	MS
	Durham City			
2	St Nicholas Durham: St Nicholas parish (48), High Bayley (6), Crosgate (41)	15 Mar 1673	95 Cert. says 103	no.13
1	St Nicholas Durham: Framwell Gate (43), St Oswald parish [Borough of Elvet] (14), The Barrony of Elvatt (50)	ditto	107	no 14, in bits
	Durham St Giles now 83			no 15

[c] Changed from 1672. Examined by justices 20 June 1674.

E179/327 Part 2
1673–4

Transcribed for this volume by Duncan Harrington FSA in 2004. He has identified the divisions within the parishes, to make comprehension easier. such identification is not present in the original documents, many of which run on so that it is often difficult to see the divisions. The ordering of these transcripts is the same as in the list. Modern forms of place-names, where they differ from those in the documents, have been added in square brackets. Each document printed here, contains some material which is not in the 1666 Assessment. A larger number of certificates were transcribed than appear in print. They will be found in the database of the British Academy Hearth Tax Research Project at Roehampton University.

The scribe can write a capital F. This seems early for this character to appear in manuscript. However, a problem arises in that some letters which are definitely a capital T, could with a bar, not present, become F. Thus such names as Toster are more likely to be Foster and Tawsett more likely to be Fawcett.

See also the note at the beginning of the listing of the contents of this file.

No 88 Printed (old no. 47)
Parish of BISHOPP AUCKLAND
[Bishop Auckland]
Dated 10 October 1673

Stockley
Jane Coulston
James Shevilay
Robt Thornburrow
Robt Brack
Ro White
Geo Jackson
Jno Bell
Edw Wilkinson
Tho Harrison
Tho Huchison
Geo Noble
Wm Blackay
Geo Fenster
Robt Porter
Maudl: Rodrup
Jno Cowhert
Anne Smith
Jane Smith
Robert Anderson
Barb: Brihangham
Nich Usher

Martin Bell

Willington
Rich Wall
Eliz Mosman
Jno Atkinson
Jno Fawall
Mrs Clackston
Jane Hull
Jane Wall
Wm Gowlin
Jane Frend
Wm Mare
Math Tayler
Isab Browne
Jno Taylor

Helmington Row
Geo Kell
Thos Jackson
Mary Walker
Rich Hall
Isab Linsay
Mary Charleton

Crooke & Bille Row
[Crook and Billy Row]
Thos Tweddall

Hedley & Cornsey
[Hedley and Cornsay]
Anne Iston
Geo Care
Robt Punshin
Wm Dixon
Wm Wright
Lau Deram
Chr Blenkinsop
Ralph Carrudas
Hump Hopper
Tho Thompson
Humph Richison
Tho Jopling
Peter Neltalor
Wd Hedley

Thornley & Helme Parke
[Thornley and Helm Park]
Robt Redshaw
Rich Bell
Tho Story
Wm Raw
Jno Garforth
Jno Wilson
Geo Bell
Eliz Garforth
Tho Garforth
Henry Lawson
Marg Hartley
Jno Stot

Wolsingham Eastside quarter
Tho Grumwell
Henry Baitson
Geo Usher
Tho Jackson
Doro Chapman
Rich Jefferson
Eliz Stafford
Wm Lawson
Tho Rutter
Perc: Collison
Jno Cowper
Ralph Dixon
Wd Stephenson
Eliz Grise
Jno Alyer
Tho Raw

Alice Fantur
Tho Maughan
Rich Marley
Wm Rennyson
Rich Kell
Henry Robinson
Ralph Harley
Tho Heighington
Margt Harrison
Margt Tog
Joseph Beastly
Ralph Trotter
Robt Willan
Tho Vary
Jno Grundwell
Mich Chapman
Robt Dunne
Allowed 101 names

Willm Threlkeld curate
Thos Bett curate
Churchwardens Robert Hodshon,
John Wharton
JPs: Will Robinson, Christo
Sanderson
Febry 3 :73 altered from 75

No. 78 Printed (old no. 55)
Parish of DARLINGTON
Dated 12 November [no year]

Blackwell
Tho Whetson
Ro Fawell
Wd Harrison
Alice Robinson
Nich Dodgson
Tho Hunter
Wm King
Jno Rolf
Wd Dobson
Jno Pyper
Robt Ward
Wd Dent
Jane Will[ia]mson
Ro Scot
Peter Goldsbrough
Anne Blymire

Tho Bigott
Anne Auckland
Leo Robinson
Corsilla[2] Rauson
Anne Law
Cuth Cornforth
Hen Kirton
Jno Harrison
Alice Adamson
Nich North
Laur Jakes
Jane Langstaffe

Oxnelfeild [Oxneyfield]
Henry Crags

Haughton [Haughton-le-Skerne]
John Collinwood
Margery Mallum
Martin Rea
Geo Thompson
Eliz Hodgson
Barth Wastall
Rich Symples
Tho Turner
Chr Jeffs
Rich Browne
Rich Walls
Tho Nansy
Math Rawlin
Robt Godlin
Wm Sissalls
Edw Harrison
Tho Mensforth
Margty Younge
Wm Stephenson
Leo Hunter
Jno Dickin
Wm Wastall
Jno Burne
Wm Kiching
Jno Pearson
Henry Wilson
Geo Pearson
Tho Chapman

Great Burden [Great Burdon]
Rich Atkin

Anth Robinson
Ralph Bowes

Barmpton
Susan Cowper
Geo Harrison
Wm Bartrum
Tho Layburne
Jno Ridley
Tho Newton
Mary Smith
Hugh Browne

Archdeacon Newton
Jno Swinbanke
Anth Man
Jno Parkin

Haughton on ye side [Houghton le Side]
Anne Darlington
Jane Burden
Wd Ande
Alice Darlington
Tho Hall
Margt Lodge
Allowed 79 names

> George Bell min:
> Churchwardens Raiph Colling.
> JPs: Will Robinson, Christo Sanderson
> Febry 3 :73

No. 74 Printed (old no. 58)
Parish of Churchmerrington
[Kirk Merrington]
Dated 10 December 1673

Churchmerrington [Kirk Merrington]
Tho Thompson
Jane Richison
Humph Clearke
Alice Banks
Robt Richardson
Wm Ayer
Jno Richardson
Chr Smith

---

[2] Query Cersilla

Hugh Dods
Anth Richardson
Wd Masterman
Anne Heighington
Fran Hevyside
Wm Haisty
Wm Mason
Wm Mason

Chiltons Great & Little
Rich Pearson
Eliz Will[ia]mson
Ralph Whitfeild
Jno Sober
Jno Sumer
Wd Fishburne
Ro Jopling
Ro Hunter
Wm Addey
Jane Hunter
Tho Musgrave
Wd Maltby
Jno Steward
Jno Morlay
Jane Richison
Geo Gibson
Wm Heron
Mich Munday
Jno Walter
Rich Harrison

Fery Hill [Ferryhill]
Anne Huchinson
Wm Boyes
Jno Stoddert
Brihan Hevyside
Alice Burden
Ralph Sweeting
William Joplinge
Tho Blaykey
Eliz Dowfoot
Jno Sanderson
Jno Carre
Jno Farrow
Edw Feaster
Wm Layburne
Anne Golson
Jno Richison
Jno Newton

Jno Humble
Ro Widdifeild

Hett
Fran Heighington
Ro Kellah
Jno Usher
Wm Walker
Henry Wood
Jno Hog
Wd Cheswicke
Ralph Cheswicke
Jno Turpin
Cuth Hopper
Wm Lister
Jno Ellison
Dor Ferry
Marton Bease
Wm Vepon
Jno Meaburne
Edw Charleton
George Hunter
Jno Sedgwicke
Edw Unthanke
Cuth Key
Jane Leet
Eliz Key
Jame Terry
Allowed 80 names

Jam: Smith
Churchwardens George Smurthwaite,
John Jepherson
JPs: Will Robinson, Christo
Sanderson
Febry 3 :73

No. 73 (old no. 53)
Parish of ... [Whitworth]
Dated 10 December [1673]

Tudhoe
Henry Sedgwick
Hen. Wheatley
Hen. Jackson
Wm. Raw
Alice Peel
Geo: Iyley

Nich. Fishburne
Jno Gills
Math Harper
Tho Pickeringe
Jno Sparke
Mary Kirkles
Margt Flecher
Emori Richison
Geo Richison
Sarah Briggs
Ambrose Bell
Jno Cawser
Margt Horner
Jent Wilson
Anne Dunne
Mary Allan
Wm Wheatley
Roger Turpin
James Elliner[3]
Wd Sparke
Chr Richison
Henry Hillary
Wd Johnson
Jno Harper
Tho Taylor
Tho Raw
Jno Brackis

Whitworth
Geo Pickering
Mary Huckwith
Wm Adamson
Tho Harrison
Tho Mainsforth
Jane Nicholson
Jno Midleton
James Hewson
Henry Sympson
Mary Adamson
Robert Widdifeild
Cuth Nicholson
James Crosby
Wm Malum
Jno Carter
James Liddall

Wm Farrow
Robt Wilson

Briars Greene [Byers Green]
Ro Taylor
Jno Emerson
Eliz: White
Mary Eltringham
Tho: White
Wm Emerson
Geo Emerson
Jno Wall
Jno Ladler
Stephen Wright
Robt Cornforth
Eliz: Fawdon
Grace Wright
Ralph Trotter

Sunderland by the Brig [Sunderland Bridge]
Jno Robinson
Isab: Allan
Robt Auld
Geo Liddall
Wm Harrison
Anne Donkin
Jane Speed
Anne Smurfoot
Robt Speed
Ambr Simpson
Mich Rickerby
Mich Ande/Aude
Nich Crooks
Jno Dixon
Eliz Dacree
Jno Burnup

Allowed 81
Will Threlkeld curate of Brancepeth
Churchwardens John Coleman
JPs: Will. Robinson, Christo
Sanderson Febry 3 1673 altered from
1675.

No. 72. Printed (old no. 60)
Parish of GAINFORD
Dated 1 October 1673

---

3 This is abbreviated so could be Ellinour/
   Ellinor.

Langton
Robt White
Ellinr Judson
Anne Spencer
Ralph Luxon
Jno Misbill
Alice Finley
Wm Musgrave
Enry Spencer
Wm Loxon
Eliz Hall
Jno Charleton
Robt Brihan
Jno Stapleton
Wm Browne
Rich Frank
Jno Browne

Ingleton
Peter Johnson
Jno Wade
Florence Wade
Wm Fenwicke
Jno Smith
Jno Wade
Tho Rand
Jno James
Jnt Nesum
Jno Farrer
Chr Dunwell
Wm White
Jno White

Cockfeild [Cockfield]
Rich Mackerish
Ro Wilson
Leo Hodgson
Eliz Sum[m]er
Christiana Lodge
Mary Brumley
Jno Chapper
Anne Smith
Ro Jefferson

Wackerfeild [Wackerfield]
Elliner Chambers
Margt Marley
Isab Sutton
Anne Bland

Jane Sedgwicke
Nich Mattison
Eliz Taylor
Wm Sutton
Henry Lamb
Anne Bowe
Jno Sutton

Hilton [Hylton[
Edw Tinkler
Margt Sympson
Tho Marley
Perc: Sympson

Morton Tinmouth
Jno Sutton

Bolam
Geo Martin
Jent Taylor
Jno Taylor
Eliz Taylor
Jno Taylor
Wm Ilay
Ro: Doul
Geo Robson
Adam Colvil
Geo Lindsay
Kath Wetherell

Summerhouse
Wd Goodson
Wm Morton
Margt Langstaffe
Kath Hadsmangh
Tho Harrison
Wd Ducklaw
Tho Abraham

Headlum [Headlam]
Jno Ratcliffe
Dor Burton
Jno Robson
Wm Errington
Jno Smith
Alice Lambert
Jno Hemldraw

Peearchbridge [Piercebridge]
Fran. Shaw
Ro White

Jno White
Fran Hodgson
Tho Harrison
Rich Cowlin
Ell: Bradshaw
Tho Newland
Wm man
Ralph Hodson
Jno Lockburne
?Powl: Largchester
Tho Bowmer
Jno Waugh
Ralph Newlands
Anne Hildreth
Geo Parkin
June Errington
Jno Cowling
Jno Smith
Ralph Parkin
Mich Rapier
Eliz Hodgson
Ed Hodgson
Fran Jobler
Edw Panshin
Mich Richinson
Jno Gray
Allowed 107 names

Edmund Fotherby vicar
Churchwardens Francis X Blackston,
John Burrall
JPs: Will Robinson, Christo
Sanderson
Febry 3 :73

No 71. Printed. (old no. 61)
Parish of GAMEFORD [Gainford]
12 October 1673

Gainford

Tho Milburne
Ro Key
Jno Browne
Wm Shirlington
Wm Thackeray
Patr Hamilton
Wm Sympson

Tho Wittars
Anth Wade
Tho Milburne
Edw Midleton
Jno Shaw
Fran Dent
Jent Watson
Jane Milburne
Jno Elwand
Anne Parcivell
Isab Abbott
Wm Tynkler
Edw Tynkler
Math Langton
Phil Boncer
Wm Parcivell
Ro Roughton
Jno Stokell
Jane Stokell
Jane Sympson
Jno Sympson
Anth Blaykston
Jno Cowling
Jno Bead

Stainthorppe [Staindrop]

Chr Docker
Anne Pearson
Eliz Hudson
Grace Aynsley
Eliz Sedgwicke
Chr Watson
Wm Cockfeild
Margt Watson
Chr Wright
Jno Frizle
Wm Branson
Stephn Wood
Tob Aynesley
Geo Robinson
Jane Robinson
Wd Thompson
William Tod
Chr Hodgson
Mary Aynesley
Geo Kirkham
Lanc: Newby
Lanc: Baddah

Wd Ridley
Eliz Robinson
Wm Watson
Jno Allon
Geo Atkinson
Tob Bayles
Wm Walker
Wm Docklaw
Wd Witherup
Cuth Hobson
Wd Farrow
Jno Viccars
Simond Layfeild
Jno Atkinson
Geo Baxter
Wd Richison
Peter Applegarth
Margt Strumwell
Jno Alder
Tho Richison
Jno Farrow
Tho Denison
Margt Aynsley
Wd West
Nich Cocfeild
Wm Baxter
Wd Helcoat
Chr Darlington
Henry Bowran
Bridget Midleton
Jno Dinsdale
Eliz Rig
Jane Wood
James Richardson
Anth Richardson
Tho Coalpitts
Eliz Rowlanson
Ralph Walker
Tho Browne

Rabye [Raby]
Wm Fowler
Alice Rowbottom
Wd Waugh
James Richinson
Jno Elgoe
Margt Arnat
Robt Outhat

Wm Smart
Edw Lee
Math Garth
Geo Hodgson
Wm Dallison
Edw Bowler
Jno Dowfoot
James Glen
Math Speck
Anne Hodgson
Wd Pickeringe
Wd Gray
Jent Tod
Chr Pearson
Eliz Aynesley
Ro Robinson
Anne Cgrimhall[4]
Tho Turner
Eliz Thompson
Mich Speck
Jno Waugh
Tho Dixon
Jno Woodmis
Charles Robson
Jane Elgoe
Wd Layfeild
Jane Grainger
Allowed 131 names

Edmund Fother[by[5]] vicar
Churchwardens Francis X Black[ston],
John Burrall
JPs: Will Robinson, Christo
Sanderson
Febry 3 :73 altered from 75.

No 70. Printed
Parish of WINSTON
14 June 1674 altered to 1673.

Isabell Tilburne 2
Prissilla Heward 1
Ann Frankeland 1
Peter Heugh 1

---

4   Could start with an exceedingly poorly written
      'O'.
5   Lost restored from 69.

Catherin Newcome 2
Sissele Harker 1
Elizabeth Morton 1
John Eiles 1
Ann Robinson 1
Christopher Bainbridge 1
John Hudson 1
Anthony Robinson 1
Edward Harlo 1
Ann Wilson 1
William Hird 1
Henry Hall 1
Richard Wilson 1
Barnard Browne 1
Nicholas Girlington 1
John Winnington 1
Allowed 20 names

Cuth Marley Rector
Churchwardens Richard Wilson,
Henry Fawell
JPs: Will Robinson, Christo
Sanderson

No. 69 Printed (old no. 62)
Parish of GAINFORD
12 October 1673

Cleatlum [Cleatlam]
Jane Barnes
Jane Smith
Dan Bruce
Chr Crawfoote
Tho Prowde
Anne Taylor
Anne Milner
Gregory Viccars
Chr Cowert
Margt Wrangham
Anne Vint
Robt Elward

Winston
Bernard Douthat
Jno Richison
Rich Wilson
Eliz Morton
Chr Race

Ellinor Bainbridge
Anne Morton
Jno Eales
Kath Newcombe
Sam Benson
Cicily Harker
Anne Heugh
Jno Franklin
Geo Huer
Isab Tilburne
Jno Brownlesse
Wm Hind
Anne Wilson
Edw Heart
Anth Robinson
Jno Hudson

Whorleton [Whorlton]
Wm Banks
Math Stephenson
Joseph Newby
Eliz Hodgson
Anne Bainbrigge
Eliz Dinsdayle
Jno Dinsdayle
Isab Soulby
Doroth Hudson
Barth Morland
George Appleby
Margt Shutt
Anne Laydman
Wm Thompson
Anth Dinsdayle

Stainton [Stanton]
Mary Milton
Wm Yarker
Jno Brathwaite
Wd Atkinson
Tho Lax
Geo Bainbrig
Ralph Bowran
Rich Johnson
Tho Harrison
Jno Robinson
Margt Wood
Robt Jackson
Martin Rackstraw
Wm Robinson

Isab Shaw
Geo Nicholson
Tho Taylor
Eliz Robinson
Margt Lazonby
Geo Peacock
Tho Viccars
Robt Nicholson
Jno Shaw

Streatlum [Streatlam]
Jane Yearker

Westwicke [Westwick]
Charles Bland
Tho Douthat
Wm Douthat

Teasdayle Forrest [Teesdale Forest]
Edw Gargat
Mich Bell
Wm Newby
Wm Walton
Wm Walton junior
Jno Walton
Wm Walton
Stephen Watson
Jno Brumell
Wd Atkinson

Newbiggin [Newbiggin on Tees]
Ursilla Lonsdayle
James Wharton
Arth Emerson
Anne Newby
Cuth Natters
Chr Allinson
Margt Allison
Geo Allison
Jno Allison
Rich Bainbrig
Allowed 95 names

Edmund Fotherby vicar
Churchwardens Francis X Blackston,
John Burrall
JPs: Will Robinson, Christo
Sanderson
Febry 3 :73 changed from 75

No. 68 Printed (old no. 63)
Parish of GAINFORD
10 October 1673

Middleton [Middleton-in-Teesdale]
Cuth Lowis
Wd Gibson
Wm Goffe
Jno Peacocke
Wd Coalpitts
Eliz Wilson
Jno Bainbrig
Tho Lind
Wm Bainbrig
Lawr Tinkler
Cuth Allison
Anth Wetherett
Henry Bainbrig
Henry Kipling

Eggleston
Richard Morton
Jacob Pynkney
Jacob Walker
Magd Locker
Tho Dixon
Kath Heedlum
Anth Morton
Chr Punshiby

Marwood
Ambr Bynks

**Forrest of Langley Dayle
[Langleydale]**
Wm Baxter
Math Yarker
Rich Bell
Peter Hodgson
Jno Emerson
Wm Jordan
Eliz Taylor
Andr Morday
James Atkinson
Mary Langstaffe
Jno Boynes
Jno Hawden
Mary Hawden
Jane Bowran

Kath Monter
Allowed 37 names

Edmund Fotherby vicar
Churchwardens Francis X Blackston,
John Burrall
JPs: Will Robinson, Christo
Sanderson
Febry 3 :73 altered from 75.

No. 67 Printed (old no. 64)
Parish Of GAINEFORD [Gainford]
12 October 73 altered from 75

Barnardcastle [Barnard Castle]
Mary Stout
Arch Barnes
Tho Keddy
Tho Wharton
Brihan Coultert
Oliver Martin
Tho Wyld
Robt Homby
Ralph Vint
Wm Hutton
Anth Hetherington
Jane Walker
Lan: Pinkney
Wd Mattison
Wm Walton
Eliz Wetherelt
Tho Browne
Anne Wharton
Margt Bradley
Leo: Westgarth
Robt Dent
Robt Hog
Robt Pearson
Margt Bradley
Edw Marley
Tho Watson
Geo Hynd
Wd Hynd
Kath Hodgson
Eliz Emerson
Margt Hynd
Anne Lonsdayle

Barth Hind
Wd Hall
Cuth Vint
Jno Newby
Robt Newby
Henry Lonsdayle
Grace Gibson
Phillis Harwood
Dor Carr
Geo Harwood
Eliz Wilson
Jno Temple
Wd Miller
Wm Portesse
Steph Smith
Robt Richison
Isab Harrison
Robt Huchison
Tho Bland
Kath Hasty
Isab Key
Isab Morley
Margt Willis
Wd Huchison
Roger Westgarth
Ferdinando [blank]
Wd Bamlet
Anne Emerson
Hen Garnet
Math Denis
Phill Vint
Wd Peacock
Eliz Denis
Phill Lonsdayle
Magd Collin
Tho Robinson
Wd Chapman
Ralph Watterman
Wm Smith
Rich Watterman
Hugh Vinter
Nich Emerson
Jno Mowbray
Jno Loadman
Ell Jackson
Jno Denis
Wm Allison

Jno Dent
James Vinter
Fran Chapman
Robt Cheesbrow
Tho Story
Cuth Bland
Tho Heslup
Jno White
Wd Baxter
Barth Horne
Amy Cowper
Wd Glover
Ambr Tynkler
Chr Grainger
Geo Kenny
Jno Allison
P[h]ill Kipling
Wm Harrison
Tho Wilson
Mich Blayklin
Hugh Barnes
Eliz Nelson
Jno Blaykleck
Isab West
Wm Chapman
Robt Cudbertson
Wd Newby
Doroth Hodgson
Peter Grainger
Chr Walton
Geo Fawcet
Tho Newby
Wd Robinson
Wm Couthert
Peter Cuthbertson
Tho Andrew
Lan: Newby
Jno Beckbanke
Allowed 117 names

  Edmund Fotherby vicar
  Churchwardens Francis X Blackston,
  John Burrall
  JPs: Will Robinson, Christo
  Sanderson
  Febry 3 1673

No. 64 Manuscript
BARNARD CASTLE
9 October 1674

James Barnes of Barnard Castle

  Jo: Brockwell minister
  Churchwardens William Vint,
  Jonathan Wharton
  JPs: Willia Robinson, Christo
  Sanderson
  9 October 1674

No. 63 Manuscript
BARNARD CASTLE
no date

Peter Horne the elder of Barnard Castle

  Jo: Brockwell curate
  Churchwardens Robt Boulton, John
  Boulton
  JPs: Will Robinson, Christo
  Sanderson
  9 October 1674

No. 62 Manuscript
BARNARD CASTLE
9 October 1674

John Glover of Barnard Castle

  Jo: Brockwell minister
  Churchwardens Will Vint, Jonathan
  Wharton
  JPs: Will Robinson, Christo
  Sanderson
  9 October 1674

No. 56 Printed (old no. 37)
Parish of GOATSHEAD [Gateshead]
12 January 1673

Pipewell [Pipewell Ward]

Tho Davill[6]
Jno Boucher
Isab Hudson
Wd Hopper
Martin Ridley
Jno Gibson
Elliner Jeake
Jno Gilbert
Jno Thompson
Anne Beautyman
Tho Hauxley
Lucy Swallwell
Geo Robson
Alice Middleton
Dor Winder
Jno Browne
Jno Foster
Wm Richeson
Jacob Coxson
Tho Hauxley
Walter Alcock
Jno Boucher senr
Ellez: Dawson
Geo Chilton
Geo Wilkinson
Tho Horswall
Chris Courting

Pant Ward

Isab Dobson
Anne Flecher
Tho Herne
Jno Struther
Isab Craggs
Tho Gibson
Ralph Athew
Tho Ridall
Kath Colburne
Tho Errington
Mich Young
Tho Williby
Tho Wilburne

Chris Wallas
Jno Dobson
Wm Watson
Anne Richeson
Jno Regnaldson
Jno Thompson
Wm Watson
Ralph Smith
Geo Nicholson
Geo Morrehead
Andrew Robinson
Fran Sadler
Ph[i]ll: Spencer
Wm Riddell
James Haddock
Wm Tod
Wm Fenwicke
Jno Gladston
Jane Blaklin
Mary Bell
P[h]ill Story
Mich Chaplin
Anne Richeson
Anne Gordon
Eliz Filling
Jane Wood
Jane Vine
Mary Hymers
Grace Nicholson
Wm Deale
Lionell Maddison
Robt Sutton
Eliz Blyth

write this on ye other side
~~South Sheelds 1st Constab~~ [South
Shields First Constabulary]
~~Geo Willan~~
~~Wd Daglish~~
~~Geo Dunne~~
~~Wd Willand~~
~~Ro Willand~~
~~Mark Thompson~~
~~Robt Nesbit~~
~~Wd Burne~~
~~Tho Curre~~
~~Jno Wright~~

---

6   Possibly Daniel.

~~Oswald Eden~~
~~Jno Grant~~
~~Thomas Browne~~
~~Jno Partridge~~
~~Edw Nicholson~~
~~Wm Clearke~~
~~Austin Ruffe~~
~~Robt Archbould~~[7]
Allowed 73 names

John Laidlor
Churchwardens John Gibson, Rob Forster
JPs: Francis Anderson, Mil. Stapylton.[8]

No. 55 Printed (old no. 35)
Parish of GOATSHEAD [Gateshead]
12 January 73

~~Witton Gilbert~~
~~Tho Trotter~~
~~Tho Jackson~~
~~Math Sheels~~
~~Jno Hopper~~
~~Wd Taylor~~
~~Tho Taylor~~
~~Tho Smith~~
~~Ralph Sanders~~
~~Alice Dawson~~
~~Margt Yealder~~
~~Tho Henry~~
~~Jno Johnson~~
~~Wm Dawson~~
~~Tho Knight~~
~~Jno Dixon~~
~~Jno Wilkinson~~
~~Jno Stoddert~~
~~Wm Lonsdayle~~
~~Isab Palliser~~

~~Burnup & Hamstreets~~
[Burnhope and Hamsteels]
~~Jno Gallilee~~

Goatshead Banke ward
[Gateshead Bank Ward]
Peter Newton
Margery Stevenson
Wm Artles
Alice Granger
Wid Rogerson
Anne Newton
Tho Tod
Isab Urwen
Robt Arrowsmith
Jno Cudbert
Robt Reed
Lanc Tayler
Jane Hering
Fran Colleson
Jno Jobison
Margt Tayler
Wm Smith
Jno London
Jno Lee
Alice Hall
Roger Lawson
Eliz Hopper
Arth Shaftoe
Tho Browell
Eden Walker
Rich Browne
Tho Foster
Math Tayler
Tho Atchinson

~~Goatshead High ward~~
[Gateshead High Ward]

Allowed 29 names

John Laidlor
Churchwardens John Gibson, Rob Forster
JPs: Francis Anderson, Mil. Staplylton

---

[7]   This listing written in a different hand on no. 61 has slightly different spellings.
[8]   Myles Stapylton JP for Durham June 1668 (C231/7 p. 327) and to administer the oath to a JP October 1672 (C231/7 p.423).

No. 54 Printed (old no. 36)
Parish of GOATSHEAD [Gateshead]
12 January 1673

Gateshead High ward

Margt Cush
Grace Garrett
Hen Eden
Fran Colleson
James Ramsey
Andrew Henderson
Margt Jawart
Tho Gibson
Elliner Younger
Tho Joyce
Wm Jackson
Wm Person
Jane Ruderfoot
Eliz Browne
Tho Browne
Tho Brockett
Robt Godruke
Tho Robson
Tho Wilson
Margt Browne
Eliz Howson
Eliz Hagg
Alice Pearce
Eliz Ward
Geo Browne
Margt Litle
Robt Anderson
Rich Willson
Tho Rea
Tho Maisterman
Geo Dinmell
James Cragg
Jane Dickinson
Thos Lambe
Robt Gorden
Elliner Winde
Rich Wood
Margt Huchison
Tho Waite
Jno Lumsdaill
Willm Bowerbanke
Isab Nattrisse
Jno Nattrisse

Anne Battailes
Margt Grainger
Peter Snagle
Tho Young
James Gladson
Wm Greene
Geo Stay
Edm Mosse
Ambros Fills
Hen Cawart
Wm Turner
Jno Heding
Jno Johnston
Ralph Ridley
James Hackworth
Chr Seals
Jno Blakey
Jno Watson
Wd Cooke
Jno Gray
Perc Dag
Mich Hunter
Wm Crinkley
Tho Sympson
Cuth Wilson
Jno Hall
Ann Hall
Jno Tayler
James Dod
Jno Parkin
Anne Johnson
Jno Bulman
Ellin Trumble
Jno Smith
Cuth Watson
Jno Tod
Margt Lonsdell
Ed Hog
Jno Howson
Roger Walker
Ed Carr
Wd Drydon
Abrah Balife
Adam Nicholson
Jno Wilson
Kath Jackson
Henry Parker

Tho Wilkinson
Alice Porter
Tho French
Wm Ellerby
Wm Tayler
Ed Willy
Willm Deamster
Ed Smith
Lanc James
Jane Coale
Ralph Thompson
Jno Trumble
Jane Crawford
Jno Lister
Wm Hering
Anne Bease
Wd Thompson
Anth Wilkinson
Char Spooner
Ed Robinson
Robt Ramsden
Anne Wigan
Andrew Cuthbertson
Cuth Hering
Tho Young
Tho Frisell
Math Cordwainer
Jane Parkinson
Jno Drew
Jno Greene
Robt Kirton
Wd Tod
Rich Fawdon
Jno Wardhaugh
Eliz Slinger
Peter Gray
Wm Scott
Robt Pincker
Mary Hope
Geo Mann
Anne Thompson
Ro Gibson
Ro Blackberd
Ed Wetherley
Tho Foster
Wm Browne
Jno Shaftoe

Chris Coulston
Rich Jackson
Chas Porter
Eliz Preston
Ralph Dobson
Cuth Clifton
Rowland Watson
Ralph Whitfeild
Allowed 145 names
John Laidlor
    Churchwardens John Gibson, Robert
    Forster
    JPs: Francis Anderson, Mil. Stapylton

No. 49 Printed (old no. 26)
Parish of CHESTER [Chester-le-Street]
8 March 1673

Chester Towne
Stephen Cowper
Chr Smith
Anth Meburne
Rich Procter
Jno Durham
Ro Currey
Edw West
Tho Smith
Geo Potts
Anth Wardroper
Charles Lavericke
Anne Davison
Anne West
Anne Thompson
Tho Rogerson
Anne Raye
Rich Shaw
Willm Mathewes
Jno Trumble
James Longerell
Isab Sumerside
Joseph Thornton
Jane Davison
Wm Weyley
Anth Smithson
Wd Errington
Marke Blaykston
Tho Chilton

David Craggs
Jno Donkin
Mary Errington
Ro Pescod
Ro Porter
Ralph Horne
Tho Steward
Tho Thornton
Edw Morley
Jno Clearke
Jno Johnson
Wd Sallett
Wd Lewin
Wm Wailes
Jno Graham
Alex Steward
Margt Laydler
Roger Heath
Jno Trummell
Thomasin Wilson
Wm Fenwicke
Anne Lupton
Geo Shawes
Jno Gelson
Nich Low
Phill Ellan
Margt Appleby
Wm Appleby
Peter Hills
Stephen Tempest
Jane Cuthbert
Robt Perkinson
Tho Andrew
Wm Turpin
Anne Fish
Wm Wortley
Anne Robson
Peter Heath
Jno Ald
Jno Haswell
Wm Smith
Tho Greenweell
Ro Dykes
Ambr Rayne
Wd Adamson
Tho Sharper
James Shutt

Marmaduke Toward

Birtley
Thomasin Johnson

Warridge [Waldridge]
Robt Rooter
Geo Jopling
Wm Addamson
Rich Brough

Harraton
~~Humph Sparrow~~
~~Wm Howed~~
~~Wm Robinson~~
~~Wm Newby~~
~~Eliz Henderson~~
~~Wd Natresse~~
~~Wm Story~~
~~Wd Dawson~~
~~Ralph Rousby~~
~~Tho Dawson~~
~~Jno Fish~~
~~Anne Nicholson~~
~~Kath Morrow~~
Allowed 82 names

James Hume curt
Churchwardens Rich Wallas, Roger
Dixson
JPs: Francis Anderson, Mil. Stapylton

No. 48 Printed (Old no. 27)
Parish of CHESTER [Chester-le-Street]
8 March 1673

Harraton
Humph Sparrow
Wm Howed
Wm Robinson
Wm Newby
Eliz Henderson
Wd Natresse
Wm Story
Wd Dawson
Ralph Rousby
Tho Dawson
Jno Fish
Anne Nicholson
Kath Morrow

Anth Newby
Robt Thornton
James Browne
Tho Browne
Tho Atkinson
Anne Howett
Wm Richison
Jane Pearson
Brihan Johnson
Anne Dawson
Mary Gibson
Wm Haddock
Jno Dodgson
Jno Dininge
Kath Pattison
Wm Stephenson
Ro Marshall
Wm Rippen
Wd Thompson
Wd Robson
Ralph Harbottle
Jno Crooks
James Bremer
Tho Little

Orpeth [Urpeth]
James Cutter
Eman Robson
Edw Coxon
Henry Pigge
Ralph Harrison
Robt Langstaffe
Christopher Jefferson
Tho Pearson
Tho Bardy
Tho Milner
Edw Maddison
Wd Charleton

Edmonsley [Edmondsley]
Wd Jackson
Mary Jopling

Pelton
Jno Fenwick
Edw Stotherd
Jno Tiplady
Edw Viccars
Tho Charleton

Plausworth [Plawsworth]
Wd Winter
Charles Mowberry
Ralph Lawson
Jno Hall
Tho Robinson
Ralph Burkall
Cuth Appleby
Ursilla Robinson
Wd Baxter
Nich Watson
Jno Lee
James Morras
Ralph Short
Thomas Clearke
Ro Watson
Jno Watson
Fran Woodmis
Robt Dixon
Ralph Harbottle
Wm Robinson
Leon Hynd
Tho Welberry
Tho Wilson
Edw Clearke
Lan Myres
Geo Harbottle
Wm Harbottle
Tho Smith
Wd Carlisle
Rowland Murton

Kiblesworth [Kibblesworth]
Geo Browne
Jno Stephenson
Wd Walker
Edw Aukland
Allowed 89 names

James Hume cur[ate]
Churchwardens Rich ?Wells, Roger
Dixon
JPs: Francis Anderson, Mil. Stapylton

No. 39 Manuscript
Parish of SEDGEFIELD
18 September 1674

Thomas Robinson
John Croft
John Ruddicke
Anne Gibson
Widow Walker
Robt Lax
Charles Bilton
Anne Gill
John Bates
Jane Hickson
M William Coltman
Christopher Dods
John Gibson
John Smith
Widow Labron
John Mason
Isabell Chipchase
Anne Chipchase
William Sparke
Margaret Bourden
Ralph Storey
Thomas Mothersley
M William Elstobb
M Cath Foster
M Alice Ward
John Emerson
William Dickson
Elizabeth Batrick
Widow Straiton
Anne Hudson
M John Ellenar
Bernard Robinson
Robt Hodshon
George Creiston
John Fletcher jun
Elizabeth Wheatley
Thomas Heavysides
John Southgate
M Robert Chipchase
John Carre
Thomas Jobling
George Benkey
Bryan Stoberd

M John Gregson
Thomas Austin jun
Thomas Sparke
Widow Hall
Ellenar Browne
James Heslopp
George Richardson
Leonard Gibson
Widow Young
William Richardson
James Coward
Thomas Coltman
Widow Appleby
John Fletcher sen:
William Chipchase
William Hart
Thomas Austin sen
Rob Richardson
John Robinson sen
Ralph Richardson
Allowed 63 names

Hammond Beaumont cler
Churchwardens Abraham X Wright,
martin X Hickson
JPs: Wm? Bellasis, Geo. Morland

Decayed since the last certificate
Richard Wrights house 2 he being then
building it
Mr Fretibs in the east end three he being
now in building it
John Smith three he being now in
building
M Mathew Brigges of Laton one which
was formerly certified for.

No. 29 Printed (old no. 21)
Parish of HARTE [Hart]
10 October 1673

Harte Towne [Hart Town]
Tho Smith
Tho Burden
Rich Wilson
Robt Toby

Wd Mensforth
Wm Wilkinson
Magd Snawden
Robt Stothertt
Anne Stephenson
Mich Tod
Jno Mensforth
Alice Meaburne
Robt Huchinson
Robt Eggleston
Margt Colsforth
James Mensforth
Robt Gibson
Tho Halliman
Peter Greenson
Jno Halliman
Eliz Nicholson
June Jenison
Mich Johnson
Isab Wright
Geo Atkinson
Wd Maughan
Jno Wright
Wm Wright
Jno Tweddall
Jno Tweddall
Lettice Cooke
John Marton
Eliz Mace
Robt Chilton
Ro Coats
Ro Turbat
Jno Key
Tho Hutton
Rich Johnson
Marke Baites
Geo Wilson
Wm Marley
Tho Rewcroft
Chr Rawlin
Anne Wright
James Mansforth

Elwicke [Elwick Hall]
Ro Swallwell
Luke Cragg
Tho Reed
Wd Speck

Geo Pattison
Anne Harrison
Jno Wood
Robt Thompson
Isab Watson
Tho Hodgson
Laurence Lavericke
Robt Lavericke
Rich Lavericke
Tho Carver
George Litleford
Isab Watson
Rich Turbeck

Dalton [Dalton Piercy]
Thomasin Corner
Jno Bell
Rich Errington
Jno Hobkirke
Andrew Bell
Rich Key
James Jackson
Robt Lavericke

Brierton & Brentoft [Burntoft]
Chr Emerson
Jno Dacrees
Tho Forrest
Lawr Dobbison
Martin Cooke
Chr Jordison
Chr Denton
Fran Richison
Tho Smith
Wm Wardall

~~Middleham~~ [Bishop Middleham]
~~Margt Wood~~
~~Wm Smurthat~~
~~Ralph Widouts~~
~~Barth Raw~~
~~Rich Beckby~~
~~Wm Rutter~~
~~Rich Moore~~
~~Wm Burton~~
~~Anne Burton~~
~~Jno Emerson~~
~~Hen Greenall~~
~~Jno Carr~~

~~Ralph Stockden~~
~~Mary Midleton~~
~~Wm Thompson~~
~~Jno Robinson~~
~~Tob Husband~~
~~Wm Mowdy~~
~~Tho Wright~~
~~Tho Robinson~~
~~Fran Mander~~
~~Jno Bochby~~
~~Ro Fisick~~
~~Eliz Mason~~
~~Margt Marre~~
~~Tho Rickerby~~
~~Wm Parken~~
~~Rich Widdifeild~~
~~Eliz Reed~~
~~Ro Cockraw~~
~~Geo Dods~~
~~Chr Porter~~
~~Willm Robson~~
~~Rich Widdifeild~~
~~Jno Stockdon~~
~~Margt West~~
~~Robt Appleby~~
~~Margt Thompson~~
Allowed 115 names

Edward Smathwate minister of Hart
Churchwardens Anthony Dunn,
Mathew Smith
JPs: John Clavering, Robt Clavering

No. 28 Printed (old no. 22)
Parish of NORTON
10 December 1673

~~Cornsforth~~ [Cornforth]
~~Ro Huchison~~
~~Fran Garret~~
~~Phill Hudspeth~~
~~Mary Chipchase~~
~~Tho Lumb~~
~~Chr Fawcett~~
~~Wm Smith~~
~~Wm Hunter~~
~~Ro Kirton~~

~~Wm Layburne~~
~~James Hudspeth~~
~~Kath Colledge~~
~~Marmaduke Tatus~~

Norton
Rich Barwick
Tho Davison
Jent Ayesleby
Tho Thompson
Tho Lister
Tho Newby
Jno Tiplady
Tho Reedhead
Robt Atkinson
Robt Bee
Tho Ripley
Tho Hainsley
Fran Smith
Joseph Wright
Rich Burrell
Jane Wright
Wm Fergison
Jno Milburne
Jno Browne
Chr Stanley
Wm Bainbrig
Anne Bainbrigge
Tho Chapman
Jent Salvage
Ralph Roe
Robt Burden
Peter Barwicke
Jno Megson
Jno Burden
Wd Fleeming
Jno Bradley
Ralph Bell
Robt Farrow
Rich Forrest
Evans Finley
Franc Robson
Henry Jefferson
Jno Wright
Chr Foster
Jane Dobson
Eliz Midleton
Tho Masterman

Wm Reay
Jane Harrison
Robt Sharpe
John Huchison
Chr Tod
Hen Burden
James Corner
Eliz Halliman
Cuth Burden
Wm Edger
Wm Tosse
Henry Browne
Patr Waltis
Jane Banbrough
Ro Barwick
Ro Sharpe
Jno Hodgson
Jno Foster
Marmad Foster
James Southorne
Fran Jackson
Tho Jekill
Tho Milburne
Ralph Blenkinsop
Alice Bayles
Ro Heighington
Isab Wright
Tho Crow
James Johnson
Robt Damis[9]

Preston super Tease [Preston on Tees]
Chr Scury
Isab Lakin
Tho Wilkinson
Isab Sturry
Anne Bowman
Jno Fewler
Wm Lakin
Jno Gent
Barb Ayer
Margt Robinson
Alice Felis
Jno Nicholson
Mary Ridley
Robt Nicholson
Mich Blaykelock

Mary Hill
Tho Robinson
Tho Thompson
Jno Steel
Wm Allison
Tho Jackson
Tho Robinson
Anth Coats
Amerill Bainbrough
Phillis Wilson
Wd Hodgson
Mary Ashton
Jno Blayklocke
Tho Ayer
Robt Reed
Evans Catherick
Tho Carter
Ellin Bell
Allowed 118 names

Tho Davison vic de Norton
Churchwardens John Gates, Tho
Thompson
JPs: John Clavering, Robt Calvering

No. 27 Printed (old no. 23)
Parish of NORTON
10 December 1673

East Harborne [Hartburn, East]
Chr Oughton
Tho Thompson
Jno Burden
Tho Glover
Leo Huggert
Ro Peers
Ro Cully
Jno Emerson
Margt Key
Jno Gent
Martin Carter
Tho Angle
Ellin Harporley
Ralph Banks

---

9   Query meant to be Davis.

Elton
James Hurdwick
Jane Watson
Anne Clearke
Anne Reed
Jno Clearke
Eliz Brasse
Barb Elston

Long Newton
~~Jno Bowmer~~
~~Anne Greenberry~~
~~Margt Clearke~~
~~Margt Newman~~
~~Brihan Clearke~~
~~Anne Wilkinson~~
~~Roger Langstaffe~~
~~Ellin Walker~~
~~Gerrard Newman~~
~~Vincent Gainforth~~
~~Margt Merrington~~
~~Wm Thompson~~
~~Jno Newman~~
~~Robt Oates~~
~~Jno Hodgson~~
~~Wd Warmouth~~
~~Jane Jobling~~
~~Jno Merington~~
~~Robt Browne~~
~~Jane Bayne~~
~~Edw Fetherston~~
~~Wm Freere~~
~~Tho Pearson~~
~~Rich Hodgson~~
~~Rich Richardson~~
~~Anth Atkinson~~
~~Willm Blayklock~~
~~Jno Richison~~
~~Doroth Richison~~
~~Robt Thorpe~~
~~Ro Young~~
~~Chr Jackson~~
~~Rich Jackson~~
~~Jno Jackson~~

Sadburye & Newbiggin [Sadberge and Newbiggin]
~~Jno Smith~~
~~Thomasin vasy~~

~~Tho Chater~~
~~Wm Ray~~
~~Wm Cully~~
~~Rich Cockerell~~
~~Margt Hutton~~
~~Jane Bell~~
~~Jane Carter~~
~~Jno Armstrong~~
~~Margery Huchison~~
~~Alice And~~
~~Jno Falton~~
~~Tho Bullman~~
~~Martin Barnes~~
~~Martin Angle~~
~~Ro Banbrough~~
~~Alice Bartle~~
~~Anne Bulman~~
~~Jno Harperley~~
~~Wm Garry~~
~~Jno Wilkinson~~
~~Fran Manre~~

Little Stainton
~~Mary Reshah~~
~~Jno Huggison~~
~~Anne Dawson~~
~~Tho Wilkinson~~
~~Tho Cooke~~

Read Marshall [Redmarshall]
Chr Armstrong
Tho Browne
Leon Sympson
Eliz Forrest

Stillington
Margt Reedman
Rich Harburne
Fran Harburne
Jno Hardy
Tho Robinson
Rich Waddisay
Margt Jackson
Jno Jackson
Valentine Martin
Geo Brignell

Carleton [Carlton]
Peter Pharoh
Doroth Tyndale

Jno Urwin
Tho Bell
Henry Hutton
Edw Bushby
Tho Ranson
Henry Gowland
Ro Wood
Rich Robson
Anth Mills
Jane Norton
Robt Hutton
Allowed 49 names

Tho Davison vic de Norton
Churchwardens John Gates, Tho
Thompson
JPs: John Clavering, Robt Clavering

No. 26 Printed (old no. 24)
Parish of MIDLETON [Middleton St
George]
20 May 1673

**Cotam Mundwell
[Coatham Mundeville]**
Chr Haukswell
Jno Hall
Chr Sureties
Chr Teasdale
Jno Dent
Jno Hodgson
Anne Dawson
Tho Johns
Tho Owen

Bishopton
Wm Charleton
Eliz Newton
Robt Anderson
Phillis Wilkinson
Jno Earle
Jno Rea
Eliz Rea
Jno Garnet
Rich Challonge
Jno Johnson
Wm Rea
Tho Farrow
Margt Denham

Ralph Heart
Marmaduke Farrow
Jno Heart
David Johnson
Jno Anderson
Robt Tod
Wm Clearke
Wm Fewler
Jno Jackson
Eliz Huttson
Mary Cowper
Mary Wilson
Jno Stotherd
Wm Sweeting
James Cuming
Barth Nicholson
Wm Eggleston
Anne Stott
Alice Robinson

Dinsdayle [Dinsdale]
Rich Phillips
Wm Ayre

Sockburne [Sockburn]
Jno Hall
Margery Willy
Tho Johnson

**Midleton on ye Row
[Middleton One Row]**
Wm Stockdayle
Chr Bowman
Tho Wilson
Wm Wilkinson
Jno Lonsdayle
Tho Bedson
JnoSavill
Wd Andrew
Ro Seymour
Anne Allison
Anne Gilman
Eliz Cully
Wm Savill
Chr Gibson
Jno Hutson
Tho Huchison
Anne Dayle
Edw Pincher

Jane Horsley
Tho Savill
Mary Savill

Ayslebye [Aislaby]
Tho Appleby
Wm Appleby
Rich Turner
Isab Duck
Chr Johnson
Jno Cooke
Tho Humble
Henry Chapman
Cuth Nicolson

Neasham
Ralph Waiting
Jno Whorleton
Jno Hevyside
Jno Stephenson
Grace Tiplady
Tho Blenkinsop
Tho Browne
Edw Stephenson
Alice Walker
Marmad Andrew
Margt Wrangham
Jno Wilson
Eliz Flecher
Leon Petty
Chr Wardall
Jno Wilson
Geo Arrowsmith
Simond Coward
Ralph Stones
Mary Lasonby
Anth Stephenson
Margt Lumley
Merill Lace
Doroth Wilson
Geo Maure
Robt Ushaw
Allowed 100 names

Geo Grayson cler.
Churchwarden Thomas Bukey
JPs: Will Robinson, Christo Sanderson

No.25 Printed (old no. 25)
Parish of NORTON
16 Feb 1673/4

Hurworth
Wm Williamson
Jno Potter
Jno Duing
Jane Walker
Edw Maure
Tho Cully
Chr Graham
Umph Steedman
Marm Jenison
Nich Whitlock
Phill Coulson
Jno Smith
Geo Farmer
Anne Gressom
Tho Coats
Rich Gressom
Ralph Algood
Robt Godlin
Tho Denham
Eliz Burnham
Mary Miteing
Anne Lodge
Geo Denham
Robt Smith
Wm Nesum
Marmad Ward
Jno Johnson
Jane Stephenson
Doroth Fenwicke
Anne Bulman
Jno Bullman
Eliz Holliman
Wm Walker
Eliz Spence
Fran Snawden
Wm Pyburne
Charles Willy
Anne Tynsdale
Anne Bellanby
Jno Brumley
Tho Martin
Mary Finley
Wm Hardy

Rich Smith
Chr Denham
Sam Ovington
Jane Anderson
Wm Arrowsmith
Jno Atkinson

Stockton burrough [Stockton Borough]
Wm Claxton
Doroth Bainbrig
Wm Kirchendle
Margery Dent
Wm Cuthbert
Wm Heron senr
Mary Sadleton
Rich Wilson
Tho Steel
Wm Stock
Jno Wilson
Jno Browne
Jane Bainbrige
Brihan Watson
Eliz Fewler
Alice Eden
Jane Denham
Eliz Denham
Jno Osburne
Ralph Crosby
James May
Rich May
Wm Middleton
Jno Maynard
Ralph Banks
Jno Heron
Mich Robinson
Margt Souley
Tho Southgate
Eliz Allison
Fran Collison
Tho Swainston

Stockton Towne [Stockton Town]
Marm Allison
Ralph Oaks
Geo Denham
Jane Clifton
Tho Baker
Grace Ellison

Margt Wilson
Fran Hedlum
Anne Crosland
Jno Bunling
Jane Potter
Wm Crosley
Jane Stephenson
Thomas Anderson
Anne Reedhead
Tho Stephenson
Tho Hudson
Tho Shorter
Wm Hewinson
Eliz Calvert
Mich Watson
Peter Smith
Jane Potter
Tho Sheraton
Anth Fletholme
Tho Watson
Ro Scadlock
Jno Thompson
Rich Story
Tho Heron
Margt Usha
Tho Fletholme
Marge Fletholme
Geo Cragge
Magd Hewison
Allowed 117 names

Thomas Davison [vicar]
Churchwardens John Gates, Tho
Thompson, Thomas Buckney
JPs: John Clavering, Robt Clavering

No 21 Printed
Parish of PITTINGTON
1 June 1673

Shadforth
John Bullock
Willi Markam
Willi Wilson
Will Hudson
Hue Bowman
John Morray

Will Man
Frances Huntly
Widow Huntly
Widow Gamsby
Mary Willson

Hall garth [Hallgarth]
Widow Story
Widow Adamson
Widow Baylie
Peter Midleton
John Nueby
John Tibelady
Will Rickebey

Pittington
Widow Hall
Miles Ubankes
Will Burden
Thos Dosson
Alex Oasten
John Roper
John Burden
Tobias Jackson
Henry Wastel
Widow Humel

Shearburn [Sherburn House]
Robert Rutter
John Gainforth
Simon Peareson
Will Jackson
Robert Cooke
Richard Pattingson
Robert Davidson
John Ferrow
George Lough
Ralph Marlye
Widow Kiede
Robert W?ende
Thomas Ruderforth
James Hesslop
Widow White
Will Shawe
John Ovington
Allowed 45 names

  Chr Thompson vicar
  Churchwardens Will Simpson, James

Swalwell
JPs: John Clavering, Robt Clavering

No. 15 Printed (old no. 9)
Parish of BISHOPP WEARMOUTH
[Bishopwearmouth]
12 March 1673

Sunderland by ye Sea [Sunderland]
Ro Boyd
Jno Thompson
Fran Sympson
Wm Younger
Eliz Lindley
Rich Sharpe
Rich Myles
Wm Watson
Jno Key
Chr Bee
Phill Randull
Wm Ellison
Wm Mawson
Rich Mooreley
Rich Harrison
Ralph Anderson
Roger Richardson
Wm Gowling
Henry Wilkinson
Tho Foster
Wm Short
Geo Jefferson
Jno Davison
Fran Wharrington
Geo Gawdy
Elliner Hart
Willm Scott
Wm Wheatley
Ellinor Thompson
Katherine Bee
Edw Grainger
Geo Hunter
Margt Brack
Fran Rodham
Wm Elliner
Math Shepherdson
Ellinor Oliver
Chr Blayerton

Jno Gilban

Wm Thompson

Tho Cole

James Moorey

Grace Ellison

Tho Davison

Mary Grainger

Jane Gibson

Margt Smith

Robt Baxter

Maudlin Palmer

Fran Pordy

Wm Thompson

Eliz Foster

Jno Syde

James Robinson

Robert Goodwin

Wm Hardcastle

Margt Gunton

James Foster

Jno Barber

Ellinor Garrett

Tho Lax

Fran Greene

Jno Mabbs

Jno Gilroy

Tho Jolins

Robert Stephenson

Anne Thompson

Eliz Langford

Tho Hardcastle

Kathe Sympson

Robt Wightman

Tho Coulson

Mary Doughty

Wm Anderson

Bridgt Hixon

Peter Anstocke

Benj Francis

Robt Brack

Mary Ridley

Wd Littleford

Wd Atkinson

Wd Story

Tho Gilroy

Jno Lee

Alex Rosse

Wm Langhorne

Jno Bee

Tho Brissel

Geo Hepper

Fran Hodgson

Wd Grainger

Eliz Dickison

Wm Turbet

Ro Pease

Wd Jopling

Rich Brewster

Wm Allon

Rich Brewster

Allowed 108 names

Tho Broughton curt

Churchwardens Thomas Wilson, James
Marten

JPs: Francis Anderson, Jo: Hall Major

No. 12 Printed

Parish of CHESTER [Chester-le-Street]

12 March 1673

*[6 columns the first and last of which are
badly damaged with information lost]*

Lumley & Lampton [Lambton]

... Rockwood

... Bell

... Robinson

... Procter

... White

... Stephenson

... [W]ilson

[Mar]gt Collins

... Stevenson

[Dor]oth Hall

... Burne

...gn Stawfoot

... Grinwell

[M]artin Barwas

...?lt Seymour

... Vynt

... Laydler

... [M]osby

... Story

... Clough
[Ral]ph Andrew
... Wind
[Jn]o Walter
[J]errard Lax
Rich Welsh
Tho Shibdon
Tho Tod
[Ro]bt Prissick
Margt Carr
Wm Currey
Jno Humble
Tho Bowmer
Geo Key
Jno Welsh
Tho Huckle
Wm Huckle
Mich Wilkinson
Ralph Tate
Rich Bell
Tho Harbottle
Tho Huchinson
James Gardner
Geo Harrison
Wd Thornton
James Aynesley
Wd Blackburne
Wd Atkinson
Fran Buck
Anne Bellas
Jno Horne
Edw Hall
Jno Garner
Rich Garner
Jno Almond
Jno Harrison
Wd Jurdison
Eliz Atkinson
Jno Feet
Robt Robinson
Chr Beednall
Jno Shaw
Jno Teckenby
Wm Butler
Tho Lightley
Edw Horne
Jno Southorne

Eliz Stout
Geo Ellinor
Wid Jefferson
Geo Bayles
Anth Allen
Tho Thompson
James Bellas
Chris Swinburne
Geo Clearke
Martin Bulmor
Jno Thorpe
Wd Burgesse
Isab Bowmer
Robt Coxon
Edw Newby
Jno Rogerson
Anne Fairne
Rich Tod
Alex Wilkison
Nich Shevill
Geo Humble
Chr Watters
Eliz Crosby
Cuth Walker
Ralph Scott
Robt Bowmer
Tho Robinson
Jno Watson
Eliz Atkinson
Eliz Sym
Jeffrey Welsh
Geo Wanlas
Peter Webb
Math Short
Willm Watson
Jno Pilkington
Wm Humble
Margt Hog
Rich Dixon
Tho Scorrer
Geo Clearke
Tho Boyers
John Robinson
Robt Clearke
Dorothy Scott
Rich Atkinson
Margt Huchinson

Geo Modby

Wm Moodby

Tho Foster

Jno Browne

Cuth Taylor

Geo Clearke

Anne Hugill

Jno Parkin

Isab Horne

Wm Ward

Geo Reed

Robt Baxter

Tho Wilson

Wm Scoome

Robt Thompson

Wm Chicken

Rich Browne

Jno Lowes

Rich Chayers

Tho Robinson

Edw Curry

Jno Laws

Rich Chambers

Jno Penelbery

James Browne

Henry Fawcett

Rich Hall

Jno Hall

Ralph Curry

Jno Sympson

Jno Raysbeck

Jno Thompson

Wm Wilkers

Isab Lawes

Robt Jackson

Emma Ford

James Lax

Robt Wallas

Eliz Rogerson

Jno Passe

Barb Robinson

Jno Bowes

Eliz Welsh

Ro Short

Jno Atkinson

Wm Midleton

Ralph Atkinson

Jno Foggett

David Key

Jno Thompson

Phill Truett

Jno Andrid

Wm Heron

Robt Hall

Wm Swinburne

Martin Parkin

Brihan Welsh

Geo Sympson

Roger Jameso[n]

Willm Smi[th]

Jno Kirtley

Chr Woole

Jno Henderson

Robt Clearke

Ellinor Bussy

Wm Sigsworth

Allowed 189 names

Jam Hume cur

Churchwardens Rich Wallas, Roger Dixson

JPs: Francis Anderson, Will Robinson

Abbreviations

CSPD	Calendar of State Papers Domestic
DRO	Durham Records Office
NA	National Archives
RCHME	Royal Commission on the Historical Monuments of England
TDNAAS	Transactions of the Durham and Northumberland Architectural and Archaeological Society
TIBG	Transactions of the Institute of British Geographers
VA	Vernacular Architecture
VCH	Victoria County History

Bibliography

Alldridge, N. ed., *The Hearth Tax: Problems and Possibilities*, (Hull, 1983)

Arkell, T. 'The Incidence of Poverty in England in the later seventeenth century' *Social History* 12 (1987), 23–47

Arkell, T., 'Identifying regional variations from the hearth tax', *The Local Historian* 33, 3 (2003), 148–74.

Barley, M., *The English Farmhouse and Cottage* (London, 1961)

Botelho, L. and P. Thane, eds, *Women and Ageing in British Society since 1500*, (Harlow, 2000)

Bowes, P., *Weardale: Clearing the Forest* (Bishop Auckland, 1990)

Braddick, M. J., *Parliamentary Taxation in Seventeenth-Century England* (Woodbridge, 1994)

Braddick, M. J. *The Nerves of State: Taxation and the Financing of the English State, 1558–1714* (Manchester, 1996)

Braddick, M. J. *State Formation in Early Modern England, c.1550–1700* (Cambridge, 2000)

Brassley, P. *The Agricultural Economy of Northumberland and Durham in the period, 1640–1750* (New York, 1985)

Brunskill, R. W., 'The Vernacular Architecture of the Northern Pennines', *Northern History* XI 2 (1975), 107–142

Calendar of State Papers Domestic. Charles II. 28 vols. (London, 1860–1947)

Chandaman, C. D., *The English Public Revenue*, (Oxford, 1975)

Chapman, V., 'The Aukside estate of Anthony Todd, freeholder, of Middleton-in-Teesdale', *TDNAAS*, new ser. 3 (1974), 75–86

Chapman, V. 'Cruck-framed buildings in the Vale of Tees' *TDNAAS* 4 (1978), 35–42.

Chapman, V., 'Heather-thatched buildings in the northern Pennines' *TDNAAS* 6 (1982), 9–12

Coleby, A. M., *Central Government and the Localities: Hampshire, 1649–1689* (Cambridge, 1987)

Coleman, S., 'The Hearth Tax returns for the Hundred of Blackbourne, Michaelmas 1662', *Proceedings of the Suffolk Institute of Archaeology*, vol.32, pt.2 (1971)

Cooper, N., *Houses of the Gentry, 1480–1680*, (London, 1999)

Cumbria Family History Society, *The Westmorland Hearth Tax 1673*, (Cumbria Family History Society,1998)

Dendy, F. W. and J.R. Boyle, eds, *Extracts from the records of the Merchant Adventurers of Newcastle upon Tyne Volume 1*, Surtees Society 93, 1894

Dewdney, J. C., ed., *Durham County and City with Teeside*, (Durham, 1970)

Dietz, B., 'The North-East Coal Trade 1550–1750: Measures, Markets and the Metropolis', *Northern History* 22 (1986), 280–94

Drury, J. L., 'More stout than wise: tenant right in Weardale in the Tudor period' in *The Last Principality: Politics, Religion and Society in the Bishopric of Durham 1494–1660* ed. by D. Marcombe (Nottingham, 1987).

Durham County Local History Society, *An Historical Atlas of County Durham* (Durham, 1992).

Emery, A., *Greater Medieval Houses of England and Wales 1300–1500, Volume I Northern England* (Cambridge, 1996)

Emery, N., 'Materials and Methods: some aspects of building in County Durham, 1600–1930' *Durham Archaeological Journal* 2 (1986), 113–120

Erickson, A., *Women and Property in Early Modern England*, (London, 1993)

Evans, N. ed, *Cambridgeshire Hearth Tax, Michaelmas 1664*, British Record Society, Hearth Tax Series I (London, 2000)

Fairless, K. J. N., 'Grange Farm – A Cross Passage House in Tyne and Wear', *TDNAAS*, 5 (1980), 81–90

Floud, R. and D. McCloskey, *The Economic History of Britain since 1700*, 2 vols, 2nd edition (Cambridge, 1994)

Fowler, J. T., ed., *Rites of Durham*, Surtees Society 107 (1902)

Gibson, J., *The Hearth Tax and other later Stuart Tax Lists and the Association Oath Rolls* (Federation of Family History Societies and Roehampton Institute, London, 1996)

Green, A., 'Tudhoe Hall and Byers Green Hall, County Durham: seventeenth and early eighteenth century social change in houses', *VA*, 29 (1998), 33–41

Green, A. 'Houses and Households in County Durham and Newcastle, *c.*1570–1730' (unpublished University of Durham PhD, 2000).

Green, A., 'Houses and Landscape in Early Industrial County Durham' in *Northern Landscapes: Representations and Realities*, ed. by T. Faulkner and H. Berry (Boydell & Brewer, forthcoming)

Halliday, S. J., 'Social Mobility, Demographic Change and the Landed Élite of County Durham, 1610–1819' *Northern History* 30 (1994), 49–63

Harrington, D. ed., *Kent Hearth Tax Assessment, Lady Day 1664*, British Record Society, Hearth Tax Series II (London, 2000)

Harrison, B., 'Longhouses in the Vale of York', *VA* 22 (1991)

Harrison, B. and B. Hutton, *Vernacular Houses in North Yorkshire and Cleveland* (Edinburgh, 1984)

Harvey, P. D. A., 'Boldon Book and the Wards between Tyne and Tees' in D. Rollason, M. Harvey and M. Prestwich, eds., *Anglo-Norman Durham 1093–1193*, (Woodbridge, 1974)

Hatcher, J., *The History of the British Coal Industry, Vol. 1, Before 1700: towards the Age of Coal* (Oxford, 1993)

Heesom, A., 'The Enfranchisement of Durham' *Durham University Journal* 80 (1988), 265–85

Hey, D., '1997 Phillimore Lecture: The Local History of Family Names' *The Local Historian*, vol. 27, 4 (1997), i–xx

Hey, D., and G. Redmonds, *Yorkshire surnames and the hearth tax returns of 1672–73*, Borthwick Institute of Historical Research (York, 2002)

Hodgson, R. I., 'Demographic Trends in County Durham, 1560–1801' *University of Manchester School for Geography Research Papers* 5 (1978)

Hodgson, R. I., 'The Progress of Enclosure in County Durham 1550–1870' in H.S.A Fox and R. A. Butlin eds, *Change and Continuity in the Countryside*, (London, 1979)

Hodgson, R. I., 'Coal Mining, Population and Enclosure in the Sea-sale Colliery Districts of Durham 1551–1801' (unpublished University of Durham PhD, 1989).

Hoffman, J. G., 'John Cosin, 1595–1672: Bishop of Durham and Champion of the Caroline Church' (unpublished University of Wisconsin–Madison PhD, 1977)

Hoskins, W. G., *The Midland Peasant: The Economic and Social History of a Leicestershire Village*, (London, 1957)

Hoskins, W. G., 'The Rebuilding of Rural England, 1570–1640', *Past and Present* 4 (1953), 44–59

Husbands, C., 'The Hearth Tax and the Structure of the English Economy' (unpublished University of Cambridge PhD, 1985)

Husbands, C., 'Hearth, wealth and occupations: an exploration of the hearth tax in the later seventeenth century' in *Surveying the People*, ed. by Schürer and Arkell, pp. 65–77.

Husbands, C., 'Regional change in a pre-industrial economy: wealth and population in England in the sixteenth and seventeenth centuries', *Journal of Historical Geography*, 13 (1987), 348–9

Hutchinson, W., *The History of the County of Cumberland*, 2 vols (Carlisle, 1794)

Hyde, P. and D. Harrington, *Hearth Tax Returns for Faversham Hundred 1662–1671*, Faversham Hundred Records, vol. 2 (1998)

Issa, C., 'Obligation and Choice: Aspects of Family and Kinship in seventeenth-century County Durham' (unpublished University of St. Andrews PhD, 1987)

James, M. E., Family, Lineage and Civil Society: A study of Society, Politics and Mentality in the Durham Region, 1500 to 1640 (Oxford, 1974)

Jarratt, M., 'The deserted village of West Whelpington, Northumberland' *Archaeologia Aeliana* 4th series, XL 1964, 189–225

Johnson, M. H., 'A Contextual Study of Traditional Architecture in Western Suffolk, 1400–1700' (unpublished University of Cambridge PhD, 1989)

Kent, J. R., 'The Centre and the Localities: state formation and parish government in England, *c.*1640–1740' *Historical Journal* 38 (1995), 363–404.

Kirby, D. A., 'Population Density and Land Values in County Durham during the mid-seventeenth century' *TIBG* 57 (1972), 83–98

Lapsley, G. T. *The County Palatine of Durham: A Study in Constitutional History* (New York, 1900)

Liddy, C. D. L. and R. H. Britnell, eds, *North-East England in the Middle Ages* (Boydell and Brewer, forthcoming).

Levine, D. and K. Wrightson, *The Making of an Industrial Society: Whickham 1560–1765*, (Oxford, 1991)

Luders, A., et. al., eds, *Statutes of the Realm* 11 vols. (Record Commission, 1810–28)

Macaulay, T. B., *The History of England* (London, 1873)

Machin, R. ''The Lost Cottages of England: An essay on impermanent building in post-medieval England', unpublished paper.

Marshall, L. M., 'The Levying of the Hearth Tax', *English Historical Review*, vol.51 (1936), 628–646

Meekings, C. A. F. ed., *Surrey Hearth Tax, 1664*, Surrey Record Society, 17 (1940)

Meekings, C. A. F. ed., *Dorset hearth tax assessments, 1662–64*, (Dorchester, 1951)

Meekings, C. A. F., *The Hearth Tax 1662–89: Exhibition of Records*, Public Record Office (London, 1962)

Meekings, C. A. F., *Analysis of Hearth Tax Accounts 1662–1665*, List and Index Society, 153 (London, 1979)

Meekings, C. A. F., *Analysis of Hearth Tax Accounts 1666–1669*, List and Index Society, 163 (London, 1980)

Morin, J., 'Merrington: Land, Landlord and Tenants 1541–1840: A Study of the state of the Dean and Chapter of Durham' (unpublished University of Durham PhD, 1998)

Mussett, P., *Lists of Deans and Major Canons of Durham 1541–1900* (Durham, 1974)

Mussett, P. with P.G. Woodward, *Estates and Money at Durham Cathedral 1660–1985* (Durham, 1988)

Nef, J. U., *The Rise of the British Coal Industry*, 2 vols (London, 1966)

Newman, C. and M. Meikle, *The Origins of Sunderland*, (VCH, forthcoming)

Ornsby, G., ed., *The Correspondence of John Cosin, Bishop of Durham, Vol. II*, Surtees Society 55 1870

Osmond, P., *A Life of John Cosin Bishop of Durham 1660–1672*, (London, 1913)

Pallister, A. and S. Wrathmell, 'The Deserted Village of West Hartburn, Third Report: Excavation of Site D and Discussion' in *Medieval Rural Settlement in North East England*, ed. by Vyner, pp.59–75.

Parkinson, E., 'The Administration of the Hearth Tax, 1662–1666' (unpublished University of Roehampton PhD, 2001)

Peters, C., 'Single Women in Early Modern England: attitudes and expectations', *Continuity and Change* 12 (1997), 325–45.

Pevsner, N. and E. Williamson, *The Buildings of England: County Durham*, (London, 1983)

Pickles, M. F., 'Labour Migration: Yorkshire, *c.*1670 to 1743', *Local Population Studies*, 57 (Autumn 1996)

Pollard, S. and D. Crossley, *The Wealth of Britain*, (London, 1968)

Purdy, J.D. *Yorkshire Hearth Tax Returns*, Studies in Regional and Local History No. 7 (Hull, 1991).

Raistrick, A. and B. Jennings, *A History of Lead Mining in the Pennines* (London, 1965)

Ramm, H.G. et. al., *Shielings and bastles* (RCHME, 1970)

RCHME, *Houses of the North York Moors* (London, 1987)

Reid, D.S., 'The Durham Church Establishment: The Gentry and the Recusants 1570–1640', *Durham County Local History Society Bulletin* 22 (1978)

Reid, D.S., *The Durham Crown Lordships* (Durham Local History Society, 1990)

Roberts, B.K., *The Green Villages of County Durham: A Study in Historical Geography* (Durham Local History Publication No. 12, 1977)

Roberts, M., *Durham*, (London, 1994) revised edition 2003.

Ryder, P. 'Fortified medieval and sub-medieval buildings in the north-east of England' in *Medieval Rural Settlement in North-East England* ed. by B. Vyner (Durham, 1990), 127–39.

Schürer, K., and T. Arkell eds, *Surveying the People* (Local Population Studies Supplement, Oxford, 1992)

Shaw, W. *A. Calendar of Treasury Books and Papers preserved in Her Majesty's Public Record Office*. Volumes 1–5, (London, 1897–1903)

Seaman, P., Pound, J., and R. Smith, *Norfolk Hearth Tax Exemption Certificates 1670–1674*, British Record Society, Hearth Tax Series, III (London, 2001)

Smith, D., 'Northumberland Hearth Tax 1664' *Journal of Northumberland and Durham Family History Society* (April 1978)

Spufford, M. *Contrasting Communities: English Villagers in the Sixteenth and Seventeenth Centuries* (Cambridge, 1974)

Spufford, M. *The Great Reclothing of Rural England: Petty Chapmen and their Wares in the Seventeenth Century* (Cambridge, 1984)

Spufford, H. M., 'The significance of the Cambridgeshire hearth tax', *Proceedings Cambridgeshire Antiquarian Society*, 55 (1962), 53–64.

Spufford, M., '2000 Phillimore Lecture: The Scope of Local History and the Potential of the Hearth Tax Returns' *The Local Historian* 30, 4 (2000), 206

Spufford, M. and J. Went, 'Poverty Portrayed: Gregory King and Eccleshall in Staffordshire in the 1690s'. *Staffordshire Studies*, 7 (1995), 1–150.

Styles, P., 'The Social Structure of Kineton Hundred in the Reign of Charles II' *Transactions of the Birmingham Archaeological Society* 78 (1962), 96–117

Surtees, R., *History and Antiquities of the County Palatine of Durham*, 4 vols. (1816–40)

Thirsk, J., ed., *The Agrarian History of England and Wales, vol 5, 1640–1750: Regional Farming Systems* (Cambridge, 1984)

Vyner, B., ed., *Medieval Rural Settlement in North-East England* (Durham, 1990)

Walsham, J., *Three reports on the state of the dwellings of the labouring classes in Cumberland, Durham and Westmoreland* (London, 1840)

Webster, W.F., ed., *Nottinghamshire Hearth Tax 1664:1674*, with an introduction by J.V. Beckett, M.W. Barley and S.C. Wallwork, Thoroton Society Record Series, 37 (Nottingham, 1988)

Woodward, D., *Men at Work: Labourers and Building Craftsmen in the Towns of Northern England, 1450–1750*, (Cambridge, 1995)

Wrightson, K., *English Society 1580–1680*, (London, 1982)

Personal Name Index

Railph 210, 215; Richard 40; Robt
91; Will 48; Willm 125; Wm 114,
168
Gowling (*Gowlin*): James 141; Wm 236,
262 *cf Cowling*
Gowre: Jno 46; Tho 71
Goyle: Tho 82
Gradon (*Graddon*): Geo 95; Henry 94;
Tho 155
Graham (*Grahame*): Chr 166, 260;
James 163; Jane 121, 131; John 154,
170, 171; Jno 15, 94, 102, 252; Mary
72, 96, 162; Mich 94, 95, 170; Peter
170; Rich 73; Richard 96; Richd
174; Roger 166; Rynion 171; Tho 84,
102, 170; Thomas 96; Wid 95; Widd
142; Will 85; Wm 126
Graine (*Grayne*): Chr 131; Peter 76
Grainger (*Granger*): Alice 106, 249;
Chr 247; Edw 262; Francis 2, 106;
Henry 18; James 18; Jane 243; Jno
13; Margt 250; Mary 263; Matthew
206; Peter 247; Robert 72; Wd 263;
Widd 106, 122; Will 39
Gramison: Bryan 2
Gramshaw: William 106
Grange (*Grainge*): Buly 46; Geo 68;
Matt 65; Ralph 49; Tho 38, 70
Granston: John 113; Raphe 174
Grant: Jno 249; John 165
Graveson: Peter 137
Gray: Abigall 174; Adam 94; Chro 107;
Cuth 68; Cuthbt 152; David 152;
Doctor 61, 93; Edw 171; Ellinor 147;
Hen 174; Henry 96; James 166; Jno
31, 32, 87, 88, 242, 250; John 44,
111, 147, 174; Maddison 31; Mathew
144; Matt 226; Matt junr 160; Mich
120; Mr 89; Mr Jno 97; Nichol 86;
Peter 86, 94, Gray, Peter 251; Ralph
56, 96; Raphe 174; Robert 26; Robt
61, 97, 107, 144, 165, 173; Tho 85,
154, 160; Wd 243; Widd 165; Will
94, 96; Wm 174
Grayson (*Graison*): Geo 260, Jno 40;
Matt 160
Greathead: Issabell 10; Jno 3, 23; Robt

19; Wid 3, 108; Will 10
Greave: Nichol 87; Wm 133
Greaveson (*Greavson*): Jane 139; Rich
139; Richard 48; Widd 139; Wm
139
Green (*Grean, Greene, Greeny*): Adam
75; Alexr 94; Bartho 165; Clement
80; Fran 263; Francis 82; Geo 12,
97, 159; Henry 53; Humphrey 33;
James 58; Jane 112; Jno 51, 97, 251;
John 146, 152; Margrett 38; Martin
5; Mr 93; Robert 76; Robt 164;
Simon 165, 168; Tho 155; Widd 59;
Will 47; Wm 250
Greenall: Hen 255
Greenaway (*Greenay, Greenway*):
Clement 152; Isab 152; Jno 63;
Lance 74; Nichol 63; Sam 75, 165;
Widd 155, 160; Willm 152
Greenbury: Ann 132; Anne 258
Greener: John 152; Roger 72, 162; Will
72
Greenhead: Hen 176; Henry 101; Wid
94
Greenlaw: James 173
Greenside: Tho 128
Greenson: Peter 255
Greensword: Geo 31; Richard 31
Greenwell (*Greenweell, Grinwell*): ...
263; Alice 63; An 28; Ann 27, 29,
129; Chris 88; Hen 134; Jane 64;
Jno 30, 34, 55, 63, 65; John 123,
126; Mary 65; Math 128; Matt 129;
Mr 93; Ms 61, 90; Ms Mary 79;
Richard 64; Robt 63, 154; Tho 11,
34, 35, 62, 252; Wid 62; Will 29, 62,
79; Willm 128; Wm 29 *cf Grenwell,
Grumwell, Grundwell, Grunwell*
Greenwin: Margrett 28; Robert 28
Gregory: Franc 109; Jno 4
Gregson: Geo 47; Jno 57; Richard 47;
Tho 57
Gregsworth: Francis 14
Grenwell: Jno, 65; Will 65 *cf Greenwell*
Gresham (*Grasham, Gressom*): Anne
260; Ninian 131; Peter 1; Richd 131,
260

Grey: Gilbt 170; Robt 174; Wm 170
Grierson (*Greirson, Greireson*), Richard
lxxx, 4; Robt 10
Griffin: John 153
Grindall: Jno 21
Grindon: Jno 29; Robt 66
Grinshaw: Margrett 10
Grisby: Geo 106
Grise: Eliz 237
Grobe: Tho 69
Grosare: Tho 155
Groves: Jno 60
Grumwell: Tho 237 *cf Greenwell*
Grundall: Jno 3
Grunden: Wid 23
Grundwell: Eliza 26; Jno 237 *cf*
Greenwell
Grundy (*Grundey, Grundye*): Ann 78;
Cuthbert 204; Edward 81; Jno 75;
Tho 60, 159, 227
Grunwell; Jno 79; Will 78 *cf Greenwell*
Grysdale: Robt 106
Gryseworth: Ambrose 37
Guddricke: Phillis 72
Gun (*Gunn*): Arthur 84
Gunton: Margt 263
Guttery: James 26
Guy: Cuth 56; Edw 87; Robt 58
Gyles: Mary 121; Richard 9

H

H'deson: Rob't 214 *cf Henderson*
Habacke: Alice 138; Geo 136; James
139
Habkirke: Elenor 173
Hackward: Tho 32
Hackworth: James 250; John 110; Widd
158
Haddby: Willm 108
Haddericke: Widd 158
Haddocke (*Haddock*): Antho 43; Chris
82; James 82, 248; Jno 79; Mr 60;
Phillip 143; Rowland 3; Stephen 56;
Wm 253
Hadley: Percivall 91
Hadon: Jno 3, 21
Hadsman: Eliz 114
Hadsmangh: Kath 241

Hadwen: Chris 20; Henry 15; Jno 31,
73; Widd 121
Haggarstone (*Haggerston*): Collonell
97; Geo 152; Wm 174
Hague: Gawen 103; Jno 103; Will 97,
99; Wm 173
Haidon: Geo 3
Haigg (*Hagg*): Eliz 250; Geo 103;
Stephen Gent 22
Hainsley: Tho 256 *cf Ainsley*
Hair: Jno 89
Haisting: Widd 46
Haith: Tho 141
Hale: Robt 127
Halelocke: John 158
Hall: Alexr 79; Alice 77, 249; Ann
85, 250; Anthony 95; Chr 106,
167; Chris gent 39; Cuth 32, 33;
[Dor]oth 263; Dorothy 128; Edw
264; Edward 4; Ellinor 8; Eliz 241;
Francis 59, 73, 107; Gawen 142; Geo
57, 61, 79, 125, 126; George 125;
Hen 136; Henry 75, 244; Hetton
55; Isabell 109; Issabell 91; James 45,
53, 54, 167; Jane 11, 153; Jno 5, 30,
32, 35, 48, 58, 62, 66, 250, 253, 259,
265; Jo: 198, 263; John 121, 145,
159, 167, 169, Mr John 91; Leo 157;
Lodowick lxxix, lxxx; Lodowick
Esqr 4; Lyell 60; Mary 128; Michaell
94; Mr junr 87, senr 87; Ms 87, 90;
Nicho 125; Nichol 44, 46, 53; Ralph
5, 32, 40, 55; Raphe 145; Rich 33,
236, 265; Robert 70; Robt 3, 56, 57,
60, 90, 145, 153; Sam 163; Tho 10,
13, 18, 29, 45, 57, 77, 104, 110, 140,
150, 161, 189, 238; Tho Gent 4; Wd
246; Wid 73, 74, 79, 88; Widow
226, 254, 262; Widd 57, 146, 147,
153, 160; Will 19, 52, 54, 75, 78, 79,
98, 102, Will Gent 65; William 15;
Willm 140; Witton 69; Wm 117,
154, 161, 171, 172
Halliday (*Helliday*): Henry 71; Mary
128; Mich 151; Robt 60, 170; Tho
101, 176; Wm 147
Halliman (*Hallyman*): Eliz 257; Jno 39,

30, 31, 53, 54, 59, 62, 65, 69, 92, 114, 119, 120, 145, 147, 168, 236, 240, 241, 242, 244; Thomas 2, 209; Wd 237; Widd 8, 127, 135, 142; Will 6, 14, 33, 38, 41, 50, 51, 73, 74, 81; Wm 110, 137, 138, 145, 240, 247

Harrowgate: Will 83

Harry (*Hary*): James 168; Jno 88

Harryman: Wm 131

Hart: Eliz 138; Elliner 262; Jno 85; John 130; Raphe 130, 136; Tho 41, 120; Widd 142; William 254; Wm 160 *cf Heart*

Hartburne: Francis 132; John 140

Hartley: Bridgett 115; Eliza 26; Jno 26, 29; Marg 237; Martin 78

Harvey (*Harvy*): James 173; Jno 5

Harwood: Bartho 12, 21; Geo 246; Phillis 246

Harygad: Nicho 164

Haselrigg: Sir Arthur xlv

Haslop: James 226

Hasly: Wm 112

Hassen: Ann 136

Hastings: Robert 83; Wid 86

Hasty (*Haisty*): Hen 176; Henry 101; Kath 246; Wm 23

Haswell (*Hasswell*): Ann 78, 142; Eliza 10; Hen 113; Jno 88, 252; John 106, 162; Mary 135; Ralph 77; Rich 78; Robt 1, 48, 52; Rodger 78; Tho 75, 135, 137; Wid 76, 78; Will 43

Hate: Wm 139

Hatherington: Geo 50, 53; John 59 *cf Hetherington*

Hatton: Jno 74; Will 12

Haueside: James 112

Haugue: Tho 99

Haukswell (*Haxwell*): Chr 130, 259

Hauxby: Jno 67

Hauxley: Tho 81, 248

Haward: John 127; Margtt 167; Rich. 186; Richard xxix, lxiv, 192

Hawd: Thomas 87

Hawden: Jno 245; Ms 93; Mary 245

Hawell: Math 108

Hawkins: Jno 84

Hay: Geo 116; Margtt 114; Ralph 65; Richard 63; Tho 227

Hayne: Tho 173

Hayson: Widd 138

Hayton: Willm 120

Head: Mary 143

Headlam (*Hedlum, Heedlum*): Antho 14; Fran 261; Kath 245; Kathar 117; Nichol 14

Headman: Katharine 114

Heads: Geo 67; Will 91

Healocke: Jno 69

Heard: Ralph 44

Hearing (*Hearinge*): Edw 149; Wm 108 *cf Herring*

Hearon: Barbara 29; Hugh 29; Robert 6; Tho 29 *cf Heron*

Heart: Edw 244; Jno 259; Ralph 259 *cf Hart*

Heaslery: Widd 136

Heath: Jno 79; Margrett 89; Mr 90; Ms 53; Peter 168, 252; Robt 166; Roger 252; Widow 226

Heaton: Hen 130; Roger 159

Heavyside (*Heavieside, Heavysides., Hevyside*): Ann 125; Antho 138; Brihan 239; Bryan 6; Fran 112, 239; Francis 34; Jno 27, 30, 260; John 126; Tho 139; Thomas 254

Hebbron: Geo 68

Hebburne (*Hebbourne*): Cornelius 96, 174; Wid 96; Widd 174

Heblethwayt: John 119; Tho 126

Hebleworth: James 157

Heckles: James 95

Heding: Jno 250

Hedley (*Headley, Hedlay, Hedly*): Geo 28, 64; Hen 121; Jno 77; John 121, 161; Mr 90; Parcivall 150; Ralph 81; Rich 155; Richard 28; Richd 146; Robt 87; Tho 28, 155; Thomas 152; Wd 237; Wid 67; Widd 154, 160; Widow 226

Hedworth (*Hedwath, Hedword*): Edw 155; Mr Francis 68; Ralph Gent 77, 80; Mr Will 68; Willm 156

Heighington (*Heighingt, Heighinton*):

Index of Places

Places in Bedlingtonshire, Islandshire, and Norhamshire which were only transferred from County Durham to Northumberland in 1844 have not been gathered together under Northumberland but have separate index entries.

Subject Index

No.	Township	Ward
1	Aislaby	Stockton South West
2	Alwent & Selaby	Darlington South West
3	Archdeacon Newton	Darlington South East
4	Auckland St Andrew	Darlington North West
5	Auckland St Helen	Darlington North West
6	Barmpton	Darlington South East
7	Barmston	Chester East
8	Barnard Castle	Darlington South West
9	Barnard Castle (det)	Darlington South West
10	Barnes High & Low	Easington North
11	Benfieldside	Chester West
12	Billingham	Stockton North East
13	Billingside	Chester West
14	Binchester	Darlington North West
15	Birtley	Chester Middle
16	Bishop Auckland Borough	Darlington North West
17	Bishop Auckland Town	Darlington North West
18	Bishop Middleham	Stockton North East
19	Bishopley	Darlington North West
20	Bishopton	Stockton South West
21	Bishopwearmouth	Easington North
22	Bishopwearmouth Panns	Easington North
23	Blackestone	Stockton North East
24	Blackwell	Darlington South East
25	Bolam	Darlington South West
26	Boldon East	Chester East
27	Boldon East (det) 1	Chester East
28	Boldon East (det) 2	Chester East
29	Boldon East (det) 3	Chester East
30	Boldon West	Chester East
31	Bourne Moor	Easington North
32	Bradbury	Stockton North East
33	Bradley	Darlington North West
34	Brafferton	Darlington South East
35	Brancepeth	Darlington North West
36	Brancepeth (det)	Darlington North West
37	Brandon & Bishottles	Darlington North West
38	Brankin Moor	Darlington South East
39	Brierton	Stockton North East
40	Broom	Durham County
41	Burdon East & West	Easington North
42	Burnhope & Hamsteels	Chester West
43	Butsfield	Chester West
44	Butterwick	Stockton North East
45	Byers Green	Darlington South East

No.	Township	Ward
46	Carlbury, Ulnaby, Thornton Hall	Darlington South East
47	Carlton	Stockton South West
48	Cassop	Easington South
49	Castle Eden	Easington South
50	Chester-Le-Street	Chester Middle
51	Chilton	Darlington South East
52	Chopwell	Chester West
53	Claxton	Stockton North East
54	Cleadon	Chester East
55	Cleatlam	Darlington South West
56	Coatham Mundeville	Darlington South East
57	Coatsay Moor	Darlington South East
58	Cocken	Easington North
59	Cockerton	Darlington South East
60	Cockfield	Darlington South West
61	Cockfield Woodland (det)	Darlington South West
62	Colliery	Chester West
63	Conside	Chester West
64	Cornforth	Stockton North East
65	Cornsay	Chester West
66	Coundon	Darlington North West
67	Cowpen Bewley	Stockton North East
68	Coxhoe	Easington South
69	Crawcrooke	Chester West
70	Crook & Billy Row	Darlington North West
71	Crossgate	Durham County
72	Croxdale & Butterby	Easington South
73	Dalton	Easington North
74	Dalton Piercy	Stockton North East
75	Darlington Town	Darlington South East
76	Dawton	Easington North
77	Denton	Darlington South East
78	Dinsdale	Stockton South West
79	Durham St Giles	Durham County
80	Durham St Margaret	Durham City
81	Durham St Nicholas	Durham City
82	Durham St Oswald	Durham County
83	Easington	Easington South
84	East Rainton	Easington North
85	Ebchester	Chester West
86	Edmondbyres	Chester West
87	Edmondsley	Chester Middle
88	Edmondsley (det)	Chester Middle
89	Egglescliffe	Stockton South West
90	Eggleston	Darlington South West

No.	Township	Ward
91	Eldon	Darlington South East
92	Elstob	Stockton North East
93	Elton	Stockton South West
94	Elvet (Barony and/or Borough)	Durham County
95	Elvet Barony	Durham County
96	Elwick Hall	Stockton North East
97	Embleton	Stockton North East
98	Eppleton	Easington North
99	Escomb	Darlington North West
100	Esh	Chester West
101	Evenwood Barony	Darlington North West
102	Evenwood Town	Darlington North West
103	Felling	Chester Middle
104	Ferryhill	Darlington South East
105	Fishburn	Stockton North East
106	Ford	Easington North
107	Foxton & Shotton	Stockton North East
108	Framwellgate	Durham County
109	Frosterley	Darlington North West
110	Frosterley (det)	Darlington North West
111	Fulwell	Chester East
112	Gainford	Darlington South West
113	Garmondsway Moor	Easington South
114	Gateshead	Chester Middle
115	Gateshead Fell	Chester Middle
116	Goosepool	Stockton South West
117	Great Aycliffe	Darlington South East
118	Great Aycliffe (det)	Darlington South East
119	Great Burdon	Darlington South East
120	Great Stainton	Stockton North East
121	Great Usworth	Chester East
122	Greatham	Stockton North East
123	Greencroft	Chester West
124	Hallgarth	Easington South
125	Hamsterley	Darlington North West
126	Harraton	Chester Middle
127	Hart Town	Stockton North East
128	Hartburn	Stockton South West
129	Hartlepool	Stockton North East
130	Harton	Chester East
131	Harton (det)	Chester East
132	Haswell	Easington South
133	Haughton Le Skerne	Darlington South East
134	Hawthorn	Easington South
135	Headlam	Darlington South West

No.	Township	Ward
136	Healeyfield	Chester West
137	Hedley	Chester Middle
138	Hedleyhope	Chester West
139	Hedworth	Chester East
140	Heighington & Old Park	Darlington South East
141	Helmington Row	Darlington North West
142	Henknowle & Coppycrooks	Darlington North West
143	Herrington East & Middle	Easington North
144	Hesleden	Easington South
145	Hett	Darlington South East
146	Hetton-le-Hole	Easington North
147	Heworth Upper, Nether	Chester East
148	High Conniscliffe	Darlington South East
149	Hilton	Darlington South West
150	Holmside	Chester Middle
151	Horden	Easington South
152	Houghton Le Side	Darlington South East
153	Houghton Le Spring	Easington North
154	Hulum	Easington South
155	Hunstanworth	Chester West
156	Hunwick	Darlington North West
157	Hurworth	Stockton South West
158	Hutton Henry	Easington South
159	Hylton	Chester East
160	Ingleton	Darlington South West
161	Iveston	Chester West
162	Jarrow	Chester East
163	Jarrow & Hedworth (det)	Chester East
164	Kelloe	Easington South
165	Kibblesworth	Chester Middle
166	Killerby	Darlington South West
167	Kimblesworth	Chester West
168	Kirk Merrington	Darlington South East
169	Kyo	Chester West
170	Lamesley & Fellside	Chester Middle
171	Lanchester	Chester West
172	Lanchester , Butsfield, Holmside	Chester West
173	Langley	Chester West
174	Langleydale	Darlington South West
175	Langton	Darlington South West
176	Layton	Stockton North East
177	Lintz Green Tanfield	Chester Middle
178	Little Stainton	Stockton South West
179	Long Newton	Stockton South West
180	Long Newton + Coatham Stob	Stockton South West

No.	Township	Ward
181	Low Conniscliffe	Darlington South East
182	Ludworth	Easington South
183	Lumley & Lambton	Easington North
184	Lynesack & Softley	Darlington North West
185	Lynesack & Softley (det)	Darlington North West
186	Mainsforth	Stockton North East
187	Marwood	Darlington South West
188	Marwood (det)	Darlington South West
189	Medomsley	Chester West
190	Middlestone	Darlington South East
191	Middleton Bounds	Darlington South West
192	Middleton One Row & St George	Stockton South West
193	Middridge	Darlington South East
194	Monk Hesleden	Easington North
195	Monkton	Chester East
196	Monkwearmouth	Chester East
197	Monkwearmouth (det)	Chester East
198	Moor House	Easington North
199	Moorsley	Easington North
200	Mordon	Stockton North East
201	Morton Grange	Easington North
202	Morton Palms	Stockton South West
203	Morton Tinmouth	Darlington South West
204	Muggleswick	Chester West
205	Murdon East	Easington North
206	Neasham	Stockton South West
207	Neasham & Aislaby (det)	Stockton South West
208	Nesbitt	Easington South
209	Newbiggin East & West	Stockton South West
210	Newbiggin East & West Thickley	Darlington South East
211	Newbiggin on Tees	Darlington South West
212	Newbottle	Easington North
213	Newfield	Darlington North West
214	Newton Bewley	Stockton North East
215	Newton Cap	Darlington North West
216	North Bailey	Durham City
217	North Bedburn	Darlington North West
218	Norton	Stockton South West
219	Nunstainton	Stockton North East
220	Offerton	Easington North
221	Old Acres	Stockton North East
222	Old Park	Darlington North West
223	Oughton	Stockton North East
224	Ouston	Chester Middle
225	Oxnetfield	Darlington South East

No.	Township	Ward
226	Page Bank	Darlington North West
227	Pelton	Chester Middle
228	Penshaw	Easington North
229	Piercebridge	Darlington South West
230	Pittington	Easington South
231	Pittington (det)	Easington South
232	Plawsworth	Chester Middle
233	Pollard Land	Darlington North West
234	Preston Le Skerne	Darlington South East
235	Preston on Tees	Stockton South West
236	Quarrington	Easington South
237	Raby with Keverstone	Darlington South West
238	Ravensworth	Chester Middle
239	Redmarshall	Stockton South West
240	Redworth	Darlington South East
241	Ricknall Heighington (det)	Darlington South East
242	Ridding	Chester West
243	Rowley	Chester West
244	Rowley & Roughside	Chester West
245	Ryhope	Easington North
246	Ryton	Chester West
247	Ryton Woodside	Chester West
248	Sadberge	Stockton South West
249	Sately (det)	Chester West
250	School Aycliffe	Darlington South East
251	Seaham	Easington North
252	Seaton	Easington North
253	Seaton Carew	Stockton North East
254	Sedgefield	Stockton North East
255	Shadforth	Easington South
256	Sheraton	Easington South
257	Sherburn House	Easington South
258	Shildon	Darlington North West
259	Shincliffe	Easington South
260	Shotterton	Darlington South West
261	Shotton	Easington South
262	Shotton Teedale Forest	Darlington South West
263	Silksworth	Easington North
264	Sledwick	Darlington South West
265	Sockburn	Stockton South West
266	South Bailey	Durham City
267	South Bedburn	Darlington North West
268	South Biddick	Easington North
269	South Shields	Chester East
270	Southwick	Chester East

No.	Township	Ward
271	Southwick (det)	Chester East
272	Staindrop	Darlington South West
273	Stainton	Darlington South West
274	Stanhope Forest	Darlington North West
275	Stanhope Newlandside	Darlington North West
276	Stanhope Newlandside (det)	Darlington North West
277	Stanhope Park	Darlington North West
278	Stanhope Quarter	Darlington North West
279	Stella	Chester West
280	Stillington	Stockton South West
281	Stockley	Darlington North West
282	Stockton Borough	Stockton South West
283	Stockton Town	Stockton South West
284	Stranton	Stockton North East
285	Streatlam	Darlington South West
286	Summerhouse	Darlington South West
287	Sunderland	Easington North
288	Sunderland Bridge	Easington South
289	The Isle	Stockton North East
290	Thornley	Easington South
291	Thornley & Helmpark	Darlington North West
292	Thorpe Bulmer	Easington South
293	Thorpe Little	Easington South
294	Thorpe Thewles	Stockton North East
295	Thrislington	Stockton North East
296	Throston	Stockton North East
297	Trafford Hill	Stockton South West
298	Trimdon	Easington South
299	Tudhoe	Darlington South East
300	Tunstall	Stockton North East
301	Tunstall	Easington North
302	Tursdale	Easington South
303	Urpeth	Chester Middle
304	Wackerfield	Darlington South West
305	Waldridge	Chester Middle
306	Walworth	Darlington South East
307	Warden Law	Easington North
308	Washington	Chester East
309	West Auckland	Darlington North West
310	West Herrington	Easington North
311	West Rainton	Easington North
312	Westerton	Darlington South East
313	Westoe	Chester East
314	Westwick	Darlington South West
315	Whessoe	Darlington South East

No.	Township	Ward
316	Whickham	Chester West
317	Whitburn	Chester East
318	Whitburn (det)	Chester East
319	Whitton	Stockton North East
320	Whitwell House	Easington South
321	Whitworth	Darlington South East
322	Whorlton	Darlington South West
323	Willington	Darlington South East
324	Windlestone	Darlington South East
325	Wingate	Easington South
326	Winlaton East	Chester West
327	Winlaton West	Chester West
328	Winston	Darlington South West
329	Witton Gilbert	Chester West
330	Witton Le Wear	Darlington North West
331	Wolsingham East	Darlington North West
332	Wolsingham Park	Darlington North West
333	Wolsingham South	Darlington North West
334	Wolsingham Town	Darlington North West
335	Wolviston	Stockton North East
336	Woodham	Darlington South East
337	common	Darlington North West
338	common	Darlington North West
339	common	Darlington North West
340	common	Darlington North West
341	common	Darlington North West
342	common	Darlington North West
343	common	Darlington North West
344	common	Darlington North West
345	common	Darlington North West
346	common	Darlington North West
347	common	Chester West